ASPECTS OF TEXT STRUCTURE

An Investigation of
the Lexical Organisation of Text

NORTH-HOLLAND LINGUISTIC SERIES

52

ASPECTS OF TEXT STRUCTURE

An Investigation of the Lexical Organisation of Text

MARTIN PHILLIPS
The British Council
London, England

1985

NORTH-HOLLAND
AMSTERDAM · NEW YORK · OXFORD

© Elsevier Science Publishers B.V., 1985

All rights reserved. No part of this publication may be reproduced, stored in a retrieval system, or transmitted, in any form or by any means, electronic, mechanical, photocopying, recording or otherwise, without the prior permission of the copyright owner.

ISBN: 0 444 87701 0

Published by:
ELSEVIER SCIENCE PUBLISHERS B.V.
P.O. Box 1991
1000 BZ Amsterdam
The Netherlands

Sole distributors for the U.S.A. and Canada:
ELSEVIER SCIENCE PUBLISHING COMPANY, INC.
52 Vanderbilt Avenue
New York, N.Y. 10017
U.S.A.

Library of Congress Cataloging in Publication Data

```
Phillips, Martin, 1944-
   Aspects of text structure.

   (North-Holland linguistic series ; 52)
   Based on the author's thesis (doctoral)--University
of Birmingham.
   Bibliography: p.
   Includes indexes.
   1. Discourse analysis.  I. Title.  II. Series.
P302.P5  1985         401'.41          84-28681
ISBN 0-444-87701-0 (U.S.)
```

PRINTED IN THE NETHERLANDS

We are absurdly accustomed to the miracle of a few written signs being able to contain immortal imagery, involutions of thought, new worlds with live people, speaking, weeping, laughing. We take it for granted that in a sense, by the very act of brutish routine acceptance, we undo the work of ages, the history of the gradual elaboration of poetical description and construction, from the treeman to Browning, from the caveman to Keats. What if we awake one day, all of us and find ourselves utterly unable to read? I wish you to grasp not only at what you read but at the miracle of its being readable.

                      'Charles Kinbote'

                                        For Marisa

PREFACE

This book is a restructuring of the main argument presented in my doctoral thesis submitted to the University of Birmingham. It explores those aspects of the structure of text which bear upon the notion of subject matter and the way in which texts create and structure realities. The reader has a psychological sensation that the text is 'about' something. I argue that this perception is not adequately accounted for at any of the levels of analysis traditionally recognised by linguistics. Rather, it rests crucially on the existence of large scale regularities in the lexical organisation of text. This patterning cannot be observed directly and it is thus necessary to adopt indirect methods for its investigation.

The book is divided into four parts. The first part outlines the theoretical background to this approach to text. The theoretical position has direct implications for the methodology of text analysis. An appropriate methodology is developed in the second part. In the course of my doctoral research, this methodology was applied to the analysis of a corpus of some ten texts. The third part is occupied with the description of this investigation and a discussion of my findings. In the final part several loose ends are identified, rather than tied up, and the broader implications of the study for linguistics considered.

The first chapter establishes the indispensable theoretical context. It is argued that the Saussurian postulates of the linguistic sign and the linearity of language imply that text can be viewed as a system of relations operating at the formal level of language substance. An analysis at this level is eminently suitable for investigating the large scale organisation of text. This suggests, however, that conventional techniques of text description are unlikely to reveal features of text pertinent to the present enquiry. This problem is considered in chapter two through a survey of a number of approaches to text analysis.

The conclusion of this stage of the argument is that an objective, statistical, computer-assisted methodology is required. There are three principal steps in the methodology. First, the raw text has to be stripped of elements extraneous to the investigation and a number of decisions relating to categories of analysis need to be taken. These preparatory considerations are discussed in chapter three. Secondly, the investigative methods proper must be established. This is done in chapter four. Thirdly, descriptive techniques for presenting the results of the analysis are needed and these are developed in chapter five. In chapter six a suitable corpus for exploring the value of the methodology in illuminating the theoretical concerns outlined earlier is identified and a pilot study described.

The next three chapters are concerned with discussing the findings of an investigation of a number of texts using the methods which have been developed. The discussion starts with a relatively narrow focus on the findings at the level of the chapter and broadens out to encompass comparisons of different classes of text. Chapter seven considers the light thrown by the findings on the notion of terminology. Chapter eight then shows how the investigation has revealed the existence of large scale lexical structures in text and explores their function in contributing to the sensation of ´aboutness´. Lastly, in chapter nine the question is posed as to whether the structuring that has been revealed is a general feature of text or specific only to certain types of text. The possibility of establishing a typology of texts on this basis is discussed. The final chapter then explores some unresolved issues raised by the investigation concerning the nature of literary text and the scope of linguistics.

An important part of the book is the appendices. Here the evidence upon which the argument is based is assembled so that it can be consulted conveniently. In this way it is hoped that the reader who wishes to verify the points made in the text or who wants to pursue further some of the implications of the argument will find sufficient data to be able to do so.

Many people have helped shape my ideas. Members of the University of Birmingham have been particularly helpful. I am most grateful for the assistance in the technical aspects of my research that I received from Alan Reed of the Computer Centre and Professor John Copas and Dr Paul Davies of the Department of Statistics and to Cathy Emmott who made the text of ´Mrs Dalloway´ available in machine readable form. Dr Michael Hoey, Dr Deirdre Burton and Jeremy Clear, all present members of the Department of English, offered many valuable insights and criticisms as did former members Dr Peter Skehan, now of London University Institute of Education, and Adriana Calderon de Bolivar of the Universidad Central de Venezuela. I owe a heavy debt to two people in particular. Professor John Sinclair´s wisdom and encouragement is in large part responsible for the project which led to the publication of this book. The unfailing enthusiasm and interest of my friend and colleague Dr Peter Roe and the continuing dialogue we have enjoyed over a number of years has made a major contribution to the work on which this book is based. I should like also to thank my employers, the British Council, for making the opportunity of research available to me and to my publishers for their sympathetic help. Finally, I am deeply grateful to my wife.

Both the writing of this book and the research on which it is based would not have been possible without her constant support. I should make clear that, whilst all those I have mentioned share in whatever merits this book may have, none has any responsibility for its imperfections. This is mine alone.

I should like to acknowledge the permissions kindly granted by Dr Mohammed Sijelmassi to reproduce the illustration of Arabic calligraphy on page 10 taken from 'The Splendour of Islamic Calligraphy' by A.Khatibi and M.Sijelmassi published by Thames and Hudson, London; by Scott Kim to reproduce his calligraphic design 'Upside Down' from 'Inversions' by S.Kim, published by BYTE Books, Peterborough, N.H. on the same page; and by Butterworths to reproduce the Chinese poem on page 11 from 'Quantitative Linguistics' by G.Herdan, published by Butterworths, London.

Martin Phillips
Bicester
23 June 1984

CONTENTS

Preface   vii

PART ONE   A THEORETICAL FRAMEWORK FOR TEXT ANALYSIS

1. Meaning, Substance and Aboutness   3
1.1 The Notion of Aboutness   3
1.2 System and Value   6
1.3 Term Meaning and Context   13
1.4 Text Structure   16
1.5 Text and Reality   22
1.6 Conclusion   27

2. Linguistics in the Study of Text   29
2.1 Levels of Linguistic Description   29
2.2 The Problem of Scale in Text Analysis   37
2.3 Statistical Approaches to Text   40
2.4 Collocation and Distribution   43
2.5 Conclusion   48

PART TWO   METHODOLOGICAL CONSEQUENCES

3. Procedures and Categories for Text Analysis   53
3.1 Text Reduction   53
3.2 Basic Analytical Categories   58
3.3 Constraints on the Analytical Procedure   64
3.4 Conclusion   66

4. Investigative Techniques for Text Analysis   67
4.1 Data Analysis: The Classical Model   67
4.2 Data Analysis: Multidimensional Scaling   71
4.3 Data Analysis: Cluster Analysis   72
4.4 Procedural Consequences   79
4.5 Data Collection and Reduction   84
4.6 Conclusion   87

5. Descriptive Techniques for Text Analysis   89
5.1 An Introduction to Digraphs   89
5.2 Further Results from Graph Theory   94
5.3 The Notion of Network   98
5.4 Conclusion   100

PART THREE EXPLORATION OF TEXT

6. Applying the Methodology — 105
6.1 The Corpus — 105
6.2 Procedural Decisions — 109
6.3 Computer Programs — 111
6.4 A Pilot Study — 114
6.5 Conclusion — 118

7. Term Meaning — 121
7.1 The Interpretation of Lexical Networks — 121
7.2 Lexical Networks in the Science Corpus — 124
7.3 Nuclear Nodes and the Structure of Networks — 140
7.4 Theories and Models of Term Meaning — 148
7.5 Conclusion — 153

8. Terms and Text Structure — 155
8.1 The Structure, Linkage and Status of Chapters — 155
8.2 The Macrostructure of Science Text — 165
8.3 The Interpretation of Macrostructure — 168
8.4 General Principles of Macrostructure — 180
8.5 A Hierarchy of Units of Relation — 192
8.6 Conclusion — 195

9. Text Structure and Text Typology — 197
9.1 The Range Index — 197
9.2 Macrostructure in Non-science Text — 200
9.3 Towards a Typology of Texts — 205
9.4 Further Structural Evidence for a Text Typology — 214
9.5 Conclusion — 216

PART FOUR ABOUTNESS REVIEWED

10. Text, Image and Reality — 221
10.1 The Problem of Macrostructure — 221
10.2 Aboutness in Literature — 224
10.3 The Scope of Linguistics — 230
10.4 Conclusion — 232

APPENDICES

1. Corpus Statistics — 239
2. Selected Lemmata — 241
3. ELEN Dendrograms — 255
4. Lexical Networks in the Science Corpus — 267
5. Nuclear Node Statistics — 291
6. Significant Chapter Linkages — 293
7. Macrostructures of the Science Texts — 297
8. Percentage of Non-collocating Nodes — 303

BIBLIOGRAPHY — 305

SUBJECT INDEX — 315

AUTHOR INDEX — 319

PART ONE

A THEORETICAL FRAMEWORK FOR TEXT ANALYSIS

CHAPTER 1

MEANING, SUBSTANCE AND ABOUTNESS

1.1 The Notion of Aboutness

I take the concept of subject matter to be problematic. The first major concern of this book is to try to throw some light on the problem. To do this a theoretical position will be described which generates a methodology for the investigation of written text. The findings which result when this methodology is applied to certain classes of text will be discussed and the extent to which these findings help us to understand the phenomenon of subject matter will be considered. In this chapter the basic problem is posed and some of its implications discussed.

Thus the kind of question which forms the subject matter of this book is what in fact we mean when we speak of the "subject matter" of such and such a book or the "topic" of chapter so and so. It seems that something is being referred to which is felt to be distinct from language but which can be summoned to consciousness only through the symbolism of language. Subject matter is the genie and language our magic lamp.

There is one ultimate fact about text. This is that it consists of elements of linguistic substance juxtaposed in linear sequence. In the case of written text, the skilled reader somehow internalises from the encounter with graphic substance a model of some aspect of ´reality´. This is what constitutes the meaning of the text. It could be argued that subject matter is the embodiment in language of knowledge and activity in the world of phenomena or in some hypothetical world. Thus unless text stands in some describable relation to such a world, it has no meaning for it cannot be relate to experience. The fundamental problem posed by text, then, is to elucidate the nature of the relationship between text and reality which allows meanings to be created in this way. How does it come about that complex non-linear conceptual structures are realised through the ultimately linear organisation of language substance? I shall refer to the psychological creation of these structures as the perception of ´aboutness´.

It is widely accepted that such non-linear conceptual structures are elaborated by the reader and are the mechanism which underlies the reader´s ability to summarise, paraphrase

and generally to state what a text is about. This ability
raises some interesting problems. It has been pointed out that
to be able to state what a book is about depends on the
processing of thousands of sentences which cannot normally be
memorised individually by the reader (van Dijk 1977a). In
general, it is the ´gist´ of a text which is recalled rather
than its wording. Studies such as those of Sachs or Clark and
Clark attest the relative subsistence of semantic memory as
opposed to the uncertainty of recall of syntactic structure
(Sachs 1967, Clark and Clark 1977).

It seems, then, that appreciation of textual meaning is a large
scale phenomenon which does not depend directly on those
structures which are responsible only for the local organisation of linguistic expression. I shall, in fact, argue that
aboutness stems in part from the reader´s appreciation of
certain global patterns of textual organisation. I call these
patterns ´macrostructure´.

Before proceeding further it is necessary to clarify some
matters of teminology. I use the term ´text´ in the broad
sense in which Muller defines it as

> "any utterance or any succession of utterances, any use
> of speech or fragment of speech, with no restriction on
> its extent, produced by a single speaker or writer and
> displaying a certain unity" (Muller 1977 p5 my trans-
> lation).

Although this definition contains an element of circularity,
since the need for a text to display "a certain unity" in fact
begs the question, I believe that this or a similar circularity
is inevitable in order to get started at all and to avoid the
danger of infinite regress. It must be assumed that text is
recognisable in order to begin to find out what it is. I shall
also have occasion to refer to objects which are often called
´texts´, usually within the context of an educational syllabus:
that is, text as artifact. Rather than use the term ´text´
ambiguously in this second sense also, I shall try consistently
to employ the term ´textbook´.

I find I do not need to use ´discourse´ as a technical term. I
hope this absolves me somewhat from undue concern for rigour
when I do use the term, which is principally when discussing
the approaches of other researchers. Indeed, I cannot use it
more rigorously than they and since there is a great deal of
confusion in this area, I feel it is justifiable to employ it
in two senses.

First, I use it to refer to the organisation of text from an
interactive perspective. In this sense it is similar to
Widdowson´s use of the term (Criper and Widdowson 1975). In
distinction to Widdowson, however, in my usage ´discourse´ does
not stand in contrast to ´text´, with the latter denoting the
purely formal aspects of the suprasentential organisation of
language. Rather I consider ´discourse´ subordinate to ´text´:

text structure subsumes discourse structure.

Secondly, I shall on occasion use it in a non-technical, everyday sense to refer to continuous stretches of spoken language. Since this book is not concerned with the spoken language, this occasional departure from Muller's definition of text, which embraces both spoken and written language, is of no consequence.

An implication of these definitions, which should in any case be obvious, is that no attempt will be made to study all the features which might possibly contribute to text structure. In general, when I refer to 'text structure' or 'macrostructure', this should be taken to mean those aspects of structure focused upon in this book. Context will make clear when such terms are being used in a different sense as characterisations of the views of others as, for example, when van Dijk's position is discussed.

Both 'text' and 'macrostructure' are relative terms. Macrostructure can be characterised at different degrees of resolution depending on the text interval chosen as focus. The scope of aboutness can consequently vary. This book is concerned primarily with the macrostructure of those stretches of text conventionally identified as textbook and chapter.

What do these preliminary considerations suggest by way of an approach to the investigation of the notion of aboutness and the hypothesised macrostructures upon which the appreciation of aboutness rests? It seems that there are clues to three classes of linguistic theory dealing with interrelated concepts. The first clue is given by the observation that ultimately text consists of elements of graphic substance in linear sequence. This fact supports a view of meaning as arising from a system of positional values of textual elements. This conception of meaning can be traced in modern linguistics to the theories of Saussure. I shall consider the relevance of Saussure's work and the implications of his views in the next section.

Secondly, it is clear that aboutness has to do with the cognitive content of text. A major clue to cognitive content is furnished by the author's selection of vocabulary. Lexical choice is a primary means by which propositions are expressed. An appreciation of how terms come to have meaning is thus of fundamental relevance to understanding how the concept of subject matter is generated by text. At the same time, theories of term meaning provide a link between the concepts of positional value and of text structure. On the one hand, it can be argued that the meanings of terms arise from their place in a system of positional values. On the other hand, register studies suggest that lexical choice provides a basis for the establishment of text typologies. Thus the field of terminological studies looks as though it may help to illuminate the notion of aboutness.

Finally, studies of text structure should be of relevance. Here it is important to distinguish between the topics studied in discourse analysis and studies adopting an approach through text linguistics. Discourse analysis, as will be seen, is concerned principally with the relationship between reader and writer. What is of prime importance here, however, is the way in which conceptual content relates to text structure. Thus investigations of text which examine the connection between cognitive content and text structure may offer valuable insights. In particular, work which postulates a relationship between linguistic patterning and the elaboration of ´cognitive schemata´ should be examined for the light it throws on the macrostructure of text.

Thus it appears that three theoretical areas may offer clues as to an appropriate approach to the problem of aboutness. The view of meaning as arising from a system of positional value ultimately rooted in the nature of linguistic substance is closely related to certain views of term meaning. Terminology itself leads to a notion of text typology and the structural investigation of text. Out of these three areas it will be possible to define a theoretical position offering a framework and suggesting the outline of a methodology for the investigation of the issues with which this book is concerned. In the next section I shall look at the first of these areas in more detail.

1.2 System and Value

Ferdinand de Saussure is one of the few modern linguists who achieves fundamental insight into the problem of subject matter. He first saw clearly that if subject matter is to be embodied in a workable linguistic system, then the structure of language cannot be isomorphic to the structure of ´reality´. This is the point of his first principle of the arbitrariness of the linguistic sign. He postulated that the linguistic sign consists of an arbitrary relationship between a ´signifie´ and a ´signifiant´. This he stated as his first principle

> "The bond between the signifier and the signified is arbitrary. Since I mean by sign the whole that results from the associating of the signifier with the signified, I can simply say: the linguistic sign is "arbitrary"" (Saussure 1974 p 67).

Thus this principle asserts that there is no necessary correspondence between the systems of language and our experience of phenomena. It would be most implausible if there were to be such a correspondence. The Kantian debate as to whether any categories are transcendentally given or are created by perception, as Slagle argues (Slagle 1974), is far from closed and the extent to which language categorises experience has been an open question since Whorf´s strong assertions in this area (Whorf 1956). Both these considerations indicate the implausibility of a direct signifier-signified relationship.

Arbitrariness of the relationship with what is represented confers great power on any symbolic system. This is seen more clearly in mathematics than in language. Mathematics is a pure formal system not even in principle concerned with any real-world phenomena, despite the popular conception of it as necessarily representing quantities, for example. If a semantics is provided for mathematical systems, however, or in other words a mapping from empirical data into the entities recognised by mathematics, then the whole power of the formal system becomes available to assist in understanding the data; theorems of the system become statements about reality. In terms of language, this is what accounts for the creativity of language; in this way, an infinite number of utterances can be created out of finite resources.

Thus few would dispute that the linguistic sign is essentially arbitrary. Sinclair observes, however, that it sounds as though Jakobson might be dissenting in his article ´Co je poesie?´ (Sinclair 1975):

> "´The function of poetry´, wrote Jacobson in 1933, ´is to point out that the sign is not identical with its referent. Why do we need this reminder?´ ´Because´, continued Jacobson, ´along with the awareness of the identity of the sign and the referent (A is A1), we need the consciousness of the inadequacy of this identity (A is not A1); this antinomy is essential, since without it the connection between the sign and the object becomes automatized and the perception of reality withers away.´" (quoted in Erlich 1980 p181)

So, in fact it is clear that Jakobson, far from asserting any necessary connection between the sign and its referent, is rather defending the arbitrary nature of the relationship against the contempt of familiarity.

It might, nevertheless, seem possible to sustain a notion of non-arbitrariness by appeal to the concept of ´appropriateness´. This refers to the aspect of linguistic choice which is considered fundamental to style. It is the literary equivalent, as it were, of the apocryphal countryman´s observation ´rightly be they called pigs´. But in my view, these considerations argue more in favour of the arbitrary nature of the relation than against it. For if the relationship between ´signifiant´ and ´signifie´ were not conventional, there could be no question of exercising stylistic choice or of creativity of the poetic sort which attaches new and unexpected meanings to familiar words.

Now, holding that the linguistic sign is essentially arbitrary entails accepting a crucial consequence. This is that signs cannot be mutually substituable and that therefore a system has to be established to keep them distinct in use. This can easily be seen from consideration of the limits to arbitrariness. First there is the situation of multiple referents mapped into identical signs. Then there is the case

of a single referent realised by a multitude of signs. Both
extreme homonymy and extreme synonymy would lead, not to an
unworkable system, but to the absence of system. Thus with
acceptance of the fundamental Saussurian tenet, the rest of
linguistics can be seen as a specification of the limits to
arbitrariness. In Saussure's words

> "In fact, the whole system of language is based on the
> irrational principle of the arbitrariness of the sign,
> which would lead to the worst sort of complication if
> applied without restriction.... If the mechanism of
> language were entirely rational, it could be studied
> independently. Since the mechanism of language is a
> partial correction of a system that is by nature
> chaotic, however, we adopt the viewpoint imposed by the
> very nature of language and study it as it limits
> arbitrariness" (op cit pp182-183).

Thus it is the distinction between signs that is crucial. The
notion of distinctive opposition seems to be a fundamental
linguistic principle operating at all levels of analysis.
Language is a system where the value of an item is determined
by its position in the system. This was also recognised by
Saussure and is embodied in his term 'valeur'. According to
Saussure, 'valeur' is the critical aspect of the meaning of a
linguistic item. He makes an absolutely crucial point when he
reasons that

> "Since one vocal image is no better suited than the next
> for what it is commissioned to express, it is evident,
> even <u>a priori</u> that a segment of language can never in
> the final analysis be based on anything except its non-
> coincidence with the rest. <u>Arbitrary</u> and <u>different-
> ial</u> are two correlative qualities." (ibid p163)

'Valeur', however, is usually supposed to refer to the
systematicity of what Saussure called 'langue', the notion of
language in the abstract embodied in the 'knowledge' of the
speech community. On this basis it is possible to claim, for
example, that the 'meaning' of nominative in a five-case system
of declension is different from its 'meaning' in, say, a
six-case system. But it arguable that the notion can be
equally well applied to 'parole', that is to any given instance
of language use. Certainly, the quotation from Saussure given
above lends itself to interpretation in this way.

This would mean that it is possible to consider meaning as
arising from the fundamental property of language which
Saussure stated in his second principle, the principle of
linearity

> "The signifier, being auditory, is unfolded solely in
> time from which it gets the following characteristics:
> (a) it represents a span, and (b) the span is measurable
> in a single dimension; it is a line." (ibid p103)

An equivalent statement can, of course, be made with respect to the written language. Thus ´valeur´ can also be seen as a property of the syntagm arising from the distribution throughout the linear stream of language substance of distinctive segments. Even syntax can be seen as a system of inferences from patterning in linear succession, although as Sinclair points out, despite the fact that

> "succession is the only ultimate relationship of elements....Syntax is rarely presented as a set of limitations upon the free combination of those elements that require to be distinguished" (Sinclair 1980a pp111-2).

It might seem a somewhat unpromising approach to text to focus on the signifier rather than the sign and on the distributional relations it contracts with its fellows. Indeed it may even be considered unreasonable to ignore in this way the understanding that has been acquired over the years of how language operates at a number of different levels of analysis. With, for example, the comparative success of grammar in accounting for a wide variety of syntactic phenomena and the promising developments in discourse analysis, there is a requirement to justify an approach to text analysis which takes an apparently more superficial approach. After all, Bloomfield attracted heavy criticism as a result of his methodological decision to exclude semantics from the purview of linguistics (Bloomfield 1935).

At the most basic level my answer to such arguments is essentially the same as Saussure´s

> "No one disputes the principle of the arbitrary nature of the sign, but it is often easier to discover a truth than to assign to it its proper place. Principle I dominates all the linguistics of language; its consequences are numberless. It is true that not all of them are equally obvious at first glance; only after many detours does one discover them, and with them the primordial importance of the principle" (op cit p100).

Given, however, this failure to accord the linguistic sign its rightful place, it is necessary to produce evidence to support the notion that there is value in redressing the balance of linguistic enquiry more in favour of a focus on language substance.

A number of pertinent considerations suggest themselves. Attention to the graphic substance itself may endow it with meaning bearing properties. In languages such as Arabic, for example, where cultural development has engendered a strong calligraphic tradition, the signifier is often developed to such an extent that it is enabled to project more meaning than that associated with the lexical content alone. Significance of this nature is conveyed by geometric designs such as the ´Al hamdu lillah´ (God be praised) reproduced in Khatibi and Sijelmassi:

(Khatibi and Sijelmassi 1976 p42)

This example may appear somewhat remote, but a similar interpenetration of meaning and substance in English has been achieved by Kim, as in the following example which appropriately reads identically upside down:

(Kim 1981 p16)

Herdan describes a property of Chinese graphic substance which has been developed to a considerable degree of sophistication in the literary form known as the Chinese language game. This consists in the creation of a poem so constructed that by systematic reordering of the characters constituting the poem, a second poem is created. Herdan gives the following example from the Huei Wen T´u or Revolving Chart of the Lady Su Huei of the Eastern Ch´in Dynasty (317-419 AD):

```
            Original                    Transformation

         永 長 麗 香              合 廻 別 才
         懷 恨 錦 羅              繡 文 人 女
         天 幽 織 綺              綺 織 幽 天
         女 人 文 繡              羅 錦 恨 懷
         才 別 廻 合              香 麗 長 永
         [D C B A]              [V B C D]
```

(Herdan 1964 p208)

Corresponding phenomena in English would be crosswords, wordsquares and palindromes where the linguistic substance is given particular prominence.

        Acrostics
        Constitute
        Realisations
        Of
        Similar
        Textual
        Inventiveness
        Concerning
        Substance

Concrete poetry also exploits the appearance of graphic form on the page to add an additional layer of meaning. How much would have been lost, for example, of the meaning of Dylan Thomas's 'Now' or 'Vision Prayer' had he adopted a more conventional format for these poems (Thomas 1982)? In general, poetry places great value on the properties of substance and employs often to great effect the meaning possibilities inherent in rhyme, assonance, metre, alliteration and onomatopaeia. The gust of air that shook the bridle of Chaucer's monk, once heard "cynglen in a whistlynge wynd als clere" can still be heard today; a rose by any other name might smell as sweet but could not rhyme with 'those' or 'enclose', though Will Shakespeare knows that as things are it always will, just as he knows the power of a pun. On the other hand, there can be a tension between meaning and substance which accounts for the kind of paradox reported in Hofstadter, such as

        This sentence no verb

(Hofstadter 1981)

The problems of decipherment of unknown languages discussed in Pope and of cryptography described by Kahn both place a premium on the formal properties of language substance (Pope 1975, Kahn 1973).

It would be a mistake to regard such features as mere eccentricities of the language system operating on the periphery of meaningfulness. On the contrary, they are manifestations of a potential central to the nature of language. This is the possibility of exploiting the medium in which language must necessarily be realised to meaningful effect. It is this property which, as noted above, renders much literary creation possible. Thus an advantage of the position I am adopting is that literature can be viewed, not as a sophisticated excrescence on an assumed more fundamental communicative function, but as rooted in the very core of language and basic to its use. Sinclair has pointed out that to be able to accomodate literature naturally within its description is an important goal for any linguistic theory (Sinclair 1983a). The significance of literature in this respect has also been noted by Foucault. He argues that

> "Through literature, the being of language shines once more on the frontiers of Western culture - and at its centre - for it is what has been most foreign to that culture since the sixteenth century; but it has also, since this same century, been at the very centre of what Western culture has overlain." (Foucault 1970 p59)

Foucault is suggesting that the "raw being" of language has disappeared from the modern perspective except in literature and thus what is in fact inherent in the nature of language appears as foreign to the culture.

Nonetheless, the realisation of this potential is not entirely restricted only to the more obvious manifestations of artistic activity. In expository prose the substantial nature of the linguistic signifier may be somewhat suppressed but its influence is still felt. Thus one can speak of prose having a rhythm or cadence; in short, of aesthetic effect. Similarly, change of type face is frequently of major significance in academic text.

More conventional analyses, however, also point in the same direction. Swieczkowski has highlighted the meaningfulness of the neglected field of word order patterning and Haas in his discussion of the zero morpheme describes with some humour the dangers of unwarranted abstraction from substance (Swieczkowski 1962, Haas 1957). Phatic communion illustrates that meaning can sometimes reside not in the semantics of the discourse but in its substance, the simple fact that something rather than nothing is said. The converse is also true and the absence of substance, that is silence, also has a role to play as Basso has pointed out (Basso 1970). Likewise, with taboo language expletives, for example, the significance is in the act of utterance, not in the denotation which may, indeed, command a physical impossibility.

To summarise the discussion so far; if ´valeur´ is a function not only of paradigmatic organisation but also of syntagmatic patterning, the conclusion is that a knowledge-free distributional analysis of textual substance will reveal the existence of systematic patterning which can be interpreted as a meaning system. An investigation along these lines might provide information about the way in which conceptual structures are elaborated on the basis of critical juxtaposition of textual elements. In other words, it offers a way of answering the question of how textual sequence leads to cognitive order. In this investigation it would be both unnecessary and inappropriate to invoke semantic criteria: the purpose of the study is to reveal the semantics of text as manifest in its macrostructural organisation. This position thus takes an essentially contextual view of meaning. It is therefore necessary to look a little more closely at theories which derive meaning from the relation of linguistic items to their context. This I shall do in the next section.

1.3 Term Meaning and Context

The contextual view of meaning is associated in British linguistics above all with the name of Firth. Firth considers meaning to be a property of a system of relations. In this he approaches quite closely in some ways to the Saussurian view of language. It is true that in a number of respects Firth rejects the Saussurian position. He has no time, for example, for the Saussurian dualisms of ´langue´ and ´parole´ or ´signifiant´ and ´signifie´. But, more importantly, like Saussure he both regards language as an essentially social phenomenon and emphasises meaning as function in context. Thus he makes statements of position which seem to assume the Saussurian notion of ´valeur´

> "The phonetic function of form, of a sound, sound-attribute, or sound-group is then its use in contra-distinction to other ´sounds´; the phonetic value or use of any sound is determined by its place in the whole system" (Firth 1935 p20).

This could have come directly from the ´Cours de Linguistique Generale .

In order to generalise his vision of language as an essentially social phenomenon, Firth proposes one of his most important abstract theoretical categories, the ´context of situation´. The term did not originate with him; he himself derives it from Wegener´s work in the last century via Malinowski´s work in the first half of this (Malinowski 1945). But he is the first to give it technical precision and to incorporate it into a comprehensive linguistic theory as a feasible category for investigation. ´Context of situation´, which Firth regards as the prime analytical category, is an abstraction of a system of relations from the life of man in society. He considers that it

> "is best used as a suitable schematic construct to apply to language events, and that it is a group of related categories at a different level from grammatical categories but rather of the same abstract nature. A context of situation for linguistic work brings into relation the following categories:
>   A. The Relevant features of participants; person, personalities
>   i. The Verbal Action of the Participants
>   ii. The Non-verbal Action of the Participants
>   B. The Relevant Objects
>   C. The Effect of the Verbal Action"

(Firth 1950 p43).

Context of situation is not, however, susceptible of direct linguistic analysis. Text is the only immediate component of the context of situation which lends itself to analysis in this way. Hence Firth's lifelong insistence on the centrality of attested language data. Recognising the difficulties presented for analysis by the abstract categories of the context of situation, he suggests that a first approach can be made by dispersing the statement of meaning over a number of congruent levels of linguistic analysis and by limiting the analysis to an examination of what he calls "restricted languages" (Firth 1956b). With this suggestion he anticipates the concept of register which was introduced formally by his students eight years later (Halliday et al 1964). A restricted language is expected to be characteristic of particular text types and can be identified through the

> "collocations of the key or pivotal words" (Firth 1957b).

In other words, the meaning of particular words depends on their linguistic context which derives ultimately from the parameters of the context of situation.

Thus Firth argues that the complete meaning of a word is always contextual. This leads him to the apparently extreme position of considering each use of a word in a new context as an occurence of a new word (Firth 1951). Conversely,

> "an isolated word which does not function in a context of experience has little that can be called meaning" (Firth 1930).

There is thus no room in this thorough-going statement of contextual meaning for the traditional Fregean notion of sense. Firth argues vigorously, for example, against the view of meaning as somehow 'contained' in words which 'express' the meanings enshrined against their written forms in dictionaries (Firth 1930). Rather, the significance that he ascribes to formal relations leads him to give prominence in very much the same way as was discussed in the preceding section to the 'shape' or 'appearance' of the linguistic element, to its plain 'face value'. In his own introduction to his collected papers for the period up to 1951 he pursues this theme

> "Words stare you in the face from the text, and that is enough; and as Wittgenstein said, a word in company may be said to have a physiognomy" (Firth 1957a pxii).

Collocational analysis thus offers the prospect of investigating language variety on the basis of lexical patterning, a possibility noted later by Sinclair (Sinclair 1966). Firth sees in the notion of collocation the linguistic basis of style, as he demonstrates in his examination of Swinburne's language (Firth 1956a, 1957c). This is an important insight because, as Schmidt argues, the analysis of text structure depends on the success with which a typology of texts can be established (Schmidt 1977).

The relationship between context of situation, text structure and text typology is also of central concern to Halliday, who regards what he calls the "generic structure" of text as ultimately determined by features of the non-linguistic context.

> "The concept of generic structure can be brought within the general framework of the concept of register, the semantic patterning that is characteristically associated with the 'context of situation' of a text." (Halliday 1978 p134)

This semantic patterning gives rise to what Halliday and Hasan refer to as

> "continuity of meaning in relation to the situation" (Halliday and Hasan 1976)

or "coherence". The concept of continuity of meaning is closely related to the notion of aboutness as Sinclair points out

> "The patterns of retrospection cover what we call topic, theme, content, subject-matter and notions. None of these can be accurately defined, because there is something ad hoc and locally interpretative about retrospective patterns in text....The reader or listener is often aware merely of a semantic coherence running through the discourse, which can be named at any time as a topic or theme." (Sinclair 1980c p257)

The important point to be grasped from the related body of work surveyed in this section is that the analysis of collocation, that is, of the syntagmatic patterning of linguistic items in the linear sequence of text, can lead to an understanding of

the nature of text structure and hence can help clarify the
basis upon which the notion of subject matter rests. The
Firthian linguistic tradition emphasises the relationship
between the overt linguistic patterning of text and the
creation of meaning at different levels of analysis. Thus it
both supports the theoretical view of text which emerged from
the consideration of the Saussurian position and offers
important methodological suggestions for the kind of analysis
that needs to be undertaken in order to elucidate the concept
of aboutness.

1.4 Text Structure

Some attempts have been made to tackle the problem of aboutness
directly within linguistics. Van Dijk, for example, asks

> "in what respect can we say that a sentence is ´about´
> something? Similar questions may be formulated for
> sequences of sentences and whole discourses. Our
> linguistic behaviour shows that we can say that a
> discourse, or part of it, was ´about´ something. That
> is, we are able to produce other discourses, or parts of
> discourses, expressing this ´aboutness´ eg in summaries,
> titles, conclusions or pronouncements in any form." (Van
> Dijk 1977a pp130-131)

It has been postulated that this ability to extract a notion of
aboutness over large stretches of text arises from the
activation by the text of conceptual ´schemata´. These are
psychological constructs which orient the reader to the text
and guide his interpretation of it. This theory is explored in
the work on the cognitive representation of narratives by van
Dijk and others (Kintsch 1977, Rumelhart 1975, Thorndyke 1977,
van Dijk 1977a). The difficulty with this approach is that
the ´schemata´ are postulated to fit the text for analysis and
are then used to ´explain´ the text. The technique begs the
question.

However, the attempt to tackle these issues led in the
seventies to the growth of the field of enquiry known as text
linguistics in which the concept of the high-level organisation
of text plays an important role. This is emphasised, for
example, by van Dijk and Kintsch

> "We distinguish between two different levels of meaning
> in discourse, viz. between that of its actual sentences
> and sequences of sentences, and that of parts of the
> discourse or of the discourse as a whole. The latter
> kind of meaning structures will be called
> macro-structures." (van Dijk and Kintsch 1977 p67)

and by van Dijk alone

> "It seems to follow that a notion such as topic of
> discourse cannot simply be explained in terms of semantic
> relations between successive sentences. Rather each of

MEANING, SUBSTANCE AND ABOUTNESS

the sentences may contribute one ´element´ such that a certain STRUCTURE of these elements defines the topic of that sequence....These and other observations have led to the assumption that we should postulate an additional level of semantic description, viz., that of semantic MACRO-STRUCTURES" (van Dijk 1977a p6).

This seems promising as far as it goes, and clearly related to the issues raised in the first section. Unfortunately, however, text linguistics started off on the wrong methodological foot. An early central tenet of the approach was that text can in some sense be accounted for within the framework of grammatical theory. From the statements of text linguists themselves, it is apparent that their basic position entails an extension of the generative grammatical model to encompass sequences of sentences. This aim is made explicit by Rieser in his review of the field

> "The methodological argument was based on the intuitively justifiable assumption that discourses should be regarded as the ´natural domain´ of a grammar rather than sentences" (Rieser 1977 p11)

and the same view is stated in various places by other advocates of text linguistics (van Dijk 1973a, Petofi 1973, 1977).

But is it in fact "intuitively justifiable" to consider text as "naturally" falling within the explanatory power of grammar? On the contrary, is it not far more likely that the systems established to account for meaning at the level of syntactic structure, and hence concerned with well-formed patterning extending over short sequences of words, will prove inadequate to offer any insight into the structure of texts, which may have no well-formedness constraint governing their composition and contain very long sequences of words? Sinclair has called attention to a fundamental theoretical confusion

> "One danger that can be foreseen is that they will assume that the descriptive categories appropriate to sentences (derived from the patterning that Saussure called <u>langue</u>), will be imposed with some ingenuity and much labour, on text (Saussure´s <u>parole</u>)." (Sinclair 1980b pp15-16)

Thus Sinclair and Coulthard argued that structures beyond the sentence in one use of the spoken language are more economically described by postulating a new level of organisation in which the categories at lower levels are available, unordered, for recombination in ways peculiar to the higher level (Sinclair and Coulthard 1975).

It is extremely plausible that a similar mechanism operates in the written language. Halliday and Hasan, for example, claim that the relationship between sentences and text is not one of constituency but of realisation (Halliday and Hasan 1976).

Hasan, describing the Systemic-Functional model of text, proffers an implicit criticism of the text linguists' position

> "at no stage does this model view the text as a ´super-sentence´. By implication it also rejects a taxonomic hierarchy with an unbroken constituency chain from morpheme to text, a view implied in Harris (1952, 1963), Pike (1963), van Dijk (1972) and others." (Hasan 1977 p228)

Indeed, Petofi himself, one of the foremost proponents of text grammar, recognises that the result of this attempt to account for semantic phenomena in terms of grammatical categories may be a redefinition of grammar. Petofi suggests that

> "one can attempt to reach this aim by enlarging the apparatus which was originally devised for the description of object language sentences. It must naturally also be clear that the resulting expanded apparatus will no longer be very similar to the original sentence grammar." (Petofi 1977 p45)

This, however, is in effect to say that the grammatical approach to text is inappropriate. There is ample evidence in Petofi's work on TeSWeST (his so-called Text-Struktur-Welt-Struktur-Theorie) of how unmanageable the expanded grammatical apparatus has to become.

The kind of redefinition of grammar that would have to take place is outlined by van Dijk, who claims that the base component of a grammar capable of describing text macro-structure can take the form of a ´text logic´ (van Dijk 1973a). The most fully developed logical theory of language is to be found in Montague's work. Whilst there may be theoretical attractions in subscribing to Montague's view that there is

> "no important theoretical difference between natural languages and the artificial languages of logicians" (Montague 1970b p222; see also Montague 1970a),

Montague is only able to account for the greatly restricted aspects of natural language embodied in the examples he constructs for the development of his argument. The explanatory power of such approaches must thus be questionable and it is, I believe, reasonable to view with suspicion any theory that hopes to account for the meaning of sentences in terms of the sum of the meanings of their parts. Speech act theory has demonstrated that language is not straightforwardly additive in this way. Thus despite Montague's discussion of pragmatics, his work shows little concern with the basic issues of how language operates to help create and maintain its social context (Montague 1968, 1970c).

Van Dijk appears to be aware of the problem and of the inability of conventional logics to handle the semantics of natural language. The most suggestive implication of his attempt to create a text logic is that even a modal predicate calculus would have to be so weakened to meet the requirements of a natural text logic that it is doubtful whether it can be considered a logic at all. Petofi recognises the difficulty and admits that

> "even if we had at our disposal all the philosophical logics necessary for the syntactic description and semantic interpretation of natural languages, and all problems within the particular logics had been solved, this would still not mean that all these logics could function without major difficulties as subsystems within a highly complex system;
> (1δ) many of the fundamental questions arising from the application of model-theoretical interpretations to natural language discourses have not yet been solved, not even within the already existing philosophical logics" (Petofi 1977 pp40-41).

He had already come to the same pessimistic conclusion earlier (Petofi 1975). Thus the redefinition of logic is no more successful than the redefinition of grammar.

Petofi's observation is the Trojan horse in the citadel of text linguistics. Despite the superficially impressive apparatus of logical calculi, the approach has achieved little and even its advocates recognise that there is a crucial lack of evidence for their theories. In their overview to a collection of papers on text grammar, Petofi and Rieser admit that the

> "empirical proofs for these intuitively reasonable assumptions still have to be provided" (Petofi and Rieser 1973 p11)

and Rieser offers an evaluation from within the school which has the ring of an epitaph

> "In hindsight it can be said that text linguistics tried to apply formal apparatuses too early, perhaps because in general the role of formalization in theory construction was grossly overrated....The precise explicitation of one's linguistic intuitions should come first, and only then does formalization make sense. Formalization alone cannot be equated with having a theory....nor can it be used - as is frequently the case - to cover up the neglecting of empirical data" (Reiser op cit p15).

Such is the price paid for ignoring Firth's emphasis on "renewal of connection with experience".

The point about the absence of data is well made. Even where empirical analyses have been undertaken, these do not extend beyond the shortest of texts (van Dijk 1973a, 1977a, van Dijk and Kintsch 1977). This does not, however, appear to deter van Dijk, who seems to regard data as a somewhat unnecessary evil in the face of which he maintains an uncompromising theoretical purity:

> "A further note of caution is that our theoretical abstractions and generalizations apply to an idealised discourse. Actual discourses that are produced, understood and accepted do not always have a fully correct textual structure." (van Dijk 1977b p6)

Thus the theory is saved by arguing that it is the data that are out of step.

At this point there is little alternative but to abandon the attempt to understand text linguistics. It is clear that although the approach raises pertinent questions, it is ill-conceived as a means of answering them. I accept that the basic insight into macrostructure is valid but draw the conclusion that any attempt to investigate it must look for evidence in the concrete patterning of linguistic substance rather than hope for insights to be generated by the abstractions of text theoretical apparatuses.

A broadly similar conclusion regarding the value of text linguistics is reached by Roe in his enquiry into the notion of difficulty in scientific text (Roe 1977a). He likewise chooses to retain the text linguists' concept of macrostructure whilst rejecting their methodology and most of their objectives. Roe's principal concern is to investigate how scientific subject matter can be said to be embodied in text. Now it will become clear in the next section that I do not accept the assumptions upon which his formulation of the problem is based. Roe postulates a notion of the "systems of science" which he sees as distinct from the various "realisation systems", mathematical, graphical and linguistic, in which he claims they are embodied. I do not, however, believe that it is possible to ascribe existential status to the former independently of the latter. Nevertheless, Roe is concerned with issues of central importance to this book. He focuses upon the conceptual structure of text, he argues pertinently that it is a global textual phenonemon and he seeks some of his evidence by means of a distributional analysis of the lexis of the texts in his corpus. For these reasons, I shall close this discussion of theories of text structure with a consideration of his work.

The main thesis in Roe's study is the claim that there is a mismatch between what he calls "the systems of science" and "the systems of the English language". This mismatch leads to what he refers to as the non-linearity of macrostructures, which he argues is a major contributory factor to difficulty in decoding science text. His argument, however, is obscured by a failure to distinguish clearly between the conceptual aspect of linguistic meaning and the interactive construction of text. Although he is primarily concerned with the encapsulation of non-linguistic reality in text, virtually the only linguistic data he offers directly in support of his thesis are examples of the organisation of the text as discourse rather than of the embodiment of topic. He sets up an impressive theoretical apparatus to explore the notion of macrostructure, constituted of such categories as "match factors", "valency" and "P-segments", but is unable to substantiate it with hard linguistic evidence. The one major example of macrostructure that he adduces concerns the genesis of what he refers to as a "mathematical sentence". This illustrates how a complex mathematical expression is derived from a number of simpler expressions introduced at different points earlier in the text. But, being concerned with the mathematical realisation system, it throws little light on how "the systems of science" are related to "the systems of the English language".

In contrast, Roe´s description of the "language of humanisation", by which he means the personalisation introduced into the text by the author in order to present the subject matter to the reader, obviously pertains to the organisation of the text as discourse rather than to the genesis of subject matter. Whilst these features are relevant to Roe´s notion of difficulty, they cannot be taken as supporting the validity of his theoretical apparatus established to account for relations obtaining among elements of what he calls the "contents" of his texts. Consequently, his theory lacks explanatory power in just the areas of most relevance to the notion of aboutness.

His concern, however, with the notion of "content" leads him to a distributional analysis of the lexis of his texts, since, as noted earlier, it is this aspect of linguistic organisation which constitutes the most obvious way in which text creates cognitive meaning. The analysis appears to offer fruitful insights insofar as it allows him to establish a concept of "systemic lexis", which he argues is that lexis which displays a systematic relationship to textual content. He reaches this conclusion on the basis of a classification of vocabularies. He identifies four categories of vocabulary. The first two are primarily methodological in application; the first vocabulary allows him to eliminate from consideration the occurence of single letters in his texts (a not infrequent phenomenon in science texts) and the second performs the same function for modal and auxiliary verbs. The vocabularies that he identifies which are most pertinent to understanding the relationship between lexis and subject matter are those he calls "Synoptic Vocabulary 3" and the "Specialised Vocabularies". These are identified on a combined frequency of occurence and coverage criterion. A token of a single type which occurs with a minimum frequency of 0.03% (ie a minimum of 3 occurences per 10,000 running words of text) in at least 5 of the 10 texts constituting his corpus is assigned to the synoptic vocabulary. The 100 most frequent items which fail to meet this criterion form the specialised vocabularies for each text.

Roe´s claim is that synoptic vocabulary 3 contains largely "non-systemic lexis", whilst he argues that

> "from a brief inspection of the Specialized Vocabularies it is possible to construct a systemic lexical profile of

each text" (Roe 1977b p68).

It would be encouraging were the matter as simple as that, but unfortunately, in my view, the classification does not support the semantic interpretation quite as neatly as Roe would have us believe. There are, on my estimate, a minimum of 46 types included in synoptic vocabulary 3 (or some 15% of the total) which look <u>prima facie</u> to be technical terms of the texts in which they occur. These terms include such items as ´angular´, ´density´, ´magnetic´ and ´velocity´. It is implausible that these do not contribute to the systematic relation between subject matter and text which Roe argues is the function of the specialised vocabularies. The problem in part arises because their classification in the synoptic vocabulary does not allow significant differences of meaning in different texts to be taken into account. And yet this must also be relevant: the term ´solution´, for example, as employed in mathematics is not at all the same as the ´solution´ found in a chemistry text, and the same is true of many other technical terms. The difficulty is that a straightforward distributional analysis of the type undertaken by Roe is insufficiently delicate to offer anything but the most general of evidence towards establishing the linguistic basis of aboutness. In conclusion, then, I do not think that Roe´s claim that "a systemic lexical profile" can be constructed simply by inspection of the specialised vocabularies can in fact be sustained, even assuming that the nature of such a profile is well understood.

1.5 Text and Reality

There is one common thread which runs through the various approaches to text discussed in the preceding sections. This is that they all make certain assumptions about the relationship obtaining between text and the non-linguistic world. Text is held to stand in a describable relation to ´reality´. Roe, for example, speaks of the systems of science as distinct from language; the Firthian tradition is above all concerned with the connection between text and its social context; Saussure´s concept of the linguistic sign is a relational one, bringing into association a signifier and what is signified.

There is thus a fundamental assumption that ´reality´ is a given and that through the systems of language it is encapsulated in text. Text is seen as a mirror of reality, perhaps a distorting one at times, but nonetheless as essentially doing no more than reflecting something which exists outside language. Texts are deemed to be a form of linguistic organisation which allows ´content´ to be embodied in language. Likewise, the notion of text typology rests upon the assumption that different classes of text can be identified by referring them to distinctive features in the non-linguistic environment. Thus all text is a kind of programme music, only interpretable by reference to external ideas, neither intrinsically complete nor self-contained.

These assumptions must be examined since they bear directly on

the central concerns of this book. The basic question of
interest is how subject matter or content is, to use a
relatively neutral term, ´actualised´ by language. The problem
is whether the conventional terms in which the question is put
and the issue approached are helpful. Jones and Roe, for
example, argue strongly that there is a need for

> "a rhetoric that reveals how knowledge is mapped into
> the print and sound systems of English" (Jones and Roe
> 1975 p2).

I agree with the perception of the need but question whether
the existential status implied for knowledge is in fact
justified. Is it necessary to postulate a pre-existent reality
which is independent of the linguistic systems which are used
to express it? Is it not more appropriate to use an
alternative mathematical, or possibly cartographic, metaphor
and to speak rather of the need to understand how knowledge is
´projected´ by the "print and sound systems of English"?

At bottom, the issue concerns the status of the concept of
reference. Lexical items, for example, are commonly held to
refer directly to the world of phenomena, as Sinclair points
out (Sinclair 1983a). Yet even Sinclair, who also speaks of
text as achieving

> "a continuous internalisation of experience, from the
> world outside to the inner space of language" (ibid p3),

locates vocabulary on what he calls the "autonomous plane" of
language. This is because vocabulary, that is, motivated
choice of lexical items, is a major means for the

> "gradual sharing of relevant experience by recalling
> previous words and phrases and reworking them in the new
> contexts provided....The stage by stage tally of the
> record of experience will be called the <u>autonomous
> plane</u> of discourse, because it is concerned with
> language only and not with the means by which language
> is related to the world outside." (ibid pp3-4)

Thus it seems that the notion of reference is an inadequate
response to the problem.

The alternative is, then, to consider text as ´projecting´ its
own reality, as, in some sense, ´creating´ a reality. This may
seem an extravagant idea, although it has long been accepted as
an appropriate way of approaching the phenomenon of literature.
This point of view has frequently been made explicit by
literary writers themselves. Writing of his poem ´I Make This
In A Warring Absence´, Dylan Thomas, for example, claims that

> "Images <u>are</u> what they say, not what they stand for"
> (see Thomas 1982 p263).

Elsewhere I have examined the implication of one of Borges´

short stories in his collection ´Ficciones´ entitled ´Pierre Menard, Autor del Quijote´ (Phillips forthcoming). In this story, Borges, through an ingenious exercise in comparative literary criticism, demonstrates that literally identical texts are capable of creating very different views of reality; that meaning lies not in the reference of the words but rather in what the reader brings to the text (Borges 1980).

It may seem, however, that this position is untenable in the case of science text. Science text, it could be argued, is above all concerned with the mapping of the conceptual structures of science into language. And yet there is suggestive counter-evidence to this view. The pages of ´Scientific American´, for example, abound with pertinent examples, such as the following

> "For the atom, the nucleus and the proton, then, the mass of the system is at least as large as the kinetic energy of the constituents and in some cases is much larger. If quarks and leptons are composite, however, the relation of energy to mass must be quite different. Since the prequarks have energies well above 100 GeV, one would guess that they would form composites with masses of hundreds of GeV or more. Actually the known quarks and leptons have masses that are much smaller; in the case of the lepton and the neutrinos the mass is smaller by at least six orders of magnitude. The whole is much less than the sum of its parts." (Harari 1983 p58)

Here a model for phenomenological reality at its most fundamental level is described. It should be noted, however, that there is no evidence in this extract that the model is simply postulated. Many of the sentences have the linguistic form of assertions of fact and the use of ´known´ to modify ´quarks and leptons´ is interesting. Note, too, how by preceding the word ´prequarks´ with the definite article existential status is thereby ascribed to them. Thus fundamental particles are apparently created by talking about them, which presumably accounts for their proliferation.
In other words, what counts as a quark, or a table for that matter, is a linguistic rather than a phenomenological question. Leech points out that

> "The extent to which, for example, the furthering of human knowledge through science is a linguistic activity has probably been underestimated." (Leech 1981 p24)

In this way, language is seen to be constructive of reality. This view finds support in contemporary sociology. Berger and Luckman, for example, ask how it is that subjective meanings become objectified and so acquire independent existence and argue that

> "language objectifies the world, transforming the

panta rhei of experience into a cohesive order. In
the establishment of this order language *realises* a
world, in the double sense of apprehending it and
producing it." (Berger and Luckmann 1967 p173)

Similar views can be found expressed in philosophy and
anthropology. Levi-Strauss, for example, makes a point of
rejecting the Cartesian direct intuition of reality:

> "Descartes believes that he proceeds directly from a
> man's interiority to the exteriority of the world,
> without seeing that societies, civilizations - in other
> words, worlds of men - place themselves between these two
> extremes." (Levi-Strauss 1977 p36)

Within linguistics this position appears to be less firmly
established. Nevertheless, it is perhaps easily overlooked
that even Saussure's distinction between the signifier and the
signified is to be taken as postulating a relationship
obtaining wholly within language. Saussure in fact disavows
the view that the signified exists apart from the signifier
when he says

> "There are no pre-existing ideas, and nothing is
> distinct before the appearance of language." (Saussure
> 1974 p154)

This view is echoed by Leech when he argues that language is
the means by which we organise experiences and thus impose
post factum a structure on them (Leech 1981). Even Firth,
apparently an empiricist par excellence, can be discovered
admitting that

> "there are no scientific facts until they are stated.
> And statement is the final stage at several removes from
> the first experience of the material. The common view
> of acts as brute and basic ultimates for everybody is
> misleading" (Firth 1953 p30).

But it is, of course, within the rationalist rather than the
empirical tradition of linguistics that statements of the
constructivist position may be expected. Thus in the French
post-structuralist perspective, Foucault uses the term
´discours´ to mean much the same sort of phenomenon as text in
the view of it that has been reached here. Inasmuch as he
offers any definition of the terms with which he conducts his
discussion, Foucault defines ´discours´ as

> "language in so far as it represents - language that
> names, patterns, combines, and connects and disconnects
> things as it makes them visible in the transparency of
> words. In this role, language transforms the sequence
> of perceptions with a table and cuts up the continuum of
> beings into a pattern of characters." (Foucault 1970
> p311)

For Foucault, then, discourse is a function of language, the function which actualises how we conceptualise experience.

The principal conclusion to be drawn from this stage of the discussion is that traditional linguistic categories established to handle the relationship between language and phenomena are unlikely to prove helpful. It was seen earlier in section 1.3 that the notion of sense was untenable for present purposes. In this section the concept of reference has been found to be similarly wanting. A view of text has emerged in which it is seen as the linguistic means by which different realities are projected. The aspect of text which is focused on in this book is its property of being a stretch of language which fulfills this function. What are the linguistic mechanisms which enable text to function in this way? This is a question which will occupy much of the discussion in later chapters.

1.6 Conclusion

There are a number of lessons which can be learnt from the preceding survey of approaches to the syntagmatic patterning of language and the analysis of text. The first is that there appears to be a crucial lack of evidence for all the key notions required by the theories of text considered here. Neither the work in text linguistics nor Roe's analysis of science text are able to substantiate the notion of macro-structure. And yet it seems to be an inescapable category. Similarly, Roe's concept of systemic lexis is suggestive but rests on flimsy empirical foundations. This failure to support theory with appropriate data is not, however, a problem of principle but of method. It will be shown later that by adopting a different approach to the analysis of text it is possible to accumulate the evidence necessary for establishing both the notion of macrostructure and of systemic lexis.

The important clue towards developing an effective methodology is given by Saussure's tenets concerning the linearity of language and the differential nature of the linguistic sign. These suggest strongly that the orthographic word can be considered as a unit of textual organisation and that a knowledge-free analysis of the terms in a text will throw light upon the way text is able to create an image of reality. The hypothesis is that such an analysis will reveal evidence of systematic and large-scale patterning which can be interpreted as contributing to the semantic structure of text and hence as constituting a major device through which the notion of content arises. In other words, it is upon the recognition by the reader of such patterning that the sensation of aboutness depends.

The third major conclusion arising from the preceding dis-cussion is that conventional linguistics has difficulty in adjusting to an appropriate perspective for the investigation of these issues. It was seen how the categories of sense and reference, which have traditionally been used to accomodate the

consideration of word meaning, entailed acceptance of
assumptions which would be difficult to sustain in the context
of the present study. The crucial concept of a knowledge-free
analysis of text viewed as a linear sequence of graphic symbols
is itself relatively unconventional. This suggests that an
original methodology is needed for the exploration of the
issues raised in this chapter. Precisely why this is so and
what the nature of an appropriate methodology might be are
questions which will be considered in the next chapter.

CHAPTER

LINGUISTICS IN THE STUDY OF TEXT

2.1 Levels of Linguistic Description

In the last chapter the problem of explaining the linguistic basis of aboutness was raised. It was seen that investigation of the problem would involve study both of large scale text structure and the contribution made to text structure by term meaning. Considerations deriving from Saussurian and Firthian linguistics suggested that an approach which treats text as a linear sequence of items acquiring formal meaning through positional value in the sequence might offer insights into the way in which the high level meaning of text is constructed. It was suggested that from within the Anglo-American linguistic tradition this led to a relatively unconventional view of text which might be easier to accomodate within the French post-structuralist approach. The kind of approach to text adopted by scholars such as Foucault, however, does not offer a recipe for the analysis of text. It may be, then, that an innovative methodology will have to be developed in order to investigate the issues raised here. Hutchins, writing from within the perspective of information science, both asks the right questions and indicates the nature of the difficulty

> "The ability to say what a text is about must be regarded as one facet of our ability to understand a text; if we do not understand a text we find it difficult to say what it is about. It is therefore somewhat unfortunate that summarisation has been neglected by linguists as much as it has by information scientists" (Hutchins 1977 p17).

The basic difficulty arises from our inability to achieve rational understanding without analysis. Where the study of linguistic meaning is concerned, this implies that language must be viewed as consisting of a number of interrelated systems operating at different levels of analysis. This is seen very clearly by Firth, who argues that his concept of the context of situation

> "is a convenient abstraction at the social level of analysis and forms the basis of the hierarchy of techniques for the statement of meanings. The statement

> of meaning cannot be achieved by one analysis at one
> level, in one fell swoop" (Firth 1950 p44)

and goes on to speak of the

> "analytic dispersion of the statement of meaning at a
> series of levels" (Firth 1957b p8).

But how many of these levels are relevant to an understanding of the macrostructure of text? In other words, what light can conventional linguistic theory throw upon the theoretical issues raised in the last chapter? To answer these questions, it is necessary to examine the scope of the different levels of linguistic analysis in turn.

The commonly recognised levels of linguistic analysis are the phonological/graphological, the morphological, the lexical, the syntactic and the discourse levels. Different theories call them by different names but it has usually been found necessary to set up qualitatively different categories corresponding to levels such as these in order to account for different classes of meaning. Halliday puts the theoretical case for these levels (Halliday 1961).

The crucial point concerning aboutness is that it is a type of meaning arising from the global structuring of text. It is thus possible to dispense immediately with consideration of the phonological/graphological level of meaning. Since written text is in the focus of attention, it can be taken that for the purposes of text analysis as conceived in the last chapter phonological meaning does not enter into consideration. It may be thought, given the emphasis placed here on the substantial nature of the linguistic sign, that a study of graphology could be of relevance. But the graphological system of language deals with the correspondence between sound and writing and the rules of orthography. In relation to the present theoretical position, it is concerned only with non-significant dialectal variation (that is, alternative spellings in British and American varieties of English, for example).

The irrelevance of graphology to the study of text structure should not be taken to embrace whatever systematicity arises from the typographical patterning of printed text. Typographical features are certainly an aspect of the substance of the linguistic sign in written text. They do not, however, operate at a unique level of linguistic analysis but rather cut across a number of different levels. Moreover, although such features make some contribution to the overall semantics of the text, it is a relatively superficial one, as can be seen from the fact that different editions of the same book can have very different typographical layouts. I do not, therefore, propose to consider typography here.

It seems equally clear that the morphological level of analysis is inappropriate to the investigation of text structure. Word morphology relates to the function of words in syntactic frames; that is, it largely reflects syntactic structuring. Syntax itself, by definition, takes the sentence as the upper bound on the analytical categories it studies. It was seen in the last chapter that the text grammarians have noted that traditional grammar, which here includes generative syntax, cannot account for intersentential cohesion. Still less can it be expected to explain large scale structures extending over long texts. The case for the applicability of syntactic categories to patterning beyond the sentence is not proven. Syntax, then, is concerned with linguistic patterning only on the local scale of the sentence and in consequence has little of interest to offer to the issues considered here.

The lexical level of analysis looks a far more promising candidate. The relationship between term meaning and ´reality´ on the one hand and textual patterning on the other was touched upon in the last chapter. The choice of vocabulary in a text is largely a function of the subject matter. It was also seen that it could be argued that lexical meaning does not inhere as if by magic in particular words but is called into existence by the functioning of lexis in text. Lexis, then, appears to be a major device for organising experience and consequently the lexical level of linguistic analysis may be expected to be an appropriate level at which to make statements of meaning of relevance to the understanding of aboutness.

Unfortunately, it appears that relatively little exists in the way of a lexical theory which considers lexis in its text forming role. A few scattered hints may be found, such as are provided in the concept of register considered in the last chapter. There is some suggestive work in the field of lexical collocation which I shall consider later (Sinclair et al 1970). Perhaps Halliday and Hasan have come closest to tackling the problem in their observations on the cohesive role of lexis in text. They recognise the cohesive role played by lexis through the devices of reiteration, lexical relations and collocations. However, it is difficult to accept that their distinction between coherence and cohesion can be sustained where the function of lexis in text is concerned. Coherence is considered to be a semantic relation whilst cohesion is a structural one. I would argue that it is precisely the fact of the semantic relations obtaining between lexical items that gives rise to the lexical structure of text. Thus when they claim that

> "Cohesion is the set of meaning relations that is general to ALL CLASSES of text, that distinguishes text from ´non-text´ and interrelates the substantive meanings of the text with each other." (Halliday and Hasan 1976 p26)

it is not clear, when it is lexical items which are forming the cohesive bond, in what way the link is structural rather than semantic and is not simply a further aspect of what they call the "substantive meanings" of the text. In my view, then, the distinction between coherence and cohesion is invalid where

lexis is concerned and consequently it seems to me that
Halliday and Hasan obscure rather than clarify the issue.

Given this kind of difficulty, it is perhaps not surprising
that the lexical level of linguistic analysis has generally
been viewed as beginning at that point in the structure of
language where

> "increase in delicacy yields no further systems"
> (Halliday 1961 p267).

But if this is the case, then nothing systematic can be said
about word meaning and lexical studies become equivalent to the
compilation of a lexicon consisting merely of a compendium of
idiosyncratic facts about individual words. This is the
traditional view and can be traced back to Sweet and Jespersen
both of whom looked on the dictionary component of linguistic
theory as concerned with particularities rather than
generalisations. In so doing they lent their authority to an
attitude that persists to this day (Sweet 1892, Jespersen
1924).

But attempts to discover structure in the lexicon do not appear
to be any more promising. Studies in the delimitation of
semantic space such as those of Fillenbaum and Rapoport or
Lehrer are more concerned with cognitive structures in the
field of psychology or the structure of reality than with the
nature of linguistic systems (Fillenbaum and Rapoport 1971,
Lehrer 1974). Lehrer's work on cooking terms, for example,
relates to an aspect of the environment which itself is
unusually well structured. It is doubtful whether her approach
would stand up in the face of a less sharply determined
correspondence between language and the world. Fillenbaum and
Rapoport recognise the nature of the difficulty

> "even these sets of findings may be open to the same
> question as to whether the findings are about the world
> or, again, findings largely concerning linguistic
> organisation" (Fillenbaum and Rapoport op cit p105).

Furthermore, it has already been claimed that a concern with
text suggests the appropriacy of an essentially distributional
analysis. I therefore agree with Muller who argues that

> "the statistics of lexis is essentially syntagmatic"
> (Muller 1977 p10)

and that

> "any statistics of a paradigmatic nature is suspect"
> (Muller ibid).

Consequently, I cannot accept without heavy qualification the
basic assumption made by paradigmatic approaches such of those
of Lehrer or Fillenbaum and Rapoport that

"the meaning of a lexical item is a function of the meaning relations obtaining between that item and other items in the same domain" (Fillenbaum and Rapoport op cit pvii).

I shall return, however, in chapter four to consider the methodological implications of Fillenbaum and Rapoport´s work which I consider to be extremely valuable in providing clues to an appropriate technique for the large scale analysis of text.

For the same reasons, the Wortfeldtheorie will not serve (Trier 1966). Katz has offered a definitive critique of this approach to word meaning

"After it is stripped of all its speculative trappings the main deficiency of this work on semantic fields is that it is carried out independently of the general study of the grammatical structure of natural languages and in a manner that is even more intuitive and informal than traditional descriptive work on syntax." (Katz 1972 p347)

Katz himself, as well as other linguists such as Lyons, has attempted to develop a set of principles in terms of which word meaning can be investigated (Katz 1972, Lyons 1968, 1977). These approaches decompose meaning into ´components´ or ´semantic markers´ each of which represents what Bolinger refers to as an "atom of content" (Bolinger 1965). But Bolinger has cast doubt upon whether the "all-or-nothing" approach of componential analysis is adequate to capture the semantics of natural language. The weakness of such approaches is that they rest on an arbitrary definition of semantics and an overly atomistic view of meaning which confines it to such matters as implicational relations between statements. While componential analysis may thus afford insight into a restricted class of logical relations among word meanings, it contributes very little to an understanding of how lexis is organised on the global scale of text to produce the sensation of semantic coherence that the reader perceives as aboutness. The same holds of other attempts, such as Gruber´s, to incorporate a lexical component within the framework of generative semantics (Gruber 1976).

The fundamental reason that lexical studies have traditionally had little of interest to say concerning the actual use of words to create text concerns the place of such studies in linguistics. The question is, as Sinclair has pointed out, whether lexical study is to be considered a branch of conceptual semantics or an aspect of text analysis (Sinclair 1983b). The former has been the historical approach and has given rise, for example, to the contemporary interest in term banks. But Sinclair argues that the term bank approach is unrealistic. Terms do not operate like that; rather, they are continuously defined and redefined by their context as the text in which they have their existence unfolds. The argument is basically the same one that has already been encountered when Firth's views were considered. Each occurrence of a word takes place in a new context and to that extent is a new word. It is only through its occurrence in a context that it has meaning at all. The attempt to preserve word meaning <u>in vitro</u> is self-defeating since the living textual environment from which the term gains its significance is lost.

> "Terms", writes Sinclair in his summary of the deliberations of the Language and Terminology section at a recent Aslib conference, "are by no means independent of text; in fact they help to create it.
> More generally expressed, each word in each text is continuously defined by its usage. One speaker....has produced the slogan "Let usage decide". In fact usage will decide, whether we like it or not." (Sinclair op cit pp69-70)

Thus the level of discourse is left as the only candidate within conventional linguistics for a suitable approach to the understanding of the macrostructure of text. And at first sight it certainly looks the most promising of all the levels considered so far. Discourse analysis is the field of enquiry currently preoccupied with the largest scale of linguistic structure. But discourse analysis takes as its starting point assumptions which, though quite probably valid, are irrelevant to the analysis of text within the perspective developed here. It finds its philosophical roots in speech act theory and is thus concerned principally with the illocutionary force of utterances. Consequently, it pays more attention to what we do with language, in a restricted, functional sense of ´do´, than to what we say. This is stated explicitly by Sinclair and Coulthard, whose influential study has largely shaped contemporary discourse studies, in their summary of Sinclair´s inaugural lecture at Birmingham University delivered in 1966

> "a case is argued for the paramount importance of dynamic situational description, an approach to language which emphasizes that we <u>use language</u> rather than <u>say things</u>, that utterances <u>do</u> things rather than just mean things" (Sinclair and Coulthard 1975 p151).

I do not wish to dispute the value of this insight or to belittle the interest of the research which it has generated. It is reasonable to argue this case for the kind of situation that Sinclair and Coulthard studied and, indeed, for many others. The problem, however, is that this position has consequences which tend to focus discourse analysis as an analytical technique on aspects of continuous stretches of language which are unrelated to the way that the issue of aboutness has been posed here.

The origin of discourse analysis in the view that language events are concerned with outcomes has led to an approach which accepts the centrality of interaction in the structuring of language behaviour. As Sinclair puts it

> "The phenomena which the level of discourse describes are those that arise when more than one participant is involved in creating linguistic structures, and where the activity is supposed to be purposeful." (Sinclair 1980c p253)

Sinclair himself points out that it is easier to view spoken discourse in this perspective than it is to regard written text as interactively constructed. Nonetheless, it is true to say that text depends for its realisation as much on the reader as it does on the writer. I would not dispute this and agree with Sinclair that it is possible, though difficult, to visualise written language as ultimately interactive in nature. I have already suggested in the last chapter that aboutness is a phenomenon in the reader which depends on linguistic clues found in the text. But I would also argue that where written expository text is concerned, the justification for its existence lies in what it says, in other words, in its subject matter content. Whilst I do not doubt that even in written text the implicit reader leaves linguistic traces which are susceptible of analysis, it is not this aspect of text which I am concerned to investigate.

Thus in my view studies of written text which accept the discourse analysis paradigm and focus on interactive features, such as those of Tadros or Cooper, miss the crux of the matter (Tadros 1981, Cooper 1983). Tadros, for example, argues

> "There is evidence that the writer does not simply present facts and ideas to the reader, but is rather concerned that these should be understood and accepted. Thus it is that the writer sometimes tries to persuade, cajole, convince and win the reader to his side." (Tadros op cit p413).

Again, I would not dispute that the manner of the writer's presentation of his argument is relevant to understanding the text. I would want, however, to ask why it is that the writer takes such pains to persuade, cajole and convince. What of the cognitive content of the argument itself? It cannot be the case that it plays no role in the structuring of the text. In considering Tadros' argument I am left with the uncomfortable feeling that not only is the propositional content of text relevant to an understanding of its structure, but is the central issue and one which in discourse analysis studies is necessarily avoided.

None of the approaches surveyed by Tadros in her exhaustive review of the literature of discourse analysis offers an adequate theoretical basis for understanding how the reader acheives an appreciation of what written text is about. Indeed, in the light of Tadros' criticism, the cynic might think that none of them seems to be adequate for what they themselves are about. Such approaches may help us to understand that the writer is, say, asserting rather than contradicting and clearly to grasp this is to advance our insight into the structure of text. But I contend that this is logically distinct from understanding what it is that is being asserted or contradicted, which is what, ultimately, the reader wants to know. It is the mechanism by which text triggers off an appreciation of content in the reader rather than the status of that content at any point in the text which concerns me.

Tadros draws attention to the kind of mistake that arises from a failure to appreciate the modal status of an utterance such as

> "The simplest way to increase food production, one might suppose, would be to bring more land under cultivation and put more people to work on it" (Tadros op cit pxvi).

But I would argue that the misinterpretation of this utterance which takes it as an assertion of fact is only possible in the light of its apparent propositional content. If the reader cannot decode the phrases ´increase food production´ or ´bring more land under cultivation´, the possibility of the discourse error simply does not arise. There is a logical priority in the notion of topic. As a result, as Bolivar has pointed out, approaches to discourse analysis such as these may illuminate internal features of text but have nothing to say about its connections to the world outside (Bolivar in progress).

Moreover, the highest unit of analysis at present generally recognised within discourse analysis is the ´event´, such as the ´lesson´, for example. The unit is, however, not very well defined and seems to depend for its recognition on the analyst´s intuitions in particular circumstances. Nor is it by any means clear whether it is applicable to written text and whether it can accomodate stretches of linguistic activity of the extent required by the theoretical considerations of macrostructure developed earlier. Certainly, Tadros came to the conclusion that the Sinclair-Coulthard model or later developments of it proposed for the analysis of spoken monologue by Montgomery could not appropriately be adapted to the investigation of written academic text (Montgomery 1977).

The various levels of analysis recognised by linguistic theory have now been considered in turn. The conclusion that is inevitably reached in the light of this discussion is that the investigation of aboutness cannot be conducted in terms of any of these levels. They are either not concerned with linguistic structure viewed on a sufficiently large scale or take as their objects of enquiry categories which are concerned with aspects of text which are not of central importance to the problem of aboutness. Conventional linguistics, then, is likely to prove unhelpful. It appears that it is necessary to look elsewhere for clues as to an appropriate methodology. It is to an examination of an alternative approach that I turn in the next section.

2.2 The Problem of Scale in Text Analysis

It has been argued that aboutness is realised in macrostructure and it became clear that macrostructure is not to be sought in the conventional components of linguistic theory which have hitherto been concerned with structuring only on the local scale. There are, of course, good reasons for this situation rooted in the historical impossibility of investigating very large stretches of language. Linguistics has traditionally been restricted to investigating the extent of language that can be accomodated on the average blackboard. Attempts to undertake analyses of cohesion over stretches of language consisting of more than a few sentences lead to the kind of triviality reported in Gutwinski (Gutwinski 1976). Harris was an early exponent of techniques for text analysis which adopt a knowledge-free distributional approach (Harris 1952). But precisely because of the difficulties of undertaking this kind of formal analysis, he was obliged to restrict himself to short exemplary texts of no more than a few sentences and to conduct his analysis in terms of ´equivalence classes´ at a level which hardly goes beyond the syntactic. He thus laid himself open to the criticism made by Hasan of treating text structure as no more than syntax writ large (Hasan 1977).

In contrast, the distribution of distinctive elements throughout the linearity of text may be expected to lead to patterns which are detectable only over considerable extents of language. Most lexical items occur infrequently. Even in a highly specialised expository text of some 50,000 running words, where particular technical terms may achieve unusually high frequencies, it is exceptional that the occurrence of a single term exceed 1% of the total. The repetition of most lexical items upon which any kind of lexical patterning must be based is an extremely rare event. Consequently, as Sinclair points out

> "Even a glance at the statistics of word occurrence suggests that to gain access to the characteristics of language one requires texts of length that puts them well out of scale of direct human observation"
> (Sinclair 1980b p15).

Observation of such patterning is difficult and requires the assistance of computers. Techniques for studying texts in this way are in their infancy.

It is at this point that it is necessary to consider a rather different approach to the investigation of linguistic phenomena from those surveyed hitherto. The fact that it is likely that large amounts of text need to be analysed in order to reveal patterning suggests that the use of statistical techniques for data analysis is appropriate. As Herdan puts it

> "This is quite in accordance with how in empirical science the quantitative treatment arises; when the masses of observation become too great for individual or

> qualitative classification, then it is time to have recourse to quantitative classification by number and measurement, and, in general, to statistics." (Herdan 1962 p97)

Thus, not surprisingly, a statistical approach to text has the blessing of statisticians. But since statistical phenomena are those which result in the perception of mass regularities arising from large numbers of individual choices, the concept appears to apply naturally to text. Indeed, the fundamental problem of linguistic analysis is how to make general statements about language which can only ever be based upon finite samples of use. This is precisely the kind of problem to which statistics addresses itself.

It is within this perspective that the major corpora of English texts have been established and analysed. The principal published corpora are the American Heritage Intermediate (AHI) corpus, the Brown corpus and the Lancaster-Oslo-Bergen corpus. I ignore studies such as those of West or Thorndike-Lorge which were undertaken before computer assistance became feasible (West 1953, Thorndike-Lorge 1944). Thus Carroll, for example, applies Herdan's findings to the analysis of word frequency data and, in particular, uses the lognormal distribution in estimating the parameters of the theoretical population from which the samples represented in the Brown and AHI corpora are drawn (Kucera and Francis 1967, Carroll 1968, 1971). He thus tackles by statistical means the crucial issue of the validation of linguistic generalisations.

Some useful insights emerge as a result of this work. In the course of his analysis of the AHI corpus, for example, Carroll develops an index of usage which combines both frequency of occurrence and a measure of dispersion to characterise the ´coverage´ of items in the frequency count (Carroll 1971). Although I have not made direct use of this index, it will become clear that the combination of frequency of occurrence with distribution is more meaningfully reflective of the structure of text than either characteristic alone. In general, however, the published corpora fail to establish a clear relationship between frequency and function. The editors of the AHI corpus certainly recognise the necessity of a functional analysis of their data but admit that the need remains unfulfilled. Consequently, it is not clear what the value is even of specialised wordcounts derived from the basic corpus, such as Zettersten's count of scientific items derived from the Brown corpus (Zettersten 1969). This means that in practice the frequency counts of the major corpora have disappointingly little to contribute to the notion of text structure.

There is also a more fundamental reason for this comparative irrelevance. All the published corpora can be criticised on the grounds of their extent and composition. Engels reports research by Frumkina which suggests that ten million words is the minimum number for a corpus which might lead to a valid word count (Engels 1965). This view might be debatable but it is certainly arguable that the potential advantages of scale inherent in the five million words of the AHI corpus, for example, are negated by the decision to restrict any one constitutive sample to a mere five hundred running words. Similarly, the smaller Brown corpus of one million words is composed of samples from a wide variety of different types of text consisting of only two thousand words each, as is its British sibling the LOB corpus described in Leech and Leonard (Leech and Leonard 1974). Such limited extracts of continuous written language are totally inadequate in extent for the investigation of macrostructure. Generalisations founded upon an heterogeneous collection of small samples are to be treated with extreme caution. Where, however, the corpus does not aspire to generality in its coverage of types of text, the composition of the corpus may not be relevant to a given study. Thus the AHI corpus is aimed exclusively at representing American school texts categorised into curricular subjects. This clearly limits its general usefulness. Moreover, even where samples of text of reasonable length and covering appropriate subject matters are available for analysis, care must still be taken to ensure that extracts are linguistically coherent if valid generalisations are to be made from them.

Thus the advent of the digital computer and the more recent provision of powerful software for the analysis of text have not of themselves overcome all the technical difficulties of text analysis. Nevertheless, the problem of scale is now at least soluble in principle. As a result, the investigation of the macrostructure of text becomes a reality in its own terms rather than either a non-question or an unconvincing extension of lower level procedures. The convergence of the need to study long texts, the theoretical focus on linguistic substance and the appropriacy of a statistical treatment clearly indicate the suitability of a computational approach. The computer is well fitted to the non-semantic analysis of large stretches of linguistic substance.

This approach is not, of course, without its detractors. Jones and Roe, for example, have somewhat disparagingly characterised statistical analyses as "text crushing procedures" which throw the interpretative baby out with the methodological bathwater by eliminating along with problems of scale

> "the communicative function that items play, the dynamic throughput of a text, the functional meaning of discourse" (Jones and Roe 1975 p19).

But this type of criticism arises through a confusion of a particular methodology with the issues which prompt its use. The critique should be directed at the triviality of the questions asked of text by the kind of studies Jones and Roe have in mind rather than at the techniques themselves. I concede that there is little point in analysing language at any level for its own sake. The investigation of language in the substance-crushing fashion of the digital computer is indeed a meaningless activity if it is undertaken in response to no higher order concerns. This is a truism reflected in the garbage-in, garbage-out aphorism. It is a principle of investigation that it should be carried out at the highest level that the analysis will sustain. This means that it must ultimately be framed in response to questions which are themselves meaningful. But meaning comes from above. The morpheme, for example, has no meaning in itself but only by virtue of its function in the higher order system of the word. Likewise, the word gains significance only as part of the larger syntagmatic system of the sentence and the paradigmatic and semantic systems of the lexicon. In the end, language and its investigation become meaningful only in relation to the real world, an insight recognised in the Firthian category of context of situation. Wilden, who is centrally concerned with the necessity of distinguishing different levels of logical typing, puts the matter succinctly

"<u>No communication can be properly defined or examined at the level at which it occurs</u>" (Wilden 1980 p113).

Ultimately, then, research must arise in response to questions located outside linguistics. Linguistics is the handmaiden of epistemology and pragmatic concerns. It does not of itself formulate interesting questions; this is the responsibility of the mistresses it serves. In the present context the epistemological relevance is provided by framing the topic in terms of the problem of subject matter and aboutness. In order to explore these notions, it has been seen that text must be analysed at least at a level where it is regarded as consisting of strings of semantically empty symbols. The amounts of data that are likely to be involved suggest that a statistical treatment may be inescapable. It is thus necessary to examine statistical approaches to the analysis of text for the extent to which they illuminate meaningful issues concerning the structure of text. The question is how far a quantitative treatment can lead to qualitative insight. I shall explore this question in the next section.

2.3 Statistical Approaches to Text

A potential problem with the applicability of studies in quantitative linguistics is the risk of triviality. Statistical approaches not infrequently display a certain naivety about the nature of the object under investigation, particularly where language is concerned. A typical pitfall is the failure to distinguish between the very different manifestations of language in its written and its spoken forms. Often a disturbing heterogeneity of evidence is adduced which is used to substantiate statistically rather than linguistically conceived arguments. As a result, such approaches fall foul of the criticism voiced in the last section and lead, not to any deep insight, but to a quantification of only the more trivial aspects of text.

Certainly the risk of such triviality often threatens to
obscure the otherwise highly original work of Herdan. His work
is fundamentally of interest, however, because he argues from a
perspective which suggests a view of language quite close to
the theoretical position outlined in the last chapter when he
says

> "The reader should observe that according to my theory of
> language structure, it is not logic which is made the
> starting point, the ´model´ of language, but the
> empirical fact of the linearity of the sequence of
> linguistic elements, and the relations of points and
> segments along that line, governed by the laws of
> projective geometry. Logic governs the relations between
> the concepts, whereas projective geometry governs the
> relations between the linguistic symbols, and thus
> provides the indication of the logical concatenation of
> the concepts. My derivation of grammar is thus
> completely immanent. It starts with the ´iron law´ of
> linearity, and explains the grammar forms as being
> subject to the general law governing the relations
> between the points and segments of the linear sequence of
> linguistic elements." (Herdan 1966 p8)

From this vantage point, he in fact makes a major contribution
to our understanding of the statistical properties of language
and most particularly in his work on type/token distributions,
first in his exploration of the lognormal distribution (Herdan
1956, 1960) and later as modelled by the Herdan-Waring
distribution (Herdan 1964, 1966).

He also argues that the Saussurian distinction between ´langue´
and ´parole´ has a natural statistical interpretation. The
distinction, he says, can be

> "made to correspond to that between the statistical
> population and the sample by letting ´langue´ stand for
> the totality of engrams in the brains of members of the
> speech community together with their probabilities of
> occurrence, and ´parole´ for random samples from it."
> (Herdan 1960 p34)

This is in fact an over-simplification since texts are in
reality non-random samples from an unknown population. This
Herdan later recognised and he modified his position
accordingly (Herdan 1966). This point is also noted by Muller
who suggests that Herdan´s interpretation of the ´langue-
parole´ dualism should only be accepted within well defined
limits. He argues that

> "the notion of probability of use should be applied only
> to a lexis of situation, and not to the lexis of the
> individual, still less to the lexis of the collectivity"
> (Muller 1977 p46).

In other words, the notion of engram-plus-probability is not in fact valid either for the individual language user or as, Herdan supposed, for the language community as a whole. It can, however, according to Muller, apply to the use of language in particular situations. This observation thus suggests the appropriateness of a statistical approach to the concept of register and with it the possibility of a quantitative basis to the typology of texts. At the same time, it makes it quite clear that large scale statistical regularity does not entail determinism at the level of individual use.

The statistical method thus becomes interesting when it facilitates qualitative statements which could not have been arrived at by any other means. This is well illustrated in the work of Zipf whose statistical approach to language was indeed elaborated to respond to a question framed outside the field of linguistics. His thesis, which attempts to establish the 'Principle of Least Effort' as a rationale for behaviour, linguistic or otherwise, cannot be accused of triviality (Zipf 1949). His substantive results are, in my view, totally unconvincing, although his most celebrated finding will provide a minor piece of evidence that I shall use when developing a methodology. This is Zipf's so-called 'law' which claims the existence of logarithmic straight-line relationship between the rank order of vocabulary items in a text and their frequency of occurrence. Herdan's observation should, however, be noted in passing that since the two variables involved are transformationally related, the 'law' cannot be regarded as a true one having explanatory force. It is not, however, either in the validity of his thesis or in the details of his results that the importance of Zipf's work lies. What he was amongst the first to achieve in linguistic research was the demonstration of the way in which a statistical methodology may appropriately be used to throw light on substantive issues. It is possible to disagree with the insight thus obtained but it is unwise to ignore the implications of the approach.

Statistical approaches to language are perhaps seen at their best when they act as contributions to forensic linguistics in, for example, authorship studies. They thus hold out the possibility of making generalisations in the field of stylistics. They offer the prospect of developing objective criteria to establish a taxonomy of texts and might consequently suggest elements of a methodology for the investigation of text structure. Yule, for example, in his pioneering statistical study of literary texts makes a number of shrewd methodological observations concerning such problems as the delimitation of the vocabulary set chosen for study, sampling technique, homograph discrimination, specification of sample size and the determination of valid inference (Yule 1944). His major contribution is the characteristic K. This is a single statistic, the value of which is independent of text length, intended to summarise the vocabulary distribution of a text. Sinclair, however, points out that it is far too global a criterion for any useful generalisations to be based upon it.

It seems, then, that on the whole work in quantitative linguistics has either been addressed to the solution of specific problems, and thus has not offered any general insights, or has promised more than it has yet delivered. There is, however, a small body of work which, from within the Firthian linguistic tradition, has used statistical techniques to good advantage and which has tackled questions of direct relevance to the theoretical issues discussed in the last chapter. It is to consideration of this work that I now turn.

2.4 Collocation and Distribution

Firth had already envisioned theoretically the possibility of analysing text as a probabilistic structure. He recognised that language operates in a matrix of conditioned probabilities. He points out that

> "We also do not feel at home unless there is a mutual expectancy, not only between the elements of language structures or of the elements of discourse in a conversation for example, or in a description, explanation or argument, but also between spoken or written words and the surrounding living space in which we breathe and move." (Firth 1959 p206)

It is clear that he views the conditioned probabilities of occurrence as structuring whole discourses in the context of situation. It has already been seen that Firth himself recognised the impracticality of an indiscriminate approach to text in general which led him to his proposals regarding the different levels of meaning. This facilitated the demarcation of distinct areas of linguistic enquiry. The concept of 'colligation', for example, arose from an early attempt by Mitchell to describe contextual meaning at the syntactic level of analysis (Mitchell 1958). Halliday further formalised many of Firth's suggestions and, what is of particular relevance here, justified the establishment of lexis as an independent level (Halliday 1966). This enabled Sinclair to take up Firth's views on conditioned probabilities by proposing a theory of lexical organisation which treated it not as a function of traditional dictionary-type relations within the lexicon but in terms of the syntagm. That is to say, lexical meaning was to be viewed as a system of positional values arising from distributional relations in the linear stream of language.

The first of two studies adopting this theoretical standpoint is that reported in Sinclair, Jones and Daley and summarised in Jones and Sinclair (Sinclair et al 1970, Jones and Sinclair 1973). Amongst the key notions introduced in this study are those of 'collocation', 'node' and 'span'. I shall examine these categories in more detail in the next chapter where questions of methodology are considered. For the purposes of the discussion at present, it is sufficient to note that 'node' refers to the lexical item in the focus of attention, 'span' relates to the number of items in the immediate context of the node and ´collocation´ is the term used to denote a common co-occurrence of items within a given span, that is the joint occurrence of a node and a particular ´collocate´.

A major concern of the Sinclair study was to give precision to the category of span upon which the whole notion of the lexical patterning of text rests. It is crucial to have a clear idea of how far the ´influence´ of a word extends into its syntagmatic environment since this determines the limits within which patterns of association are to be sought. Sinclair´s finding was that a span setting of four orthographic words on either side of the node yields optimum results. This result will be considered in more detail in the next chapter. A further key notion developed in this study is the possibility of identifying sets of lexical items based upon their frequency of syntagmatic association rather than on the concept of paradigmatic substitution. Sinclair had already posited the notion of ´cluster´ (Sinclair 1966) and in the later study a first attempt was made to identify a lexical set on the basis of the collocational patterning of lexical items. The authors of the study concluded that

> "This survey has shown that evidence of the lexical organisation of the language can be found by studying the patterns of significant collocation. There is thus good reason to expect that intuitively satisfying lexical sets could be formed based on collocational information from a very large body of natural language and using a clustering technique similar to the one developed during the project for identifying the meanings of ambiguous words." (Sinclair et al 1970 pp77-78)

This conclusion is of major importance since it suggests the possibility that by means of an objective distributional methodology, the existence of hitherto only suspected

> "forms of organisation in the language to which grammatical classification is irrelevant" (ibid p77)

could be revealed. It is a contention of this book that such forms of organisation are intimately connected with the creation of text macrostructure and that therefore the notion of aboutness can profitably be investigated by pursuing the mode of enquiry outlined in the Sinclair study. I do not believe, however, that the particular statistical approach adopted in this research is appropriate but I shall defer discussion of this aspect of the study to chapter four where I consider statistical techniques in detail.

The only other significant study adopting this general theoretical position is that of Berry-Rogghe (Berry-Rogghe 1970). She is concerned with the computational methodology of identifying significant collocations and with relating the resulting information on collocational patterning to conventional approaches to semantic theory. She makes some interesting suggestions of detail, such as proposing a more flexible notion of span in terms of a variable number of pure lexical items dependent on the grammatical category of the node. It is fair to say, however, that her results do not represent any significant advance on the position reached by Sinclair and his colleagues.

Both the study by Sinclair and that by Berry-Rogghe suffer from similar disadvantages. Major shortcomings are the small size of the corpora used and the questionable nature of their composition. The principal corpus used by Sinclair was 135,000 running words of spontaneous conversation which was supplemented by some 12,000 running words of 'scientific' text culled from a journal of popular science. It is clear that the extent of continuous language activity represented by any one sample in this corpus is inadequate to sustain an investigation of the macrostructure of text. Moreover, the extent to which science journalism can be regarded as representative of the specialist register of science is also open to question.

Berry-Rogghe's corpus is even less acceptable. It consists of a mere 71,595 running words whilst her treatment of it reveals gross linguistic naivety insofar as she accepts dramatic text as an adequate substitute for genuine conversation. She appears not to appreciate the fundamental difference in the contexts of situation which account for conversation as opposed to drama, not the least of which is the absence in the creation of the latter of factors pertaining to real-time control. The otherwise interesting work by Geens on his theatrical corpus and the investigation by Zipf, which I have already discussed, suffer from the same fallacy (Geens 1978, Zipf op cit).

A second weakness of these studies is that, having outlined the notion of lexical set, they make little attempt to assess its significance or to evaluate its role in text. There is a frustrating sense that the problem is abandoned just at the point where it begins to present real interest. Both studies are more concerned with investigating the concept of collocation per se than with answering any major higher order questions. Thus the following intriguing suggestion made by Sinclair was not followed up:

> "It is evident that there is a need for a taxonomic study of English. Firstly it would be of value to find the factors of the language, where by this we mean certain characteristics of the language which we can quantify and use to compare one text with another. Texts in English might then be classified using these factors" (Sinclair et al 1970 p36).

This point will be taken up in chapter nine and thus the present investigation will go some way towards meeting Lehrer's criticism of the collocational approach as non-explanatory. By relating the phenomenon of collocation to that of text macrostructure a beginning can be made on the explication of aboutness and the form of an explanation outlined for what Jones and Sinclair describe as

> "the relationship between the physical evidence of
> collocation and the psychological sensation of meaning"
> (Jones and Sinclair 1973 p15)

which was one of the main motivations prompting them to embark on this line of enquiry.

It must be borne in mind, however, that both the Sinclair and the Berry-Rogghe studies were undertaken before the advent of large scale integration microchip technology. This simple fact placed severe constraints on the amount of text processing that could be done. Thus these early investigations were essentially programmatic in nature. They pointed up the need for a taxonomic study of English, emphasised the irrelevance of grammar to such an enterprise but admitted that the relationship between the basic syntagmatic category of collocation and the structure of texts represented a major loose end in the programme. In fairness, both the size of the corpora and the goals of the enquiries were realistic for the period. Despite these constraints, the value of the work of Sinclair and his colleagues in opening up the field of distributional text analysis can hardly be exaggerated.

Since these early efforts Moscovich and Caplan have developed an approach concerned with

> "effective techniques for the systematic study of
> co-occurrence of text elements" (Moskovich and Caplan
> 1978 p108)

which they call Distributional Statistical Analysis (DSA). The aim of this method is to investigate text through analysis of the distribution throughout a text of linguistic items in different categories. Although this is clearly related to the concerns of this book, the results they report are in fact relatively uninteresting. This is largely because the approach suffers from a fundamental problem inherent in any straightforward frequency count approach. This is the flaw of equating frequency of occurrence with functional importance.

The difficulty lies in the use of significant frequency of occurrence relative to some interval of text as the basic analytical tool. This concept limits the extent to which useful generalisations about text structure can be made. By definition, if a linguistic item occurs with significantly high frequency in one text interval, it cannot occur significantly in all the intervals in the text under investigation. If it occurs with similar frequencies in all text intervals, then its occurrence in any one interval can no longer be regarded as significant. This then makes it difficult to make interesting statements about the relations among different text intervals on the basis of the distribution of the item in question since nothing can be said about the non-significant occurrences. There is no principled way in which the significant occurrences can be related to the non-significant ones. Consequently, it is difficult to make a comprehensive statement about the structure of the text. The simple distributional approach captures too crude a feature of the distribution of the textual elements and as a result it is possible to make only relatively weak claims about text structure.

A second problem with DSA, at least as it has been described, is that it appears to focus on the identification of paradigmatic sets. This is what Moscovich and Caplan appear to mean when they refer to the concept of a "semantic centre". Their hope is to infer from the distributional analysis the structure of semantic fields relevant to the text. The aim of deriving the characteristics of ´langue´ from those of ´parole´ is a worthy one; indeed, it is the only way to proceed. But I argued in the last chapter that for an understanding of ´parole´, which is what I am concerned with, the paradigmatic approach is unsuitable.

Despite these criticisms, I subscribe fully to the general statement of position made by Moscovich and Caplan, which I consider of sufficient importance to warrant quoting at length:

> "Association maps of text elements provided by DSA have some characteristics that make them absolutely indispensable for the kind of objective text study that modern semantics and stylistics purport to strive for:
>
> 1) they are obtained directly from the text and are not creations of a subjective judgement; they include only elements found in the text and no other elements that might be taken from other sources;
> 2) they are generated by an algorithmic procedure that can be repeated by a computer on any new corpus of texts;
> 3) they reveal various facets of the meaning of a word in a given body of texts;
> 4) they detect not only semantic links between text elements but statistical links as well; the latter are more varied and cannot be detected by any other method.
>
> Difficulties that stand in the way of a wider application of the DSA are threefold:
>
> 1) the comparative novelty of the method and the need for further development and testing of its techniques;
> 2) the high cost of input and computer processing of large text corpora;
> 3) the psychological difficulty for users involved in the use of any new technique.
>
> In view of the complexity of the field and the need for an immense outlay of human and financial resources involved in the application of DSA to analysis of large samples of text, closer international cooperation in the field remains a priority. Work on DSA is still scattered throughout many disciplines (artificial intelligence, computational linguistics, psychology, philosophy,

information retrieval, literary studies) and there is
little knowledge of work done in various countries and a
very negligible exchange of ideas." (Moscovich and
Caplan 1978 pp147-148).

I consider that with a clearer specification of objectives and
a consequent refocussing of the methodology, the approach
represented by DSA holds out promise of achieving real insight
into text structure. The research reported in part three of
this book can be construed as a contribution to the programme
implicitly outlined in the above quotation.

2.5 Conclusion

This chapter has reviewed the contribution that a number of
approaches to linguistics make to text analysis. It was first
seen that the conventional levels of linguistic description
fail to address themselves to appropriate questions and are
thus unlikely to throw light upon the issues of interest here.
With the possible exceptions of the lexical level and discourse
analysis, the components of linguistic theory are all
concerned with the structuring of language on the local scale
rather than with the organisation of whole texts. Lexis,
however, has traditionally been studied in terms of the
paradigmatic structures of semantics whilst discourse analysis
tends to focus on the way in which the attention of the reader
or listener is focused on the text rather than on how text
creates the notion of conceptual structures on which the
participant's attention needs to be focused.

In large part, then, the scale of linguistic enquiry is
inadequate to achieve an understanding of how texts achieve
their ends. It was seen that this was an historical problem
arising from the difficulty of devising the techniques of
indirect observation that are needed in order to investigate
text on the macro-scale. With the application of computers to
linguistic analysis, statistical procedures become usefully
available for handling the large quantities of data involved.
On the whole, however, statistical approaches to text have
promised more than they have delivered. Little by way of a
general theory of text has emerged from this work.

The most promising application of statistical techniques was
found to lie in the studies of text within a collocational and
distributional approach that were discussed in the last
section. The study by Sinclair in particular introduced the
seminal notions of collocational analysis. But the
investigations that have been undertaken hitherto raise more
questions than they answer. They opened a gateway onto
uncharted territory without venturing very far in its
exploration. Their value is that they provide a number of
pointers as to how the investigation of the large scale
structuring of text can proceed.

It also became clear, however, that none of the approaches
which have been discussed offers a ready-made methodology for

the investigation of the issues that I raised in the first chapter. Consequently, I conclude that an original methodology is required for this purpose. The considerations involved in developing such a methodology will occupy the next part of this book.

PART TWO

METHODOLOGICAL CONSEQUENCES

CHAPTER 3

PROCEDURES AND CATEGORIES FOR TEXT ANALYSIS

3.1 Text Reduction

In the course of the discussion hitherto the conclusion has been reached that the investigation of aboutness cannot conveniently be conducted in terms of the levels of conventional linguistic theory. It also emerged that a statistical distributional analysis of text at what could appear to be a relatively superficial level might prove to be the most appropriate way of obtaining insights into how text is structured so as to generate the sensation of subject matter. Thus this conclusion has substantial methodological implications.

The first consequence is that the linguistic carriers of locally organised meaning in text can be eliminated from the analysis. The initial step, then, in the elaboration of a methodology is to reduce the text for analysis by excluding such items from consideration. In order that as few objectively unverifiable claims as possible need be made about the categories to which particular text constituents might be assigned, it is desirable that each decision to eliminate an element of the text from the set of items for investigation should be justifiable on formal linguistic grounds. No semantic intuitions about such matters as the ´degree of lexicality´ of a linguistic item, for example, or the ´vocabulary class´, whether ´technical´, ´sub-technical´ or ´general´, to which it belongs, should be allowed to enter into the text reduction procedure. On this basis it is possible to proceed with the process of reducing the text by identifying items to be eliminated. A series of ´filters´ must be devised through which the text can be conceptually passed; at each pass the markers of meaning at a particular linguistic level will be extracted. This will leave a residual text consisting of elements distinguishable from each other purely on the basis of their graphic form. I characterise the process as a conceptual one since it is not necessary physically to prepare a reduced text. The analytical procedure can be designed to access a natural language text but to recognise in it only the residual elements which would be left were such a filtering operation actually to be performed.

These filters should be set up in accordance with explicit principles operating at the graphological, morphological, syntactic, lexical and discoursal levels of meaning. At the graphological level the spelling distinctions among different varieties of English can often be ignored. This relatively trivial requirement can mean, for example, that the differences in the orthographic conventions of the British and North American varieties of English are not taken into account. Thus variants such as ´behaviour´-´behavior´ will be treated as the same item. Where intertext comparisons of subject matter organisation are made, it could be important to exclude this intrusive element of irrelevant meaning. In other cases, however, where no comparisons of this nature are required, the principle will be satisfied vacuously.

Morphological variation among lexical items conditioned solely by syntactic factors also has to be deleted. In other words, the set of elements for investigation must be reduced to the form of lemmata. Since, as has been argued, syntactic organisation is irrelevant to the concept of text macro-structure, it is necessary to exclude the morphological markers of syntactic function by lemmatising the text. Besides being a theoretical requirement, lemmatisation has practical advantages as Quillian points out

> "Removing all inflections during encoding permits all nodes in the memory model to represent canonical forms of words; this is of importance in reducing the model´s overall size and in locating conceptual similarities within it." (Quillian 1968 p243)

The fact that this filter applies to lexical items does not mean that the categorisation of certain elements in the text as such must be assumed and that in consequence the requirement for the formal justifiability of any categories is violated. The filtering process can be conceptualised as ordered such that discoursal and syntactic meaning are first eliminated and then the syntactically conditioned morphological variation of the residue is excluded. In this way, no ´knowledge´ of what constitutes a lexical item is implied at this stage.

Thus as well as the morphological markers of syntactic relations, individual linguistic items required to articulate the syntactic structure of sentences must also be eliminated. These are identified by their membership in what Halliday terms "closed systems" recognised on the basis of distributional criteria (Halliday 1961). This filter removes articles, demonstratives, pronouns and pronominal adjectives, modal and auxiliary verbs, conjunctions, interrogative pronouns and adjectives, prepositions and such adjuncts as intensifiers and interjections. Moreover, although the basic analytical procedure rests upon the notion of proximity in the linear stream of language substance, no concept of sequence should enter into the method. Thus meaning arising from word order relations must also be excluded. In this way meaning at the syntactic level is eliminated from the analysis.

Meaning is eliminated at the lexical level of analysis by

requiring that distinct text items be distinguished by means of their formal shape and not their semantic content. This means that homographs should not be distinguished. It will be seen in part three that this approach to text analysis can produce suggestive evidence of the possibility of objective homograph discrimination on the basis of distributional features. But such discrimination cannot be an *a priori* requirement; rather it should emerge naturally from the analysis by the application of the investigative procedures. The only way of interpreting the results of the investigation for the light they throw on the notion of aboutness, however, is by considering the semantic relations revealed by the distributional analysis. In other words, lexical meaning has to be reintroduced after the macrostructure has been revealed. But it must be emphasised that this is an interpretative procedure and not an analytical one.

Finally, the explicit markers of discourse structure must be eliminated. These are also identifiable as closed system items. This filter removes the conjunctive elements of textual cohesion described by Halliday and Hasan and thus excludes from consideration such items as 'however', 'furthermore', 'nevertheless' and so forth (Halliday and Hasan 1976). This discoursal filter, in conjuction with the syntactic one, also eliminates the markers of the semantics of logical relations. This agrees with the decision arrived at in the last chapter to reject the narrowly defined 'semantic component' as a feasible source of structural information about text.

In theory all the linguistic items identified by the criteria embodied in the preceding filters can be exhaustively enumerated by means of a list. Thus the procedure for text reduction can be summarised as follows: items which are members of closed sets do not belong to the class of elements contributing to the macrostructure of text and are not therefore elements of the set of objects whose behaviour in text should be selected for observation. The statement is somewhat idealised because it is only in theory that closed sets can be considered as closed. Both Halliday and Sinclair have postulated that all language items can be placed on a cline of degrees of lexicality (Halliday 1966, Sinclair 1966). In other words, the distinction between closed and open system items is by no means as clear cut as the terminology suggests. Nevertheless, it is convenient and necessary to make the assumption for the procedural requirements of the theoretical position outlined earlier to be met. In cases of real uncertainty, which in practice are relatively rare, the criterion suggested by Sinclair of positional freedom can always be invoked (Sinclair et al 1970).

Furthermore, even if it were not possible to justify the text reduction procedure theoretically, as I have done, some form of eliminatory measures would have to be invoked on an *ad hoc* basis. For otherwise, if an attempt were made to search for regularity of distributional patterning using the natural text, the likelihood is that any evidence of organisation would be completely swamped in the 'noise' of competing word occurrences. The combined effect of very high frequency items such as 'the', 'a' and 'and' and the large numbers of <u>hapax legomena</u> contained in a typical text would mean that patterning attributable to the creation of subject matter would be extremely difficult to detect.

If, then, the exclusion filters appear inescapable, it is as well, nevertheless, to be aware of two types of error that can be made. It is possible to
1. exclude items that should be included or
2. include items that should be excluded.

These two possibilities exactly parallel the type I and II errors of classical statistics. In one sense, there is little that can be done about the first type of error. It arises in any case as a result of the need to reduce the amount of data investigated to manageable proportions. In practice it is impossible to examine the textual behaviour of every candidate for observation on the grounds of sheer quantity. It has to be accepted that many items which the filters will identify as meriting investigation will have to be omitted. In other words, this is hardly an error but an inevitable price to be paid for devising implementable procedures. It helps, however, to put the risk of making genuine type 1 errors into perspective. The issues involved in data reduction will be discussed in the next chapter.

Either type of error is likely to arise in attempting to apply the syntactic filter to items which could be called lexico-syntactic homographs or when the discourse filter operates on lexico-discoursal homographs. These terms refer to items which, when taken out of context, on one reading would be categorised as full lexical items and on another as either grammar words or discourse markers respectively. 'Just' is an example of the former and 'course' of the latter, while 'still' is three ways ambiguous, as the following constructed examples indicate

Lexical:	The law attempts to punish the guilty without rewarding the just.
Syntactic:	Mr Jones has just fallen over.
Lexical:	A short course on FORTRAN will be held next week.
Discoursal:	It is always possible, of course, to propose an alternative explanation.
Lexical:	The hunters remained completely still for over an hour.
Syntactic:	He is still a member of the debating society.
Discoursal:	Still, the gardens do need a drop of rain, I suppose.

There are two possible responses to this kind of problem. The first is to try to develop finer criteria for drawing the required distinctions so that fewer items are inappropriately accepted or rejected by the filters. The second solution is to trust the procedures to resolve fuzzy cases at a later stage.

The first approach could be implemented by using Winter's classification of vocabularies to exclude at least some of the fuzzy items, though it would by no means exclude them all (Winter 1977). Winter identifies three vocabularies responsible for the signalling of relations between clauses. Vocabulary 1 consists of the subordinators whilst Vocabulary 2 comprises sentence connectors. Winter's thesis is that there exists a third vocabulary of lexical items which, like the members of the first two vocabularies, form a closed system.

> "The open system words refer to their items in the real world, which may be seen or unseen; Vocabulary 3 words refer to their open-system words in the utterance."
> (Winter op cit p88)

The purpose of Winter's discussion is to establish the closed system membership of Vocabulary 3 items. He is concerned to show that Vocabulary 3 items can be recognised in that their meanings are such as to associate them with what he terms the "closed system semantics" of the subordinators and connectives. If this is the case, then Winter's work should provide further criteria for filtering out from the text some quasi-lexical items which are in fact operating at the syntactic or discoursal levels of analysis.

Thus Winter proposes four semantic criteria for identifying Vocabulary 3 items. There are, however, considerable difficulties in determining precisely what these criteria are and how they are differentiated. In fact, they all appear to amount to the same thing, the single notion that Vocabulary 3 items are recognisable as paraphrases of the subordinators and connectives.

> "So far we have discussed the paraphrase relations in describing the closed-set as Criterion 1 and the typical vocabulary of questions as Criterion 2, and will again be discussing paraphrase relations when we discuss anticipation as Criterion 4. All Criterion 3 means is that one of the defining features of Vocabulary 3 is that it directly or indirectly paraphrases the connection meanings of Vocabulary 1, the subordinators, and Vocabulary 2, the sentence connectors." (Winter ibid p42)

But he has already argued that

> "Criterion 1 rests on two observations. The first is that most of Vocbulary 3 cited above directly or indirectly paraphrases the connective semantics of Vocabulary 1 or 2 or both." (Winter ibid p28)

Thus it is not entirely clear quite how many distinct criteria there really are. This is presumably because in each case Winter appeals to intuitions about meaning relations.

Thus while Winter's work is an interesting contribution to the interpretation of what may be called the microstructure of text, it is insufficiently rigorous to help increase the discriminatory power of the text reduction filters. Indeed, it is more than likely that if Winter's criteria for Vocabulary 3 were incorporated into the filtering procedure, it would be weakened thereby rather than reinforced. Attempts to refine further the principles upon which text reduction is based may thus well introduce problems of demarcation more complex than those which they were intended to resolve.

I consequently conclude that the second response to the problem is more appropriate. This is to trust the analytical procedure itself to resolve doubtful cases. It is intuitively likely that no formal mesh can cope entirely satisfactorily with the blurred outlines of polysemy or the possibility that all closed set items (with the probable exception of one and two letter words) have open set homographs. As a result, there may always be a certain element of type 2 error in any analysis of this nature. However, I contend that it is entirely likely that items such as those classified by Winter as Vocabulary 3, which cannot be eliminated from consideration in advance on account of the informality of the recognition criteria, will be identified objectively by the methodology itself. Vocabulary 3 items belong to the metalanguage of text and consequently can operate to articulate virtually any subject matter area. If the methodology is successful in revealing subject matter as a function of macrostructure, then it may be expected that Vocabulary 3 items will not show up in the analysis. Thus a successful methodology will also clear up residual areas of fuzziness in the data.

3.2 Basic Analytical Categories

As a result of the operation of the exclusion filters described in the preceding section, a conceptual reduced text is arrived at which is effectively stripped of all meaning other than the formal meaning that might arise from the distributional patterning of the residual text elements. These are exclusively open system items distinguished from each other by distinctiveness of graphic form rather than semantic identity. One consequence of this procedure is that the possible form of the analysis is restricted to one of three types.

The first possibility is an analysis of the relative frequencies of occurrence of the selected elements in the text taken as a whole; that is, an analysis of the frequency distribution of the text. This approach can be quickly dismissed. An analysis of the frequency distribution permits only a synoptic view of the text as a static entity. It can offer little insight into the dynamics of text construction and allows only the crudest characterisation for the purpose of relatively superficial intertext comparisons. This was essentially the nature of the objection to Yule's characteristic K. Such an approach offers no prospect of insight into macrostructure which must be concerned with the relations obtaining among distinct sections of text. I noted in the last chapter that the Index of Usage developed by Carroll represents a superior approach and that both frequency and distributional criteria need to be incorporated into the analysis.

The second conceivable procedure is to analyse the distribution of the selected text elements relative to appropriate intervals of text. I have, however, already criticised this technique in the discussion of the distributional statistical analysis proposed by Moskovitch and Caplan. There is no simple relationship between the distribution of an item through text and its function and to suppose that there is leads, as I have suggested, to difficulties of analysis. There is, for example, a good case to be made out for the importance of relatively low frequency items in certain circumstances, particularly when, for instance, their distribution is highly localised or their environments are markedly restricted. Phenomena such as these could easily be missed by the straightforward DSA approach.

This leaves as the only viable possibility an analysis of the distribution of the selected text elements relative to each other in some suitable text interval, which may, but need not, be the whole text. I submit that the possibility of a far more revealing analysis is offered by the investigation of the behaviour of the residual text elements for whatever patterns of association they may contract with each other as a function of repeated co-occurrence. Adoption of this approach also has the advantage of suggesting immediately two investigable questions. What configurations, if any, arise as a result of the association of distinct elements in the linear stream of text? How are such configurations related to each other?

In order to begin to answer these questions, the answers to three further questions which are presupposed must first be given. It is not possible to identify patterns of association in text without first determining the extent of text over which patterns are to be validly identified; the kind of elements which are to be considered as associating with each other; and the environment within which co-occurrence of elements is to be identified with association. The first question relates to the category of 'interval', the second to that of 'unit' and the third to the category of 'span'. I shall now consider each of these categories in turn.

It should be evident that the interval within which the search for patterns of association is to be conducted cannot coincide with the whole text. If the whole text were adopted as the interval, the procedure would reduce to the first of the analytical techniques rejected above. At the other extreme there is reason to believe that an interval restricted to a sequence of no more than eight orthographic words would prove unhelpful since, as will be seen shortly, the interval would then overlap with the category of span.

Thus the upper and lower bounds within which the text interval must be identified have been fixed. There are two possible approaches. A purely arbitrary segment of, say, five or ten thousand running words could be adopted and the analysis undertaken on that basis. Alternatively, an attempt could be made to identify an interval which might reasonably be suspected of playing a functional role with respect to text macrostructure. In view of the exploratory and relatively innovative nature of the approach developed here, it is perhaps prudent to maximise the chances of obtaining useful results by adopting the latter approach. As with the question of fuzziness in the data discussed in the last section, it is a reasonable hope that the methodology will confirm intuitions about meaningful text intervals.

Bearing in mind the lower limit on the category of interval, the first possibility which suggests itself is the sentence. The sentence, however, is too restricted in extent to be a realistic choice. Moreover, as a syntactic unit its boundaries are determined by grammatical constraints which have already been rejected as irrelevant to macrostructural organisation.

The next higher unit which suggests itself as a possible interval is the paragraph. The paragraph, however, is not firmly established as a viable linguistic category. I remain unconvinced by such desperate attempts as those of Longacre to argue for it grammatical status (Longacre 1977). Recent work in the Soviet Union is also relevant. In his review of Soviet research, Gindin points out that

> "It cannot be gainsaid that at the present stage of development of written and printed speech the distribution of paragraphs can be thought of by language speakers as being <u>more</u> or <u>less motivated</u> and that a ´good´ division into paragraphs is one that accords with the inner structure of the text, which involves among other things the division into SEs [ie supra-sentential entities]. ´To accord with´ does not mean ´to coincide with´ but rather ´to coincide with or deviate <u>justifiably</u>´" (Gindin 1977 p266).

In other words, the paragraph is at best a very flexible unit, the relationship of which to macrostructure is by no means constant. It is clear as well that Gindin leaves open the possibility of ´bad´ paragraphing. It is also interesting to note that Bolivar in her work on newspaper editorials observes that orthographic paragraph boundaries are not significant in her texts (Bolivar in progress). Whilst paragraphing in journalism is perhaps peculiarly unsystematic, it is nonetheless clear that the safest course is not to consider the paragraph seriously as a candidate for the category of interval.

A ´section´ may be defined as the segment of a chapter bounded by major headings, where a major heading is the highest level boundary marker after that of the chapter in a possible hierarchy of boundary markers in the text. A major heading is identified by such typographical features as placement, the use of a numbering system, distinctive type faces and spacing. In this definition, the section appears to be a promising candidate for an analytical interval. It is, however, too flexible in extent to permit valid intertext comparisons and, indeed, may simply not exist as a category in certain types of text. It is not, in consequence, generally acceptable as the exponent of the category of interval.

Thus it is the chapter as conventionally recognised which presents itself as the first stretch of continuous text at less than the level of the whole textbook which can feasibly be adopted as a workable interval. I am aware that it is a somewhat notional entity and that many factors may enter into an author's decision to create chapter boundaries. Roe has discussed the relative invalidity of the notion of chapter in connection with his corpus (Roe 1977a). Nevertheless, it is arguable that the chapter has status as a conceptual unit in the mind of the author and it cannot be ignored that it is a primary 'given' in the structure of most texts. It would in consequence be unwise to ignore its significance. It seems to me, therefore, entirely reasonable to accept it as a useful heuristic interval. It is always possible to reassess the status of the chapter in the light of actual results. Some practical effects of the decision to adopt the chapter as interval will become more apparent when the findings of one particular study are discussed in part three of this book.

The next decision which has to be taken concerns the identification of the elements whose associative behaviour within the chapter as interval is to be observed, that is the category of unit. It has already been established that the fundamental unit of analysis in this study is the lemma. It is the occurrence of any form of the lexeme referring to the concept of, for example, 'rotation' which is significant for the notion of aboutness rather than the particular form the word takes at a given point in the text. The occurrence of the lexeme is the aspect of authorial control which results from the choice of topic. The morphological realisation of the lexeme in any given instance, however, is conditioned by inescapable factors of the linguistic system to which the writer has no choice but to conform in order to produce well-formed strings. In the example given above, the concept of rotation may be carried by any one of 'rotate', 'rotates', 'rotating', 'rotated', 'rotation', 'rotations', 'rotational', 'rotationally'. The relation between the grammatical constraints which give rise to these realisations and the concepts embodied in the author's subject matter are highly indirect.

A basic issue raised by the decision to accept the lemma as unit concerns what definition of word is adopted. Muller has discussed the principles involved in lemmatisation and both he

and Herdan have pointed out the theoretical and practical
difficulties involved in lemmatisation arising from the
mismatch between orthographic words and meanings (Muller 1963,
1977, Herdan 1964). Polysemy or homography on the one hand,
where one orthographic word carries several meanings, and
polymorphemic items on the other, where one meaning is carried
by several orthographic words in association, both present
difficult cases when deciding how to attach a given word in a
text to a particular lexeme. This is another case where
ultimately an arbitrary decision has to be made and adhered to
as consistently as possible. I believe that the only
currently practicable definition of the word for computer-
assisted studies is the orthographic word, that is a string of
characters bounded by spaces or punctuation marks. This is the
definition used for all practical purposes by the major
frequency counts as, for example, the introduction to Kucera
and Francis makes clear (Kucera and Francis 1967).
Lemmatisation, then, should be undertaken by conflating
syntactic variants of the orthographic word.

This decision has interesting consequences. It means, for
example, that the lexical elements of semantically distinct
phrasal verbs are conflated, since the distinguishing particles
are eliminated from consideration by the process of text
reduction. I have already emphasised, however, that word
meaning is irrelevant to the formal analysis. Any distinction
of meaning among, say, ´put out´, ´put up with´, ´put down´ or
´put off´ will be revealed by the differing patterns of
association with other lemmata into which the various
occurrences of ´put´ enter irrespective of the presence or
absence of the particle.

Some borderline cases will still present themselves, including
the treatment of antonyms and related phenomena. It is fairly
clear that pairs such as ´possible´ and ´impossible´ should be
treated as belonging to different lemmata. The issue is more
clouded, however, with such cases as ´inverting´/´non-
inverting´, ´dimension´/´dimensionless´ or ´power´/´under-
powered´/´powerful´/´powerless´. Again it may simply be a
matter of taste whether such examples are regarded as variants
or distinct; the appropriate response is to take an intuitively
reasonable decision and to apply it uniformly. As Halliday and
Hasan conclude, in the end it may not matter much where the
lines are drawn provided they are drawn consistently (Halliday
and Hasan 1976). Henceforth in this study the citation form of
orthographic words, that is the token, will be identified by
enclosure within single quotation marks, eg ´word´ and the
canonical form or lemma, that is the type, by underlining, eg
<u>word</u>.

The third required decision concerned the necessity of a
category intermediate between the interval now defined as the
chapter and the unit of the lemma. It is the pattern of
association among units within the text interval that needs
investigation. For this purpose a further category is
evidently required at a lower level than the interval.

Otherwise, merely by virtue of their occurrence in the interval, all units would be considered as associating with each other. There is a sense in which this is indeed the case. It will be seen later how the chapter, and indeed the whole text, can be viewed as a configuration of elements in its own right. But in order to sharpen the notion of patterns of association, the environment within which co-occurrence is recognised must be delimited.

At this point, to facilitate further discussion, it is convenient to introduce some definitions. The ´node´ is the word whose behaviour is being investigated. A ´collocate´ of a node is a word which co-occurs with the node in the text and a ´collocation´ is a node-collocate pair. Collocation is recognised within an environment of a number of words preceding and/or succeeding the node, for example, the five preceding and the five following words. This environment is termed the ´span´. This is the intermediate category and the point at issue is what constitutes the optimum span size.

Before this question is considered, it should be noted that I am using the term ´collocation´ in a more abstract sense than is often the case. ´Collocational meaning´ is not infrequently used to refer to that aspect of meaning which arises from the idiosyncratic association of words in stock phrases consecrated by the language. A typical example would be the fact that ´old people´s home´ is acceptable while, in normal circumstances, ´old people´s house´ is not. I am not, however, interested in such ad hoc facts about English. In this study the term ´collocation´ is used to refer to the general event of co-occurrence within a specified span. This more technical use shades off into the more conventional one when such co-occurrence happens with a certain degree of predictability, but this aspect is not central to my concerns.

In the discussion of the work of Sinclair and his colleagues the point was made that determination of the optimum span size was a major objective of their study (Sinclair et al 1970). Their conclusion was that the influence of the node does not extend appreciably beyond a span of four orthographic words on either side of the node. That is to say, no significantly interesting information about the behaviour of the node is gained by taking into account its collocation with words occurring at distances greater than this threshold. Whilst it is desirable that Sinclair´s findings should if possible be replicated, there are also good reasons for accepting his findings as they stand. The procedure used to determine the optimum span size involves considerable statistical analysis and the development of the necessary software and the amount of computation needed to arrive at an independent result for a different and reasonably large corpus would entail a major study in its own right.

I have, however, explored to some degree the validity of Sinclair´s findings in a small-scale study which used a less theoretical, more pragmatic procedure. A chapter from a first year undergraduate textbook in classical mechanics was selected at random and submitted to collocational analyses at each span setting from three orthographic words on either side of the node (3X3) up to eight orthographic words on either side (8X8). The changes among the different sets of results as span size increased were then examined to determine the minimum span setting which offered the maximum amount of useful information, in other words, to identify the point of diminishing returns. The conclusion reached was that within the range of span settings from 3X3 to 5X5 the stability of the results was such as to suggest that a reasonable solution had been found. There was no particular reason for choosing one of these three span settings over the others. Given the very different natures of the corpora used in my study and that investigated by Sinclair, this is a particularly interesting finding which suggests strongly that a setting of 4X4 can be safely adopted as appropriate for most purposes. Thus there is empirical evidence to support any decision to adopt the span setting used by Sinclair (Phillips 1983).

3.3 Constraints on the Analytical Procedure

The essential categories required by the analysis of interval, unit and span were discussed in the preceding section. I am now in a position to describe in outline the steps in the procedure that is need for exploring the patterns of association of the textual units. The first step is to total over each occurrence of each node the number of its co-occurrences with each collocate within the span. That is to say, the frequencies of collocation for each node-collocate pair must be determined. These frequencies should be summed as appropriate to reflect the lemmatisation of nodes and collocates.

Following this, the frequencies of collocation have to be examined to see whether any groupings of the data suggest themselves, that is, whether certain sets of lemmata tend to associate with each other with particular frequency. The actual technique that needs to be used at this step will be described in detail in the next chapter. The configurations for each text interval thus arrived at will form the basis for comparing intervals with each other. Patterns of association can be compared across intervals and similarity of patterning will constitute evidence of macrostructural organisation. The results of this stage can then be used to develop the approach to text classification described in chapter nine.

It is necessary to place a number of constraints on the procedure as described. The first is that although the text is reduced in order to identify the units constituting the set of nodes and collocates for investigation, thereafter the identification of patterns of association has to operate upon the natural text. There are two reasons for this constraint. First, if the text were reduced for the collocational frequency count, the span setting would be invalidated and there would be no appeal to Sinclair's work for justification. The span of plus or minus four orthographic words is only valid for natural text whilst it will be recalled that the process of text reduction involves both the elimination of non-lexical items and the lemmatisation of the remainder. In theory it is possible to take advantage of Berry-Rogghe´s results concerning span size where span is measured in terms of lexical items only (Berry-Rogghe 1970). But this would introduce the second reason for working from the natural text, which is the enormous practical difficulties involved with any other technique.

There are two ways of avoiding use of the natural text. The first is to tag each token in the text for category. At its simplest this could be a ´retain´ or ´reject´ label; at a more sophisticated level, tokens could be tagged for grammatical class. This, however, involves a great amount of pre-editing work which negates much of the advantage of a computer-assisted study. There is, of course, some point in such text editing when a permanent corpus the uses of which cannot be exhaustively predicted is being established. As the work on the LOB corpus has shown, however, this is a major enterprise in its own right and not to be undertaken lightly.

The alternative to pre-editing is the development of automatic tagging techniques. The elaboration, however, of mechanised text reduction procedures would equally constitute a major research program in its own right. It would represent a major contribution to computational linguistics. Consequently, in most cases it would not be practical to consider Berry-Rogghe´s suggestions regarding span size. Moreover, her span size varies with the word class of the node, which further complicates the procedure and increases the length of the chain of abstraction from the data in the text to the conclusions derived from them. The chain of inference is already fairly lengthy. Thus I consider it more prudent that the findings of the study should be directly referable to the natural text, leaving the reduction of the text purely as a technique for identifying the set of items for investigation.

Thus simple realism suggests that lemmatisation should normally be a <u>post factum</u> procedure operating on the output of the frequency analysis. It must be pointed out, however, that basing the analysis on the natural text does not necessarily mean accepting all the textual features contained in the text. It is perfectly reasonable, for example, to ignore strings composed of non-alphabetic characters, that is numerical or symbolic strings. Nor is there any requirement to recognise any boundaries within the text between those determining the orthographic word and the chapter. In other words, it should be accepted that collocational patterning transcends sentence boundaries.

A further major constraint upon the procedure is that no node should be given preferential treatment in the process of determining patterns of association. It may well prove in practice that one node enjoys a privileged position but this clearly is something to be established by the procedure rather

than to be incorporated as an assumption of the methodology.
This represents an inelegancy in the studies by Sinclair and
Berry-Rogghe. In both cases sets of lexical items were
´seeded´, as it were, by singling out a particular node as
focus and building up a pattern of association from the
perspective of that node. As a result, it is impossible to
assess the extent to which the configurations which they
arrived at accurately reflect lexical organisation in their
texts. Their choice of initiating node made have distorted the
objective patterns of association present in their texts.

The consequence of this argument is that in the analytical
procedure the collocational patterning of all nodes must be
examined simultaneously in order to determine on as objective
a basis as possible which nodes are to be considered as
initiating patterns of association or, indeed, whether the
notion of initiation is in fact appropriate. This constraint I
shall refer to as the requirement of simultaneity. It is a
major constraint to which the analytical procedure must conform
and is a persuasive argument for the use of a statistical
technique. No other approach has the power to allow the
behaviour of a large number of nodes to be scanned
simultaneously.

3.4 Conclusion

In this chapter the categories required by the approach to text
analysis discussed in earlier chapters have been established
and an outline of the kind of procedure that needs to be
developed has been given. The first consequence of the
theoretical position reached as a result of the discussion in
the first two chapters is that the carriers of local meaning in
text have to be eliminated from consideration. A set of
principles for appropriate text reduction was developed which
enables the identification of the linguistic items whose
behaviour in text is to be observed.

The analytical procedure involves the specification of three
fundamental categories, interval, unit and span. These were
discussed in turn and justifications developed for adopting the
chapter as interval, the lemma as unit and a span of four
orthographic words on either side of the node as the extent of
text within which collocations would be recognised. Finally,
an outline of an appropriate analytical procedure was given.

Having thus described the basic elements of the methodology, it
is now appropriate to consider in more detail the investigative
techniques. These, as has already been indicated, will be
statistical in nature. The descriptive techniques needed for
presenting and interpreting results also need to be considered.
I shall discuss statistical methods in the next chapter and a
possible approach to the description of findings in chapter
five.

CHAPTER 4

INVESTIGATIVE TECHNIQUES FOR TEXT ANALYSIS

4.1 Data Analysis: The Classical Model

The implementation of the analytical programme outlined in the previous chapter can conveniently be considered under two headings, the statistical and the computational. Statistical methods are required to analyse the data of the reduced text to determine patterns of association of textual units. Three feasible data analysis techniques are discussed here. In this section the classical statistical approach used in previous studies is criticised. Then an alternative approach known as Multidimensional Scaling is considered and rejected and finally a technique called Cluster Analysis is reviewed in some detail and found to offer a suitable means of implementing the statistical analysis. Following this, the computational procedures involved in collecting the data for analysis and reducing them to manageable proportions are described.

It will be recalled from the last chapter that the fundamental information that needs to be extracted from the reduced text is the frequencies of collocation of each unit considered as node with every other unit occurring as collocate within the span of plus or minus four orthographic words. The crucial step in the analysis is the search for patterns of association in these collocational data. One way of doing this is to suppose that the parametric techniques of classical statistics provide an appropriate model for the linguistic phenomenon of interest. This involves making the fundamental assumption that the feature of text being studied behaves in a manner which can be characterised as that of a stochastic (ie probabilistic) variable describable by a known distribution. In any given analysis two assumptions are consequently needed. First, that a particular distribution appropriately describes the behaviour of the linguistic feature studied. Secondly, that the text being analysed is a true random sample of the population described by this distribution.

If these assumptions are made, it then becomes possible to use the distribution descriptive of the population to predict the behaviour of the linguistic feature in question in a given text. The theoretical prediction can be compared with the behaviour actually observed in the text to determine to what extent deviations from the predictions of the model are attributable to purely random fluctuations. It is customary to

set an arbitrary level beyond which it is considered that the
chances of deviation being assignable to random factors are
sufficiently small to warrant the inference that a causal
mechanism is at work. In other words, the linguistic behaviour
in the focus of attention is tested for significance.

This position was adopted by the two previous studies concerned
with collocational patterning by Sinclair and Berry-Rogghe
discussed in the last chapter (Sinclair et al 1970,
Berry-Rogghe 1970). In essence, they both assumed that the
chances of collocations occurring could be described by a known
statistical distribution and that the texts they investigated
were random samples of an homogeneous population. They
differed in that the Sinclair study adopted the Poisson
distribution as its model whilst Berry-Rogghe considered the
normal distribution to be an adequate approximation. The
simplification proposed by Berry-Rogghe is in fact justifiable
when a large number of items is involved.

Thus both Sinclair and Berry-Rogghe tested each of their
collocational frequencies for significance and only accepted
into their analyses those collocations which were thus shown to
be significant. Their arguments that the existence of
syntagmatic lexical sets could be detected were based on a
manual sort of the significant frequencies of collocation.
This approach to the problem of discerning patterns of
association in the data has its attractions. Provided that the
assumptions required by the method are reasonable, there is a
satisfying rigour in the procedure. Well-understood methods
are used and the technique is comparatively straighforward with
few intuitive judgements being required. Significance testing
lends itself to algorithmic implementation. But two questions
need to be asked about the method. To what extent are the
assumptions reasonable ones? And, how are the significant
collocational frequencies which are obtained to be handled?

The second of these questions can be dealt with quite quickly.
I noted in the last chapter that neither Sinclair´s study nor
Berry-Rogghe´s meet the constraint of simultaneity. The
classical model can only go so far. It does not lead to the
automatic identification of lexical sets but leaves these to be
inferred from the data. Hence the necessity that the two
earlier studies were under of a manual sort of the
collocational data. It might, of course, be possible to
develop techniques for revealing lexical sets based on the
evaluation of different levels of significance in the data.
This would not, however, be particularly easy to implement and
would introduce a further degree of arbitrariness into the
solution. It is not surprising that this possibility was not
explored. As implemented in previous studies, then, the
classical approach stops short of the analysis required here.

But there are more serious objections to this approach. It is
questionable whether the assumptions made are in fact
justifiable and thus whether classical significance testing is
appropriate for the investigation of this aspect of language.

There are at least four points on which the position described above can be criticised. First, it can be argued that significance of collocation is relative to the length of the text sample. If the sample is long enough, then every collocation will achieve significant frequencies. In this case, the concept of significance itself ceases to be particularly meaningful.

In order to understand why this is so it is necessary to grasp three pertinent notions. These are the expected frequency of collocation in an equivalent random text, the true frequencies of collocation in the real text and the observed frequencies of collocation in a sample of the real text. The more the sample approximates to the text from which it was drawn, the more the discrepancies between the real text and the equivalent random text will be observed in the sample. Since significance testing involves precisely comparing expected frequencies of collocation if they occurred randomly with observed frequencies, it follows that the longer the sample, the greater the number of collocations that will be judged significant. The concept of significance thus becomes increasingly less meaningful as text length increases.

Secondly, the form of significance testing used in studies of this nature assesses the likelihood of the joint occurrence of two events. The events dealt with in collocational analysis are the occurrences of two words within the same span. But it is arguable that two different notions of joint occurrence are involved, one relevant to the statistical procedures and the other pertaining to linguistics. The statistical notion applies to cases where both ´x´ and ´y´ can be predicated of the same entity. An example would be the likelihood of someone´s living in London and having a motor accident in the coming year. There are grounds for thinking that the linguistic notion is philosophically quite different. In this case the concept concerns the likelihood of two items occurring at different points in the text. There is no ´same entity´ of which the fact of the two word occurrences can be predicated. It seems likely that the strict linguistic counterpart of the statistical notion would be the chances of node ´x´ and node ´y´ occurring simultaneously at the same span position, which is clearly an impossibility. Thus it is doubtful whether the linguistic phenomenon of collocation is conceptually compatible with the statistical procedure.

Thirdly, the classical model assumes that the probabilities of occurrence of words in a text are independent. This is clearly not the case. Probabilities of word occurrence are conditional probabilities. That is to say, given the occurrence of a particular word, the occurrence of other words is thereby rendered more or less likely. Sinclair explicitly admits that the assumption of independence is a simplification motivated by considerations of practicality (Sinclair et al 1970).

The most fundamental objection to the classical model, however, is that it is most implausible that texts can be viewed as random samples of a population described by a theoretical stochastic distribution. It was seen in chapter two that Herdan found it necessary to revise his views upon this point. Not dissimilarly, Sinclair confesses that treatment of collocational phenomena within a classical model is problematic because

> "any text which is a non-random sample from an unknown population causes great problems for the statistician." (Sinclair et al op cit p12)

In other words, he concedes that the essential assumptions of the study are made more on grounds of methodological convenience than because they are warranted by the phenomena under investigation. But this is to admit that parametric techniques, that is techniques based on an underlying distribution, are inappropriate.

It seems, then, that the rigour of the approach to which I referred above is in reality only a pseudo-rigour. The need to make arbitrary decisions in the course of implementing the methodology is avoided only by basing the methodology on some rather strong assumptions which have been seen to be unjustified. It is interesting to note that Herdan reaches a similar conclusion. He observes that

> "Although applicable in general, significance tests are not always to the point in the particular sphere of linguistics. For this reason the need arises for more appropriate statistics, whose evidence would weigh more heavily than that of the conventional significance tests" (Herdan 1960 p9).

What is the alternative? It is, as Siegel has pointed out, to adopt a non-parametric technique, which by definition does not depend upon assuming particular properties of the data for its application (Siegel 1956). There is, however, a price to be paid for this emancipation from the classical approach. The decisions which were swept under the methodological carpet with the broom of a stochastic model now have to be faced squarely. A justified position has to be taken on a number of issues which do not arise with parametric techniques.

A further consequence of rejecting the classical model is that a methodology is being abandoned which fundamentally claims to be explanatory in nature in favour of one which is merely descriptive. There is no longer any underlying statistical theory of collocational behaviour in terms of which the observed phenomenon of collocation can be explicated. In other words, what is frequently regarded as statistics proper proves to be inadequate for present purposes and recourse has to be had to the weaker methods of data analysis. These should not, however, be considered as necessarily inferior, as Sibson has persuasively argued

> "My candidate for inclusion in a Greater Statistics is a part of what has sometimes been called ´data analysis´: the study of systems of <u>objects</u> and <u>descriptions</u>, with a view to the extraction of information-rich summaries of the original data and possibly the construction of hypotheses within the subject involved." (Sibson 1972 p311)

This seems to me to be an admirable statement of objective and one entirely appropriate to the field of text analysis.

The decision to adopt a non-parametric technique does not, however, eliminate the need to identify a method whose philosophy is in accord with whatever intuitions may be held about the structure of the data. Broadly speaking, it is possible to conceive of the data as, for example, spatially organised. Collocational frequencies can be imagined as constituting a set of data points located at various ´distances´ from each other; the more similar the collocational patterning, the closer the relevant points in the analytical space. Alternatively, the data might be supposed to form a taxonomy in which collocations group into sets which themselves are members of larger groupings and so on. Such a taxonomy could be hierarchical in form. Detailed consideration of these issues will be deferred, however, until after I have surveyed the two non-parametric methods which appear most promising. These methods are Multidimensional Scaling and Cluster Analysis. These are both distribution-free methods, as Chatfield and Collins point out (Chatfield and Collins 1980). After consideration of both methods, it will become apparent that it is preferable to adopt one of the Cluster Analysis techniques. The reasons for this will emerge from the following discussion of the two approaches.

4.2 Data Analysis: Multidimensional Scaling

Of the techniques which adopt an underlying spatial model of the data, Multidimensional Scaling (MDS) was considered as possibly the most relevant to text analysis. It is described in a number of places, Shepard and Everitt both offering helpful introductions (Shepard 1962a, 1962b, Everitt 1978). Use of this technique would involve conceiving of the set of collocational frequencies of a node as its coordinates in multi-dimensional space. MDS attempts to collapse the number of dimensions in the original data set to the minimum number which optimally preserves the relative positions of the points. It may then be possible by inspection of the resulting relations among the data points to identify dense areas in the data corresponding to association of textual units. In other words, the simplest configuration is sought consistent with introducing a minimum amount of distortion into the data. Solutions of low dimensionality are looked for; typically, it is hoped that a two-dimensional solution can be achieved since this allows groupings in the data to be represented graphically.

If the technique is successful in achieving an acceptable solution, it is then possible to attempt to develop an interpretation of the resultant dimensions in terms of latent ´components´ or ´factors´ which can be postulated as accounting for the structure of the data. For example, the study reported in Fillenbaum and Rapoport, which is one of the few instances of the application of this method to linguistic problems, attempted to interpret the solution obtained as the various dimensions of semantic space with reference to which different lexical items could be located (Fillenbaum and Rapoport 1971). They suggested that in this way it was possible to arrive at a description of the subjective lexicon.

Problems, however, can be anticipated with any attempt to apply MDS to the investigation of the theoretical issues in text analysis discussed in earlier chapters. Any solution other than a two-dimensional one would present considerable difficulties of interpretation. It is intuitively rather improbable that the large number of interpoint distances involved are reducible to this dimensionality without unacceptable distortion of the structure of the data. It is also implausible that a meaningful interpretation can be assigned to any restricted set of dimensions that might be uncovered. For example, it makes sense to attempt such an interpretation for paradigmatic studies such as those of Fillenbaum and Rapoport, where it might be possible to locate colour terms on such dimensions as ´hue´, ´saturation´ and ´brightness´. It is not at all clear, however, what a comparable set of dimensions might mean for syntagmatic data. For text analysis, then, it is necessary to seek an alternative approach. This is offered by the various techniques which are collectively known as Cluster Analysis.

4.3 Data Analysis: Cluster Analysis

Two previous studies suggest that the use of Cluster Analysis might prove a fruitful means of investigating the theoretical issues in the structure of text of interest here. One of the principal objectives of the study undertaken by Fillenbaum and Rapoport referred to in the last section was to evaluate Cluster Analysis in comparison with Multidimensional Scaling. Although, as has already been pointed out, their work concentrated on the area of subjective semantic space, and only very limited data sets of the order of only twenty cases were involved, their results are nevertheless of considerable interest. These showed that Cluster Analysis gave results which were consistently more readily interpretable than those obtained from MDS (Fillenbaum and Rapoport 1971). The second study of relevance is Kintsch´s small scale investigation of narrative text (Kintsch 1977). He successfully used Cluster Analysis to recover from the text the organisational categories postulated by his theory.

There is thus some empirical support for the validity of applying Cluster Analysis to linguistic problems involving relationships between words or the structure of texts. A further consideration is that Cluster Analysis meets the criterion of simultaneity. In the technique no particular data point is allowed to prejudice the structure of the clusters identified by its being arbitrarily selected to initiate the discovery procedure. At each stage in the analysis all points are considered simultaneously.

Cluster Analysis is the generic name for a number of related techniques which may differ in their underlying model of the data. Some techniques adopt a taxonomic view of the data and may build up a hierarchical structure of groupings in the data by progressive fusion of individual data points. Others are spatially oriented procedures such as the density search techniques. Reasons will be adduced for preferring one of the agglomerative hierarchical cluster techniques. In methods of this kind each lemma can be conceived of as characterised by the set of values comprising the frequencies of collocations of the lemma as node with its collocates. Thus identity of patterning of the collocational frequencies would indicate identity of the nodes, since there would be no formal criterion for distinguishing between them; they would be operating in identical environments. It is thus possible to summarise this information about each node in the form of a similarity coefficient and this is the first step in the clustering procedure. Replacement of the original variables by a simpler statistic preserving the essential information contained in the data is a common way of handling problems in the analysis of multivariate data.

An objective criterion is then selected on the basis of which to evaluate the distortion introduced into the data by fusing pairs of nodes. Fusion is considered on the basis of the similarity coefficients and that fusion which results in the optimal value for the objective criterion is adopted. The criterion is a statistic chosen to ensure that the intra-cluster similarities are greater than any cross-cluster similarities and thus to optimise the formation of clusters. After each fusion a new similarity coefficient may be computed for the new cluster just created. The fusion process is then repeated. Thus the initial ´n´ nodes are considered at the outset as ´n´ separate clusters and are grouped at progressively ´weaker´ values of the criterial statistic until all nodes are grouped in a single cluster. At each stage all of the $n(n-1)/2$ possible pairings of data points are considered for fusion.

Other Cluster Analysis techniques operate in a comparable fashion. Divisive hierarchical techniques, for example, can be viewed as acting in an inverse manner to the procedure just described. They initially treat the data points as a single set and make progressive divisions of the data until the ´n´ data points each constitute an individual cluster. Density search techniques posit a somewhat different underlying model in that they search for ´dense areas´ in the data but the principle of clustering according to a density criterion is not dissimilar to what I have already described.

The value of the objective criterion can be used as a touchstone of the 'strength' of clustering. If, for example, it is chosen such that it represents a quantification of the information loss as a result of clustering, then lower values of the statistic will reflect a minimum of information loss. This would mean that there is a high degree of similarity among the nodes clustered and hence the clusters can be considered as tightly constructed. The converse would hold for high values of the statistic. Thus the statistic can be used as a guide to the number of clusters to accept as a solution. Since Cluster Analysis procedures cluster continuously from the start number of data points to the end number (either 'n' or 1 in both cases), then a decision has to be made as to which level of clustering should be accepted as a 'cut-off'. This is the problem inherent in all hierarchical clustering techniques of devising a 'stopping rule'. I shall return to this topic below. At this point it should simply be noted that the cut-off level can be specified in terms of a threshold value of the criterial statistic.

There is an advantage in using one of the techniques which treats each fusion as a new data point. This is that it makes the decision to cluster relative to the current state of the clusters as a whole and not to the individual nodes in the clusters. For example, if the procedure has clustered <u>potential</u> with <u>energy</u>, a further lemmar, <u>function</u> say, will be evaluated for clustering relative to the cluster formed by <u>potential+energy</u>. Similarly, if <u>conservative+force</u> have already been clustered, then these items will be evaluated as a single unit relative to <u>potential+energy</u> as a whole. This approach increases the robustness of the solution. A cluster cannot be formed simply because a set of lemmata, which might otherwise show no patterns of intercollocation, all happen to collocate frequently with the same node. This follows from the fact that group rather than individual characteristics are considered, that is the total collocational behaviour of each lemma is taken into account. Conversely, if a cluster is revealed where one node co-occurs with a set of collocates none of which intercollocate, this would be an interesting result.

This is an important point since the criticism is sometimes made of Cluster Analysis that it is a Procrustean technique, that is that it will always assign structure even in cases where the data are unstructured. Fillenbaum and Rapoport have noted that

> "particular procedures for the analysis of data (and for obtaining data) <u>may force or impose a structure on the data</u>. We take this to be one of the central methodological problems in this area." (Fillenbaum and Rapoport op cit p238)

and warn that

> "if we use a hierarchic clustering technique we will end up with a taxonomic structure, even if the data really

fall into distinct nominal classes." (ibid p239)

Various objective techniques have been suggested for evaluating results and minimising the risk of accepting spurious solutions. Gnandesikan and his colleagues suggest four major methods for the analysis of clustering results (Gnandesikan et al 1977). The difficulty, however, with such suggestions is that they involve considerable computation. Thus, although they are intended to help solve applications problems, they in practice introduce unhelpful complications into a procedure which was originally adopted to simplify the complexities of data analysis.

Although there is clearly some force in these objections, I believe that the risks of accepting inappropriate solutions and the problem of evaluating results in the case of textual data are in fact more apparent than real. First, I do not think it is inevitable that Cluster Analysis imposes a structure on the data. For example, it is to be expected in any set of collocational data derived from a typical corpus that a number of lemmata will show no tendency to enter into associations. Cluster Analysis will group these lemmata together by default because of their very weak or non-existent collocational patterning. This is instantly recognisable in practice in the Cluster Analysis solution as a relatively large group of data points clustered at a single value of the criterial statistic and consequently showing no evidence of internal structure. In terms of the graphical representation in which the results of hierarchical clustering techniques are conventionally presented, a typical pattern would be as follows

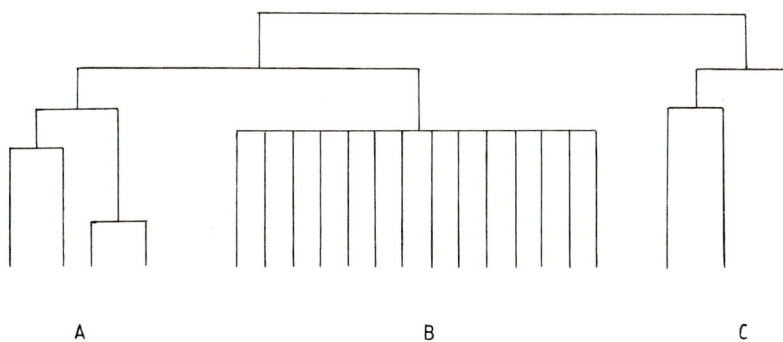

where it is precisely the lack of structure in cluster B which indicates that the other groupings do not arise from any inherent tendencies of the clustering technique to impose a solution.

Secondly, use of a computational procedure does not mean that there are no safeguards against suspect solutions. It is always possible in cases of doubt to check the clustering results against the original data. Only if a cluster is identified for which there is no supporting evidence in the frequencies of collocation does a problem arise. In practice such verification invariably supports the decision to reject clusters of type B above and confirms the validity of the simpler clusters. It thus gives grounds for confidence in the reasonableness of the more complex clusters where, because of the large numbers of intercollocational frequencies involved, the solution cannot be arrived at or confirmed by direct inspection of the data.

Another difficulty with Cluster Analysis, which has already been briefly mentioned, is that of deciding on the number of clusters which accurately reflect groupings in the data. Here objective procedures have also been suggested, such as the algorithmic ´stopping rules´ proposed by Mojena (Mojena 1977). It usually turns out, however, that proposals of this nature introduce spurious procedures into the analysis. The initial step in applying Mojena´s first stopping rule, for example, is to eliminate outliers from the set of data points. The distribution of a criterial statistic for distinguishing a cut-off level is then calculated. But the procedure begs the question, since the distribution should be based upon the complete data set otherwise assumptions about where the cut-off might lie are already built into the method.

Again, however, I consider that there is a danger of overestimating the problem as it applies to textual organisation which is itself not a matter of clear cut certainties. Between the upper bound of chapter, where the number of clusters can be considered to equal one, and the lower bound of the individual tokens in the text, where the number of clusters is ´n´, there can be no uniquely ´correct´ number of associations into which these tokens enter. It is a question of emphasis whether each token is considered as associating with every other by virtue of their joint occurrence in the same text interval, whether each is felt to be a separate entity, or whether some intermediate level of configuration is focused upon. The problem of stopping rules in Cluster Analysis directly mirrors the nature of lexical organisation in text.

It is also arguable that it is inappropriate to make a fetish of uniqueness of solution. Herdan makes a telling point about the rigorous procedures of classical significance testing

> "While established techniques are important in any branch of experimental statistics, knowing when to use them and when not to use them is more important. What should be done is almost always more important than what can be done exactly. Hence new developments in experimental statistics are more likely to come in the form of <u>approximate methods</u> than in the form of exact ones."

(Herdan 1966 p11)

I would argue, then, that the dangers of Cluster Analysis are exaggerated, at least as far as textual data of the type of interest here are concerned. If Cluster Analysis is accepted as an heuristic technique and no claims are made for the absolute validity of its solutions unless supported by independent reasoning, then the investigation of text structure will be on safe ground. Linguistic analysis enjoys the inestimable advantage that the solutions obtained can be required to be intuitively sensible. This is the view of Fillenbaum and Rapoport who argue

> "it seems at least possible that even if there are doubts about aspects of the organisation revealed by a structural analysis, because of some Procrustean properties of a given technique, nevertheless, if the results appear to be intelligible one might still have considerable confidence that the sorts of meaning properties that seem to be involved have been correctly identified." (op cit p241)

This view is shared by professional statisticians, as Everitt indicates

> "Many authors argue that the validity of clusters should be judged qualitatively, by subjective evaluation and interpretability" (Everitt 1980 p96).

Cluster Analysis has thus been justified in general terms as appropriate for the investigation of the syntagmatic organisation of text. It is still necessary, however, to make a choice from the variety of techniques available. In his survey of the field, Everitt categorises Cluster Analysis methods in four main groups, Hierarchical, Optimisation, Density Search and Clumping techniques, and a fifth miscellaneous class (Everitt 1980). Within each group there are a number of methods differentiated by such factors as the kind of similarity coefficient recommended and the type of criterion used for clustering.

Two criteria that any technique must meet can be stated immediately. It must be implemented as a computer program and, for convenience, as an option within the CLUSTAN software package (Wishart 1978). Secondly, the output from the procedure should be representable in graphical form for ease of interpretation. This often takes the form of an inverted tree diagram or 'dendrogram'.

Optimisation and divisive hierarchical techniques can be discounted at once since they typically require large amounts of computer time and for this reason are not implemented in CLUSTAN. Clumping techniques appear attractive in that they allow for the possibility of overlapping clusters. It is consequently claimed, with some plausibility, that they are particularly appropriate for problems in linguistic classification (Needham 1967). Two considerations, however, argue against this choice. First, it is as yet unclear whether any groupings at all exist in the kind of data of interest here. This is an hypothesis to be confirmed rather than an established fact to be explored. Secondly, there must be some uncertainty about whether any Cluster Analysis technique will prove successful since none has hitherto been applied to the analysis of syntagmatic patterning. This means that it is prudent to adopt a relatively straightforward Cluster Analysis technique rather than to introduce unnecessary sophistication by permitting non-discrete clusters which might obscure the clarity of whatever results are obtained.

The decision thus reduces to a choice between a hierarchical or density search technique. The former is represented in CLUSTAN as a range of options under the rubric HIERARCHY and the latter is exemplified principally by the DENSITY procedure. There is no obvious reason, however, for preferring one of these techniques over the other. In favour of a hierarchical technique, it can be argued that there is a degree of conceptual congruence between the notion of syntagmatic patterns of association in text and clusters formed by an agglomerative hierarchical procedure. The notion of lexical set is a classificatory one and suggests the possibility of such phenomena as class inclusion or union which a taxonomic technique might justifiably be used to explore. Taxonomies, and in particular, taxonomic hierarchies, have stood linguistics in good stead in many areas. Although it may be reasonable to assume that the macrostructural organisation of lexis may prove to be different from other levels of linguistic structure, the success with which a hierarchy of units has been used to account for certain aspects of discourse patterning is encouraging. Fillenbaum and Rapoport, moreover, have argued that

> "one of the major virtues of a hierarchical clustering procedure is that in addition to yielding clusters it also reveals how these are successively merged into larger and larger clusters, and in so doing provides information about the weighting or importance of the features involved, the later the merging with regard to some property the more significant that property as a differentiating factor." (op cit p188)

This argument seems to support intuitive feelings about the way words might associate syntagmatically in text, forming first local patterns of association which themselves contract further associations until the whole text can be viewed as a kind of multi-layered extended semantic network.

The point that Fillenbaum and Rapoport make also relates to the notion of information as inversely proportional to predictability, that is, Shannon´s concept of ´redundancy´. This suggests another point of contact between text organisation and clustering schemes. The list of collocational frequencies of a node can be viewed as a set of transition probabilities for that node. Consequently, as has already been noted, the more similar the pattern of collocational frequencies for two nodes, the less distinguishable they can be considered in their ´instantial´ meaning.

There are thus grounds for supposing that a hierarchical clustering technique would be a reasonable choice. At the same time, it can be argued that despite the difference of the underlying model, the DENSITY technique can be viewed as essentially equivalent to a hierarchical method. DENSITY will identify dense areas in the data. Within each such dense area, it will then attempt to identify further distinguishable regions of density. This is not dissimilar to the notion of hierarchical division. Consequently, a decision to opt for one technique rather than the other becomes a question largely of whichever proves the more convenient in practice and the interpretability of the results produced. These are matters which can be decided only empirically and which in the present case were put to the test in a pilot study described in chapter six. The reasons which prompted the final preference for a hierarchical technique will be given there.

Among the various hierarchical techniques available, one method stood out as likely to be superior to the others. This was WARD´S METHOD of minimising an objective function (Ward 1963). It is recommended by Wishart as

> "possibly the best of the HIERARCHY options" (Wishart 1978 p33)

and in an evaluation of seven different clustering methods Mojena concluded that

> "Method 7 (Ward´s error sum of squares) gave a superior performance across all data sets" (Mojena 1977 p361).

It is also claimed that Ward´s method is robust against possible mismatch between its conceptual assumptions and those held about the data. In contrast, an alternative hierarchical method, the NEAREST NEIGHBOUR (SINGLE LINKAGE) technique, is well known for the problem of ´chaining´. This is the tendency to cluster objects together at a relatively low level when they are linked by a chain of intermediate data points, rather than to establish genuine groupings. I conclude that Ward´s method is a suitable choice for the statistical technique to determine patterns of association in the collocational data.

4.4 Procedural Consequences

The decision to approach the analysis of the data in this way has further consequences. The first of these is that the collocational data must be conceived of as forming a matrix. The rows of the matrix are given by each lemma as node and the columns represent each lemma as collocate. Thus the entry in

the ijth cell, that is the cell in row i column j, is the
frequency of collocation of the ith node with the jth
collocate. Since the set of nodes is identical with the set of
collocates, the matrix will be square and symmetric about the
leading diagonal. In other words, all the information is
contained in the upper triangular matrix. A second consequence
is that CLUSTAN requires that the data be submitted as a
rectangular matrix in FORTRAN F format. A useful introduction
to the properties of matrices is provided by Coulson, whilst
Calderbank describes the pertinent features of Fortran (Coulson
1969, Calderbank 1969).

A problem arises as to how to treat the entries on the
principal diagonal of the matrix. These represent the
frequencies of self-collocation, that is the number of times a
node co-occurs with itself as collocate within the span. The
nature of the problem can best be illustrated graphically.

		1	2	3	collocates (variables)
nodes (cases)	1	0	10	12	
	2	10	0	15	
	3	12	15	...	

In this fragment of a matrix of collocational frequencies,
nodes 1 and 2 collocate with each other ten times but neither
node self-collocates. Since the matrix is treated by the
procedure as a set of values of variables for a number of
cases, the program will take cases 1 and 2 as being quite
dissimilar with respect to the first two variables. Thus the
corresponding nodes will be clustered only if there are
sufficient examples of similar frequencies of collocation with
other collocates, as is the case in the example with collocate
3. Presentation of the collocational frequencies in their raw
form is thus misleading since it obscures the fact that nodes 1
and 2 share the primary feature of collocating with each other.

A related problem is that the apparent agreement of nodes 1 and
2 as regards their collocational behaviour with collocate 3
must be referred to the individual frequencies of occurrence of
the nodes concerned. If, in fact, node 1 occurs in the text
twelve times, for example, and node 2 one hundred times, then
the apparent similarity of their frequencies of collocation
with collocate 3 disappears. Collocate 3 is then found in the
environment of node 2 in only 15% of its occurrences whereas
the occurrence of node 1 totally predicts the occurence of
collocate 3, if for the sake of simplicity the case where the
collocate occurs more than once within the span is excluded.

These problems can be resolved by normalising the data. This
is done by transforming the raw frequencies of collocation such
that a value of 1 is assigned to each cell in the diagonal and

all other frequencies of collocation are scaled in proportion to fall within the range 0-1 inclusive. This is tantamount to the assertion that no node can be considered as more similar to any other node than it is to itself. In theory, then, only in cases of perfect collocation, where node and collocate only ever occur in each other's environment, will this condition be met by different nodes. In practice, the picture is slightly complicated by the infrequent case of repetition of collocation within the span, but this does not affect the validity of the procedure.

The scaling can be done additively by, for example, letting

$$f'_{ij} = \frac{f_{ij}}{f_i + f_j - f_{ij}} \qquad (1)$$

where f_i is the frequency of occurrence of the ith node, f_j the frequency of the jth node and f_{ij} is the frequency with which the two nodes collocate. Alternatively, a multiplicative procedure can be used, such as that embodied in the following formula

$$f'_{ij} = \frac{f_{ij}}{\sqrt{f_i f_j}} \qquad (2)$$

For most purposes it will be appropriate to scale additively using formula (1). This measure has the advantage over the multiplicative approach of having a straightforward interpretation. The normalised frequency represents the number of instances of collocation expressed as a proportion of the non-collocating occurrences of both nodes.

There is also support for this measure in the literature. In an evaluation of association measures, Jones and Curtice commented favourably upon its performance (Jones and Curtice 1967). Moscovich and Caplan, referring to it as formula IX, say

> "it may be assumed that formulas of the type VI, VII, VIII and IX that are based on the evaluation of the statistical significance of the excess of the observed co-occurrence over expected co-occurrence are more preferable than the formula V based solely on the value of the observed co-occurrence as they provide a procedure for filtering the most significant connections." (Moskovich and Caplan 1978 p125)

Since this method of normalisation weights collocational frequencies relative to the frequency of occurrence of both items in the collocation, this means that the notion of 'directionality' discussed by Sinclair is accommodated within the procedure (Sinclair 1966). Sinclair suggests that it is of greater importance to 'omen' that it collocates with 'good' than it is to 'good' that it collocates with 'omen', given their very different probabilities of occurrence in the language at large. Thus 'omen' is more predictive of 'good' than vice versa.

Incorporating this insight into the procedure has the further practical consequence that the collocational behaviour of low frequency items will not be swamped by the potentially obscuring presence in the text of high frequency items. As a corollary, it allows some very high frequency items to be admitted into the study without undue risk of thereby obliterating the patterns of association contracted by less frequently occurring nodes. This is of some significance in science text where a number of highly characteristic lemmata are likely to occur with particularly high frequencies. In one chemical engineering text, for example, the lemma <u>react</u> alone accounts for some 1% of the running words. It would obviously be undesirable to have to exclude an item which is so intuitively typical of this text on the grounds that its exceptionally high frequency of occurrence might conceal the patterning of other less frequently occurring nodes.

I would argue, then, that there is no point in following Berry-Rogghe's proposal that

> "a collocate which appears ten times in the text and collocates with the node in each of these occurrences should be considered more highly significant than a collocate which appears only twice in the text and collocates twice with the node" (Berry-Rogghe 1970 p48).

To a certain extent, of course, low frequency items are intrinsically advantaged due to the relative overestimation arising from the integral nature of occurrence frequencies. An increase in frequency from 1 to 2 represents a doubling whereas an increase from 100 to 101 is a mere 1% advance. Carroll has observed that this is a problem inherent in the statistics of 'parole' (Carroll 1968). I think the more cogent argument, however, is that a high frequency node has an intrinsically greater chance of contracting significant collocations than a low frequency node in any case. Thus it is a distortion to assign less significance to the collocations of low frequency nodes as Berry-Rogghe proposes. It is plausible that a node occurring five times will do so with five different collocates in a given span position, but it is highly unlikely that a node occurring five hundred times will have as many different collocates in the same position.

So far in this section I have been discussing the general consequences of deciding to analyse the collocational frequencies using a Cluster Analysis technique. A consequence of the choice of Ward's method in particular must now be

mentioned. It will be recalled that CLUSTAN computes a
similarity coefficient to summarise the collocational behaviour
of each node. In effect, the matrix of normalised frequencies
submitted to CLUSTAN is replaced with a smaller matrix of
similarity coefficients. A wide variety of similarity and
distance coefficients is available within CLUSTAN but in
practice the choice is pre-empted if Ward's method is adopted.
Wishart points out that Ward's method

> "is only meaningful or defined where distance
> coefficients (ICOEF=1 or 2) have been computed with
> CORREL" (Wishart 1978 p32).

This assertion means that a particular form of coefficient
which characterises the 'distance' between each pair of data
points must be used.

The coefficient in question is the Euclidean metric. This is
defined as

$$d_{ij} = \sum_{k=1}^{p} \{(X_{ik} - X_{jk})^2\}^{0.5}$$

where d_{ij} is the distance between points i and j and X_{ik} is the
value of the kth variable for the ith entity. In this case,
the values of the variables are the collocational frequencies,
the set of entities comprises each lemma taken as node and the
summation is performed over the p collocates of each node i and
j, which may include the case of self-collocation.

Again, there is encouraging support for the Euclidean distance
coefficient in the literature. Fillenbaum and Rapoport
assessed the results from Multidimensional Scaling using both
the Euclidean metric and an alternative, the City Block metric.
They report consistently lower stress values, which is a
measure of the distortion of the data introduced into the
solution, for the Euclidean metric.

The use of Ward's method also entails acceptance of the error
sum of squares (E.S.S.) as the objective criterion determining
which fusions are made. The E.S.S. increases in value as the
strength of the clustering decreases. The E.S.S. is given by

$$E.S.S. = \sum_{clusters} \sum_{within\ clusters} [\sum_{k=1}^{p} (X_{ik} - X_k)^2]$$

where X_k is the mean of the kth variable of all the entities
within a cluster. What this means, according to Ward, is that
at any stage of an analysis, the loss of information resulting
from clustering can be measured by the total sum of squared
deviations of every point from the mean of the cluster to which
it belongs. Thus, in intuitive terms, the E.S.S. measures the

´tightness´ of the clusters. At each step in the analysis, the union of every possible pair of clusters is contemplated and the two clusters are combined whose fusion results in the minimum increase in the total value of the E.S.S. over all clusters.

4.5 Data Collection and Reduction

It has been seen that Cluster Analysis operates upon a matrix of collocational frequencies. These are provided by a computational analysis of the text to be investigated. Collection of relevant data involves three steps. The first step is to identify and eliminate from consideration all closed system items. Next, the remaining items have to be lemmatised. Lastly, the collocational behaviour of the set of units thus arrived at must be quantified. The first of these steps necessitates the production of a complete vocabulary listing for the text involved. The third step entails obtaining a listing of the frequencies of collocation of each member in the set of lemmata with every other. The information required by these two steps dictates a particular computational methodology.

There are at present two major software packages for text analysis in general use in Britain. The first of these is OCP or the Oxford Concordance Program (Hockey and Marriot 1980). The second is CLOC, which is an acronym derived from the term CoLOCation (Reed 1978). The need for collocational information rules out the use of OCP since no routine is currently incorporated in the package for this purpose. CLOC, on the other hand, can produce collocational frequency counts and contains in addition a number of options which make it eminently suitable for the kind of analysis envisaged.

I have described CLOC in some detail elsewhere and shall therefore restrict myself to a brief survey of the main features of the package which make it suitable for the data collection required by the approach to text analysis developed here (Phillips 1984). CLOC can produce wordcounts, concordances and co-occurrence statistics as well as collocational frequencies for a set of nodes defined by the user and within a span extending up to a maximum of twelve words on either side of the node. The collocations can be printed out either in context or as a condensed listing consisting of only the nodes and collocates together with their individual and joint frequencies of occurrence. Both the choice of nodes for input to the routine as well as the selection of collocates for output can be controlled by the user. Nodes may be specified by an exhaustive listing whilst both nodes and collocates can be selected by giving a list of exclusions or by means of a frequency criterion.

An extremely important feature of CLOC is the facility it offers for specifying searches in terms of word patterns. Thus the form ´kn.w*´, for example, identifies all strings beginning with ´kn´ followed by exactly one arbitrary character followed by ´w´ followed by any number of arbitrary characters, including the zero case. This specification would thus select all the syntactic variants of the lemma know. This means that CLOC has a limited capacity to lemmatise the text automatically. The package itself cannot, of course, decide whether a word is to be lemmatised and if so to which lemma it is to be attached. This information must be provided explicitly in a control file which must be created by inspection of the word frequency count for the text in question. A degree of caution has also to be exercised when taking advantage of this lemmatisation facility. In many cases it may be possible to conflate all the syntactic variants of interest only by specifying a pattern which is over-inclusive and which thereby incorporates unwanted words into the lemma. For example, the pattern ´act*´ will identify all occurrences of ´act´, ´acting´, ´action´, ´active´ and so forth, but will also include in the same search ´actual´ and ´actually´, which may not be what is intended. Consequently, it is usually necessary to maintain an exclusion list to ensure that words are appropriately lemmatised.

The output from CLOC is, however, unlemmatised. That is to say, the patterns specified in the control file are reconstituted into the various forms of the matching words from the text. This is a useful safeguard since it allows unanticipated words which undesirably match the pattern to be filtered out manually. It does mean, however, that the output must be relemmatised before any further processing of the results takes place and the collocational frequencies of the individual constituents of each lemma summed appropriately. The resulting frequencies must then be manipulated into the matrix form required by CLUSTAN for its input. This entails the use of a specially written computer program.

The number of frequencies of collocation that it is practicable to submit to CLUSTAN for analysis is relatively limited. A square matrix of only one hundred lemmata contains a potential ten thousand collocational frequencies. In a two-dimensional array the number of cells increases as the square of ´n´; thus doubling the number of lemmata to two hundred quadruples the number of cells to 40,000. CLUSTAN is quite reasonably limited to a maximum of two hundred cases and even so the investigation of a 200X200 matrix can still be quite expensive in terms of computer time. But a text of some 60,000 running words typically has a vocabulary of between three and seven thousand different types. Thus even a set of two hundred nodes for investigation is of modest size. In other words there is a significant problem of data reduction. Whilst application of the text reduction criteria developed earlier markedly reduces the number of vocabulary items, on a rough estimate some 1,500 lemmata at least remain from a typical text as candidates for investigation. It is consequently necessary to develop rational principles by which to reduce the quantity of data for analysis whilst preserving the maximum amount of relevant information about the text.

This can be done by appropriate random sampling. When taking a sample in this way, it is hoped that the distribution of frequencies in the sample will be similar in form to that of the population from which the sample is drawn. The sample can then be considered as typical of the population with some confidence. This will normally be the case if three conditions are met. First, exceptional features associated with the extremes of the population should be eliminated. Secondly, the the population distribution needs to be reasonably smooth over the majority of its extent. Finally, the sample must be of reasonable size relative to the population.

The population distribution to be sampled consists of the number of items occurring ´x´ times in a text. The three conditions are or can be met without undue difficulty in the case of this kind of distribution. It is desirable to set upper and lower cut-off limits for the portion of the distribution to be sampled. In this way all the very high frequency closed system items are excluded on the one hand and the low frequency items which are intrinsically unlikely to display collocational behaviour on the other. Herdan offers statistical confirmation of the reasonableness of treating the frequency distribution in this way. He suggests that the form of vocabulary distributions is such that three distinct probability density functions can be postulated to account in turn for the high, middle and low frequency regions of the distribution (Herdan 1964). Thus by setting upper and lower cut-off limits the first condition is met in a statistically valid manner. Zipf´s ´law´ shows that the distribution of words ranked according to frequency of occurrence is a bilogorithmic straight line over the portion of the distribution of interest and thus the second condition obtains (Zipf 1949). Finally, by the combined operation of the text reduction principles and the use of upper and lower cut-off limits, it is possible so to arrange the procedure that up to 60% of the remaining text items ´at risk´ can be sampled. Thus the final condition can also be met.

After the cut-off limits have been applied to the distribution for a text of some 60,000 running words, a central population of between three and five hundred lemmata remains. Given the constraints on the size of matrices accepted by CLUSTAN, it is clearly necessary to reduce this number by sampling. The question is to determine by how much. It has already been suggested that on the grounds of computational efficiency it may be desirable to restrict the number of cases to something less than the maximum of two hundred accepted by CLUSTAN. Sibson, who writes with considerable authority in the area of Cluster Analysis, claims that

> "Sixty objects is a convenient figure to keep in mind for the capacity of a method which is to be used routinely" (Sibson 1972 p313).

This is confirmed by my own experience; I have found that typically matrices of fifty to eighty cases represent about the upper practicable limit both in terms of the amount of manual data preparation required and the processing time of the computer.

On the other hand, it can be assumed that in any text interval only a proportion of the lemmata selected for investigation will in fact display collocational behaviour. Moreover, any collocational frequency can be required to reach a certain criterial level before it is considered of interest. Consequently, the set of lemmata can in practice be allowed to exceed the optimum size suggested by Sibson. Needham points out that in linguistic classification

> "if we go to make a similarity matrix, we shall find that an object only has non-zero similarities to very small proportions of the other objects" (Needham 1967 p47).

This is certainly true of collocational behaviour. Thus it is possible to allow the sample to approximate the CLUSTAN limit of two hundred entities in the expectation that at the very outside only about half of these will in fact give rise to frequencies of collocation. The lemmata in the central portion of the distribution can be sampled by assigning a number to each and then picking them out according to a list of pseudo-random numbers generated by the computer.

The price paid by adoption of a sampling procedure is a loss of information available to the analysis. There is thus a possibility that only a partial or distorted reflection of the patterns of association in the data will be obtained. This is to be regretted but not unduly so; the alternative is simply to abandon the attempt to extract information about this aspect of textual organisation. On the other hand, a significant advantage accrues from random sampling. Since no linguistic assumptions are allowed to influence the final choice of lemmata, there is a corresponding gain in objectivity. If the procedure results in the discovery of patterns of association, the evidence will carry conviction.

4.6 Conclusion

In this chapter the statistical and computational procedures which are appropriate to the analysis of text within the theoretical framework developed in the first part of this book have been discussed. It was seen that classical techniques of statistical significance testing do not appropriately apply to text and that a non-parametric procedure of data analysis is more suitable. Of the possible techniques, Cluster Analysis appears to offer the greatest chance of producing suggestive results and Ward's method in particular was singled out as robust and effective.

Two major consequences stem from the decision to use a Cluster Analysis technique. The first of these is that the data must be presented in matrix format and the second is that there must be a limitation on the amount of data submitted for analysis.

The first of these consequences itself has implications for the manipulation of the data. Not only must computer programs be written to transform the data into this form but steps must also be taken to ensure that the procedure does not misinterpret the data through the peculiarities of the matrix format. It was seen that it is necessary to normalise the data in order to avoid certain problems of interpretation. This also requires the development of a simple computer program for this purpose.

The practical limits on the quantity of data that can be submitted for analysis are quite severe. This stems from the fact that one of the points of using Cluster Analysis is that it allows a simultaneous analysis of all frequencies of collocation to be undertaken. It was argued that this is desirable in order not to prejudice the identification of patterns of association. The price to be paid for this objectivity is that only a relatively small proportion of the candidate lemmata in a typical textbook can be investigated. As a result, it is necessary to develop a sensible procedure for restricting the number of lemmata for analysis. The main considerations in sampling the data were discussed and it became apparent that it is possible by judicious selection to obtain a sample which will reflect fairly the principal characteristics of the frequency distribution of the text.

At present only one software package exists in Britain which is capable of extracting collocational data from text. This is the CLOC package developed at the University of Birmingham. The main features of this package were described. Thus by using CLOC to obtain the raw data and CLUSTAN to analyse them, it is possible to derive information about the large scale lexical patterning of text. The next step is to display the results thus obtained in a readily interpretable form which reveals clearly the structural relations existing in the data. In other words, a technique for the description of structure is required. This forms the topic of the next chapter.

CHAPTER 5

DESCRIPTIVE TECHNIQUES FOR TEXT ANALYSIS

5.1 An Introduction to Digraphs

Previous chapters have developed a theoretical view of text and explored a methodology for the empirical investigation of this view. The objective of such an investigation would be to seek patterns of association among selected lemmata in the text. These would furnish evidence for the existence of a level of macrostructural organisation. If this level can be established, it may be expected to throw light upon the way in which text generates the notion of subject matter and thus to help explain the nature of the relationship between text and reality. In order to examine the relations obtaining among any lemmata which the analysis reveals as tending to enter into patterns of association, it is necessary to adopt a technique for describing empirical structures. The relevant considerations are discussed in this chapter.

To facilitate structural statements and to establish a basis for making comparisons among patterns of association identified in different parts of a text, the representation of patterns must be formalised. This will then offer the possibility of making the kind of generalisations upon which the notion of macrostructure must rest. A suitable representational system can be found in graph theory. Patterning of the type that it is anticipated may be found in text can be treated as the empirical realisation of the mathematical objects studied by the theory of directed graphs. For convenience, this branch of discrete mathematics is usually known as ´digraph theory´. This abbreviation should be clearly distinguished from the term ´digraph´ in linguistics, which refers to a quite different concept. In this book ´digraph´ will always denote the mathematical object.

A helpful introduction to graph theory will be found in Wilson but it is Harary and his colleagues who provide the most cogent justification for studying the data in this way (Wilson 1979, Harary et al 1965). They state that

> "digraph theory is useful to the researcher interested in the structural properties of any empirical system, for it provides concepts, theorems, and methods appropriate to the analysis of structure" (Harary et al op.cit. p3).

By choosing a suitable coordination of pertinent aspects of data with the abstract objects of digraph theory, useful rigour will be introduced into the key notions required for their understanding and a precise vocabulary will be available for their description. Other benefits which may accrue in the longer term include the fact that

> "digraph theory and associated branches of mathematics provide techniques of computation and formulas for calculating certain features of empirical structures" (ibid p3).

That is to say, graph theory allows structural phenomena to be quantified.

Most important, perhaps, is the property of digraph theory that it forms an axiomatic system and from its axioms a large number of logically derivable theorems follow. If the empirical structures found in text satisfy the axioms of digraph theory, then its theorems become valid assertions about structural properties of the data and thus furnish a powerful tool for furthering understanding of those data. Although it is the relatively modest application of digraph theory as a means for representing structural relations in the data which will be of principal relevance here, from time to time some of the theorems of the theory will be invoked to make precise important intuitive notions. This exploitation of digraph theory is complementary to the use of Cluster Analysis. Digraph theory alone cannot determine which textual units enter into patterns of association. It has been argued that Cluster Analysis is indispensable for this. But having isolated such patterning, digraph theory permits the rigorous exploration of its properties.

The use of graph theory is not entirely unprecedented in linguistics. The particular form of graph known as a ´tree´ is, of course, well established both in linguistics and mathematics as a representation for grammars. Simmons has applied the concept of a ´network´, which is a particular type of digraph which I shall examine in the next section, to the development of a theory of language comprehension in terms of conceptual nodes and semantic relations among them (Simmons 1973). He conceives of

> "semantic nodes as representing human verbal concept structures and semantic relations connecting two such structures as representing the linguistic processes of thought that are used to combine them into natural language descriptions of events" (Simmons op.cit. p63).

This is a relatively sophisticated application. My interpretation of the formal structures will be considerably more straightforward than that of Simmons.

I shall now outline the principal features of digraph theory which are relevant to present concerns. In this I follow the

DESCRIPTIVE TECHNIQUES FOR TEXT ANALYSIS 91

description in Harary et al (Harary et al op.cit.). A digraph is defined as an entity which satisfies the following axiom system:

The primitives are:

P1: A set V of elements called 'points' (or 'nodes' or vertices').

P2: A set X of elements called 'lines' (or 'arcs' or 'edges').

P3: A function f whose domain is X and whose range is contained in V.

P3: A function s whose domain is X and whose range is contained in V.

The first two primitives are self-explanatory; they specify the points and lines of which a digraph is composed. The second two relate the lines to the points by means of two functions 'f' and 's' which identify the 'first' and 'second' points of each line respectively. Thus if 'l' is a line in X, then f(l) identifies the point from which the line emerges and s(l) the point to which the line extends. In other words, the lines of a digraph are 'directed' and the direction of a line is conventionally represented on the graph by an arrowhead. Lines are considered to be 'parallel' if they connect the same two nodes and are identically directed.

The axioms of digraph theory are:

A1: The set V is finite and non-empty.

A2: The set X is finite.

A3: No two distinct lines are parallel.

A4: There are no loops.

The first two axioms exclude the possibility of infinite graphs and state that all graphs must contain some point. Axiom two, however, does not exclude the possibility that the set of lines may be empty. Thus the two graphs below are both digraphs:

Graph 5.1 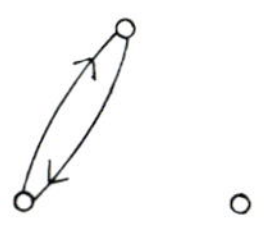   Graph 5.2

Graphs of this type are called 'disconnected' and Graph 5.1 is 'totally disconnected'. It will be seen later that such graphs have their application in the description of text structure.

Axioms three and four exlude the following graphs:

Graph 5.3   Graph 5.4

Graph 5.3 is not a digraph because it contains parallel lines 'uv', a case which is excluded by axiom three. Graph 5.4 is not permitted on account of the loop 'vv'. It will be seen that this latter constraint can be legitimately relaxed to good purpose later in the investigation.

Where every pair of points in a digraph is connected by two lines, which by axiom three must therefore be oppositely directed, the digraph is called 'symmetric'. If the direction of the lines in a symmetric digraph is not in fact important, the convention can be adopted of replacing the two directed lines with a single undirected line. The resulting diagram can then be referred to simply as a 'graph'. Thus a symmetric digraph such as that represented in Graph 5.5 will normally be represented as the graph illustrated in Graph 5.6:

Graph 5.5   Graph 5.6

An interpretation can now be provided for a graph, that is, a coordination of the empirical entities being investigated with

DESCRIPTIVE TECHNIQUES FOR TEXT ANALYSIS   93

its points and lines. Lemmata can be made to correspond to the points of a graph and the occurrence of collocation to the lines. Thus the following graph

a   b

Graph 5.7

indicates that lemma **a** collocates with lemma **b**. As an example of how this works in practice, the graphical representations of two empirical patterns of association derived from the study reported in part three of this book are illustrated below:

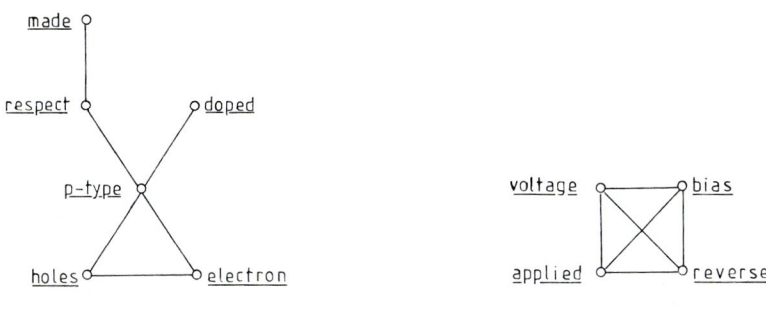

Graph 5.8   Graph 5.9

Both graphs are taken from a text on electronics and clearly indicate that certain terms in the text tend consistently to associate with each other in distinctive groupings.

The structural relations represented by the lines of the graphs can be obtained from inspection of the collocational frequencies output by CLOC. The orientation, however, of the graphs on the page, the physical distance between each pair of points and whether straight or curved lines are used to connect the points are arbitrary. In other words, the graphs can be presented in several isomorphic forms. Thus Graphs 5.10 and 5.11 below contain exactly the same information as the preceding two graphs. The only differences involved relate to purely geometric properties with which the analysis is not concerned; the topological characteristics remain unchanged.

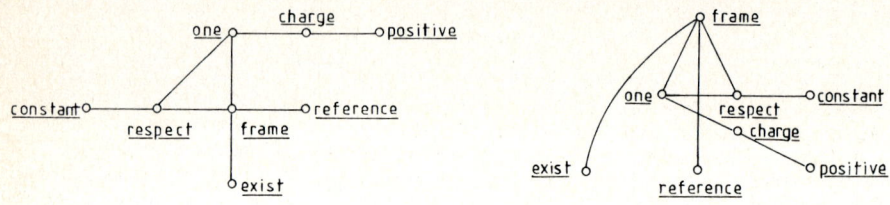

Graph 5.10   Graph 5.11

It can be seen that the use of graph representation immediately clarifies the relations obtaining among nodes and collocates in a way that is impossible with a straightforward listing of frequencies. But to explore the internal structure of such patterns of association in greater depth, further results from digraph theory are required. These will be surveyed in the next section.

5.2 Further Results from Graph Theory

A useful concept associated with the structure of graphs is the notion of ´reachability´. This is arrived at by first defining a ´path´ as an alternating sequence of distinct points and lines which begins with a point and where each line is preceded by its first point and followed by its second point. This means that the directionality of the lines is significant. Symbolically, a path can be represented as

$$v_1, v_1v_2, v_2, v_2v_3, \ldots, v_{n-1}v_n, v_n$$

where v_i is a point and v_iv_j is the directed line from point v_i to point v_j. The concept of a path enables ´reachability´ to be defined. If there is a path from a point ´u´ to a point ´v´, then ´v´ is said to be ´reachable´ from ´u´.

The concept of ´reachability within a certain distance´ can now be introduced. The ´distance´ between two points is the number of lines that must be traversed in proceeding from one point to the other. With each point ´v´ in a digraph two numbers can be associated which represent the maximum distance from ´v´ and the maximum distance to ´v´, symbolically $d(v,u)$ and $d(u,v)$. The ´outnumber´ of a point ´v´ is the largest of the numbers $d(v,u)$ for all ´u´ in the digraph. Similarly, the ´innumber´

of a point 'v' is the largest of the numbers d(u,v) for all 'u' in the digraph. It should be apparent that the smaller these numbers are, the more 'central' is the location of the point 'v' in the graph. Thus the 'outcentre' of a digraph can be defined as the point with smallest finite outnumber in the digraph. The 'incentre' of the digraph can be defined in a similar manner. In the graphs of interest here, which will normally be symmetric, the outcentre and incentre will coincide.

These properties of digraphs allow the internal structure of associations of textual units to be explored. It is now possible formally to distinguish between the central and peripheral nodes in a pattern of association. Using another of the patterns identified in part three of this book derived from a text on classical mechanics for exemplification, some of the power of these notions can be seen. Consider the pattern graphed below:

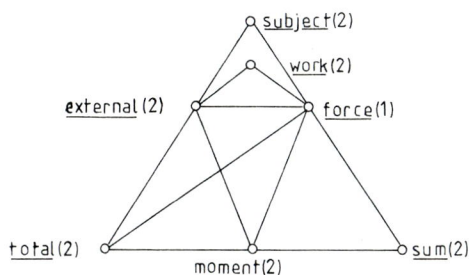

Graph 5.12

Whilst the relations among the different nodes in this pattern are clearly revealed by the graphical representation, it is not immediately apparent whether all the nodes enjoy equal status or whether one plays a more fundamental role in the structure than any of the others. By assigning innumbers and outnumbers to the various nodes as appropriate, it can be determined that the lemma force is central. The ability thus objectively to identify nodes which are central in such groupings is of considerable linguistic significance and a definite advantage resulting from this application of graph theory.

The possibility of completely disconnected graphs was mentioned in the preceding section. Conversely, graphs may be completely connected. A graph is said to be completely connected when every point in the graph is connected to every other point.

The ways in which the points of a graph are interconnected is known as the 'connectivity' of the graph. Connectivity can also be an object of study and it will be seen that it can be of use in characterising the empirical forms of patterns of association.

Following Wilson, the question can be posed 'How connected is a connected graph?' (Wilson 1979). One way of providing an answer is to determine the number of lines which need to be removed from a graph in order to disconnect it. This notion gives rise to the concept of the 'disconnecting set' of a graph. The disconnecting set of a graph is the set of lines whose removal disconnects the graph, that is leaves at least one point in the graph isolated from all the other points. A 'cutset' is a disconnecting set which does not include a proper subset which is a disconnecting set. In other words, a 'cutset' of a graph cannot itself be reduced in size by the omission of any of its constituent lines and remain a cutset. This is not to say, however, that other cutsets consisting of different combinations of lines may not exist for the same graph nor that a given cutset necessarily consists of the minimum number of lines whose removal is needed to disconnect the graph.

With these preliminary concepts established, it is now possible to introduce the crucial notion of the 'line-connectivity' of a graph. This is defined as the size of the smallest cutset of the graph, that is the minimum number of lines required to disconnect the graph. For a graph 'G', it is represented symbolically by $\lambda(G)$. In the case of a completely connected graph 'G' on 'p' points the value of $\lambda(G)$ will equal p-1, since in order to isolate any point in the graph all the lines connecting it to the p-1 other points in 'G' must be removed. It is thus possible to develop an expression to measure the extent of connectivity of a graph. The ratio of the line-connectivity of a graph to that of a completely connected graph on the same number of points is what is required, that is

$$c = \lambda(G)/p-1$$

where 'c' can be called the 'connectivity index'. For a completely connected graph, the index equals 1.

To illustrate these notions two of the graphs which have already been introduced in the last section can be used as examples. Graph 5.8 is a graph on 6 points. A completely connected graph on this number of points would have a line-connectivity of 5. In fact, it can be readily seen that the actual line-connectivity for this graph is 1, since the graph can be quite simply disconnected by removing either of the lines connecting the nodes made or doped. Thus the connectivity index for this graph has a value of 0.2, that is the ratio 1/5. In contrast the connectivity index of Graph 5.9 has a value of 1 since this graph is completely connected. The ratio involved is 3/3.

In the context of text analysis, one point of thus measuring the connectivity of a graph is that it represents a way of quantifying the extent to which the collocates of a node themselves intercollocate. It is potentially of importance to be able to do this since what is thereby measured is the relative status of the lemmata in terms of their power to attract collocations. A comparatively low value of the connectivity index of a graph corresponding to a particular pattern of association in a text tends to indicate an inequality in the way the nodes concerned are operating in the text. Such a finding is likely to suggest productive hypotheses about the function of different textual units.

Finally, it was noted in the first section of this chapter that the restriction formulated in axiom four that a digraph cannot contain any loops could also usefully be relaxed. By doing so it becomes possible to represent the case of self-collocation within the span. Thus Graph 5.13 below is identical with Graph 5.8 discussed in section one, with the exception of the additional information that the node electron in fact collocates with itself:

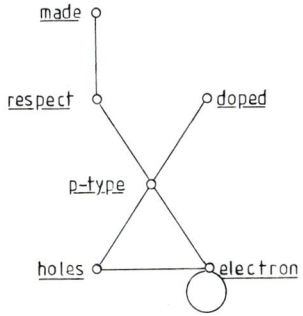

Graph 5.13

It will be seen in part three that the phenomenon of self-collocation may have implications for the establishment of a typology of texts. I shall not, therefore, pursue its discussion further at this stage.

There is a further notion within graph theory which is of use in analysing the data derived from text by the techniques which have already been outlined. This is the possibility of assigning values or 'weights' to the lines of a graph. This will open up a new perspective on the structure of any patterns of association which might be found in text. This possibility is considered in the next section.

5.3 The Notion of Network

Further insight into the properties of patterns of association in the data may be obtained by relaxing some of the constraints on the form of the graphical representation, as was suggested in the first section. In particular, a more delicate appreciation of the internal structure of such patterns can be achieved by assigning a 'weight' to each line in the relevant graph which is proportional to the 'strength' of the collocation represented by the line.

This procedure gives rise to a new set of mathematical entities called 'networks'. A network may be defined as a graph on a finite set 'V' of points, with its set of lines identified as usual as 'X', but where a 'weight', denoted w(l), has been assigned to each line. If the graph is irreflexive, that is if w(uv) is not the same as w(vu), then the object is a weighted digraph. In the case of collocational data, the weighting which suggests itself naturally is the frequencies of collocation. Since, however, these frequencies are relative to the frequencies of occurrence of the collocating items, it is more useful to use the empirical probabilities of collocation as weights.

If each line in the digraph representing a pattern of association is labelled with the probability obtained by dividing the frequency of collocation for which it stands by the frequency of occurrence of the lemma represented by the first point to which the line is incident, a weighted digraph or network is obtained. In this network lines directed outward from a point represent the probability in the text of the relevant lemma co-occurring with the collocate represented by the second point on the line. Similarly, lines directed inward to a point stand for the probability that a particular collocate will co-occur with the node. Given that lemmata will occur with different frequencies in the text, it should be clear that the weights assigned to the two lines joining a pair of points need not be identical. Outdirected lines will correspond to what van Buren has called the 'Active Prediction Ratio' and indirected lines to his 'Passive Prediction Ratio' (van Buren 1967). Thus in this way, the directionality of collocational relations recognised by Sinclair and mentioned in the last chapter can be incorporated into the representation of structure. Some examples of such networks taken from the study reported in part three are given below:

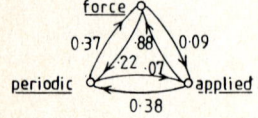

Graph 5.14

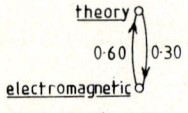

Graph 5.15

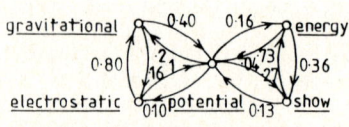

Graph 5.16

DESCRIPTIVE TECHNIQUES FOR TEXT ANALYSIS   99

It should be noted that since the values assigned to the outdirected lines from a node represent the empirical probability of a particular collocation from the set of all collocations of the node in the text being found, the probabilities will not normally sum to unity in a given analysis. This simply means that the node sometimes occurs in the text without collocating with any of the collocates participating in the particular pattern of association represented in the graph. This, of course, is to be expected.

Armed with the apparatus just described, it is possible to explore the internal structure of patterns of association in greater detail. It is now feasible to pursue the investigation in terms of the notion of directionality, the concept of strong and weak collocations and the relative strength of patterns of association. By way of illustrating the potential power of the techniques developed here, I shall briefly consider what light may be thrown upon an area which is germane to the aspects of text analysis focused upon here but not in the centre of attention. I believe that the concepts introduced here could profitably be used to investigate the structure of scientific terminology.

It could, for example, be argued that the class of collocations where both weights on the two lines representing the collocation equal or approach unity is likely to represent an idiom or the polymorphemic expression of a single concept. A typical example would be the use of the term ´quantum mechanics´ in physics. Where one only of the lines has a relatively high weighting, in excess, say, of 0.5, it may still be the case that the existence of a polymorphemic item articulating a conceptual structure viewed as a unit has been revealed. The difference would be that elements of the linguistic item can also actualise other conceptual structures at different points in the text. Examples derived from a text on classical mechanics would be:

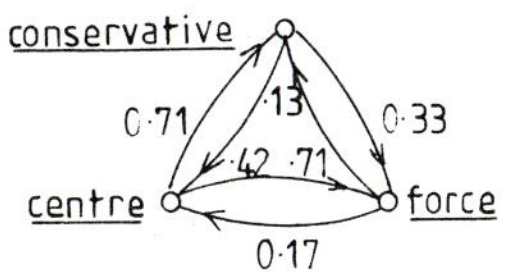

Graph 5.17

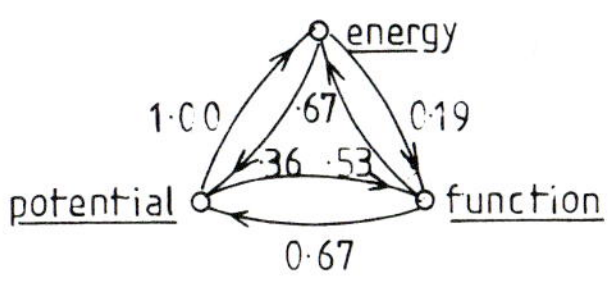

Graph 5.18

Note that in Graph 5.17 the occurrence of centre predicts that of conservative and force about seven times in every ten, suggesting that a nominal group such as ´central conservative force´ actualises an established concept in mechanics, which is indeed the case. Similarly, the occurrence of potential in

Graph 5.18 totally predicts _energy_, meaning that ´potential energy´ is a key concept in the text. There would seem, then, to be some promise in such an approach to the analysis of scientific terminology.

I do not propose, however, to develop these topics further here since this book is principally concerned with the macrostructure of text rather than the structural characteristics of terminology. It will be seen in part three that the concept of network is of use in establishing the patterns of cross-chapter similarity on which the notion of macrostructure rests. For this purpose, the apparatus developed hitherto in this section is sufficient. Before, however, leaving the subject of descriptive techniques entirely, I propose to give terminological recognition to the fact that the mathematical definition of a network offers an appropriate descriptive device for the kind of patterns of association of interest here. It will be recalled that the text reduction process is theoretically equivalent to the production of a text consisting entirely of lemmatised lexical items. Bearing this in mind, I shall no longer refer to groupings of these text units by the cumbersome term ´patterns of association´ as I have done up to now. Instead I shall refer henceforth to ´lexical networks´. In the light of the discussion conducted in this chapter, this term seems to me accurately to reflect the nature of the phenomena that the methodology described hitherto is designed to investigate. An incidental advantage of using this term is that it both relates the phenomena of interest to and distinguishes them from those described by the term ´lexical set´. A lexical set is a paradigmatic concept whilst a lexical network is a syntagmatic one.

5.4 Conclusion

With this chapter I have come to the end of the survey of the methodological implications of the theoretical position developed in part one. In chapter three the preliminary steps in an approach to text analysis were reviewed. It was seen that these involve eliminating from the text all the carriers of local meaning. A set of reduction principles was proposed through which the text can be filtered. This procedure conceptually leaves a text consisting only of lemmatised lexical items.

Chapter four then discussed the procedures needed to analyse this reduced text. The basic statistic that needs to be obtained is the frequencies of collocation of the residual text units with each other. This can be achieved by use of the CLOC text analysis software package. These frequencies can then be submitted to the CLUSTAN package for processing by Ward´s method of Cluster Analysis. It was argued that Cluster Analysis offered a better prospect of obtaining evidence of the existence of patterns of association in the text than other statistical methods. The issues involved in limiting the amount of data to manageable proportions were also discussed. The solution was seen to lie in a combination of selecting the middle band from the frequency distribution of types in the text and then randomly sampling the types in that band.

Finally, in the present chapter a technique for describing and presenting the structural relations in the results obtained from Cluster Analysis was outlined. It emerged that any empirical patterns of association discovered in the data could be considered theoretically as lexical networks. It is thus possible to develop a representation for lexical networks in terms of the methods of digraph theory. It was argued that this approach facilitates the exploration of the structure of lexical networks and hence of the macrostructure of text.

The theoretical argument suggests that there may well be interesting discoveries to be made by approaching the analysis of text in this way. It is an empirical question, however, whether such networks in fact exist in text and are discoverable using the techniques developed in this part. It is necessary, then, to undertake an empirical analysis both to explore the validity of the methodology and to substantiate the category of macrostructure. It is hoped that light will thereby be thrown on the phenomenon of aboutness and that in consequence the theoretical position arrived at in part one will be justified by empirical evidence. A detailed discussion of such an investigation occupies the next part of this book.

PART THREE

EXPLORATION OF TEXT

CHAPTER 6

APPLYING THE METHODOLOGY

6.1 The Corpus

In the present part of this book I shall describe the implementation of a study of text aimed at exploring the theoretical issues raised in the first part and framed in accordance with the methodology developed in the second part. In this chapter the procedural decisions required by the methodology in the particular circumstances of this study are considered. In the remaining chapters of this part the findings of the study are discussed, the evidence for macrostructure marshalled and the consequences of these results reviewed.

The first step in implementing the methodology was to determine the criteria to be used in establishing a corpus of texts for the study. A fundamental decision that had to be taken early in this process concerned the optimum size for the corpus. The interest of obtaining maximally valid generalisations, which argued in favour of as large a corpus as possible, had to be balanced against considerations of practicality.

In his study of scientific text, Roe claims that one million running words represent an adequate database from which to derive tenable generalisations (Roe 1977a). Roe's view is supported by a suggestive comment by Twaddell in his introduction to Kucera and Francis to the effect that

> "There are pedagogical questions that may well be within the proper scope of a megaword corpus. For example, what kinds of clumping of vocabulary items take place and in what proportion?" (Kucera and Francis 1967 pvii)

In practice, Roe was unable to live up to this ideal and his study appeals to samples from ten texts amounting in total to approximately half a million words. Roe's experience is thus suggestive of the upper practicable limit on the number of texts which can usefully be analysed within a reasonable time span by a single individual. Accordingly, it was decided that a corpus consisting of a maximum of ten textbooks would be of realistic size.

A second important decision in establishing the corpus had to do with the subject matter categories to be admitted. Two considerations suggested that science text would constitute a suitable object for investigation. Pragmatic factors relating to an interest in the pedagogy of English for Specific Purposes meant that a study of science text was seen as offering the possibility of producing results of practical value. But there was also a significant theoretical reason for focusing on science text. In an exploratory study such as this one where there is comparatively little in the way of previous research on which to base the approach, it is prudent to take what opportunities are available for maximising the chances of obtaining interesting results. This was the view held, for example, by Sinclair and Coulthard when they deliberately chose a well structured manifestation of spoken interaction for a first enquiry into discourse analysis (Sinclair and Coulthard 1975). It seems fairly obvious that lexis plays a significant role in science text and that it is likely to pattern in ways which contribute to the structure of the text. These theoretical intuitions about science text suggested that it might prove an appropriate choice of object for the investigation. Consequently it was decided that the primary category in the corpus would consist of a number of science textbooks.

For the purposes of this study Roe's definition of science text as

> "any title appearing on an official recommended reading list for students of science or technology at tertiary level" (Roe ibid p19)

was adopted. The acceptance of the restriction to tertiary level textbooks was motivated by considerations of relevance to the pedagogic concerns of English for Specific Purposes language teaching and the recognition that the scope of the enquiry had to be restricted to a manageable field. At the same time, it became clear that the corpus could not be restricted to this category of text only. If patterns of association of textual units were in fact discovered in science text, this would prompt the question whether the phenomenon is restricted to this particular class of text or whether it is a more general characteristic of the written language. It was therefore decided to include a number of texts from other genres, collectively referred to here as ´non-science´ texts, in the corpus.

It was also recognised that there could be a need to estimate the significance of any results obtained. One way of doing this would be to compare the results derived from the science and non-science texts with those obtained from equivalent texts generated on the basis of a random sequence of items, where equivalence means that the frequency distributions of the types in the random texts are comparable in form to those displayed by natural language texts of the kinds investigated. Thus equivalent random texts formed a third class in the corpus. In the light of these considerations, the composition of the corpus was fixed at five science textbooks, three non-science texts and two randomised texts.

The choice of individual science texts was restricted for reasons of practicality to a selection from those available in the Birmingham University corpus. The following selection criteria guided the choice:

>(1) all texts should be at the level of first year undergraduate studies;
>(2) the final selection of texts should represent as broad a coverage of fields of scientific enquiry as possible;
>(3) each text should where practicable deal with a well-defined field of enquiry;
>(4) the sample of each text available on computer file should ideally be the whole textbook (with the acceptable omission of prefatory matter and appendices) or, failing that, should constitute a coherent sub-text.

Application of these criteria resulted in the following choices:

A. Whole text except for prefatory matter and appendices

>(1) Ahmed H and Spreadbury P J Electronics for Engineers. Cambridge University Press, 1973.
>
>This text is described by the authors as follows: "This introductory textbook on electronic circuits covers the early part of degree level courses taken by electrical and electronics engineers and the material on electronics which is usually contained in other first degree courses in engineering at universities, polytechnics and technical colleges" (Back cover). The entire text with the exception of the preface and the appendices is contained in the sample.
>
>(2) Kibble T W B Classical Mechanics. McGraw-Hill, 2nd edition, 1973.
>
>This is a "textbook intended for use in the first or second year of an Honours degree course in physics" (Back cover). The sample on computer file represents approximately 87% of all the printed matter in the book and comprises everything except the preface and appendices.
>
>(3) Gareth Morris J A Biologist's Physical Chemistry. Edward Arnold, 2nd edition, 1974.
>
>"This book has been written in response to a need encountered when teaching elementary biochemistry to students reading for a degree" (Preface pvii). The 74% of the text incorporated in the computer sample comprises chapters 1-10 inclusive, excluding the prefatory material, the appendices and the worked examples and problems at the end of each chapter. Although this text could be construed as inter-

disciplinary in nature in that it treats only of such
aspects of physical chemistry as are judged to be of
relevance to the student of biology, it was included as
being the only readily available undergraduate textbook
dealing with chemistry.

B. Coherent sub-texts

(4) Levenspiel O *Chemical Reaction Engineering*.
Wiley, 2nd edition, 1972.

The author comments "I find that chapters 1-8, 11 and 14
form a reasonable basis for undergraduate instruction"
(Preface pvi). The computer sample contains chapters 1-8
in their entirety which, as Levenspiel suggests, form a
clearly defined component of the text. Chapter 9
onwards is considered as suitable for a graduate
programme.

(5) Sonntag R E and Van Wylen G J *Introduction to
Thermodynamics: Classical and Statistical*. Wiley,
1971.

Only 35% of the whole text is represented in the computer
sample but this covers chapters 1-9 completely, with the
exception of the problems to chapter 9. The authors´
comments on the organisation of their text indicate that
these chapters, which treat only of classical
thermodynamics, can form a coherent whole.

Henceforth, for convenience, these texts will be referred to by
the acronyms which identify the computer files on which they
are held. These are, following the sequence given above, ELEN,
CMEC, BIPC, CREL and THRM.

For the composition of the non-science category of the corpus,
it was decided that two works of fiction and one of non-fiction
would be appropriate. Within these limits it was felt that
useful breadth of coverage could be achieved by choosing two
novels, one of which should be an overtly ´literary´ work and
the other a carefully written but more popular narrative. It
was also considered that further interesting contrast could be
obtained by choosing a work of popular science as the
non-fiction text.

The final selections of non-science texts were:

(6) Woolf V *Mrs Dalloway*. Granada Publishing, 1976.

The publisher´s description on the back cover gives an
indication of the reasons for this choice: "With this
book she finally broke from the form of the traditional
English novel, establishing herself as a writer of
genius." Fortunately, although Virginia Woolf broke
sufficiently with traditional forms to eliminate
classical chapter boundaries, she retained the principle

of chapter divisions which are clearly identifiable as
increased spacing in the text. The whole text is
available on computer.

(7) Greene G   The Human Factor.   Penguin, 1978.

"The Human Factor is a thrilling story of tension and
intrigue" (Back cover). The computer sample contains
the whole text up to and including chapter 5, section 1,
or some 70% of the total. The part omitted deals with
the principal protagonist´s escape from London to
Moscow, which represents in structural terms a ´coda´ to
the main narrative. The sample can thus be considered
as constituting a coherent unit covering the whole of
the plot.

(8) Evans C   The Mighty Micro.   Gollancz, 1979
(hardback) and Hodder and Stoughton, 1980 (paperback).

"The impact of the microchip revolution. This could be
the most important book you ever read - it might even be
the last...". Unfortunately, the prediction emblazoned
on the front cover of the paperback edition proved
false. However, consolation was taken in the fact that
the 72% of the text contained in the sample covers the
majority of the principal themes of the book.

These three texts are identified as MRSD, THF and TMM
respectively.

The third category of the corpus comprised randomised versions
of one text from each of the two preceding categories. ELEN
and TMM were used as the basis for constructing equivalent
random texts identified as ELENRND and TMMRND respectively.
The procedure for creating these texts will be described in
section three when the computer programs used in the course of
the study are discussed.

6.2 Procedural Decisions

Within the overall context of the decision to analyse this
corpus using a Cluster Analysis technique, a number of specific
decisions of detail had to be taken. The process of text
reduction followed exactly the procedure described in chapter
three. The unit of analysis adopted was the lemma and the
interval chosen for the main study was the chapter, again as
discussed in chapter three. In fact, a small scale study was
also undertaken using the section as interval. The point of
this was simply to determine whether lexical networks are
identifiable within this relatively restricted extent of text.
The findings of this investigation have been reported elsewhere
(Phillips 1983). The main conclusion was that networks could
be identified even within this limited interval. The extent of
span adopted was four orthographic words on either side of the
node for the reasons given earlier. In addition, a number of
computer programs were specially written to facilitate the use

of CLOC for the purposes of the study, including providing an
interface to convert the output from CLOC into the form
required for input to CLUSTAN. These will be described in the
next section.

In chapter four the use of Ward´s method of Cluster Analysis
was recommended. It was also seen, however, that there might
not be much to choose between an agglomerative hierarchical
method of this type and the density technique based on an
underlying spatial model. It was argued that the choice would
ultimately depend more on questions of convenience than of
principle. These are matters which can be decided only
empirically and for this reason, as well as to test the
feasibility and usefulness of Cluster Analysis in general, the
pilot study described in section five of this chapter was
undertaken. I shall outline there the reasons which led to the
final choice of Ward´s method for the main study.

It was also seen in chapter four that certain procedural
decisions have to be made as a consequence of choosing to use
Ward´s method. The first of these concerns the type of scaling
procedure used to normalise the data. I chose to scale using
the additive formula given in chapter four section four. More
consequential decisions, however, are enforced by the need to
restrict the amount of data submitted to the method to
manageable proportions. The general criteria governing the
approach to data reduction were discussed in chapter four
section five. It is now necessary to describe their specific
application in the case of the study to be described here.

It became apparent that the only practicable way of limiting
the quantity of data was by a process of random sampling and
that such an approach was entirely justified by the nature of
the frequency distributions involved. The procedure involves
first establishing upper and lower cut-off points in order to
sample from the smooth central region of the distribution. In
practice, the limits determining the portion of the
distributions of the texts in the corpus to be sampled were set
at absolute values of three hundred occurrences for the upper
limit and ten occurrences for the lower. The actual values of
the cut-off points for any given text in the corpus were
adjusted in proportion to the length of the text.

There was a possible disadvantage in ignoring all items with a
frequency of occurrence below ten. It is conceivable that a
number of nodes might have existed in a particular text all
attachable to the same lemma and all having frequencies of
occurrence not exceeding nine but jointly achieving a frequency
of at least ten. If there were no other node with a frequency
of occurrence falling within the cut-off points which was
attachable to the same lemma, then clearly the fact that this
lemma existed would not have been recognised by the procedure.
Consequently, a candidate for admission to the set of items for
investigation would have been overlooked. It was felt,
however, that the chances of this happening were sufficiently
low and the effect of not taking into consideration any such

APPLYING THE METHODOLOGY   111

cases so negligible as not to justify complicating the
procedure to allow for this eventuality.

Two considerations suggested that it was not necessary, or
perhaps even appropriate, to demand equality of sample size
from each text in the corpus. First, it was felt that the
methodology for investigating lexical networks ought to prove
itself sufficiently robust to withstand some variation in
sample size. Secondly, the number of items from a sample
actually exhibiting collocational patterning was unpredictable
and would certainly vary from text to text. To that extent,
then, there would be an inherent variability of the feature
under investigation irrespective of the sample size. In any
case, quantitative comparisons across samples could always be
made by relativising to the sample sizes involved. Thus the
number of lemmata sampled from each text was allowed to
fluctuate around the CLUSTAN limit of two hundred entities.

It was suggested in chapter four that the amount of information
obtained from the analysis could also usefully by restricted by
setting a minimum value that a collocational frequency would
have to meet before being accepted as data. In the main study
this threshold was set at the lowest practicable value. It was
decided that only collocations achieving a frequency of two or
more in the text interval would be accepted into the study. In
this way a maximum of information about patterning in the text
was retained whilst rejecting the large amount of data on nonce
collocations, which for present purposes was irrelevant.

It will be recalled that the output from CLOC is unlemmatised.
It should therefore be noted that the requirement of a minimum
of two occurrences of a collocation implied that each
constituent form of any given lemmata would have to collocate
at least twice. Collocations consisting of two constituents of
a lemma each of which co-occurred once with the same collocate
lemma were thus not acceptable. This is perhaps a slight
inelegance in the method but has the advantage, in contrast, of
being quite a strong constraint on the acceptability in the
study of collocational patterning. Consequently, confidence in
the robustness of any lexical networks revealed by the
methodology would be increased.

Statistical data relating to the frequency distributions of the
texts in the corpus, the values of the sampling cut-off points
for each text and the size of the samples will be found in
appendix one. The sets of lemmata sampled by the procedure and
submitted to the analysis are listed for each text in appendix
two.

6.3 Computer Programs

It was found convenient to design two classes of computer
program to facilitate the study. The first class was concerned
with the process of data selection and the preparation of
control files for submission to CLOC. The second class
comprised the programs which were written to simplify the

interfacing of CLOC to CLUSTAN. All these programs were written in BASIC-PLUS-2 to run on a DEC-2060 computer.

Three programs were developed to aid the process of selecting nodes from frequency counts produced by CLOC and incorporating them into CLOC control files. The first of these was called LEMMACOUNT. It allows the user interactively to select or reject each node in a frequency listing or to defer a decision by requesting a concordance to the node. If the node is selected, the user is given the option of conflating it with other nodes. In other words, the program requests instructions for lemmatisation. The user is prompted to give a name to the lemma thus created which is expected to take the form of a CLOC pattern specification. The frequency of occurrence corresponding to the new lemma is calculated from the frequencies of the constituent nodes. Thus the output from LEMMACOUNT consists of a file of selected lemmata together with their frequencies of occurrence and a second file of nodes for which a concordance is to be requested at a later stage.

This program was designed to interface with two further programs which automatically create CLOC control files. The first of these was called CONCORDCOMMAND and, as its name suggests, creates a control file for a CLOC concordance job using those nodes on which a decision is deferred under LEMMACOUNT. The second program, called COLLOCATECONTROL, forms a similar CLOC control file with the selected lemmata in readiness for running a collocational analysis. In both cases information relating to the nature of the particular job to be run is elicited interactively from the user.

These programs were used primarily in the course of the pilot study reported in the next section. At that exploratory stage it was felt appropriate to undertake lemmatisation on a chapter by chapter basis and this was considerably facilitated by these three programs. In the main study a single global control file was created. If CLOC fails to find an occurrence of an item specified in the control file, it simply reports the fact. This means that a single control file applicable to all the chapters in a text can, if it is so desired, be formed whether or not every item included in the control file occurs in each chapter. Thus the control file represents a kind of lowest common multiple of the whole text. This saves an appreciable amount of time when preparing data for submission to the computer and to a large extent obviates the need for computer assistance at this stage. Consequently this was the approach adopted in the main study.

The second group of programs are concerned with facilitating the interface between CLOC and CLUSTAN. They take a reduced collocational analysis output by CLOC, that is a listing consisting only of nodes and collocates together with their individual and joint frequencies of occurrence but including none of the context in which the collocations are found, and convert it into a square matrix of normalised collocational frequencies in FORTRAN F5.3 format. FORTRAN format is required

by CLUSTAN. The particular format chosen means that each
frequency in the matrix is expressed as a five digit number in
which three digits follow the decimal point. It was felt that
this allowed the normalised frequencies of collocation to be
expressed with adequate but not meaningless precision.

The first program was called NEWMATRIX. It accepts a CLOC
collocational analysis as input and outputs the frequencies
only in matrix form. This involves summing the frequencies of
the lemmatised nodes. This is done by matching each node in
the collocational analysis against a canonical form held in a
separate file accessed by the program. This file might, for
example, contain the form ´HEATEDHEATING´ with which ´heat´,
´heated´ and ´heating´ can all be matched. As a result, the
frequencies of these three forms would be summed. On the other
hand, if the file contains as distinct entries ´SOLUTE´ and
´SOLUTION´, then each will be treated as an unlemmatised node.

A certain amount of care needs to be exercised with string
manipulations of this type. In the first example above, if the
collocational frequency file also contains the node ´eat´, then
it will be matched both to the correct canonical form (which
might be, for example, ´EATSEATINGATE´) and spuriously to
´HEATEDHEATING´. This means that the frequency for the lemma
eat will be correct but that for heat will be in excess of the
true frequency by the frequency of node ´eat´. The solution
adopted in this study was to edit the data so that nodes were
kept unambiguously distinct. In this case, for example, ´eat´
was consistently edited to the unique form ´xat´. It is
necessary to be constantly alert to the possibility of
unintentional conflations.

The matrix output by the NEWMATRIX program forms the input to a
second program called NORMALISE. This simply normalises the
frequencies in the matrix using the additive formula given in
chapter four. It then outputs the resulting matrix with each
frequency conforming to the BASIC print format "###.###". In
other words, the program normalises the data in the matrix and
manipulates it to conform to the FORTRAN F5.3 format.

One further program was developed for the main study. In the
first section of this chapter it was mentioned that a category
of equivalent random texts was required in the corpus for
purposes of comparison. The program called NEWRANDOMTXT was
developed to generate such texts. This it does by using a
random number generator to select words from the CLOC wordlist
of a given text with a probability corresponding to the
empirical probabilities represented by the frequencies of
occurrence of the types in the list. The output file thus
consists of a text composed of randomly ordered words each
occurring with a frequency approximating within the limits of
random fluctuation to the corresponding frequencies of
occurrence in the source text.

6.4 A Pilot Study

It should be clear from the discussion of Cluster Analysis in chapter four that the proof of this particular theoretical pudding lies in its empirical eating. Chatfield and Collins in their book on multivariate statistics make the same point somewhat more prosaically:

> "The ´success´ or ´failure´ of different methods on particular sets of empirical data may have more influence than theoretical criteria in the selection of a method for a particular type of data" (Chatfield and Collins 1980 p228).

Thus rather than use the type of algorithmic evaluation procedures for Cluster Analysis proposed by Gnandesikan, it was decided to evaluate the competing claims of Ward´s method and Density Search using a more straightforward technique of assessment (Gnandesikan et al 1977). If, as Fillenbaum and Rapoport suggest, the inherent assumptions of different techniques could prove problematic in the cases of particular types of data, then different techniques should lead to different solutions for the same data set (Fillenbaum and Rapoport 1971). If, on the other hand, different techniques lead to substantially similar results, whichever technique proves more convenient in practice can then be used with some confidence. Thus a standard method of evaluating Cluster Analysis techniques is to submit to the procedure data whose structure is known in advance. The technique is judged according to how well it manages to recover the structure.

It was this line of reasoning that led to the design of a pilot study in which both Ward´s method and the Density Search technique were used. A set of lemmata was chosen which on the basis of prior knowledge of the conceptual organisation of the field of science involved might reasonably be expected to associate in predictable ways. The procedures followed for the definition of the data set and those used in analysing the data must be clearly distinguished. In the pilot study the selection of data followed different principles from those used in the main study and described in chapter four. The choice was deliberately biased in order to optimise the chances of obtaining structured data and consequently of providing an easily interpretable test of the Cluster Analysis procedures. In the main study, as I have been at pains to indicate, care was taken precisely to avoid prejudicing the selection of data in this way so that any structure in the results could be interpreted as a genuine reflection of organisation in the text and not as arising from bias in the choice of objects for investigation. The procedures for analysing the data, however, which were what needed validating, were identical in both the pilot and main studies. Thus the pilot study constituted a valid test of the Cluster Analysis techniques.

CMEC, the classical mechanics text, was chosen as the text for investigation in the pilot study as it was felt that its subject matter was relatively accessible and that if would not therefore present undue difficulty in the identification of key concepts. Thus it offered the prospect of comparatively easy specification of a potentially structured data set. Approximately 130 lemmata which were judged representative of the conceptual content of the text were identified. It was hypothesised that these lemmata would associate in reasonably predictable ways. One analysis was undertaken using the whole text as interval. In addition individual data sets were defined for each of the thirteen chapters in the text and a further analysis using the chapter as interval was performed.

A few items found in very obvious collocations were included in these sets of lemmata. Examples are <u>quantum</u> and <u>mechanics</u> or <u>magnetic</u> and <u>field</u>. These were chosen in order to provide an immediate check on the analytical procedure. Any candidate technique would be required at least unfailingly to recover these collocations. Following the steps described in the preceding part of this book, frequencies of collocation of these lemmata with each other within a span of four orthographic words on either side of the node were obtained from CLOC. These frequencies were then manipulated by the programs discussed in the previous section into a normalised and formatted matrix and submitted to analysis by both Ward´s and the Density procedures in CLUSTAN. The set of lemmata used in the pilot study and a detailed listing of the findings can be found elsewhere (Phillips 1983).

The results were extremely encouraging and amply confirmed the usefulness of undertaking an analysis of the corpus using Ward´s method. The first, and perhaps most inportant finding was that the clusters identified by both techniques were intuitively reasonable. There was little problem in providing an interpretation for the groupings of lemmata in terms of the concepts of classical mechanics. The very obvious collocations, for example, such as <u>quantum mechanics</u> mentioned above, were recovered by Ward´s method at pleasingly low values of the Error Sum of Squares. Clusters were revealed which centred on the lemmata <u>energy</u>, <u>momentum</u>, <u>oscillation</u>, <u>charge</u> and <u>force</u>. These clusters appear to reflect in a relatively straightforward way the conceptual concerns of the text. Whilst a failure to find such congruence between the results and intuitions about the subject matter would not necessarily have constituted an argument for the invalidity of the solution, the fact that they did correspond provides strong support both for the theory of collocational meaning and the efficiency with which Cluster Analysis can recover that meaning. There thus appeared the first intimation of aboutness realised in text macrostructure.

Whilst the clusters identified by the two analytical techniques were not identical, the clustering trend was broadly similar in both cases. In particular, there was good agreememt about which lemmata constituted the more central items in each lexical network. Differences pertained principally to the more peripheral items, that is, lemmata clustered at relatively high

E.S.S. or low values of the density statistic. In other words, disagreement was confined largely to the less typical members of a cluster. Density showed a tendency to form larger clusters than Ward´s method but it was noted that these were almost invariably unions of two or more clusters which Ward´s method kept distinct. Thus on the whole there were very few cases of incompatible cross-classifications in the two methods. The difference, then, was mainly one of the level of delicacy at which clusters were formed, with Ward´s method being a somewhat more delicate technique. It seemed reasonable to conclude from this that the correspondence arrived at by the two methods was such that it could only have arisen as a function of latent organisation existing in the data and not as a result of any Procrustean properties of the techniques used.

Some unexpected insights into collocational behaviour emerged from these results. One case can be cited by way of example. Both <u>electric</u> and <u>charge</u> were included in the set of lemmata investigated but the results showed that they were rarely found in each other´s company. <u>Charge</u> was grouped with <u>distribution</u>, <u>density</u>, <u>point</u> and <u>uniform</u>.
<u>Electric</u>, on the other hand, tended to collocate with <u>dipole</u>. It is possible to offer a plausible explanation for this unexpected result. In a text on classical mechanics <u>charge</u> can only ever refer to the concept of an electric charge. Thus the qualifier is redundant and consequently is rarely used to specify the nature of the charge. On the other hand, the distribution of charge densities on spherical bodies is a topic of some importance in classical mechanics. Similarly, classical mechanics is frequently concerned with systems of bodies and one of the important two-body systems is the electric dipole. Thus the Cluster Analysis solution obliged rejection of the obvious psychological associations based on everyday experience in favour of ones constructed as a function of the subject matter. This was not merely reassuring evidence of the objectivity of the Cluster Analysis approach. It also suggested that useful qualitative results could be expected.

Since the lemmata chosen for investigation were selected on semantic criteria and not by the objective sampling technique used in the main study, a number of lemmata were included which had frequencies of occurrence in the text below the lower cut-off limit of ten occurrences which was adhered to in the main study. The matrix of frequencies of collocation obtained in the pilot study indicated clearly that such lemmata collocated only relatively rarely with the other members of the data set. The density of entries in the collocational matrix for lemmata occurring less than ten times was minimal. In other words, almost no information would have been lost to the analyis by excluding these lemmata from consideration. This was taken as significant empirical confirmation of the reasonableness of the decision to adopt a lower cut-off limit when sampling the frequency distribution of a text in the corpus.

The proportion of nodes collocating in each chapter was remarkably stable. On average about half the lemmata selected from a given chapter entered into collocations. This was despite the fact that the choice of lemmata was made relative to each chapter and that the constitution of the data set thus varied from chapter to chapter. It could be speculated that this finding reflects some kind of average degree of organisation required by a coherent text. It had, however, a more practical consequence in that it furnished evidence in support of the decision taken in the main study regarding the optimum size of sample. It meant that a choice of some two hundred nodes from the whole text could be reasonably made in the expectation that in any one chapter around one hundred nodes at most would show collocational patterning. As a consequence, the data set to be submitted to CLUSTAN would be of manageable size. At the same time, appreciable numbers of lemmata in each chapter formed a ´ragbag´ cluster. This was taken as further evidence that the techniques were not producing spurious solutions arising from the artificial imposition of structure.

Finally, the pilot study provided a timely reminder that the use of computational procedures is no guarantee against error. Through faulty coding in the text file, over which it was not possible to exercise control, hyphens were occasionaly omitted. This meant that it was not always possible to distinguish among the occurrences of ´centre´, ´centre-of-mass´ and ´mass´. Consequently, although it would have been preferable to treat these as distinct lemmata, it was possible consistently to differentiate only the two extreme terms. It was interesting to note, however, that the clustering results themselves suggested that ´centre´ was being used in two different patterns, collocating with ´force´ in such phrases as ´central conservative force´ and with ´mass´, where it represented in all probability an occurrence of the polymorphemic item. This is suggestive evidence in favour of the possibility of the automatic discrimination of homographs proposed by van Buren as well as for the validity of the point made in chapter three when the text reduction procedure was discussed (van Buren 1967, 1968). There it was suggested that the clustering technique itself might be expected to clear up any residual areas of fuzziness in the data. This finding tended to confirm the reasonableness of the supposition.

Whilst the trend of the two techniques was to cluster in similar ways, it has already been noted that Ward´s method on the whole discriminated more clusters. It thus tended to confirm the view held by Fillenbaum and Rapoport that hierarchical techniques are often preferable because they can reveal the genesis of structure in the data with clarity (Fillenbaum and Rapoport 1971). Ward´s method, moreover, generally clustered a greater proportion of the nodes than the Density Search technique and thus provided more information about the lexical networks discernable in each chapter. It is possible that with greater experimentation in the setting of values for the various parameters of the density method, a greater number of clusters would have been discovered with this technique also. Since, however, the choice in the end rests on issues of interpretability and convenience, the pilot study demonstrated clearly both that Ward's method of Cluster Analysis is effective and preferable to Density Search on both counts.

6.5 Conclusion

In this chapter the implementation of the methodology in an empirical study was described. First the factors determining the composition of a suitable corpus were considered and the texts composing the corpus were detailed. The corpus consisted of five representative science texts, two novels, one text of popular science and two equivalent random texts. The latter were generated by means of a specially written computer program which preserved a typical frequency distribution for science text but ensured a random ordering of the words in the resulting texts.

A number of decisions have to be taken when applying the methodology to a particular corpus. These include determining the band of frequencies from which the sample of lemmata for investigation will be drawn and specifying the criterial level which instances of collocation must achieve in order to be accepted into the study. The decisions taken for the study reported here were discussed in section two of this chapter. Following this, the computer programs which were specially written for the investigation were described. It was seen that these were designed to facilitate the preparation of the data for submission to CLOC and to manipulate automatically the output from CLOC into a form acceptable to CLUSTAN.

Finally, the findings of a pilot study of structured data were discussed. This pilot study was undertaken with two objectives in mind. First, it was intended to explore in a preliminary fashion the potential shown by Cluster Analysis for revealing the existence of lexical networks in large stretches of continuous text. Secondly, it was used to evaluate two techniques, Ward's method and Density Search, in comparison with each other. The findings of this pilot study demonstrated convincingly that Cluster Analysis was able to provide persuasive evidence for the existence of lexical networks which corresponded well to intuitive assumptions about the way the subject matter of the text investigated was constructed. Consequently, it was concluded that Cluster Analysis was likely to be a valuable tool for the kind of investigation envisaged here. It also emerged that Ward's method in particular afforded the prospect of achieving results of sufficient delicacy for it to be possible to interpret the findings in a reasonably straightforward manner.

Thus the methodology which had been developed earlier in the light of the theoretical view of text presented in part one was found in practice to offer the possibility of a meaningful and appropriate analysis of text. The results of applying this methodology to all the texts in the corpus forms the topic of the remaining chapters in this part.

CHAPTER 7

TERM MEANING

7.1 The Interpretation of Lexical Networks

The analysis of the science texts in the corpus according to the methodology developed in the preceding chapters produced unequivocal evidence of the existence of lexical networks at the level of the chapter. In the light of Needham's comment that

> "if we were to select the material at random, it would probably turn out that the data was (sic) so sparse that nothing useful could be found" (Needham 1967 p47)

this is an extremely interesting result. The selection of objects for investigation was, of course, guided by the theoretical considerations discussed in the first part of this book, but the final choice of lemmata was made by random sampling. It will be recalled that the results of the analysis are obtained in the first instance in the form of the dendrograms output by CLUSTAN. It is not practicable for reasons of space to reproduce here all the dendrograms obtained for each text but by way of illustration the set of dendrograms for the analysis of ELEN is presented in appendix three. From inspection of these examples it can be clearly seen that there is evidence of structure in the form taken by the dendrograms. They reflect the progressively more extended groupings into which lemmata enter in the chapter as the clusters become less homogeneous.

In chapter four I described an appropriate procedure for fixing a cut-off point to determine the number of clusters identified within a dendrogram, and hence their configuration within a chapter. On the sample dendrograms in appendix three the cut-off level is indicated as a horizontal dotted line superimposed upon the graph. Application of the cut-off to the Cluster Analysis results revealed in each chapter of the science corpus a number of independent patterns of association among lemmata. These are syntagmatic lexical networks. This is crucial: the analysis has revealed the existence of only indirectly observable categories in text. **The first major result of this study was the discovery of the existence of these networks.**

The number of lexical networks identified in each chapter is sufficiently large to be considered as satisfactory evidence of the effectiveness of the procedures adopted. Had the decisions relating to the text reduction process, for example, been inappropriate, the result would have been that few discrete groupings would have been identified. The chapter would have appeared as a relatively homogeneous network of undifferentiated relations. In this context, the presence in virtually all chapters of ELEN of a ´ragbag´ cluster should be noted since it constitutes further confirmation of the genuineness of the other clusterings. The same is true of the other science texts in the corpus.

With each terminal node in the dendrograms its corresponding lemma can be associated. In other words, a semantic label can be given to these nodes. It then becomes a relatively straightforward matter to perceive how the syntagmatic organisation of lemmata into lexical networks relates to the conceptual concerns of the texts. **Thus the second major result of this study is that the lexical networks identified by the analysis are meaningful.**

By the claim that the lexical networks are meaningful, I mean, then, that they are constructive of subject matter. Now I know of no entirely objective way of establishing the meaningfulness of the networks that have been identified. To do so would require a means of determining the subject matter of a text independently of the lexical networks. It is precisely my point that it is the recognition of such patterns of lexical association which gives rise to the notion of aboutness. Thus there is a danger of circularity. It need not, however, be vicious and I believe the following considerations are persuasive. If in each text interval it can be shown that

> (1) nodes which are intuitively representative of the subject matter of the interval are associated by the analysis;
>
> (2) the nodes are clustered into interpretable groups; and
>
> (3) the major groupings correspond to clues provided by the author to the content of the interval

then I submit that it can safely be inferred that the lexical networks represent forms of linguistic organisation which are determinant of subject matter.

The clues a scientific writer typically provides to the content of a given text interval are those furnished by tables of contents, chapter and section headings, introductions and explicit chapter summaries. The kind of correspondence that it is reasonable to expect may be established between such clues and the lexical networks is one of semantic compatibility. That is to say, an intuitively satisfactory interpretation placed upon the configurations of nodes cannot be incompatible with the propositional content of introductions and summaries or with the implied propositions contained in headings and titles. Incompatibility would arise if, for example, there were no identity of lemmata between the two categories of ´network´ and ´clue´ or if lemmata were associated in ways clearly different from what is implied in the clues.

It could be objected that since the investigation of the syntagmatic behaviour of lemmata was selective, some lemmata would inevitably have been omitted from the analysis which would have been required to confirm the correspondence between a given lexical network and the topic of the text interval in which it was latent. This argument is trivially true and consequently not particularly interesting. I consider that it can be more cogently argued that if such a correspondence can be established even with the omission of such lemmata, this may be taken as convincing support for the position adopted here. It will have to be admitted that the argument for the meaningfulness of lexical networks is persuasive if it can be shown that subject matter can be established even on the basis of an incomplete data set. Indeed, it will be seen that in many cases the lexical networks so strongly suggest the actualisation of conceptual structure that the point can readily be predicted at which lemmata missing from the analysis would have been integrated. Thus I do not view the constraints imposed by the methodology as making the analysis more problematic. On the contrary, they reinforce the argument.

It may also be expected that a number of lemmata will enter into lexical networks which appear to be more concerned with the general structure of well-formed text than with the construction of subject matter. I do not think this need give cause for concern. The possibility of more general items being clustered with technical lexis in this way must be accepted as an almost inevitable consequence of the fact that lexical networks do not exist in isolation. They are embedded in the context of ´non-systemic´ lexis and structural items required for the articulation of sentences. It will not be surprising, then, if such items occasionally achieve sufficient regularity of patterning within a text interval to figure in the findings of the analysis. What would give significant pause would be the case where the same non-systemic items consistently appeared in identical environments in a number of text intervals or if they were to figure as central members of the lexical networks in which they occur. Provided, however, that the majority of lexical networks are constituted mainly of lemmata which associate to construct subject matter and that when other items do appear they tend to do so as peripheral rather than central members, then the validity of the interpretation of lexical networks as constructive of subject matter will not be impeached. It will be seen later that both these conditions are normally met. Consequently, I conclude that the structural role of non-systemic items is minimal.

The networks identified in the science corpus will be found in appendix four. These may be compared with the sets of sampled lemmata given in appendix two. The comparison indicates the extent and kind of structuring found in the data. I shall now substantiate the claim that these lexical networks actualise subject matter by considering some of the results from each of the science texts in turn. It will become apparent that the three conditions which I earlier placed on the interpretability of lexical networks do in fact hold. The findings of the study are too extensive, however, to be presented in full and it is consequently not possible to discuss all the results for each text in detail. I shall consider here two representative samples from each text. The reader is invited to judge for himself the further generalisability of my argument by exploring the full set of results which I have presented elsewhere (Phillips 1983).

7.2 Lexical Networks in the Science Corpus

(i) Networks in ELEN

The principal clues to topic in this text are provided by chapter titles and section headings. The first example is taken from chapter two, which is entitled "The p-n Junction and the Field-effect Transistor". It is divided into the following sections:

      2.1 Introduction
      2.2 The p-n junction
      2.3 Forward and reverse biased p-n junctions
      2.4 Depletion layer width and junction capacitance
      2.5 The field-effect transisitor (unipolar transistor)
      2.6 Principle of operation
      2.7 Characteristics of the field-effect transistor
      2.8 Field-effect transistor amplifier
      2.9 Amplification of signals
      2.10 Small signal parameters of the f.e.t.
      2.11 The common source amplifier (A.C. analysis)
      2.12 Simple bias circuit for the f.e.t.
      2.13 Input and output impedance
      2.14 Coupling of f.e.t. amplifiers and amplification of
           low frequency signals
      2.15 Amplification of high frequency signals
      2.16 The source follower
      2.17 The metal oxide semiconductor transistor (MOST)

It is possible to discern a number of focal areas in this segmentation. First, sections 2.2-2.4 are concerned with the structure of transistors formed by the introduction of microscopic amounts of impurity into a wafer of silicon, a process known as ´doping´. Secondly, sections 2.5-2.7 relate to the structure and functioning of a particular type of transistor, the field-effect transistor (f.e.t.). Thirdly, the use of the f.e.t. in amplifier design is discussed in sections 2.8-2.13. Fourthly, a variety of further topics is considered in sections 2.14-2.17 of which the most salient is the amplification of signals of different frequencies.

Inspection of the results for this chapter reveals that the

lexical networks below are amongst those identified. They are
presented in the graphical representation developed in chapter
five.

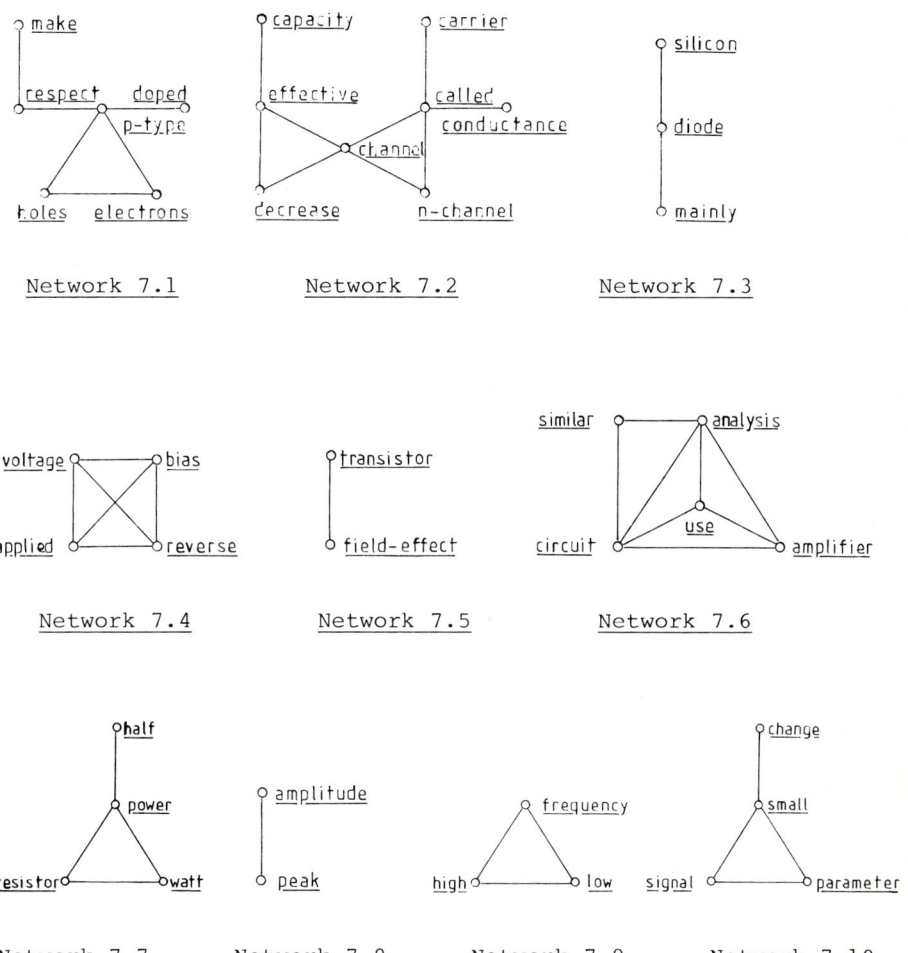

I submit that an obvious interpretation of these networks
suggests itself. Networks 7.1-7.5 account for the topic of the
first two groups of sections, transistor design and the
operations of the f.e.t. Networks 7.6 and 7.7 are clearly
concerned with the issues of amplifier design treated in the
third group of sections. Networks 7.8-7.10 all relate to the
discussion of the amplification of signals conducted in the
final group of sections. There is thus a convincing
correspondence between the patterning of the lemmata revealed

by the analysis and the subject matter of this chapter. This
is all the more striking given that none of <u>junction</u>, <u>source</u>,
<u>coupling</u>, <u>impedance</u> or <u>output</u> was included in the analysis, all
of which would have contributed appreciably to a clarification
of the correspondence in this chapter.

A second example can be taken from chapter four entitled
"Operational Amplifiers and Linear Integrated Circuits". Again
I list the section headings:

4.1	Introduction	
4.2	A review of the properties of real and ideal amplifiers	
4.3	The terminology of integrated circuit differential amplifiers	
4.4	The inverting operational amplifier	
4.4.1	Gain	
4.4.2	Input and output impedance of the inverting amplifier	
4.5	The non-inverting operational amplifier	
4.5.1	Gain and output impedance	
4.5.2	Input impedance	
4.6	The differential operational amplifier	
4.7	Some applications of operational amplifiers	
4.7.1	The voltage follower	
4.7.2	The adder amplifier	
4.7.3	Integrating and differentiating amplifiers	
4.8	Frequency response of operational amplifiers	
4.9	Offsets in operational amplifiers	
4.9.1	Input offset voltage	
4.9.2	Input bias current and input offset current	
4.10	Common mode rejection ratio	
4.11	Slewing rate and full power response	
4.12	Linear integrated circuits	
4.13	The advantage of integrated circuits	
4.14	Design and construction of integrated circuits	
4.14.1	Resistors	
4.14.2	Capacitors and inductors	
4.14.3	Transistors	
4.14.4	Diodes	
4.15	Isolation of devices in integrated circuits	
4.16	A comparison of circuit design concepts in integrated and discrete circuits	

It is clear from the title that the subject matter of this
chapter comprises two principal topics: operational amplifiers
and a particular kind of circuit design, the integrated
circuit. Inspection of the section headings suggests that the
types of amplifier involved can be classified as inverting,
non-inverting and differential. It also appears that the
design of integrated circuits involves the consideration of
various circuit components including resistors, capacitors and
inductors.

I consequently take it to be of great significance that the

TERM MEANING   127

analysis of this chapter reveals that there are two major
lexical networks. One is centred on the lemma amplifier and
the other on the lemma circuit. There are, of course, a number
of other networks but those represented below seem amply to
confirm the notion that the lexical network is constructive of
topic.

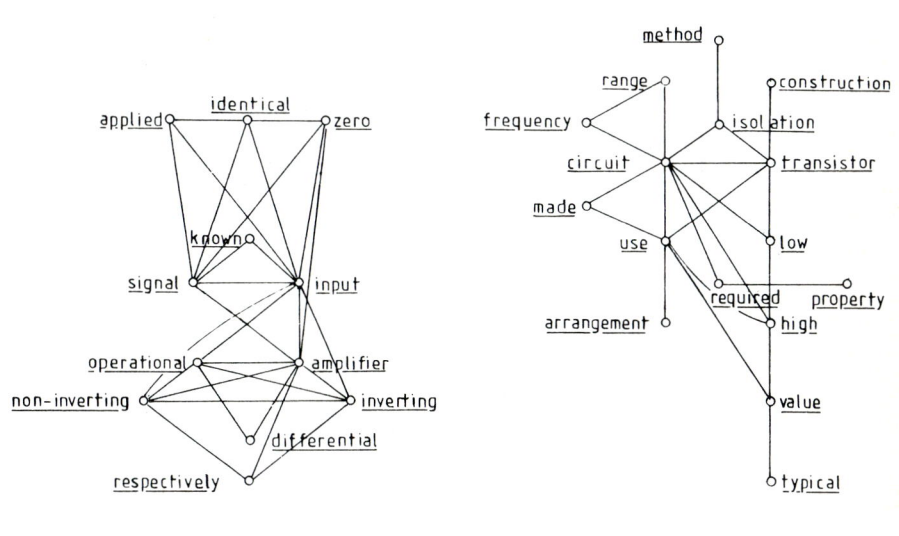

Network 7.11   Network 7.12

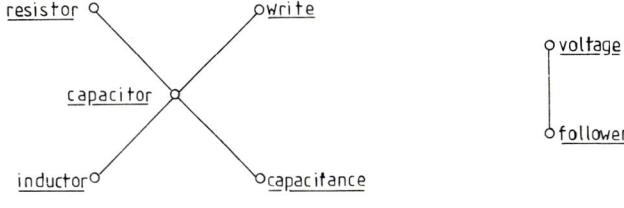

Network 7.13   Network 7.14

In the light of these results, there seems to me to be no doubt
that in this text the empirical structures that have been

revealed are meaningful and that they provide major clues to the notion of aboutness. In order to demonstrate that these findings are not a mere idiosyncracy of this particular text, however, I shall now turn to the next textbook in the corpus.

(ii) Networks in CMEC

The existence of meaningful lexical networks in CMEC can be illustrated by reference to the first chapter. It will be recalled that the text deals with the subject of classical mechanics. The following statements are taken from the summary that the author provides for this chapter:

> "We have chosen to regard position and time (relative to some frame of reference) as basic....The first law contains the definition of an inertial frame with the physical assertion that such frames exist while the second and third laws contain the definitions of mass and force....These laws, supplemented by the laws of force, such as the law of universal gravitation, provide the equations from which we determine the motion of any dynamical system." (Kibble 1973 pp11-12)

This quotation gives an indication of the nature of the discussion conducted in this chapter. If the two largest lexical networks in this chapter are examined, the following configurations are found:

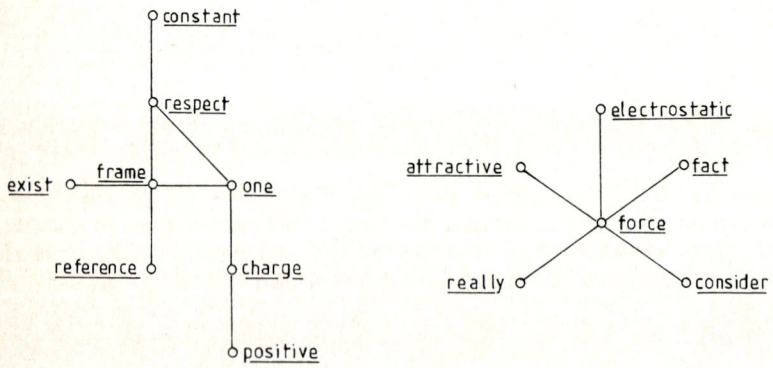

Network 7.15   Network 7.16

Following Kibble's summary, I suggest that network 7.15 relates to Newton's first law whilst network 7.16 is concerned with the second and third laws. The terms position, time, inertia and mass were not included in the sample studied but it can fairly straightforwardly be predicted that the first three would have

TERM MEANING   129

been clustered in network 7.15 and the latter in network 7.16.

As a further illustration, chapter five, "Rotating Frames", may
be considered. Here the findings are somewhat more complex. I
give first Kibble's section headings, followed by extracts from
the summary to the chapter:

        5.1 Angular Velocity; Rate of Change of a Vector
        5.2 Particle in a Uniform Magnetic Field
        5.3 Acceleration; Apparent Gravity
        5.4 Coriolis Force
        5.5 Larmor Effect
        5.6 Angular Momentum and the Larmor Effect

"In problems involving a rotating body – particularly the
earth – it is often convenient to use a rotating frame
of reference....
These are the centrifugal force, directed outwards from
the axis of rotation, and the velocity-dependent
Coriolis force....
Rotating frames are also useful in any problems involving
a magnetic field." (ibid pp87-88)

The principal lexical networks revealed in this chapter are
graphed below:

      Network 7.17   Network 7.18   Network 7.19

```
o  magnetic                          o  earth
|                                    |
|                                    |
o  uniform                           o  surface
```

       Network 7.20   Network 7.21

Inspection of these results suggests that there can be little doubt that the analytical procedure is recovering the principal conceptual domains of the chapter. There is a fairly obvious and direct relation between network 7.17 and Kibble's sections 5.3 and 5.4. Network 7.18 articulates the theme implied in the quotations from the summary. Network 7.19 corresponds to section 5.6, which contains a discussion of the precession of axes of rotation whilst network 7.20 relates to section 5.2. Finally, network 7.21 corresponds to the concerns of the chapter as a whole as indicated by the quotations.

Again, lemmata omitted from the analysis do not appear to have affected the validity of the results. It appears that easily interpretable results have been obtained despite the omission of such items as <u>centrifugal</u>, <u>axis</u>, <u>field</u> and <u>Larmor</u>. This only serves to strengthen the conviction that lexical networks construct subject matter. The inclusion of these items would simply have added further clarification to the correspondence between the groupings of lemmata and Kibble's clues to subject. Moreover, the integration of the omitted lemmata can be easily predicted. <u>Centrifugal</u> is likely to belong to network 7.17, <u>axis</u> and <u>Larmor</u> to network 7.19 and <u>field</u> clearly to 7.20.

It seems, then, that the lexical networks identified by the analysis are equally constitutive of their respective topics in domains as diverse as electronics and classical mechanics. I shall now survey some representative findings from the remaining science texts to demonstrate that this is the case for all the areas of science covered by the texts in the corpus.

(iii) Networks in CREL

The examples for this text are drawn from the first and last chapters in the sample. The first chapter constitutes an introduction to the topic of chemical reaction engineering. This is indicated explicitly in the title of the chapter, which is simply "Introduction", and by the kind of statement made in the opening section. In CREL the first section of the chapter, although not marked as such, always serves as a survey of the

TERM MEANING   131

material to be covered. Levenspiel says in this section:

> "Every industrial chemical process is designed to produce
> economically a desired product from a variety of
> starting materials through a succession of treatment
> steps....Chemical reaction engineering is the synthesis
> of all these factors with the aim of properly designing
> a chemical reactor." (Levenspiel 1972 pp1-2)

The section headings are:

    (1)   Thermodynamics
    (2)   Chemical Kinetics
    (3)   Classification of Reactions
    (4)   Variables Affecting the Rate of Reaction
    (5)   Definition of Reaction Rate

Amongst the lexical networks identified in this chapter, the
following simple networks are of particular interest:

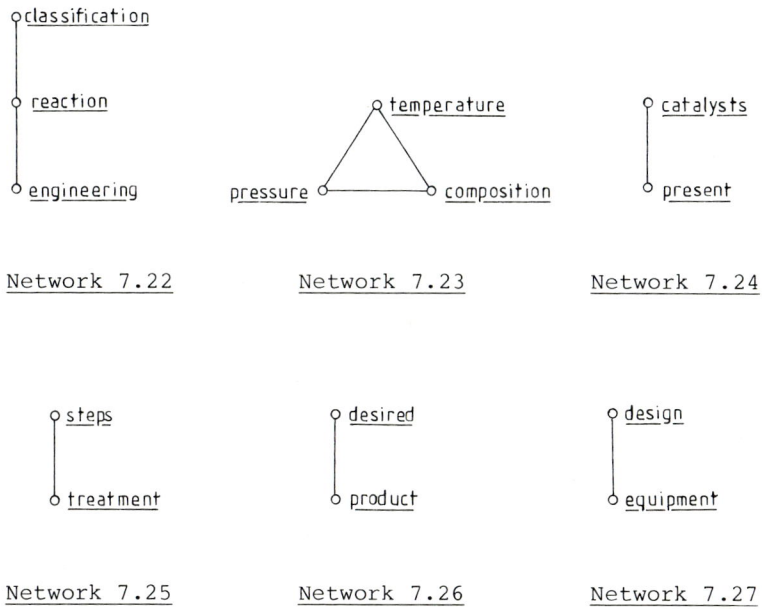

Network 7.22   Network 7.23   Network 7.24

Network 7.25   Network 7.26   Network 7.27

Network 7.22 fairly obviously relates to the topic of the third
section which is both literally and figuratively central to the
whole chapter. Network 7.23 picks out the variables
influencing rate of reaction, which is the subject of the
fourth section. In this context, it is no chance that the
analytical procedure should have recognised the importance of

the co-occurrence of <u>present</u> and <u>catalyst</u> which constitute
network 7.24. The presence of a catalyst in a chemical
reaction speeds up the rate of the reaction. Networks 7.25 and
7.26 relate to the topic adumbrated in the first part of the
quotation from Levenspiel's introduction, whilst network 7.27
relates to the second part. Thus even in a relatively
unspecific introductory chapter and where the lexical networks
identified contain few members, the correspondence between
networks and subject matter is good.

Chapter eight, entitled "Temperature and Pressure Effects", is
considerably more complex. Here are the section headings:

    (1)   Single Reactions
    (2)   Heats of Reaction from Thermodynamics
    (3)   Equilibrium Constants from Thermodynamics
    (4)   General Graphical Design Procedure
    (5)   Optimum Temperature Progression
    (6)   Heat Effects
    (7)   Adiabatic Operations
    (8)   Nonadiabatic Operations
    (9)   Comments and Extensions
    (10)   Exothermic Reactions in Mixed Reactors - a
              Special Problem
    (11) Multiple Reactions
    (12)   Product Distribution and Temperature
    (13)   Temperature and Vessel Size (or τ) for Maximum
              Production
    (14)   Comments

It should be noted that the first part of the chapter, "Single
Reactions", is concerned largely with temperature effects and
heats of reaction. The second part, "Multiple Reactions",
deals more with techniques for obtaining optimum production of
products. These concerns can be seen to be actualised by the
following lexical networks identified in this chapter:

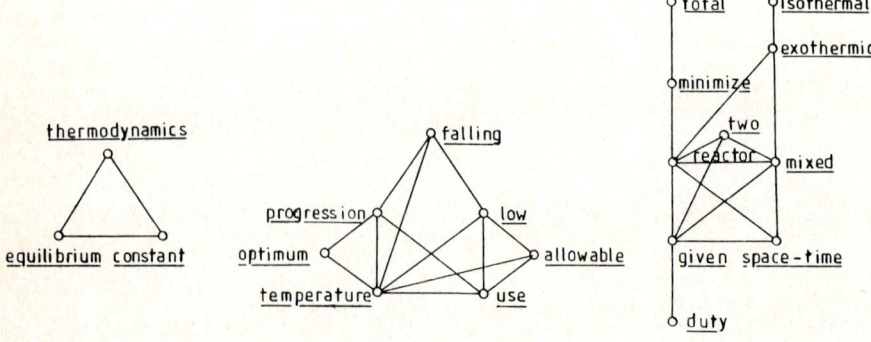

      Network 7.28   Network 7.29   Network 7.30

TERM MEANING   133

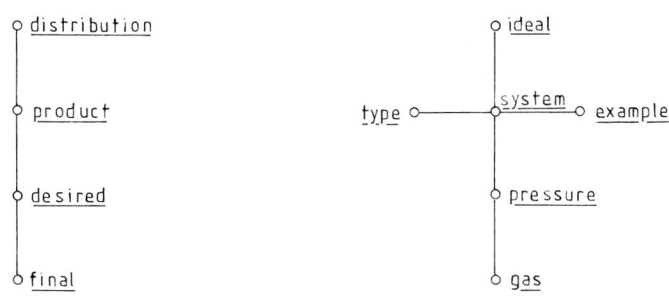

          Network 7.31   Network 7.32

Here networks 7.28-7.30 correspond to the principal topics of the first part of the chapter and networks 7.31 and 7.32 to those of the second part. In addition, network 7.32 indicates that pressure, the other variable mentioned in the title, also figures prominently in the structuring of this chapter.

The analysis of CREL thus tends to confirm the earlier findings from ELEN and CMEC.

(iv) Networks in BIPC

In contrast to the examples from CREL, which were drawn from the extremes of the sample, I shall consider now two consecutive chapters from BIPC, chapters four and five. Gareth Morris provides no consistent summaries to his chapters and his sectionalisation is complex and extensive. The simplest approach to illustrating the kind of clues he provides to his topics is to list only the major section headings. These are indicated in the text by capitalisation.

The title of the fourth chapter is "Some Properties of Aqueous Solutions" and the principal section headings are:

      (1)   Vapour Pressure
      (2)   Solutions of Non-electrolytes
      (3)   Osmosis
      (4)   Solutions of Electrolytes
      (5)   Solubility of Salts

Relevant lexical networks identified in this chapter are as follows:

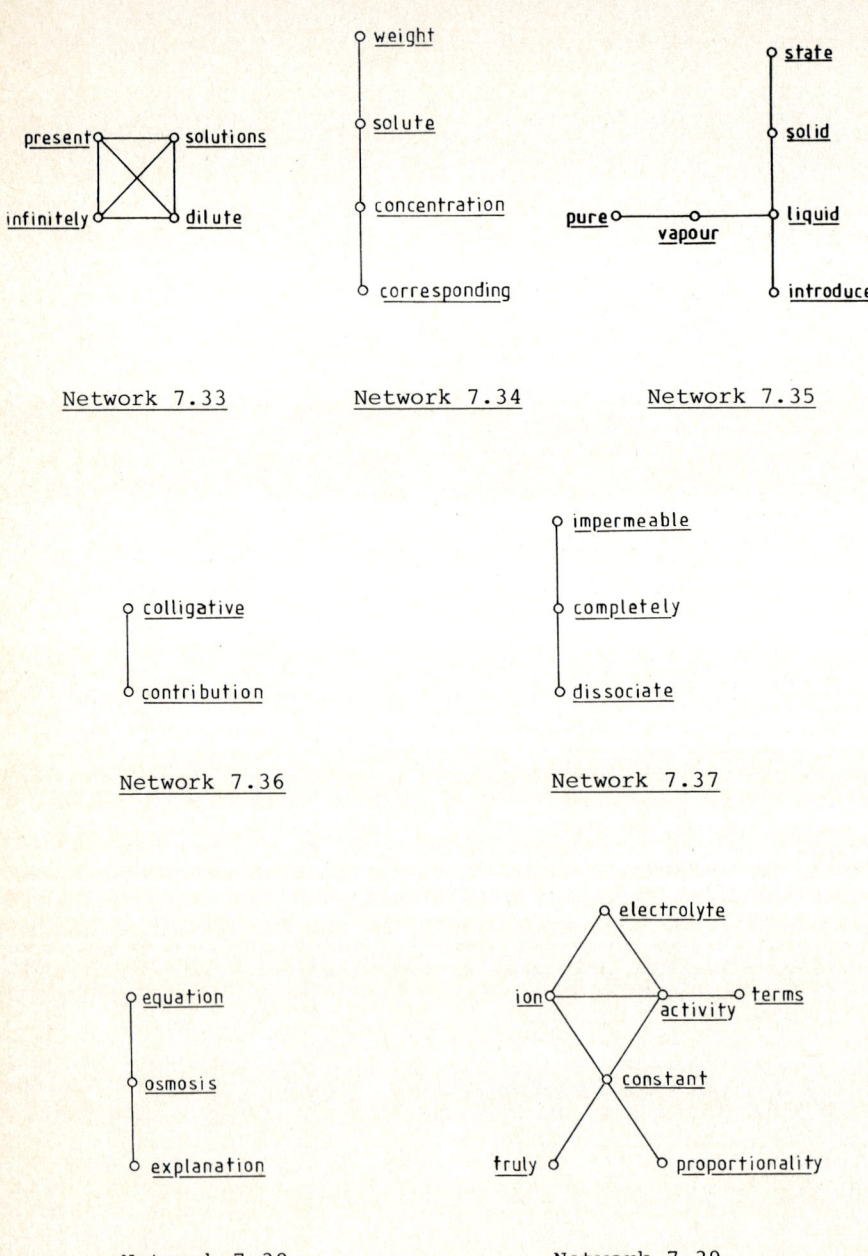

Networks 7.33 and 7.34 obviously relate to the topic of the
chapter as a whole whilst network 7.35 appears to be more
closely related to section one. Of particular relevance to
section two is network 7.36. A sub-section of this section is
entitled "Calculation of the molecular weight of a solution
from the magnitude of the colligative properties of the dilute
solutions". Networks 7.37 and 7.38 are both concerned with the
topic of osmosis, network 7.37 relating to the properties of
membranes. Network 7.39 actualises the main concerns of the
fourth section. Some of the sub-sections of this section are:
"Ionization of electrolytes in aqueous solution"; "How the
ionic strength of a solution of an electrolyte affects the
value of the mean activity coefficent"; "Calculation of the
degree of ionization of a weak electrolyte". Further, five
other sub-sections make explicit reference to colligative
properties of solutions.

Chapter five has the title "Acids, Bases and Buffers in Aqueous
Solution". The major section headings are:

    (1)   Acids and Bases
    (2)   The Interaction of an Acid with a Base
    (3)   Buffer Mixtures and their Buffer Capacity
    (4)   The Dissociation of Polyprotic Weak Acids
    (5)   pH Indicators
    (6)   The pH´s of Dilute, Aqueous Solutions of Salts

Pertinent sets identified are:

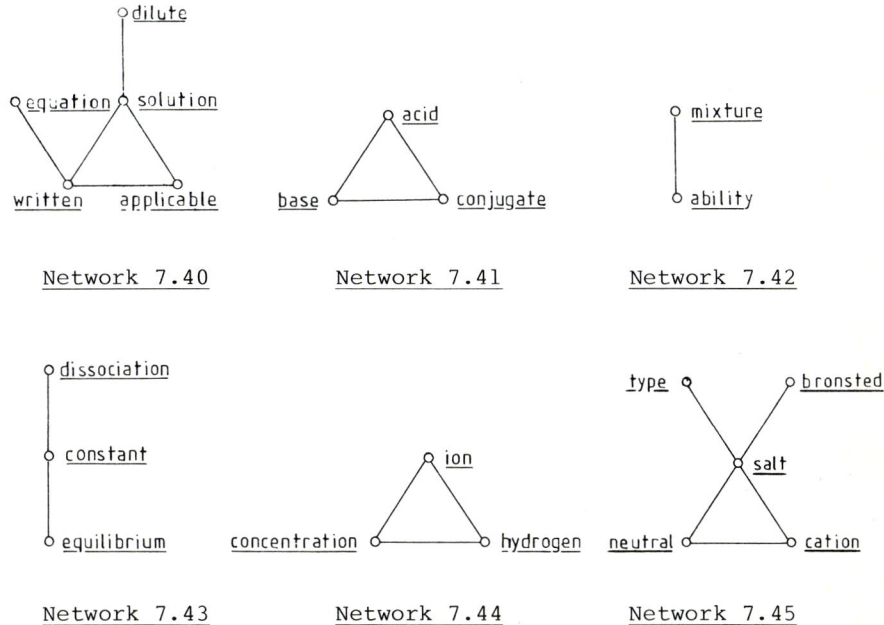

Again, I observe that network 7.40 seems to apply to the topic of the chapter as a whole. Network 7.41 clearly relates to sections one and two. Network 7.42 appears to be concerned with the topic of section three. <u>Buffer</u> is not in the set of lemmata investigated but it may be predicted that it would have been clustered in this network. Networks 7.43-7.45 would seem to relate to sections four, five and six respectively. It should be noted that pH is an expression which refers to the concentration of hydrogen ions in a solution.

Thus BIPC furnishes evidence that is substantially similar to that observed in the other texts.

(v) Networks in THRM

The final two examples are taken from contrasting chapters in THRM. The first is a general survey chapter and the second is a chapter dealing with a specific topic. Sonntag and Van Wylen tend to provide only relatively high-level section headings. That is to say, the title of each section gives only a broad indication of the contents. Moreover, although each chapter begins with an introduction, this too is usually brief and fairly general. Nevertheless, despite the increased difficulty of interpretation that this implies in order to establish the correspondence between lexical networks and topic, it will be seen that there is no incompatibility between the empirical structures and the clues provided by the authors.

The first set of results comes from chapter two which is entitled "Some Concepts and Definitions". The introduction to the chapter includes the following definition:

> "Thermodynamics is the science that deals with heat and work and those properties of substances that bear a relation to heat and work." (Sonntag and Van Wylen 1971 p17)

Section headings are as follows:

    (1) The Thermodynamic System and the Control Volume
    (2) Macroscopic vs Microscopic Point of View
    (3) Properties and State of a Substance
    (4) Processes and Cycles
    (5) Units for Mass, Length, Time and Force
    (6) Energy
    (7) Specific Volume
    (8) Pressure
    (9) Equality of Temperature
  (10) Zeroth Law of Thermodynamics
  (11) Temperature Scales
  (12) The International Practical Temperature Scale

The most relevant lexical networks that were identified are:

TERM MEANING

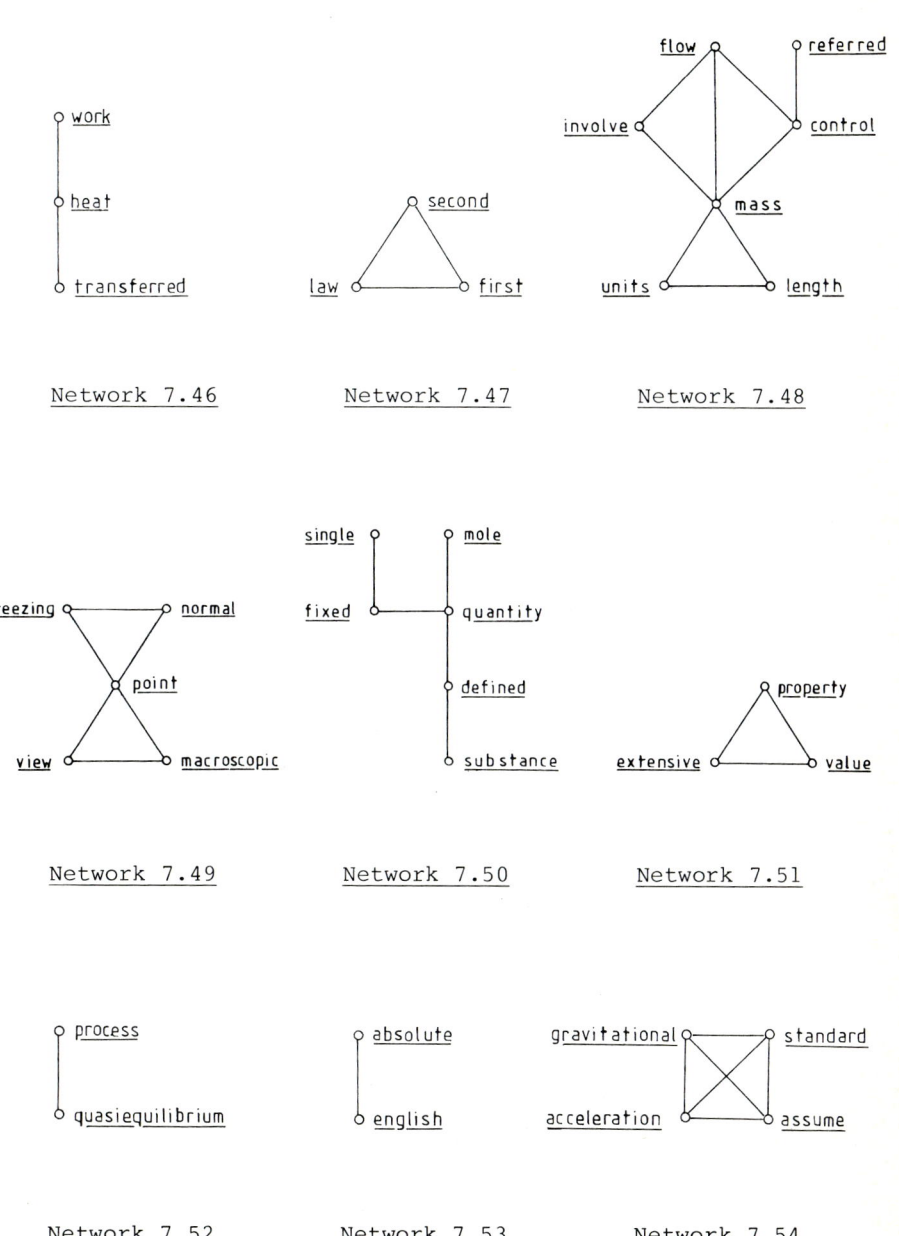

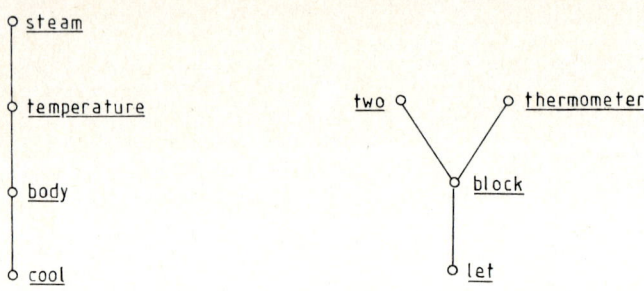

Network 7.55   Network 7.56

It appears that networks 7.46 and 7.47 relate to the topic of the chapter, and indeed of the textbook, as a whole. The remaining lexical networks then suggest the following correspondences. Network 7.48 relates to both sections one and five; network 7.49 clearly relates to section two; network 7.50 both relates to section three and is concerned with the topic of systems of measurement which is introduced in section five; network 7.51 is also concerned with section three; network 7.52 relates to section four. Network 7.53 refers to systems of units and network 7.54 is concerned with the description of how force is measured. Thus both these networks relate to section five. Network 7.55 is concerned with the topics of sections nine and ten. It should be noted that the zeroth law of thermodynamics concerns the conditions under which equality of temperature is recognised. Network 7.56 refers to the way in which temperature scales are established by measuring the electrical conductivity of blocks of copper and thus contributes to the actualisation of the topic of sections eleven and twelve. It is worth noting that none of energy, pressure or volume was included in the lemmata investigated. Hence there is little support in the data for sections six, seven and eight.

The more specific chapter selected as an example is chapter seven entitled "The Second Law of Thermodynamics". The section headings are:

(1) Heat Engines and Refrigerators
(2) Second Law of Thermodynamics
(3) The Reversible Process
(4) Factors that Render Processes Irreversible
(5) Heat Transfer through a Finite Temperature Difference
(6) Mixing of Two Different Substances

TERM MEANING   139

    (7)   Other Factors
    (8)   The Carnot Cycle
    (9)   Two Propositions Regarding the Efficiency of a Carnot Cycle
   (10)   First Proposition
   (11)   Second Proposition
   (12)   The Thermodynamic Temperature Scale

The following pertinent lexical networks were identified:

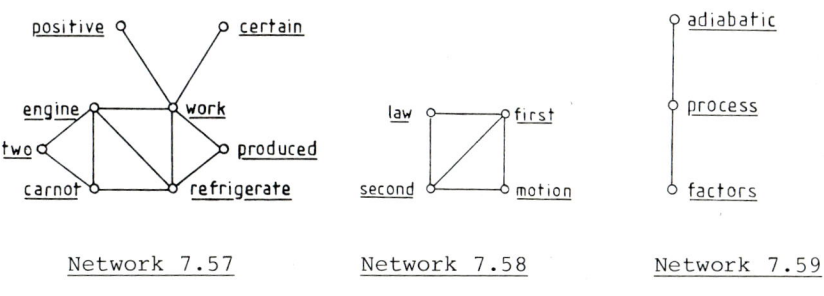

Network 7.57   Network 7.58   Network 7.59

Network 7.60   Network 7.61

The patterning in this chapter is somewhat more difficult to interpret in relation to the generalised section headings provided by the authors. Nor does the introduction to the chapter offer any useful clues. Nevertheless, I think it reasonable to propose the following correspondences. Network 7.57 relates primarily to sections one and eight. Network 7.58 is likely to be latent in the whole of the chapter but is of particular relevance in section two. Network 7.59 is fairly obviously involved in sections three and four whilst networks 7.60 and 7.61 relate principally to section five.

There are a considerable number of further lexical networks in this chapter which can be related to topic but to do so would require rather more exegesis than is reasonable in the interests of establishing a point which is already adequately made by the networks I have considered in these sections. From the evidence discussed it can be safely inferred that the results from THRM lead to the same conclusion as that arrived at from the review of the other texts. The lexical networks that have been identified in this text are constructive of subject matter and thus constitute a major means whereby the sensation of aboutness is perceived by the reader.

7.3 Nuclear Nodes and the Structure of Networks

It is unnecessary to pursue the demonstration further. Even in the samples discussed in the preceding section, there is enough evidence to place beyond reasonable doubt the validity of the claim that associations of lemmata identified on the formal criteria of collocational frequency are a major means by which the conceptual meanings of text are constructed. This interpretation is supported by Benson and Greaves in a small-scale study of the descriptive and instructional literature accompanying a hi-fi system (Benson and Greaves 1983). Thus on the basis of the regular co-occurrence of items separated from each other by relatively small numbers of intervening words, groupings of lexical items could be discerned which clearly articulate the principal cognitive content of the texts. The existence of such networks provides, then, a major clue to the way semantic structures are derivable from the linear sequence of text.

These results are by no means obvious. They demonstrate that network membership is determined by the need to construct meanings rather than, as might be supposed, being a simple function of the frequency of occurrence of the various realisations of the lemmata in a text. In CMEC, for example, on a straightforward frequency basis it might be predicted that force, with a frequency of 460, would collocate regularly with energy (f=297) or body (f=252). The evidence of the lexical networks, however, clearly indicates that this does not happen. Similarly, the high frequency lemma force occurs in every chapter and expresses a concept fundamental to the subject matter of the text, as Kibble himself implies in his introduction. It might consequently be expected that this lemma would belong to a network in every chapter. The evidence shows that this is not the case either. Similar observations can be made for the other texts. These assertions can be verified by reference to the full results presented elsewhere (Phillips 1983).

A second non-trivial result implicit in this evidence stems from a feature of the graphical representation of lexical networks. It will be recalled from the discussion of graph theory in chapter five that a formal procedure exists for distinguishing between the centre and the periphery of networks. The central position of a lemma in a network implies that it tends to attract significant co-occurrences with the largest number of participating lexical items. The network

exists largely because of the critical occurrence of the
central term. In this sense, the central lemmata can be said
to ´organise´ the networks in which they occur. The concept
for which such a lemma is the label is crucial to the
structuring of the reader´s understanding of the pertinent
aspect of reality. I shall henceforth refer to such central
lemmata as ´nuclear nodes´. In many cases, more than one node
is identified as nuclear in the same network. In this case I
shall refer to the ´set of nuclear nodes´ of a lexical network.
It should be noted that nuclear nodes are central by virtue of
the structural associations of lemmata revealed in the networks
and not necessarily on account of the frequency of the
collocational relations they contract.

The third major finding of this study is that **there is a
restricted number of nuclear nodes accounting for the lexical
organisation of the texts.** This brings to mind the observation
in Yule´s early study of literary vocabulary to the effect that

> "The use of vocabulary is concentrated very heavily on to
> a relatively very small proportion of the whole" (Yule
> 1944 p12).

Thus in ELEN, for example, out of the original 199 lemmata
investigated, on average only nineteen per chapter are nuclear.
Comparable figures for the other science texts, in round
figures are twenty five nuclear nodes per chapter in CMEC,
twenty seven in CREL, thirty six in BIPC and thirty two in
THRM. These figures could be reduced even further if the
´strength´ of collocations were to be taken into account. It
would then be possible to distinguish between the elements in a
set of nuclear nodes with two members and thus to specify one
or the other as the unique nucleus. This is a possibility I
shall consider later.

It can also be deduced from the data that the overwhelming
majority of nuclear nodes are ´content words´ or, to use Roe´s
term, ´systemic lexical items´ (Roe 1977a). I have not
attempted to distinguish rigorously between ´systemic´ and
´non-systemic´ lexis. It emerged from the discussion of Roe´s
work in chapter two that the criteria for drawing these
distinctions are by no means clear. In order, however, to
arrive at an approximate notion of the proportions of nuclear
nodes accounted for by different types of item, I propose to
adopt an intuitive semantic classification of vocabulary based
on function. Those lemmata which appear to be concerned with
the expression of content I shall consider to be A-items, so
called because they operate on Sinclair´s autonomous plane of
discourse (Sinclair 1983a). Lemmata whose semantics suggest
that they refer to the text itself and are thus principally
concerned with the on-going construction of text will be
counted as I-items, that is, items that operate on Sinclair´s
interactive plane of discourse.

If these intuitive categorisations are applied to the data,
then it emerges that at most only 20% of the nuclear nodes in

any text in the science corpus are I-items and that the proportion may be as low as 6%. These figures can be confirmed by inspection of appendix five. I also give there the average number of nuclear nodes in each text interval and the number of distinct nuclear nodes in each text. The graphs below plot the distribution of nuclear nodes in the texts, that is, the number of new nuclear nodes introduced in each text interval.

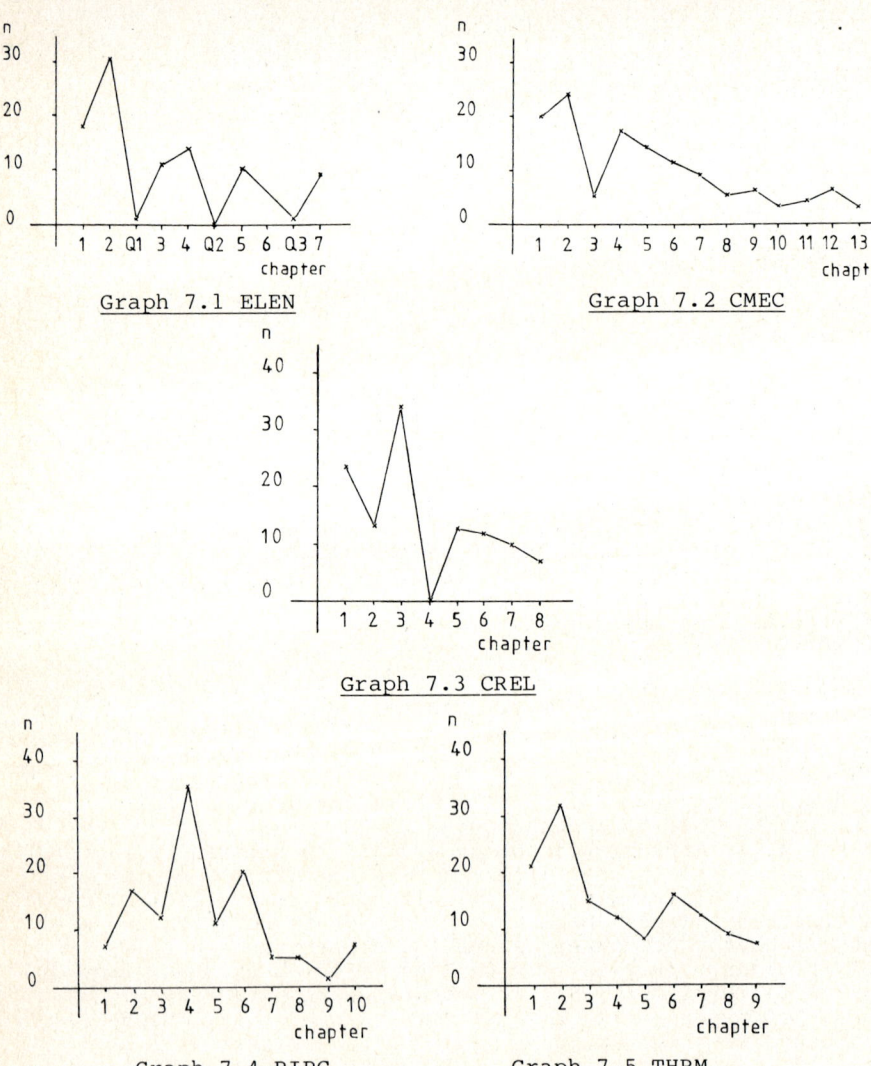

It can be seen from inspection of these graphs for the science texts that the bulk of the nuclear vocabulary occurs early in

the texts and that the incrementation falls off markedly from
the third or fourth chapter onwards. It would seem that the
majority of the total vocabulary is required in order to be
able to discuss any topic within the general field of a
particular scientific subject matter. In consequence the
development of topic throughout the course of a textbook calls
upon only relatively few fresh vocabulary items.

It may seem that this conclusion is contradicted by the graph
for BIPC which indicates that the bulk of the nuclear nodes in
this text is not introduced until chapter four. It should be
recalled, however, that the early chapters of this textbook
contain material which is relatively independent of the main
body of the text and which could easily have formed the subject
of separate appendices. The first chapter is entitled
"Mathematics Revision", the second "SI Units and their Usage"
and the third "The Behaviour of Gases". It is not until
chapter four, which treats of "Some Properties of Aqueous
Solutions", that the subject matter proper of ´A Biologist´s
Physical Chemistry´ is clearly established. The observed
distribution of nuclear nodes in this text does not, then,
contradict my interpretation.

The inference from these findings is that whilst certain
aspects of the discourse structure of text may be attributable
to the operation of interactive plane items, the lexical
structure of text is in general the responsibility of a
restricted set of vocabulary items concerned with organisation
on the autonomous plane. The items which operate on the
interactive plane to guide the reader through the complexities
of the conceptual relations expressed in this way appear only
relatively infrequently as nuclear. I interpret this to mean
that in most instances nuclear nodes represent the foundations
of cognitive structures critical to the construction of subject
matter.

A few networks might seem to offer counter-evidence to the
interpretation I am putting forward. In chapter five of CMEC,
for example, the following network is found, in which the lemma
small must be accepted as nuclear.

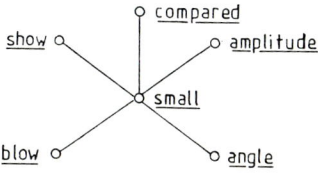

Network 7.62

In this case it might be objected that all that is being demonstrated here is the fact that <u>small</u> occurs in this chapter mainly as a qualifier for a variety of different, and largely non-technical, headwords. The intuitive expectation, however, is that it is the headwords that should enjoy the prominence rather than the qualifier. This network appears to be more revealing of grammatical than of semantic relations. Two considerations, however, suggest that this interpretation is inappropriate. First, in this text three of the other lemmata in the network, <u>amplitude</u>, <u>blow</u> and <u>angle</u>, are all used in specific contexts and must consequently be considered technical terms of the subject. In other words, the relations revealed by the network are as much to do with cognitive content as with any of the networks discussed earlier. Secondly, the quantification of phenomena and their measurement are of considerable importance in science in general and are certainly significant in mechanics. Thus it is not surprising that a term which implies a scale of measurement should enjoy nuclear status. The conclusion I draw is that there is no fundamental difference between the principles accounting for the structure of this network and the interpretation of the other networks which I have developed in this chapter. It must also be realised that networks of the type illustrated in the graph above are exceptional.

In addition to the finding that the set of nuclear nodes for a given text is comparatively small, these results reveal a further significant feature of the structure of lexical networks. In her early study of collocations, Berry-Rogghe expressed the view that intercollocation of the collocates of a node is a relative rarity (Berry-Rogghe 1970). If this is indeed the case, then it may be expected that in the results from the present study the tendency of lemmata to collocate with the set of nuclear nodes will far outweigh their tendency to intercollocate. Using the concept of the connectivity of a graph which was developed in chapter five, it is possible to rephrase this expectation rather more precisely. Despite the fact that any pattern of intercollocation among the lemmata in a lexical network is in principle possible, it may be anticipated that in fact observed networks will generally display only relatively low connectivity. It will be recalled from chapter five that the lower the line-connectivity of a graph, the fewer the intercollocations within the corresponding lexical network.

First, it should be clear that lexical networks consisting of two lemmata only do not present any interest. These are necessarily completely connected by the nature of collocational data. For the remaining lexical networks identified in this study, consisting of a minimum of three lemmata, a mean connectivity index was calculated for the networks in each of the fifty text intervals in the corpus. In only thirteen of the text intervals did this mean connectivity index exceed the value of 0.5. That is to say, in only a quarter of the chapters in the science corpus did the average number of collocations within a lexical network exceed half the

theoretically possible number. Moreover, when the value of
0.50 is exceeded, it is normally by only a very small amount.

This finding provides further powerful evidence of the
organising role played by the relatively restricted number of
nuclear nodes. It is clear that Berry-Rogghe's surmise was
justified. At least as far as the data produced by this study
are concerned, it can be asserted that a relatively small
number of critical nodes tends to 'attract' other lemmata and
thus to create configurations which realise the conceptual
structures of the text.

In contrast, the graphs of the relatively few lexical networks
which have a comparatively high value of the connectivity
index must be considered of particular interest. Two
interpretations can be given to highly connected graphs of
networks. In most cases they represent networks which are of
exceptional significance for the construction of subject
matter. In a few instances, however, the structure of the
network may arise as a consequence of the presence of a
homograph. I shall now consider each of these possibilities in
turn.

Consider first the lexical networks graphed below:

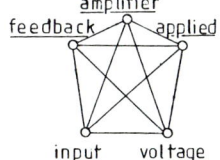

Network 7.63 ELEN   Network 7.64 CMEC   Network 7.65 CREL

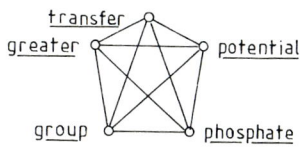   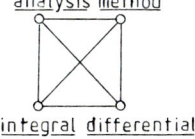

Network 7.66 BIPC   Network 7.67 THRM

These are the largest completely connected graphs of networks
from each of the texts in the science corpus. In the case of
ELEN and BIPC the examples are unique, that is no other
completely connected graphs were identified by the study. For
the other texts I have chosen a representative graph from the
small class of those on four points which are completely
connected.

It can easily be seen that the lexical networks represented
here are of particular importance for the construction of
conceptual areas central to the fields of science dealt with by
these texts. Network 7.63 comes from ELEN chapter five and
needs no comment. Network 7.64 is taken from CMEC chapter
eight. This network obviously actualises a notion of critical
importance to the analysis of systems of bodies as it is
undertaken in classical mechanics. Network 7.65 from CREL
chapter three relates to the expression of the methodology for
analysing rate equations. This is a central notion in chemical
engineering. Network 7.66 taken from BIPC chapter nine is the
least obviously interpretable of the networks presented here.
The chapter from which it is taken is concerned with "The
Application of Thermodynamics to Biochemistry". The network
graphed above actualises the notion of ´group transfer
potential´. This is a concept involved in the explication of
the ´free energy change´ for ´high energy compounds´. This
network is of significance in the discussion of the chemistry
of living organisms considered from a thermodynamic point of
view and is thus crucial in Gareth Morris´ text. Finally,
network 7.67 from THRM chapter seven is indisputably
appropriate in a text on thermodynamics. These networks thus
provide firm evidence for a relationship between tightly
organised networks, where every member collocates with every
other, and the expression of topics of particular importance to
the subject of the text.

It appears to be occasionally the case, however, that
intercollocations may occur arising from the occurence in a
single text interval of a homograph in more than one of its
contexts of use. There is a clear example in CMEC chapter six:

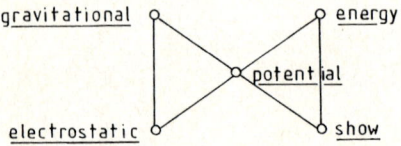

Network 7.68

TERM MEANING   147

Here the ambiguity of <u>potential</u> is clearly revealed. Its use
in the group ´potential energy´ can be opposed to its occurence
both in ´gravitational potential´ and ´electrostatic
potential´.

A rather more complex instance is found in CMEC chapter two.

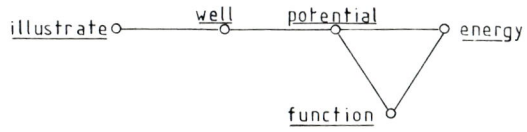

Network 7.69

In this case <u>potential</u> operates ambiguously in ´potential
energy function´ and ´potential well´. It may seem that <u>well</u>
itself is ambiguous between its use in the latter nominal group
and the verbal group ´well illustrated´. In fact, the
reference is to the graphical representation of a potential
well.

A final example may be taken from THRM chapter two. It is
graphed below:

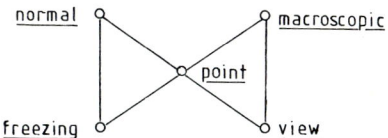

Network 7.70

Here it can be clearly seen that <u>point</u> is used in two senses
in this text interval. It is defined both by the group
´macroscopic point of view´, which is the topic of a section in

this chapter, and by ´normal freezing point´. Thus the finding that intercollocation of the collocates of the nuclear nodes is comparatively unusual is reinforced by the recognition that when it does happen it either occurs because topics of particular significance are thereby articulated or because of the presence of a homograph.

7.4 Theories and Models of Term Meaning

In the preceding sections it has been demonstrated that there exists in science text a vocabulary which is critical in terms of its function of constructing subject matter. It also became clear that this vocabulary is quite restricted in extent. In effect, of the three and a half thousand or so types which constitute a typical first year undergraduate science textbook, perhaps only five per cent are required to articulate the crucial concepts. This finding penetrates beyond the simplicities of word frequency to an assertion of the functional significance of a limited subset of the vocabulary of a given text.

It has been seen that the critical items are closely and complexly interrelated in lexical networks. This brings to mind the Saussurian notions of ´valeur´ and ´solidarite´. What I am calling the ´critical vocabulary´ of text consists of numbers of lexical items which are mutually defining and which tend to behave as bound rather than free entities. This means that it makes no sense to suggest that the meaning of an item such as ´circuit´ can be defined in isolation. Taking the use of this term in ELEN as an example, its meaning can only be fixed by appreciating that it stands in a certain relation to ´amplifier´, ´components´, ´use´, ´input´, ´voltage´, ´transistor´ and so on. This is suggestive evidence for a contextual theory of lexical meaning.

The essentials of a contextual theory of word meaning have been proposed by Anthony in his "spectrum intersection theory" (Anthony 1975). He postulates that a word has a range of meaning potential. On any particular occasion of use it acquires a unique meaning by virtue of its association in text with other lexical items. He refers to the unactualised word with its complete range of meaning potential as a ´repertory´ word. A particular meaning is picked out by the intersection of the meaning potentials of other words in context to create what he calls a ´discourse´ word. The contextual meaning of words arises, then, out of a system of mutually defining relations. It has already been seen that similar notions have been expressed by Firth as well as by Sinclair, Simmons, who suggests the possibility of a set-theoretic interpretation of "semantic network structures", and by Quillian (Sinclair 1966, Simmons 1973, Quillian 1968). Quillian argues that

> "To define one word, the dictionary builder always uses tokens of other words. However, it is not sufficient for the reader to consider the meaning of the defined word as simply an unordered aggregation of pointers to

the other word concepts used in its definition. The
configuration of these word concepts is crucial; it
modifies the meanings of the individual word concepts
that make up its parts and at the same time creates a
new gestalt with them, which represents the meaning of
the word being defined." (Quillian op cit p234)

The lexical networks identified in the present study furnish
strong evidence in support of these views. An example from
CMEC chapter one is graphed below.

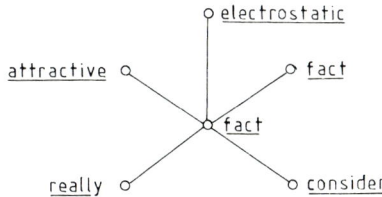

Network 7.71

Here it can be argued that the ´meaning´ of <u>force</u> is just that
region of its meaning potential in the language which is
specified by its intersection with the meaning potentials of
<u>attractive</u> and <u>electrostatic</u>. This rules out, for example, the
kind of interpretation for force which is implied by the
collocations ´task force´ or ´police force´. Only in
exceptional circumstances would the latter happily intersect
with the meaning potential of ´attractive´. Similarly,
<u>attractive</u> is delimited by <u>electrostatic</u>, thus eliminating the
possibility of any facetious reading. These data thus provide
evidence for Leech´s argument that

> "Within a semantic approach based on conceptual meaning,
> all these observations suggest that meaning-in-context
> should be regarded as a narrowing down, or probabilistic
> weighting, of the list of potential meanings available
> to the user of the language." (Leech 1981 p68)

In the light of the evidence I have provided, I would differ
from the views expressed by Anthony and Leech in only one
respect. I do not accept that contextual meaning is
necessarily a matter of narrowing down a fixed meaning
potential. The intersection of the meaning potentials of other
words in the context is capable of creating new meanings and
hence of adding to the meaning potential of a repertory word.
This is crucial for it is the mechanism by which new meanings
are acquired and in particular underlies the creation of the

complex of semantic relations to which the term subject matter is usually given.

The insights into term meaning that have thus been gained can be formalised. As has been seen, the meaning of a node is delimited by its collocates. But the meaning potential of the collocates is in turn restricted by their intersection with their own collocates. These thus indirectly determine the unique meaning of the original node at a particular point in the text. This can be represented by the following graph:

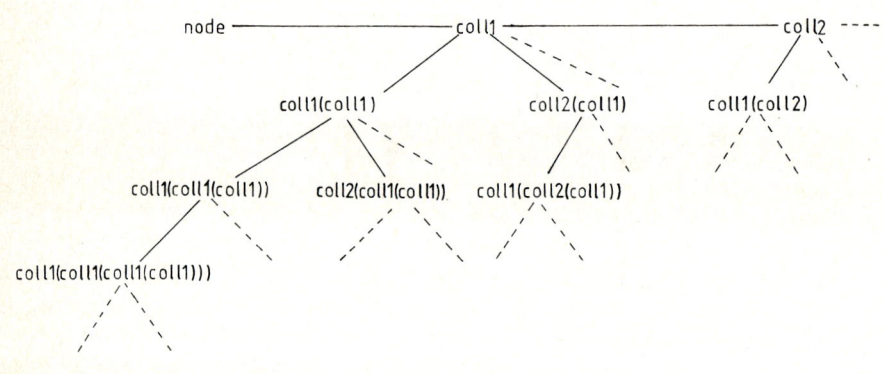

Graph 7.6

Thus the contextual word meaning of a node at a particular point in a text is a function of the particular choices made to realise the above schema.

It is also possible to see in the data of the study evidence in support of Pike's theories of language. He has argued that it is necessary to perceive language as particle, wave and field in turn (Pike 1959). Pike's principal considerations are drawn from the areas of grammar and phonology. I suggest that there is now lexical evidence for the validity of his position. The approaches to word meaning embodied in traditional semantics have tended to treat words as discrete items. This is the particulate view. I believe there is now evidence which suggests that a wave model of lexical behaviour is appropriate.

The model is suggested by consideration of the categories fundamental to any exploration of text, the ´type´ and the ´token´. The fact that for a given text this distinction can be made is a consequence of the repetition of like events. In other words, the occurrence of tokens in a text can be viewed as a periodic phenomenon. For the sake of simplicity, I shall make the assumption that such repetition is regular. This is clearly an oversimplification, although for large bodies of language not unduly so. In any case, it does not affect the validity of the argument.

Periodic phenomena can be conceptualised as waves. Consider a sine wave:

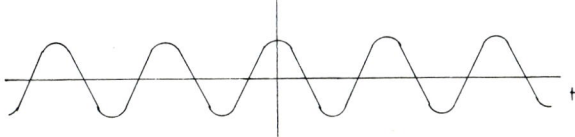

Figure 7.1

The horizontal line represents the ´time base´. The number of repetitions of like events, the number of peaks or troughs for example, in a given time interval is called the ´frequency´. The height of the waves above or below the horizontal line is called the ´amplitude´.

Now consider two waves of slightly different frequencies:

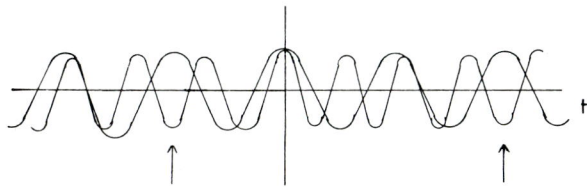

Figure 7.2

The two waves coincide exactly at the origin. They are said to be ´in phase´ at that point. Moving away from the origin they get ´out of phase´. Thus these waves get successively in and out of phase.

Physical theory informs us that any complex waveform can be
viewed as the addition of a numbr of simple sine waves. In
the example below, the result of the addition of two waves is a
wave of lower frequency:

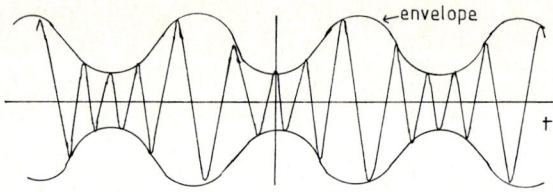

Figure 7.3

The resultant wave is called the ´modulation function´ or
´envelope´. Large numbers of different waves could be added
together to produce highly complex modulation functions.

If a suitable linguistic interpretation for some of the
concepts of wave theory is provided, it will serve as a model
for the lexical behaviour which has been revealed by the
present study. A wave corresponds to the occurrences in a
stretch of text of a lemma. The time base may be interpreted
as the real-time time base of speech or the linear ordering of
written language. The notion of frequency corresponds to the
frequency of occurrence in the text of the lemma.

On this interpretation, the collocation of two lemmata is then
represented by the point where two waves are in phase. If two
waves of the same frequency are locked in phase, this
corresponds to the case where two lemmata have the same
frequency of occurrence and are without exception found in each
other´s environment; a polymorphemic item perhaps. If two
waves of the same frequency are locked 180 degrees out of
phase, this would mean for lemmata that they occur with the
same frequency but never collocate, within whatever span is
appropriate, in the text in question. When the frequency of
one wave is an integral multiple of the frequency of a second
wave and they are in phase, this corresponds to the case where
the occurrence of one of the lexical items completely predicts
that of the other but not reciprocally, as is the case with
´kith´ and ´kin´ for example. The normal case where the
frequency of collocation is less than the frequency of
occurrence of either of the individual lemmata is the
interpretation given to two waves of slightly different
frequencies which move successively in and out of phase. The
modulation function can now be interpreted as the occurrence of
a collocation.

The usual cautions which Nagel reminds us apply when
constructing models must be observed (Nagel 1961). Some of the
concepts of the theory remain uninterpreted in the model. For
example, words are particulate in nature insofar as they either
occur or not. Waves, in contrast, are continuous. In
consequence, there is no interpretation for the notion of
amplitude. On the other hand, uninterpreted features of the
theory may prove valuable heuristically in the discovery of new
facts about language. Conversely, there is at least one notion
from lexical theory which has been of crucial importance in my
study and which seems to be unrepresented in the model. This
is the notion of span. This lack represents a weakness in the
model unless a theoretical property of waves can be found which
can receive this interpretation. Enough has been said,
however, to demonstrate that the aspect of lexical behaviour
revealed by the findings of this study is capable of receiving
an interpretation which is supportive of Pike´s view of
language as particle, wave and field.

7.5 Conclusion

In this chapter the results obtained from the analysis of the
science texts conducted with the chapter as interval have been
presented and discussed. It was shown that in each text there
was convincing evidence for the existence of lexical networks
which are intimately concerned with the construction of subject
matter. From this it emerged that a relatively small number of
lexical items, which I have called nuclear nodes, are primarily
responsible for the lexical organisation of text.

These findings were further seen to provide support for two
views of term meaning as a function of textual occurrence.
First, the evidence of the lexical networks lent itself to an
interpretation which directly confirmed the contextual view of
word meaning. Secondly, a dynamic view of lexical behaviour
was developed in which the occurrence of lexis in text was
modelled as a wave phenomenon.

Thus two fundamental points emerge from this stage of the
analysis. It is clear that term meaning should be viewed as a
function of the syntagmatic lexical relations obtaining in
text. There is now empirical evidence in favour of Sinclair´s
argument against the approach to term meaning which sees it as
a branch of conceptual semantics (Sinclair 1983b). In other
words, the establishment of term banks rests upon inadequate
theoretical foundations. Secondly, it is apparent that terms
help to construct text. Networks arise from the large-scale
patterning of lexical items over stretches of text which in the
present study reached the chapter in extent. They play the
crucial functional role in text of constructing subject matter.

It is thus likely that lexical networks have an important part
to play in the macrostructure of texts and consequently in the
creation of the sensation of aboutness. In order to
investigate this possibility it is necessary to examine the
extent to which networks are stable throughout the whole text

within which the text interval was defined in which given networks occur. The problem whether the findings at chapter focus have implications for the macrostructure of textbooks as a whole leads me to a description of a further set of findings from the study reported here. Their discussion will occupy the next chapter.

CHAPTER 8

TERMS AND TEXT STRUCTURE

8.1 The Structure, Linkage and Status of Chapters

In the last chapter I demonstrated the existence of patterns of association within the chapter as interval which took the form of lexical networks. At the end of the discussion I raised the question of how such networks relate to patterning elsewhere in the text. In this chapter, then, I shall focus on the evidence that the study provided for the functioning of networks in the large scale structuring of text. I shall first discuss the relationship of networks to the structure of the chapter and then examine the evidence for the existence of macrostructure in text. I argued that the notion of macrostructure relates to the perception of aboutness. The nature of this relationship will be considered for each of the science texts in the corpus.

Lexical networks have been considered hitherto for the light they throw on the construction of subject matter. It is also possible to examine them for the role they play in structuring the text interval in which they occur, which in the case of this study means the chapter. The hierarchical form of the dendrograms from which the lexical networks are derived provides a clue to their interpretation as elements in the structure of the chapter. It suggests that the chapter can be conceived of as organised at a series of stages, where each stage consists of associations of units from previous stages.

The lemma, represented by a vertical line ´|´, can be taken as stage zero. At stage one associations of lemmata occur:

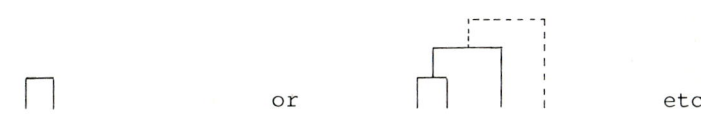

Figure 8.1   Figure 8.2

Stage two consists of associations of units from stage one:

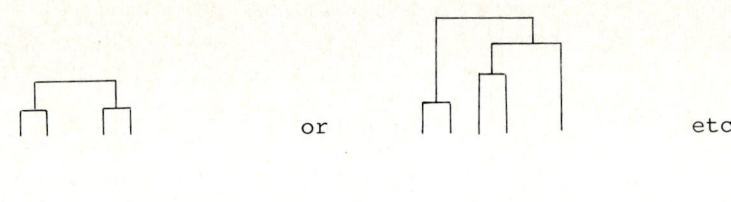

Figure 8.3   Figure 8.4

Stage three is composed of associations of units from stages two or one

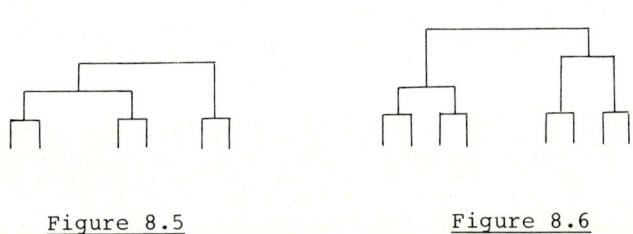

Figure 8.5   Figure 8.6

and so on. At any stage beyond zero, a configuration can be regarded as a lexical network.

These stages can be illustrated by observing the development of a relatively simple lexical network in CMEC chapter thirteen. At stage one the following associations occur:

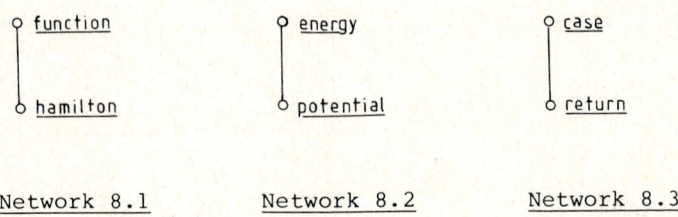

Network 8.1   Network 8.2   Network 8.3

At stage two networks 8.1 and 8.3 merge

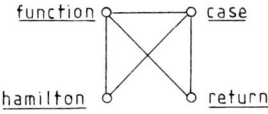

Network 8.4

and at stage three network 8.2 is added

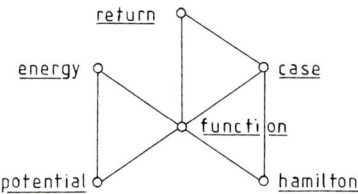

Network 8.5

It should be noted how at stage two function and case are identified as nuclear whilst by stage three function is revealed as the prime organising node.

It is now possible to define the text interval from the point of view of lexical organisation. It corresponds to the disconnected digraph formed by the union of the subgraphs which result when the influence of the nuclear nodes is exhausted. The only connectivity beyond the lexical networks I have identified is the trivial one provided by the ultimate fusion of all networks into the 'ragbag'.

From these considerations I conclude that lexical networks contribute to the organisation of the chapter. The chapter can be viewed as consisting of a number of dense regions of conceptual space. Does this mean, then, that despite the fact that the chapter was accepted as a methodological convenience and despite Roe's finding that the textual apparatus of typical science text calls into question the validity of chapter boundaries (Roe 1977a), these findings constitute objective evidence for the chapter as an identifiable structural unit in text? To answer this question it is necessary now to turn to the results from the study bearing upon the structuring of text at the level of the whole textbook, that is to the evidence for text macrostructure.

The exploration of macrostructure was guided by the following line of reasoning. If an individual linguistic item occurs in different intervals of a text with a statistically significant frequency of occurrence, then it is legitimate to infer a linguistic cause. This is the fundamental insight of distributional-statistical analysis. If this is true of the occurrence of individual linguistic items, then it must be equally so of the partial or total repetition of networks. The constraints on the occurrence of networks are by definition greater than those on the appearance of individual lexical items. Consequently, the presence in different intervals of a text of networks which can be considered in certain fundamental ways as similar would be an unusual and therefore significant event. If this phenomenon were in fact to be observed, then it would have to be viewed as furnishing persuasive evidence for the notion of macrostructure. The investigation of such relationships among text intervals constitutes a particular realisation of an objective set by Herdan. He emphasised the importance of studying what he termed "vocabulary connectivity", suggesting that

> "In this way the global frequency distribution of words is reduced to a network of connecting links between the segments of a text - not only neighbouring segments but also distinct ones - and the confusing mass of morphemic relations to a few points characterising that network" (Herdan 1962 p108).

In the study it was, however, anticipated that it would be unreasonable to demand absolute identity of lexical networks from one interval to the next. It is intuitively improbable that networks actualising the same general conceptual area will be in one-for-one correspondence in all points, except for the very simplest. Factors relating to the local organisation of text are likely to have the effect that within an intuitively perceived stability, a certain amount of variability of network membership will be observed. Moreover, the relationships obtaining between networks within an interval are bound to vary as a result of the progression of the argument in the text. This will be reflected in the constituency of the networks. As a result, networks articulating fundamentally the same conceptual area in different text intervals are likely to show some variation as a function of the influence of different networks in each interval. It is highly probable, for example, that the more peripheral nodes of lexical networks will be subject to fluctuation as a result of these factors. Similarly, the presence of a new lexical network or the absence of an old one from a particular text interval will affect the total patterning in extremely complex ways which, in the present state of understanding of these phenomena, can only be a matter for conjecture. It was concluded, however, that the observable result was likely to be a tension between variation and uniformity in lexical association.

It was necessary, then, to formalise intuitions about the stability of network structure by developing a notion of similarity which could be used to compare networks with each other. Two features of network structure are fundamental to a concept of similarity for networks. First, networks can be compared in terms of the number of corresponding lemmata, that is nodes coordinated with identical lemmata. Secondly, they can be compared in terms of the relative position in the networks of corresponding lemmata.

With these notions in mind, two criteria for similarity were established. The criteria apply simultaneously. The first is as follows:

> (1) Networks must have a minimum of two corresponding lemmata in common.

It would perhaps have been preferable to require that a certain proportion of the lemmata in a pair of networks should correspond rather than a minimum absolute number. A proportional measure would allow the relative size of networks to be taken into account. It was judged, however, that it would have given rise to difficulties in interpreting non-integral proportions and that it was simpler to insist simply on a requirement of minimal identity of collocational behaviour. It might appear that this criterion is relatively weak, given that it specifies that only two lemmata need correspond. If the actual textual phenomenon that is represented as a network is considered, however, it will be realised that it is by no means a weak requirement. It means that identical pairs of lemmata must be regularly found in each other's environment in different text intervals. It is thus in fact quite a strong constraint on similarity.

Further, the first criterion receives crucial reinforcement from the second, which is as follows:

> (2) At least one of the corresponding lemmata must be a member of the set of nuclear nodes in each network.

This criterion thus ensures that at least one of the corresponding lemmata occupies the central position in the network and is thus of critical importance to the existence of the network. The requirements for the recognition of similarity are thus that a minimum number of lemmata be identical and that the networks should have at least one organising lemma, which may of course be the unique nuclear node, in common. It was felt that taken together these two criteria provided an adequate guarantee of similarity in terms of the fundamental organisation of the networks.

Given these constraints, a further problem could arise in the case where the criteria might suggest similarity on the grounds of identical lemmata which happen to occupy different positions in their respective networks. One lemma, for example, might be nuclear in one network whilst the corresponding lemma in the other network might be peripheral; or both lemmata might be peripheral. This might raise a question as to the meaningfulness of the similarity. In these cases, the following further criterion could be invoked:

> (3) A threshold value of the conditional probability of collocation of a peripheral lemma with any nuclear node in the same network must be achieved before the peripheral lemma can be considered as corresponding to the identical lemma in a different network.

In other words, the prediction ratios mentioned in chapter five could be used to determine the 'degree' of membership of a lemma in a network. Such a measure can be viewed as essentially a fuzzy set membership function (Zadeh 1965). Although Zadeh explicitly denies that his functions are probabilistic, there is no reason why lemmata should not be conceived of as having different degrees of membership in lexical networks depending on their probabilities of collocation. Although the development of a fuzzy set theoretic model of lexical behaviour represents a worthwhile challenge for further research, it was not found necessary in the present study to invoke this criterion in anything other than an informal manner to check the validity of the occasional intuitively felt relationship between lemmata. In practice, the joint application of the first two criteria proved adequate to ensure that relationships were established only among associations of lexical items which projected substantively similar aspects of the conceptual content of the texts in which they occurred.

By way of example, the use of these criteria allows the networks represented below, taken from CMEC chapters three and eleven respectively, to be treated as essentially similar. This is indicated on the graphs by lines linking the corresponding nodes on the graphs.

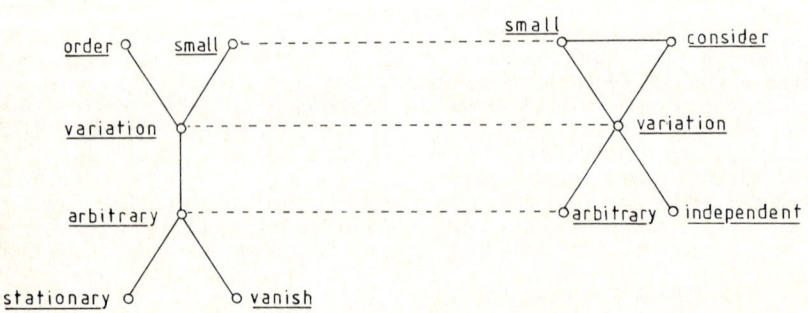

Network 8.6   Network 8.7

TERMS AND TEXT STRUCTURE   161

These networks reveal that in both chapters the notion
expressed by ´arbitrary small variations´, though operating in
slightly different contexts in the two cases, is of
significance. This seems to be entirely reasonable. More
interesting is the case in which the criteria establish that a
network arises as the union of two or more networks which may
each occur independently in other text intervals. The example
below comes from CMEC chapters two, five and twelve.

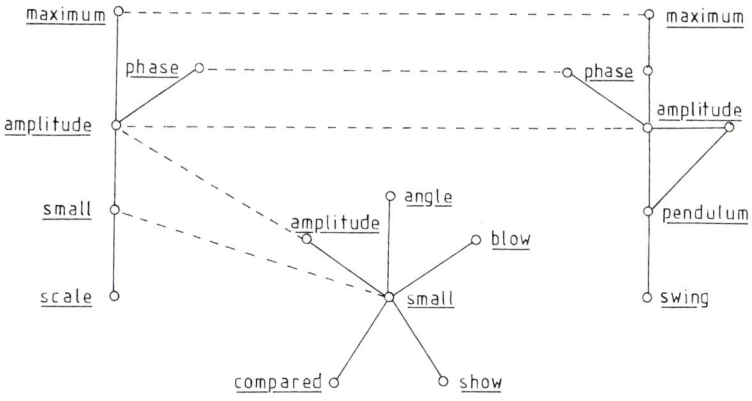

Network 8.8

In this case, different aspects of the core notion of ´ampli-
tude´ are taken up at different points in the text. The
pattern of linkages resulting from the application of the
criteria described above for all the texts in the corpus can be
found elsewhere (Phillips 1983).

Similarities among networks established on this basis lead to
an overall pattern of linkage among text intervals. This level
of patterning can be more clearly revealed by constructing what
I call second and third order graphs, where lexical networks
within a text interval represent first order graphs. A second
order graph is one in which the nodes represent complete
networks and the lines are interpreted as standing for the
relationship of similarity. Thus the linkage diagrammed
earlier in networks 8.6 and 8.7 can be more simply represented
as follows:

Graph 8.1

The numbers associated with the points identify the chapter in which the relevant network occurs. It will be noted that the relation of similarity is represented by a single directed line from the node standing for the network which occurs in the later text interval to the node corresponding to the similar network found earlier in the text. The implication is that repetition of similar lexical networks is a retrospective phenomenon.

Considerable interest has been generated recently concerning patterns of prospection relating to the interactive construction of text. Both Tadros and Cooper have pointed out that a writer may make a commitment at one point in the text to be fulfilled later (Cooper 1983, Tadros 1981). In this example from CREL

> "The first of the two ideal steady-state flow reactors is variously known as the plug flow, slug flow, piston flow, ideal tubular, and unmixed flow reactor" (Levenspiel 1972 p97).

A prediction is set up that at some later stage the second type of steady-state flow reactor will be discussed. A lexical item or association of lexical items, however, cannot per se be predictive. Nothing about the occurrence of "steady-state flow reactors" in CREL chapter five above predicts its later reappearance. It may be highly probable that such items will be repeated, but this cannot be predicted with certainty. To put it another way, they need not be repeated and the text may still be well formed. In contrast, if the prediction set up in the quotation from Levenspiel above were not fulfilled, it could be legitimately claimed that the text was in some sense inadequate. The repetition of lexical items, on the other hand, actualises the meaning potential stored in the reader's mind as a result of previous occurrences of the item. The new encounter is located with respect to earlier and, in retrospect, provisional patterns of use. I am thus concerned with retrospective patterning and this is reflected in the diagrammatic representations.

It is highly likely that most chapters in a given textbook will display some linkage with each other. Indeed it would be surprising if this were not the case with science text viewed from a lexical standpoint. It was consequently necessary to develop a notion of significant linkage in order to reveal whatever patterning might be latent in an otherwise undifferentiated mass of interrelationships. The problem was to determine how many linkages represented by second order graphs should be required in order to consider two text intervals as significantly related. There are at present no theoretical arguments that can be adduced to help resolve this question. There appeared to exist, however, an interesting discontinuity in the data which proved useful as the basis for an empirical criterion. This discontinuity occurred between the number of times chapters displayed one second order link and the frequency of two or more such linkages. In CMEC, for example, there is a total of twenty three single linkages between chapters but only eight double linkages. Beyond that, only nine times are chapters linked by more than two ties. The figures for the other science texts are comparable.

A conservative criterion would, then, be to require that chapters must be connected by a minimum of three second order links in order to qualify as significantly related. It is again a case of identifying that level of analysis which retains the maximum of information about the text without obscuring the latent patterning in a mass of detail. This requirement is a fairly strong one. The representation of chapter linkages for the texts in the corpus resulting when all single and double linkages are ignored will be found in appendix six. The lines in the remaining graphs are weighted with the number of linkages they represent. I call these third order graphs. It will be seen later that on the basis of such third order graphs it is possible to establish the nature of the macrostructure of each text.

The complex patterns of relationship obtaining among the chapters in the texts as revealed by my findings cast some doubt upon the validity of the notion of the chapter as an independent unit of textual organisation. It will be recalled that in chapter three the chapter was accepted into the analysis as an heuristic unit. It seems that in the light of my results it is indeed not possible to ascribe to it any more secure a status. Lexical patterning clearly transcends chapter boundaries in non-trivial ways.

This conclusion strongly supports the views expressed by the authors of the texts in the science corpus regarding the relative lack of independence of the chapters in their works. They all to a greater or lesser degree treat the integrity of their own chapter divisions with cavalier disrespect. I quote here some of the more obvious examples.

ELEN "Certain sections of the book have been marked with a . These are considered to be too advanced for some first year students and may be omitted on first reading" (Ahmed and Spreadbury 1973 pxii).

CMEC "Chapter 6, which could be omitted without substantially affecting the remaining chapters, deals with potential theory" (Kibble 1973 pxii).

CREL "....in my teaching of a one-term course to students with a physical chemistry background I leap over Chapters 1, 2 and 3 in a lecture or two plus a few representative problems mainly as a means of presenting definitions of terms. Then since Chapters 6, 7 and 8 reinforce the ideas of Chapter 5, I only very briefly outline this material and right away plunge into the problem-solving. Finally, in Chapter 14 I leave out the sections on product distribution and fluidized bed design" (Levenspiel 1972 pvi).

BIPC "Since pH is of prime interest to all biologists, Chapters 5 and 6 are devoted directly or indirectly to the topic, complemented (necessarily in my experience) by a section of Chapter 1 which describes the meaning and use of logarithms" (Gareth Morris 1974 pviii).

THRM "An alternative to covering all the material in order is to spend the first term on classical thermodynamics (Chapters 1-5 plus 7 and 8, or 1-9 and/or 10 and/or 11 depending on the length and credit hours of the course)" (Sonntag and Van Wylen 1971 pix).

Historically, the chapter was conventional in nature. Its origins in literature can be traced to a number of contributory factors which tended to impose a more or less regular segmentation on the writer´s production. The oral narrative tradition would have given rise to a need for natural breakpoints in the course of the recitation which have left a trace as conventional divisions in written text. The sectioning arising from the epistolary style of early novels carried over into later established narrative technique. Publication by instalments, a common practice in the eighteenth and early nineteenth centuries, obliged the novelist to segment his text. Something of this original conventionality in the nature of the chapter survives in modern science text. There is no linguistic reason for the existence of chapters rather than, say, the division of a continuous text into sections. There is perhaps a psychological basis insofar as large stretches of unbroken text might prove daunting to the reader, particularly in a pedagogic text. A tendency to avoid continuous text in excess of thirty to forty pages can be discerned. Closely related to this is the force of tradition, which should not be underestimated. Textbooks are traditionally divided into chapters and a publisher might well not be sanguine about the marketability of a textbook not so divided.

There is perhaps one rather more motivated basis for the chapter in science text, though again not a linguistic motivation. Since in all the science texts in the corpus the chapter boundary coincides with the provision of problems, it seems that a major reason for the existence of chapter divisions is the necessity to take stock from time to time of the ground covered and to give the student the opportunity to consolidate his newly acquired knowledge. Again, however, it should be noted that the particular location of problems is not usually clearly motivated. In many texts worked examples are scattered at various points through the chapter. Any one of these could have been developed into a major boundary by expansion with additional unworked problems. Thus it seems that the prime reason for the existence of chapters in science textbooks is pedagogic rather than structural. It is perhaps not unreasonable to suggest that it is a vestige in written expository text of the spoken lecture format. This is, of course, simply conventionality in another guise. It is thus

not surprising that linguistic techniques of analysis are
unable to establish the chapter as an independent unit. In any
case, a synchronic approach is unlikely to produce evidence in
support of a diachronic hypothesis.

8.2 The Macrostructure of Science Text

From the third order graphs of significant chapter linkages in
appendix six, it is possible to derive a representation of the
overall pattern of connectivity among chapters in a text. This
is the patterning that I call macrostructure. The macrostructures of each of the science texts in the corpus are
presented in appendix seven. Each chapter is represented by a
node labelled with the title of the corresponding chapter and
the interchapter linkages are represented by connecting lines.

In this section I shall introduce some notions in terms of
which the macrostructures of science texts can be interpreted.
This interpretation, which will be undertaken for each of the
science texts in the corpus in the next section, requires
something of a reorientation of approach. Hitherto what may be
termed a ´process´ perspective has been adopted in order to
reveal macrostructure. By this I mean that the identification
of related sections of text from the clues provided has been
retrospective. Chapter linkage has been viewed in terms of
similarities obtaining between networks directed from the
network occurring later in the text to the earlier network.
This perspective corresponds to that of the reader for whom the
text is an experiential phenomenon and who cannot, therefore,
predict the macrostructure of the text from the features
investigated here. It is likely, of course, that he will be
forewarned about the macrostructure by the text itself. This,
however, arises from metacommunication in the text taking place
on the interactive plane of discourse and does not therefore
contradict my point.

To interpret macrostructure, however, it is necessary to adopt
a ´product´ perspective. This means that the text must be
considered as a whole in which internal relations can be viewed
as prospective or retrospective as best suits the interpretation. In a process perspective the fact that the last chapter
echoes topics introduced in the first chapter, for example, can
only be recognised once the final chapter has been reached. In
the product perspective, in contrast, this relationship is
given simultaneously with all the other relationships obtaining
in the text. Consequently, it can equally well be viewed as a
prospective relation. The product perspective thus corresponds
to the writer´s and the analyst´s position. The reader is also
analyst insofar as he continually reinterprets the ground
covered in the light of current knowledge. And this is the
crux; the product perspective is crucial to interpretation.

In the light of these consideration, I propose that three basic
patterns of relation can be postulated to account for the
macrostructures presented in appendix seven. I call these
distinct patterns of relation ´segments´. The three segment

types are the 'sequential segment', the 'synoptic segment' and the 'isolated segment'. Each type of segment articulates the text in a different manner and lends itself to a particular interpretation. The first of these, the sequential segment, is defined as consisting of a sequence of linked chapters beginning with a chapter which displays only prospective links and ending in one with only retrospective connections and containing at least one intermediate chapter. A synoptic segment consists of a pair of non-consecutive chapters, the first displaying only prospective links and the second only retrospective ones. Finally, an isolated segment, as its name suggests, consists of a chapter which is not linked to any other.

All three types of segment can be identified in the following example, which is a fragment of the macrostructure of CMEC.

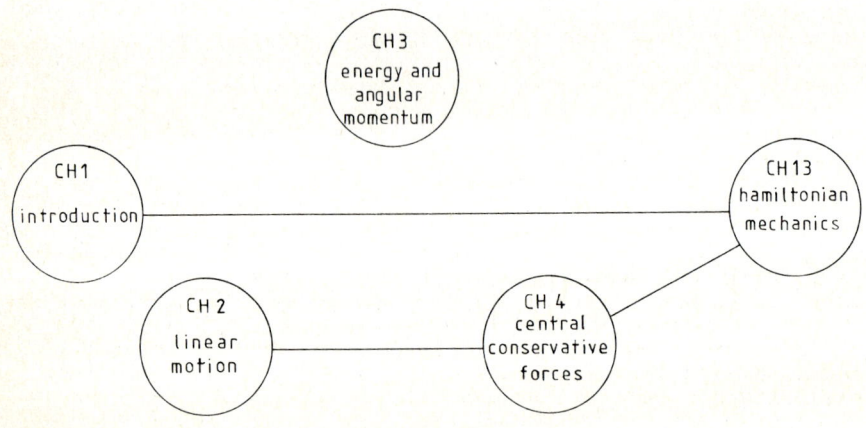

Figure 8.7

Here, chapters two, four and thirteen form a sequential segment, chapters one and thirteen form a synoptic segment and chapter three constitutes an isolated segment.

These three categories were identified on formal grounds. But they have functional significance. I suggest that they can be interpreted as follows. The sequential segment represents the development of topics of fundamental importance in the text. It often embodies a conceptual 'core', that is the expression of the major aspect of the subject matter. When the sequential segment consists largely of consecutive chapters, it suggests that in this respect the division of the text into discrete chapters is not conditioned by the dictates of the subject matter, as was discussed in the last section. The synoptic segment appears to be concerned with the development of one particular aspect of the subject matter, a sub-theme for example.

Synoptic segments can exist in parallel with sequential segments, as has already been seen in the case of CMEC. This provides crucial evidence for Roe's concept of non-linearity in science text (Roe 1977a). Roe argues strongly that science text cannot be viewed as a linear cumulative construct but that various configurations of chapters are feasible depending upon the purposes of the user in relation to the content of the text. It has already been seen that this view is encouraged by the science text authors themselves. I indicated in chapter two, however, that all of Roe's evidence is drawn either from the mathematical arguments of his texts or from the clues provided on the interactive plane by the author for the benefit of the reader in, for example, the introductory textual apparatus. What I have now established is that there can be an intrinsic discontinuity in the exposition of the subject matter of such texts for which there is linguistic evidence on the autonomous plane. Patterning on this plane is indicative of the way in which a vision of the world is constructed in text. Neither the vision nor text is linear.

There is some evidence for a somewhat different genesis for a particular class of synoptic segment. A unique function is performed by the synoptic segment consisting of the first and last chapters of a textbook. The first chapter often presents an overview of the whole text, raising the topics and problems which will receive detailed treatment later. The last chapter may fulfill a summary function or simply draw upon most of the topics treated earlier. As the most developed statement of the subject, it synthesises the diverse aspects covered in the course of the entire book. Consequently, these chapters have more in common with each other than they do with any of the other chapters in the textbook. This was clearly revealed in the macrostructures of the science texts.

Finally, an isolated segment can arise where a chapter deals with facets of the subject matter which are of general relevance to the whole text rather than crucial for the development of a particular aspect. In a sense, this kind of isolated segment is the *reductio ad absurdum* of the class of synoptic segment just discussed. It represents the case where the 'general' synoptic segment consists of a single chapter. A consequence of this function is that their position in the sequence of chapters is relatively unmotivated. Examples have already been quoted of authors indicating that the point at which such chapters are taken is largely a matter of taste. It will be seen that this interpretation is unequivocally valid for two of the isolated segments in BIPC and for several in CMEC and CREL. There still remains the possibility of a more straightforward interpretation in some cases. An isolated segment can represent the treatment of a comparatively self-contained aspect of the subject matter. This seems to be above all the case with BIPC and in the next section I shall discuss a possible reason for this.

I am arguing, then, that the segments constitutive of macro-structure correlate with important topic structuring functions and that they therefore have semantic significance. In a variety of ways, the content of the text is organised into a large-scale pattern. This pattern is revealed by the global lexical associations which enable the reader to discern different relations among the various aspects of the subject matter of the text. The result is that awareness of the macrostructure facilitates the reader's understanding of what the text is 'about', that is of the way in which a number of conceptual topics are more or less closely related in fairly complex ways.

Some confirmation for this view of the role of macrostructure in accounting for the phenomenon of aboutness may be obtained by investigating the extent to which the empirically observed macrostructures of the science texts correspond to the view of the organisation of each text put forward by its author. A correspondence between the author's statements about the structuring of his subject matter and the structural segments of macrostructure identified in the analysis would constitute <u>prima facie</u> evidence for the validity of the argument proposed here. It cannot, of course, be expected that my analysis will correspond with the author's description in all respects. In general, I would argue that it is prudent to treat with a certain amount of scepticism an author's statements regarding his text. There is usually more to a text than meets the eye even, or perhaps especially, of its 'onlie begetter'. If not, critics would be unemployed. This is perhaps trivially true of literature but I suspect it is also the case to a certain extent with expository text.

On the other hand, my analysis focuses on only one aspect of textual organisation. It was never intended to take account of all the factors contributing to the structuring of text, many of which an author might have in mind when describing his text. Nevertheless, it is not unreasonable to expect that if macrostructure is a genuine level of textual organisation, then the findings of this study will at least be compatible with the conventional opinions of the texts as expressed by the authors and may even throw light on the validity of their statements. At the same time, should a clear instance of incompatibility be revealed, the macrostructural data will not simply disappear. An explanation for the discrepancy would have to be sought either in inaccuracies of the analysis or inadequacy of the author's appreciation. It is, then, to the interpretation of the macrostructure of each science text that I now turn.

8.3 The Interpretation of Macrostructure

(i) The Macrostructure of ELEN

Ahmed and Spreadbury describe the structuring of their text as follows:

"....in Chapter 1, a discussion of the general principles

> of signal handling in electronic circuits, such as gain,
> input and output impedance, frequency response and
> coupling of networks, precedes the descriptions of
> circuits using active devices. Since these topics recur
> frequently throughout the whole subject of electronics
> they can subsequently be referred to with little
> repetition of ideas....The principles of negative and
> positive feedback are explained in chapters 5 and
> 6....These principles together with those of basic
> amplifiers described in Chapter 1 are held by us to be
> fundamental and ageless, and should provide the core of
> any electronics course. Chapters 2, 3 and 4 on f.e.t.s,
> bipolar transistors and integrated circuits
> respectively, describe how to realise amplifier blocks
> to fit into any system....These chapters may be read in
> any order. Chapter 7 describes more advanced circuits
> and applications....we have included multiple choice
> tests after chapters 2, 4 and 6...." (Ahmed and
> Spreadbury 1973 ppxi-xii).

This is a fairly sophisticated view of the text. It is conceived of as simultaneously integrated and modular. Some chapters are considered to act as foundations to the field as a whole while others stand in relative independence. The non-linearity of certain parts of the text is stressed but at the same time there is a strong implication that it falls naturally into internally coherent segments signalled by the location of multiple-choice quizzes.

The macrostructure of ELEN is reproduced in Figure 8.8 on the next page. Inspection of this figure suggests an interpretation which is broadly compatible with the views expressed by Ahmed and Spreadbury. The fact that chapters two, three, four and seven form a sequential segment is evidence for the arbitrary nature of the chapter divisions involved. The topics of these chapters are interrelated and there is no particular motivation, except in the case of the last chapter, for the ordering finally adopted in the text. This seems to be entirely in accord with the comment made by the authors regarding the order in which the earlier chapters may be read. Secondly, the authors' appreciation of chapter one as basic is supported by its analysis as an isolated segment. It will be recalled from the previous section that one reason that was postulated for the existence of isolated segments is that they treat of topics of general relevance to the text as a whole.

Finally, I believe it is possible on the basis of the macrostructural evidence to view the text as composed of three major themes. If for the moment the role of the final chapter is discounted, then three strands of development of topic can be discerned. It can be seen that chapters four, five and six each terminate a line of development. It seems plausible to suggest that one strand is formed by the general consideration of amplifiers and their circuitry. A second strand is composed of the notions which give rise to negative feedback. The third strand leads to the development of the concept of positive

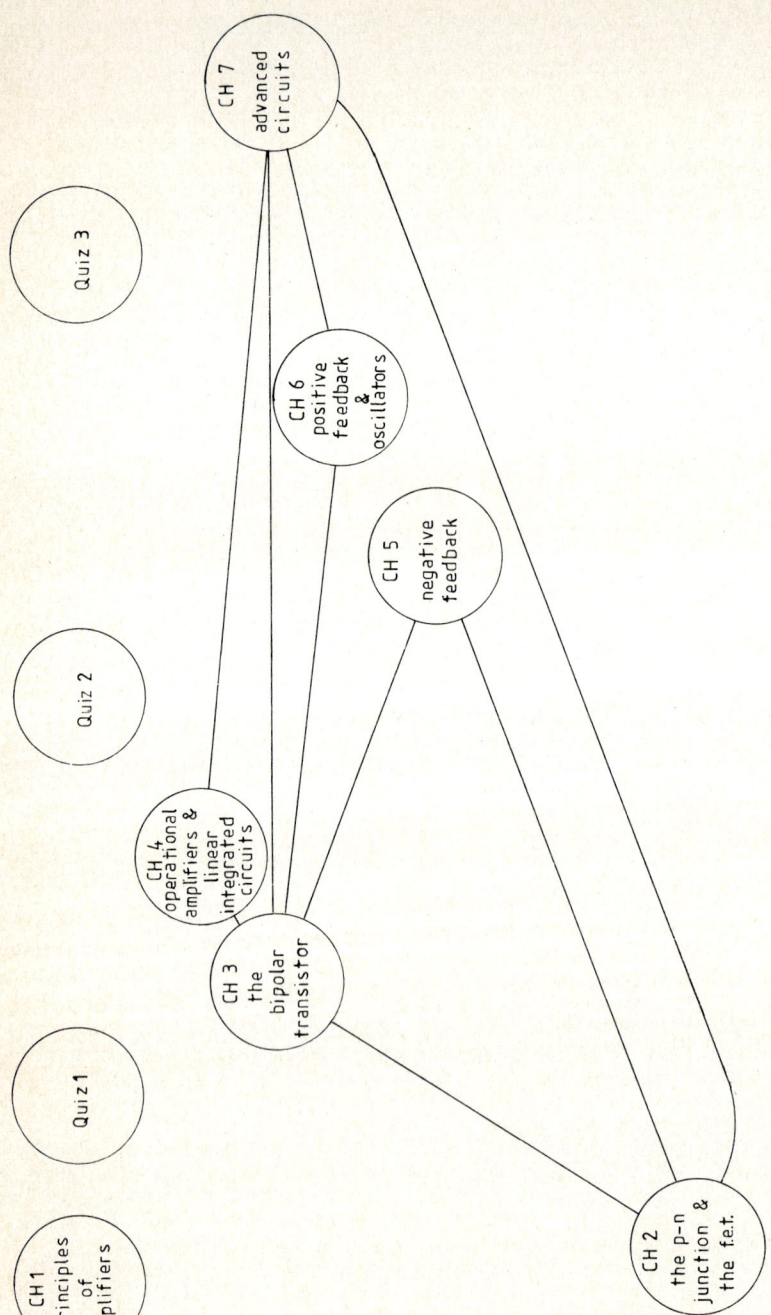

Figure 8.8 Macrostructure of ELEN

feedback. Without pressing the interpretation too far, there is evidence in the macrostructure for viewing these as distinct aspects of the subject matter of this text, given that there are no direct linkages between chapters four, five and six, each of which presumably represents the most fully worked out statement of the respective topics. It is therefore satisfying to note that Ahmed and Spreadbury consider "the principles of negative and positive feedback" as well as "those of basic amplifiers" as "fundamental and ageless" and that they "should provide the core of an electronics course". There can be little doubt that the macrostructural evidence is entirely compatible with the authors´ view of their text. If to the preceding considerations is added the observation that the text is clearly articulated by the quizzes, which are revealed as isolated segments, then I think it can be convincingly argued that the formal analysis of macrostructure is related quite unproblematically to the authors´ notions regarding the structuring of their work.

The macrostructural analysis, however, additionally suggests an element of teleological organisation not explicitly stated by the authors. Earlier I chose temporarily to overlook the role of the final chapter, which treats of advanced circuits. It is arguable that this chapter is a global organising element insofar as two of the three strands of development in the text might be construed as existing for the purpose of facilitating the exposition of the principles of advanced circuits. Thus there appears to be an overall logic to the structure of this text transcending the apparently arbitrary choice of chapter divisions described in the authors´ resume. The macrostructural analysis thus offers an insight into the organisation of the text not otherwise available.

(ii) The Macrostructure of CMEC

In contrast to the authors´ perception of ELEN, Kibble´s view of his text is rather more conventional:

> "The first chapters are primarily concerned with the mechanics of a single particle, and Chapter 6, which could be omitted without substantially affecting the remaining chapters, deals with potential theory. Systems of particles are discussed in Chapters 7 and 8, and rigid bodies in Chapters 9 and 10. The powerful methods of Lagrange are introduced at an early stage, and in simple contexts, and developed more fully in the last three chapters of the book. The final chapter contains a discussion of Hamiltonian mechanics...."
> (Kibble 1973 pxi).

This is a far more linear view of the text which does not seem to be so well supported by the evidence of the macrostructure presented in Figure 8.9. Nevertheless, there are some crucial points of contact.

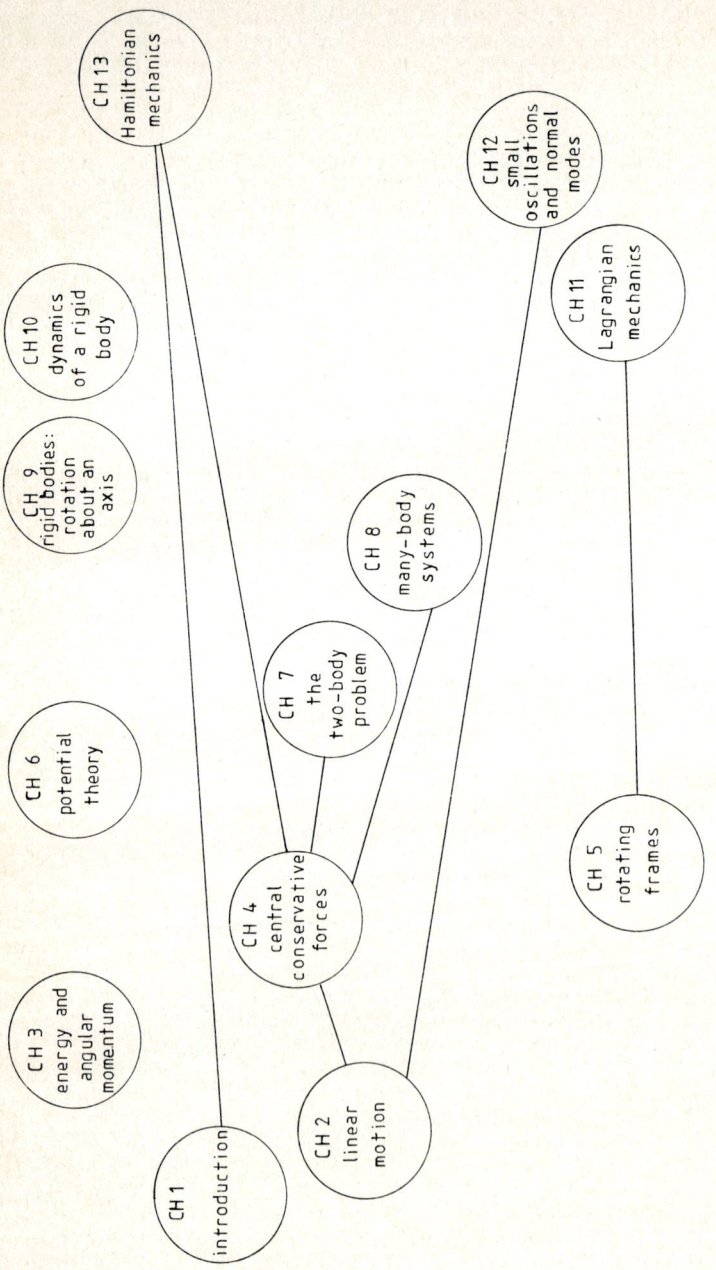

Figure 8.9 Macrostructure of CMEC

First, there appears to be a good correspondence between Kibble's description and the occurrence of isolated segments. The quotation above singles out chapter six as easily detachable from the succession of topics and this is confirmed by the macrostructural analysis. Similarly, it is clear that Kibble considers that there is a second conceptual break after chapter eight. In my analysis this coincides with the isolated segments formed by chapters nine and ten. Further, I have already suggested that in the majority of cases isolated segments treat of topics of general relevance in the text. The remaining isolated segment, chapter three, deals with a topic of general relevance; 'Energy and Angular Momentum' is clearly not concerned with the discussion of a particular facet of classical mechanics but with conceptual principles fundamental to the whole field.

In other respects the macrostructural analysis reveals aspects of the text not mentioned by Kibble but which make good sense in terms of classical mechanics. Chapters seven and eight seem each to conclude a basic line of development, in a somewhat similar manner to what has already been seen in the case of ELEN. The crucial notions of linear motion and central conservative forces having been established in chapters two and four, Kibble can then tackle the topic of the motion of members of systems of bodies, which is among the fundamental problems of classical mechanics. One sequential segment leads to the treatment of the two-body system, which is the simplest system of this kind. The other sequential segment leads to the more complex case of many-body systems. The macrostructure indicates that these two classes of system are only indirectly related in the text by the way they draw upon a common pool of ideas presented earlier. Many-body systems cannot, however, be viewed as a straightforward extension of the two-body case.

Finally, there is evidence for two synoptic segments. The first of these, that consisting of the first and last chapters, illustrate the case described earlier as a theoretical possibility where the survey function of the initial chapter relates it most closely to the integrative role of the final chapter. The other synoptic segment is formed by chapters five and eleven. Here the treatment of a distinct sub-theme related to the topic of rotational motion can be discerned. The concepts of rotating frames of reference and the precession of axes of rotation introduced in chapter five are of particular relevance to the topics treated in chapter eleven which include the 'Precession of a Symmetric Top' and the 'Pendulum Constrained to Rotate about an Axis'.

It is thus primarily the linear conceptualisation of the first five chapters which appears to be oversimplified in Kibble's appreciation. In other respects the analysis corresponds acceptably. It is not surprising that in order to treat of the motion of a single particle, concepts are introduced which reappear when more complex systems are considered. Consequently, the topics of the first five chapters are less discrete than Kibble's summary makes it appear. Thus the macrostructural analysis of CMEC not only confirms some crucial points in the author's view of his text, but also furnishes insights into structural relationships which have their logic in the treatment of the subject matter but which are not explicitly stated in the author's description.

(iii) The Macrostructure of CREL

The macrostructure of CREL is considerably simpler than that of either of the texts considered hitherto. This is also reflected in the author's explicit comments on the structure of his text which take the form of a brief description of how he exploits it in his teaching. Levenspiel has already been seen to say:

> "I leap over chapters 1, 2 and 3 in a lecture or two plus a few representative problems mainly as a means of presenting definitions of terms. Then since chapters 6, 7 and 8 reinforce the ideas of chapter 5, I only very briefly outline this material and right away plunge into problem solving" (Levenspiel 1972 pvi).

This is hardly a detailed description of the conceptual structure of CREL but it does provide a few useful clues. It is clear that Levenspiel regards the first three chapters as containing basic definitional material of general relevance to the main development later. He makes no mention of the function of chapter four, but it seems that the chapters from five onwards in his view form a coherent body.

Levenpiel's view receives satisfactory confirmation in the macrostructural analysis, which is diagrammed on the opposite page. The first two chapters are both isolated segments as might be predicted from the author's description. In addition chapter four, which is apparently of so little functional significance that it does not even receive a mention in Levenspiel's description, is also revealed as constituting an isolated segment. Its title, 'Introduction to Reactor Design', is another tell-tale clue. It can thus be regarded as a further introductory chapter of general relevance but not specifically related to any other section of the text.

It is also clear from the macrostructure that the author's view that chapters five to eight form an identifiable group is entirely justified. These chapters constitute a sequential segment realising the principal theme of the text. There is a logic in the development from the discussion of single ideal reactions in chapter five and reactor design for such reactions in chapter six proceeding to the consideration of multiple reactions in chapter seven. Finally, both single and multiple reactions are dealt with in chapter eight concerned with 'Temperature and Pressure Effects'.

Chapter eight is also involved in the one piece of evidence provided by the macrostructure which does not directly support the author's view. Chapter three, which from Levenspiel's

TERMS AND TEXT STRUCTURE 175

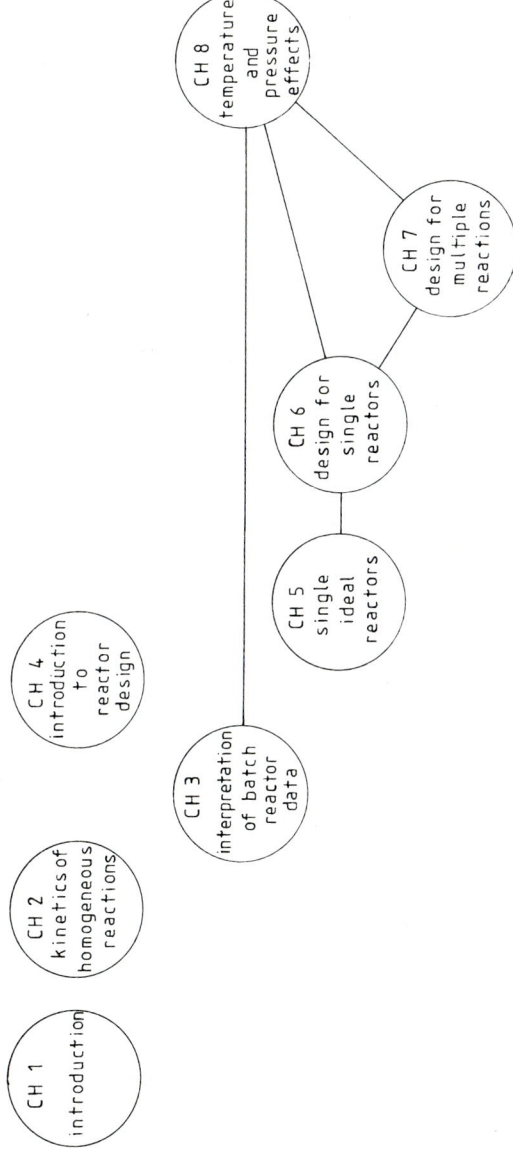

Figure 8.10 Macrostructure of CREL

description might be expected to be an isolated segment, in fact forms a synoptic segment with chapter eight. Whereas the sequential segment consisting of chapters five to eight appears to create a conceptual core to the text concerned with reactor design, the synoptic segment formed by chapters three and eight seems to constitute a sub-theme related to the interpretation of data obtained from reactors in the quest for a suitable rate equation for reactions. Temperature and pressure effects may be expected to play a crucial role in this. There is thus an acceptable rationale for the existence of the synoptic segment.

CREL, then, also demonstrates that the macrostructure revealed by the analysis sustains an interpretation in functional terms which both substantiates the author's view of the structure of his text and is reasonable in the light of conceptual relations which might be expected to obtain within the subject matter.

(iv) The Macrostructure of BIPC

This text displays the simplest macrostructure of all the science texts, as can be seen from the diagram on the opposite page. All but three chapters form isolated segments and the three exceptions constitute a simple sequential segment. With this evidence in mind, Gareth Morris' comments on the structure of his text are particularly revealing:

> "It will be obvious from its limited coverage that it is not intended as a comprehensive textbook of physical chemistry, nor as the basis for a course intended to convey disciplinary instruction in physical chemistry....its content falls into 'natural' sections that are virtually self-contained....Since pH is of prime interest to all biologists, Chapters 5 and 6 are devoted directly or indirectly to this topic" (Gareth Morris 1974 pviii).

It is unnecessary to stress the substantiation for Gareth Morris' "self-contained" sections by the high proportion of isolated segments in the macrostructure. I would simply like to draw attention to the reason for this state of affairs implied in the author's description. It is precisely because this text is not intended to be "a comprehensive textbook of physical chemistry" but rather selects discriminately from this field just those aspects considered to be of relevance to first year biology students that it is possible for Gareth Morris to regard his subject as consisting of "'natural' sections". Whatever conceptual coherence the field of physical chemistry might display will be disrupted in the interests of creating a cross-disciplinary text. It is also interesting to note that the first two chapters stand clearly apart from the themes of physical chemistry. They deal with independent revision topics in mathematics and systems of units rather than physical chemistry proper.

It is even more striking that of the three chapters forming the sequential segment, the relationship between two of them is

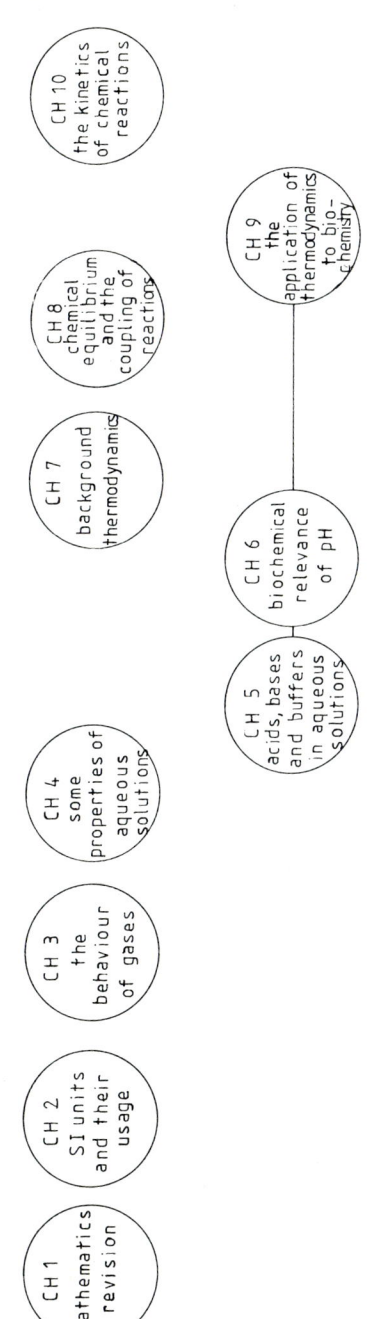

Figure 8.11 Macrostructure of BIPC

explicitly recognised by Gareth Morris. The term pH refers to the activity of ions in solution and it is thus evident that it forms a unifying theme linking chapters five and six, as the author makes clear. There is, however, no particularly obvious reason which would explain the presence of chapter nine in the sequential segment. Inspection of the networks actually responsible for creating the linkage suggests that the expression of notions relating to ´dilute solutions´ and ´equilibrium constants´ is a unifying factor but this is hardly illuminating.

Apart from this single problematic aspect, the correspondence between the macrostructure and Gareth Morris´ description is remarkably close. The reasonableness of the interpretation provided for the macrostructure of this text affords considerable support for the validity of the analytical procedures used in this study and for the value of the insights so gained into the large-scale structure of text.

(v) The Macrostructure of THRM

It was seen that BIPC has a highly discrete macrostructure. In complete contrast to this, THRM appears to be a text organised around an essentially homogeneous topic that can be developed in a fairly straightforward, cumulative manner. The macrostructure diagrammed on the opposite page illustrates how, with the exception of the first three chapters, each chapter is linked to every other. An approach to interpreting the macrostructure of THRM would be, then, to distinguish chapters one to three as being relatively less integrated from the core of the text carried by the sequential segment formed by chapters four to nine. There are, strictly speaking, two sequential segments. One is formed by chapters one, three and four to nine. The other consists of chapter two with chapters four to nine. It is the fact that chapters four to nine are common to both segments and that chapters one and three, on the one hand, or two on the other, can be conceived of as alternative approaches to this common core that is significant.

Taking the essential elements of the sequential segment first, then, it can readily be seen that there is no particular difficulty in providing an interpretation. First, it may be considered significant that chapter four, which is entitled ´Work and Heat´, initiates the segment. An indication of the absolutely basic role played by these concepts has already been given by Sonntag and Van Wylen in their second chapter which offers the definition of relevant concepts. There they state that

> "Thermodynamics is the science that deals with heat and work and those properties of substances that bear a relation to heat and work" (Sonntag and Van Wylen 1971 p17).

It is not surprising, then, to find that a chapter explicitly dealing with these two fundamental notions should initiate the

TERMS AND TEXT STRUCTURE 179

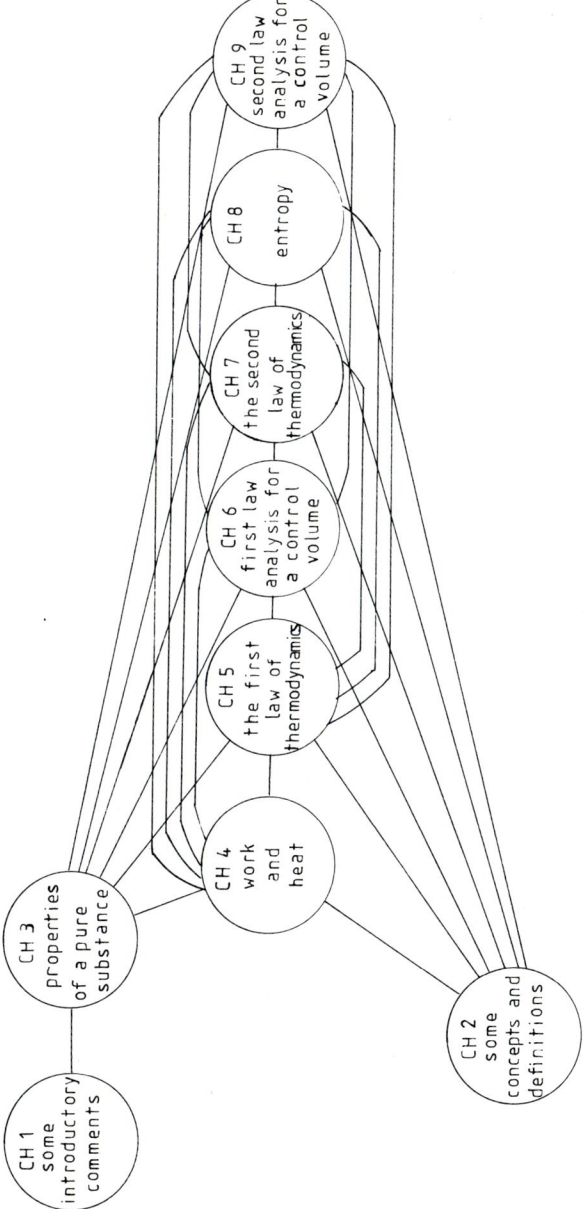

Figure 8.12 Macrostructure of THRM

segment that actualises the principal subject of the text.

Secondly, it is clear from the topics covered in each chapter as revealed by their titles that the logic of the development of this subject requires the sequential treatment that is revealed in the macrostructure. The text moves in a linear sequence from discussion of the first law of thermodynamics to its application in the analysis of a closed system, the ´control volume´. After this, the second law of thermodynamics can be considered. This requires somewhat more elucidation and consequently the concept of entropy, which is the subject of the second law, receives particular attention. The application of the second law can then be discussed in the same way as was done with the first law. In this progressive unfolding of the subject along a single track there is no requirement to, as it were, either pause at any wayside halts to take on board relatively isolated sub-topics or to sidetrack the development through the consideration of secondary themes.

The first three chapters stand apart insofar as they break the smooth sequencing of the presentation of topic. This is because, as is apparent in their titles, they are concerned with prerequisite topics rather than with the principal subject of the text. It might have been expected that, in common with the evidence provided by the macrostructures of the other science texts, these three chapters would have constituted isolated segments. I suggest, however, that in the particular case of classical thermodynamics, the authors are led to such an integrated treatment of the subject matter that even the introductory material exhibits a relatively high degree of lexical relatedness to the main argument.

8.4 General Principles of Macrostructure

The interpretations for the macrostructures of the science texts in the corpus developed in the last section were text specific. In this section an attempt will be made to take the exploration a step further by seeing whether it is possible to propose general principles which, when applied in specific instances, give rise to the macrostructures of individual texts. In particular, they must account for all the macrostructures observed in the study.

In order to achieve this kind of generality, it is necessary to move to a higher level of abstraction at which common features in the observed macrostructures can be observed. It may seem that the results presented in the previous section are unpromising material. The macrostructures discussed there appear to be individual and distinctive and the interpretations that I offered might be construed as closing off the possibility of generalisation. Clearly it will not be easy to detect general features and in consequence the view I shall develop here is somewhat tentative. I believe, nevertheless, that it is possible to explain the various manifestations of macrostructure in terms of a relatively simple formalisation and as the result of the operation of certain underlying

TERMS AND TEXT STRUCTURE 181

generative principles.

As a first step in this direction I recall the distinction made earlier between the ´process´ and the ´product´ perspectives. The adoption of a product perspective is required by interpretation and, in this instance, suggests a general categorisation of chapters in terms of their macrostructural role. I shall first propose a logical classification and then relate this to a categorisation that seems to be imposed by the empirical findings.

Two types of distinction can be usefully made. First, chapter linkages may be viewed as ´prospective´ or ´retrospective´. Secondly, a link may be from a chapter to none, one or more than one other chapter. These notions generate all the logical possibilities of interchapter linkage. The possibilities are listed below.

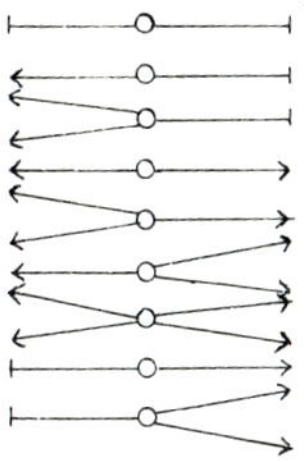

		Retrospective links	Prospective links
(1)		none	none
(2)		one	none
(3)		more than one	none
(4)		one	one
(5)		more than one	one
(6)		one	more than one
(7)		more than one	more than one
(8)		none	one
(9)		none	more than one

<u>Figure 8.13</u>

It can be seen from this figure that the logical possibilities fall into four groups. The first group has a single member consisting of the chapter with no links, (1). The other three groups are those chapters with no prospective links, (2) and (3); chapters with both retrospective and prospective links, (4), (5), (6) and (7); chapters with no retrospective links, (8) and (9).

Inspection of the empirical data discussed in the previous section suggests a slightly different scheme. It will be seen below, however, that it is easily relatable to the logical categories just described. I propose that with respect to its structural function a chapter can be assigned uniquely to one of five categories. These categories, together with their criterial of identification, are:

    (1)   source: a chapter linked only to one or more subsequent chapters.

    (2)   medial: a chapter linked to one or more preceding chapters and only one subsequent chapter.

(3) pivot: a chapter linked to a preceding source and several subsequent chapters.

(4) goal: a chapter linked only to one or more preceding chapters.

(5) isolate: a chapter with no links to any other.

These categories will be denoted by the initials S, M, P, G and I. This scheme then gives the following empirical realisation of the logical categories:

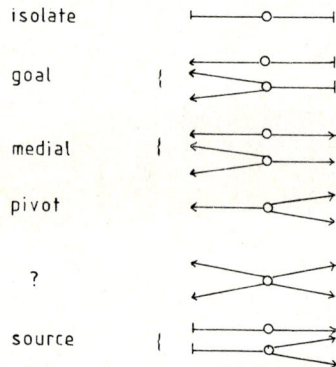

Figure 8.14

There are two points of interest here. First, the logical group consisting of chapters having both prospective and retrospective links has been split between the categories of medial and pivot. This corresponds to an important distinction in the macrostructure of text between chapters which maintain the continuity of the argument, whether or not they draw their material from one or more preceding chapters, and those which set up the possibility of a subsequent diversification of the argument. The structural role of the latter type, that is the pivot, appears intuitively to have the greater importance. It will be seen later in this section that pivot is indeed a critical macrostructural category.

Secondly, no empirical realisation of the type (7) logical category was found. This I take to be of considerable significance. On general principles, it is to be required that at least one logical possibility be excluded by theory. If every possibility were allowed within the theory, then the predictive power of the theory may be trivial. As soon, however, as the theory excludes a logical possibility, it acquires explanatory force.

In the particular case under consideration, a plausible

explanation for the exclusion of category (7) can be offered. I suggest that it is highly unlikely that a single chapter will serve the dual function of integrating material from several preceding sections of text only to fragment the argument by distributing the flow of information among a number of subsequent chapters. The point of its integrating function would be negated were this the case.

This means, moreover, that a test for the theory of macrostructure that I am now developing can be proposed. The theory predicts that no text will display a macrostructure in which a chapter is linked to more than one chapter both retrospectively and prospectively. Consequently, a suitable falsifying instance would be the discovery of such a chapter. Now I do not believe in Popper's notion of the single critical experiment but rather accept with Lakatos that research programmes tend to exist in "a sea of anomalies" (Popper 1979, Lakatos 1978). At the same time, the discovery of such a counterexample would clearly entail the need for modifications to the theory. Thus, although I would agree with the falsificationalists that no theory can be conclusively proven to be true, I suggest that until a number of counterinstances is produced, further examples of macrostructure will constitute corroborating evidence for the theory.

It is now possible to represent the macrostructures discussed in the previous section in the more abstract notation which has been developed here. First, however, it is convenient to adopt a simplifying assumption. If two consecutive chapters ´b´ and ´c´ are linked to each other and both are linked to an immediately preceding third chapter ´a´, thus

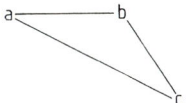

Figure 8.15

then it will be assumed that this configuration arises from a transitivity principle. That is, ´a´ appears similar to ´c´ because ´a´ is similar to ´b´ and ´b´ is similar to ´c´. In such a case, the link ´a-c´ will be omitted from the representation, thus

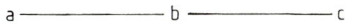

Figure 8.16

It is reasonable to suppose that this kind of configuration arises from the exposition of a topic across a number of chapters and that, in consequence, there is nothing distinctively significant about the ´a-c´ link. It merely reflects the fact of a conventional division of a continuous exposition into chapters. The convention adopted here affects primarily the representation of THRM, as will be seen shortly.

The macrostructures of the five science texts can now be represented as follows, where the numbers identify the chapters:

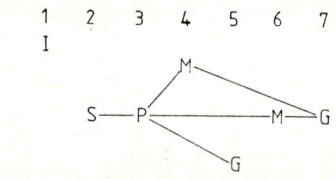

Figure 8.17 ELEN

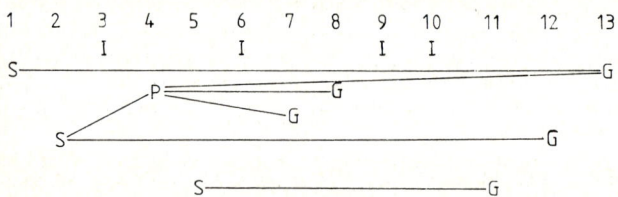

Figure 8.18 CMEC

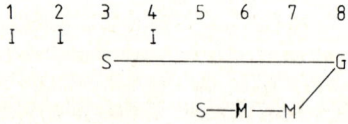

Figure 8.19 CREL

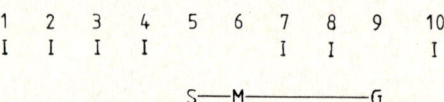

Figure 8.20 BIPC

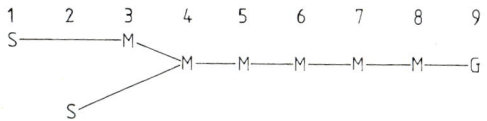

Figure 8.21 THRM

Three comments on these diagrams are in order. First, it will be recalled that the sample available in the corpus covers the entire textbook only in the cases of ELEN and CMEC. In the remaining cases the text is truncated and consequently the assignment of chapters to categories must be provisional. It is required, however, that the partial evidence provided by the remaining three texts should be consistent with the view of macrostructure to be developed.

Secondly, the quizzes have been ignored in the representation of the macrostructure of ELEN. It was noted in the last section that these are all isolated segments. It was consequently felt that nothing was to be gained by including these uncharacteristic and idiosyncratic features in the interpretation.

Finally, the simplifying convention discussed above applies to chapters two to nine and chapters three to nine in THRM. In other words, within these limits each chapter is linked to every other, with the exception that chapters two and three are not themselves linked to each other. In a sense, the segmentation into chapters of the stretch of text from chapter four to chapter eight (and possibly beyond) is arbitrary. To put it another way, no particular structural significance attaches to any of these chapters individually. The representation is intended to capture this without overburdening the diagram in unnecessary complexity. This analysis has the advantage that it enables a rigorous definition of the segments in terms of which the individual macrostructures were interpreted in the last section to be developed. A ´sequential segment´ can now be defined as any sequence of macrostructural categories beginning with a source and ending with a goal which includes either one or more medials or a pivot. A ´synoptic segment´ consists simply of a source linked to a goal with no intermediate category intervening. Finally, an ´isolated segment´ is formed by an isolate.

Despite the increased clarity of statement conferred by this more abstract conceptualisation, the macrostructures represented in figures 8.16-8.20 still appear quite heterogeneous and there would at first sight seem to be little prospect of deriving from them any general principles of formation. Closer inspection, however, suggests that an initial distinction can be drawn between those macrostructures which contain a pivot and those which do not.

Examples of texts which do not have a pivot in their macrostructure are BIPC and THRM. A general representation of the macrostructures of these texts can be provided by the following formula, where parentheses indicate optional repetition of an obligatorily occurring category:

$$(S) - (M) - G$$

This means that the first type of macrostructure must consist of an arbitrary number of sources followed by an arbitrary number of medials leading to a unique goal.

It might, however, be objected that it is the chance incompleteness of the sample for both BIPC and THRM that accounts for the lack of pivot and that the distinction proposed between the two classes of macrostructure is invalid. In the present state of knowledge, this objection is hypothetical but I think it unlikely that the criticism has force. First, if the macrostructure of these texts were to include a pivot, it might be expected to occur at a relatively early point in the text. The pivot is a category which diversifies the treatment of the subject through its prospective links to a number of subsequent chapters. This is a feature that may be anticipated to appear early in the development of the subject, following immediately on whatever introductory or ´framing´ material is included. The evidence from ELEN and CMEC confirms this view. In both cases the pivot is located in an early chapter. Secondly, in BIPC at least the sample falls only slightly short of the full text. The first ten out of the total of twelve chapters are included. It is thus impossible for either of the missing chapters to be categorised as a pivot. Chapter eleven can by its location only be an isolate, medial, goal or, what is most unlikey, a source. The possibilities for chapter twelve are more restricted still. It can be only an isolate or a goal. Although it is possible that an earlier chapter turns out to be linked to one of the missing chapters, this is intuitively highly unlikely. The trend of the macrostructure suggests strongly that the category of medial will simply be repeated. This is also the likelihood in THRM.

Accepting, then, the presence or absence of a pivot as probable if not conclusive justification for two types of macro-structure, the second type containing a pivot can now be considered. This is exemplified by ELEN and CREL. Using the same convention for parentheses as above and with braces indicating an optional element, the macrostructures of these two texts can be represented in general form as follows:

TERMS AND TEXT STRUCTURE   187

$$(S) - \{M\} - P - \{M\} - (G)$$

This means that texts in this category are constituted of an arbitrary number of sources leading to a single pivot which leads to an arbitrary number of goals. A medial may optionally intervene between any S - P or P - G sequence. I do not exclude the possibility of discovering macrostructures containing more than one pivot, though the present corpus provides no evidence of such a case.

Two classes of macrostructure have thus been distinguished on the basis of the presence or absence of a pivot. Another classification, however, can be developed based on the presence or absence of isolates and plurality as opposed to singularity of sources and goals. This categorisation is independent of the first in that it gives rise to a cross-classification, although the possibility of multiple goals can only arise in the class of macrostructures containing a pivot. Thus if the presence of a relatively high proportion of isolates is taken as criterial, the texts classified so far are found to form two new classes. BIPC and CMEC are grouped together, having an above average number of isolates, whilst THRM and ELEN form a class for the opposite reason. This classification is maintained for those macrostructures containing a pivot if the singularity or plurality of sources and goals is taken as criterial. Thus not only does CMEC have a relatively large number of isolates, it also displays considerable plurality of sources of goals. ELEN contrasts with CMEC in both respects.

There appear, then, to be two distinct dimensions along which the macrostructure of science text can be classified. These are numbers of pivot (P) and proportion of isolates and/or sources and goals (I/S.G.). The classification arrived at so far can thus be represented as in figure 8.22:

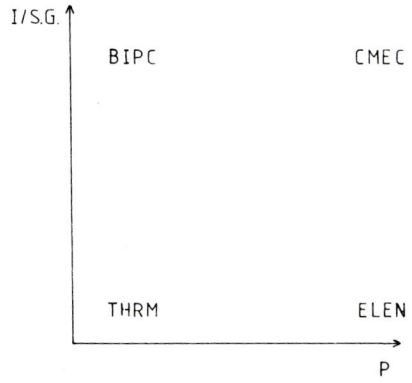

Figure 8.22

If it proves possible to interpret the two dimensions in figure 8.22 in terms of underlying ´factors´, this will mean that the objective of the present section has been achieved. For such an interpretation would be a statement of the immanent principles which account for the apparently diverse manifestations of macrostructure observed in the corpus. I shall now propose such an interpretation.

The vertical dimension of increasing proportion of I/S.G. corresponds to the increasing ´differentiation´ of the subject matter. Differentiation refers to the degree to which the subject can be presented as an homogeneous body of knowledge as opposed to a compendium of distinct, though possibly interrelated lines of enquiry. In a highly differentiated text, the subject matter is presented as a number of distinct topics. These topics may be treated in isolation as, for example, are the ´Heat´, ´Light´, ´Sound´ and ´Electricity and Magnetism´ of the school physics textbook. The topics may be related to each other, without for that losing their individual identity. At a higher level of exposition in physics, for instance, atomic, nuclear and particle physics all represent distinctive lines of enquiry though all are related through the concepts of quantum mechanics. A high degree of differentiation reveals itself in macrostructural terms, in the first case as the presence of a relatively large number of isolates and in the second as a high proportion of sources and goals.

On the other hand, a weakly differentiated text results when the subject matter is presented as a relatively homogeneous conceptual field with few distinctive features. This may be true, for example, of textbooks on microbiology or calculus. It is possible that the text may explore more than one line of development but all lines tend to lead to the same end and represent variations on the same basic topic rather than genuinely distinct conceptual areas. The text is comparatively integrated and the motivation for segmentation is correspondingly weak. Consequently, a low degree of differentiation results in a macrostructure with few isolates and a limited number of sources and goals.

The horizontal dimension determined by the presence of pivots corresponds to the possibility of ´serialisation´ in the presentation of the subject matter. Serialisation refers to the degree to which the subject matter lends itself to sequential exposition. In other words, it concerns the extent to which the text can be processed in sequence with a minimum of cross-reference. This possibility can arise from two causes. The exposition of the subject matter may be straightforwardly cumulative with each chapter building on the totality of its predecessors. Alternatively, the text may be so highly differentiated that it is segmented entirely into isolates. In this case there is no possibility of cross-reference and the text can only be processed sequentially, although the sequence is of course arbitrary. In this respect ´serialisation´ must be distinguished from Roe´s concept of linearity which always implies a determinate ordering (Roe 1977a).

Thus in texts characterised by the absence of a pivot the
organising principle along this dimension can be conceived of
as one of 'serial' development. The text moves sequentially
from source through intermediate chapters to a final goal.
There is a sensation of teleology. In contrast, texts which
include a pivot in the macrostructure may be characterised as
embodying a principle of 'parallel' development. Clearly,
given the inescapable ultimate of the successivity of textual
substance, this does not mean that different aspects of the
subject are treated simultaneously. It does imply, however,
that more than one aspect is kept in view over a number of
chapters. First one topic is discussed, then a second followed
possibly by further development of the first topic before a
return is made to the second topic, and so on. Thus several
aspects of the subject matter may be treated in an overlapping
manner over a number of chapters. The development 'leap-frogs'
rather than runs in 'relay'.

The two dimensions should not be confused. It must not be
supposed that increasing integration implies increased
serialisation or that a high degree of differentiation of the
subject matter, for example, necessarily implies parallel
development. This will become clearer by considering the
distinctions revealed among the four texts when they are
classified according to the place occupied by their
macrostructures in the scheme developed so far. This is done
in the figure below:

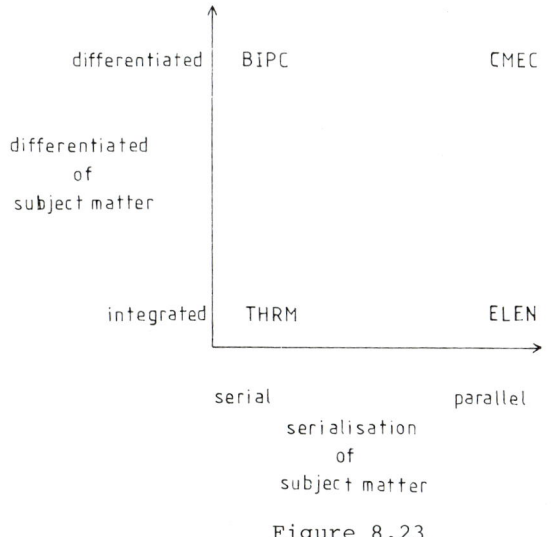

Figure 8.23

The subject matter of the sample of THRM in the study is
classical thermodynamics, the study of heat and work in closed
systems. The principal distinctions made in this subject

crystallise around the three laws of thermodynamics. These are the zeroth law, concerned with the measurement of temperature; the first law, dealing with the conservation of energy; and the second law, embodying the principle of the overall increase in entropy. These laws can be presented in sequence and can all be discussed in terms of idealised closed systems. The subject matter of the text can be regarded as homogeneous and cumulative. Consequently, a macrostructural organisation which is basically integrated and serial is a possibility. This accounts for the position of THRM on the graph above.

In electronics a relatively small number of concepts inform the whole subject and are discussed, in ELEN at least, in terms of virtually a single notion, that of amplifier circuits. Thus, like THRM, ELEN also deals with a comparatively homogeneous subject matter. Unlike THRM however, it is not possible to treat electronics in the same straightforward additive fashion. The concepts of positive and negative feedback, for example, whilst drawing upon an identical substrate of ideas, do not lend themselves to cumulative treatment but represent alternative topics. Thus an integrated text is not necessarily serially organised. In contrast to THRM, then, ELEN displays parallel development.

In complete opposition to ELEN stands BIPC. Whereas ELEN is integrated and parallel, BIPC is differentiated and serial. It was noted in the last section that Gareth Morris´ view of his text as treating of a number of relatively self-contained topics was entirely consistent with the evidence provided by the macrostructural analysis. In other words, the text is highly differentiated. At the same time, there are comparatively few points of contact among the various matters treated. It was seen that the text includes topics as varied as mathematical fundamentals, the behaviour of gases, ionic activity in solution and chemical kinetics. There are few, if any, unifying principles underlying this heterogeneity. There is little question of interrelation and consequently no requirement for parallel treatment. The text is thus serial in development. It is perhaps no chance that this conclusion should be reached of what is the only cross-disciplinary text in the corpus. Gareth Morris presumably selected just those aspects of chemistry which he considered of relevance to student biologists. He is not concerned with whatever latent conceptual unity a chemist might see in his subject.

This is in marked contrast to CMEC which shares the feature of differentiation with BIPC but where the relatively heterogeneous topics are complexly interrelated. Although classical mechanics, which is the subject of CMEC, relies upon a small number of concepts, these are used to account for a wide variety of phenomena. Using the basic concepts of position and time, together with a number of derived concepts such as force and mass, CMEC treats of topics as apparently diverse as the motion of the earth and the formation of tides, oscillatory movement and the phenomenon of resonance, the interaction of electrically charged bodies and elastic

collisions. Thus the context of the discussion is constantly
changing. At the same time these topics are interrelated at a
more abstract level, in part through their all drawing upon the
same fundamental notions and in part through the general
relevance of Lagrangian techniques, which Kibble explicitly
draws attention to. Thus, like ELEN, CMEC displays parallel
development. In contrast to ELEN, however, it is a relatively
differentiated text. But if in this latter respect it
resembles BIPC, it differs in that it is not serially
organised.

Thus THRM and CMEC form one pair of polar opposites whilst ELEN
and BIPC constitute a second pair. In the first pair the
integration and seriality of THRM are opposed to the
differentiation and parallelism of CMEC. In the second pair,
the contrast is between the integration and parallelism of ELEN
as opposed to the differentiation and seriality of BIPC. These
four texts have thus been treated as ideal polar types. It
should be recalled, however, that the two dimensions of
interpretation are continuous. In other words, it is
reasonable to expect in practice gradations of integration and
seriality.

Bearing this in mind, it is now possible to locate the text
which has been omitted from the discussion hitherto. CREL has
a macrostructure which places it somewhere between the extremes
represented by THRM and BIPC along the dimension of
differentiation. It has some isolates whereas THRM has none;
but these amount to a considerably smaller proportion of the
total text than is the case with BIPC. There is no immediate
difficulty in locating CREL along the horizontal axis of
serialisation. There is no pivot in the macrostructure of
CREL. There is, however, a faint suggestion of the possibility
of parallel development in the comparative independence of the
S - G segment formed by chapters three and eight. It may be
that an analysis of the whole text up to the final chapter
fifteen would in fact result in the recategorisation of an
earlier chapter as a pivot. This must remain an intriguing
possibility for further investigation. For the present the
available evidence allows me to complete the classification as
in figure 8.24 on the next page.

I have argued that the observed variety of macrostructure can
be successfully accounted for in terms of the interaction of
two basic principles of large-scale text organisation. These
principles represent linguistic options in the creation of
subject matter. The subject matter may be viewed as
homogeneous or heterogeneous and the text will be
correspondingly integrated or differentiated. At the same
time, the text may construct the subject matter serially,
rather as a computer might execute jobs sequentially, though in
some cases the sequence might be arbitrary. Alternatively, the
text may develop topics in parallel, just as a time-sharing
system cycles round the current state of many jobs in a multi-
user environment. My claim is that all science textbooks can
be described in terms of these two principles and that they are

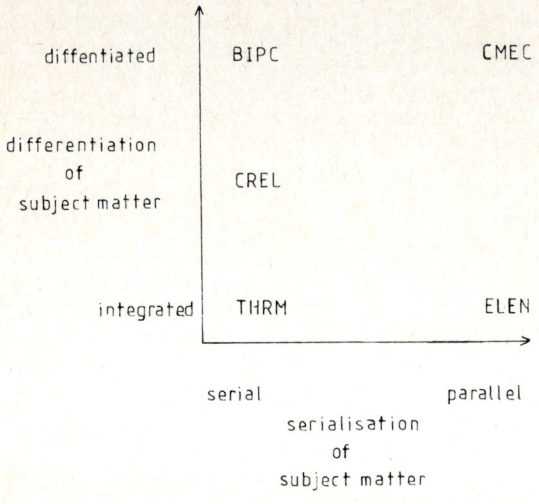

Figure 8.24

explained by the possibilities of articulation inherent in the field of knowledge of which a particular text is an actualisation.

Thus I have both substantiated and amplified the view of science text developed by Roe (Roe 1977a). It will be recalled that I criticised his position in chapter two on the grounds that it rests on inadequate empirical foundations. The present study has furnished the missing evidence. I would claim in addition, however, that in its postulation of theoretical principles my analysis adds an explanatory dimension missing from Roe's descriptive study. As a result, a coherent and illuminating view of science text begins to emerge as well as a theoretical apparatus for the description of text structure. It is to a consideration of the implications of the study for linguistic theory that I turn in the next section.

8.5 A Hierarchy of Units of Relation

In the course of this study I have introduced a number of different units which were required by the analysis. They are, from the fundamental category of lemma to the high-level notion of macrostructure, all relatively unfamiliar in linguistic analysis when compared to the well established categories of syntax, for example. Some, such as the categories of macrostructural description discussed in the preceding two sections, have been introduced for the first time. For a theory to be internally consistent it must state not only what categories are established but also how they are related to each other. The relationships among the categories needed at various stages of the analysis were described as they were introduced but the time has now come to present a comprehensive summary.

Although the area of linguistic activity that has been explored has required a distinctive methodology, it is nonetheless possible to conceive of the units postulated in the course of the investigation as related in a taxonomic hierarchy, which is a form of organisation well understood in other branches of linguistics. The point of a taxonomic hierarchy is that the categories at the different levels are similar in kind and consequently the levels are related to each other by the same type of relationship which is that of constituency. In grammar, for example, the rank scale of units is a taxonomic hierarchy. Morpheme, word, group and clause are all slot-filling units and enter into constituency relations with each other.

As far as the lexical structure of text is concerned, the situation is somewhat more complex. If, following Halliday's view, lexis is considered to be 'most delicate grammar' (Halliday 1961), this implies that the phenomena categorised as lexical will present a greater apparent heterogeneity than is the case in grammar. The more delicate the analysis, the more varied the appearance of its objects. The systematic study of lexis is in consequence more abstract than that of grammar. This was evident in the present study insofar as it was found necessary to adopt an indirect methodology and the objects of investigation were relations rather entities.

This latter point is crucial. A taxonomic hierarchy of units of textual analysis does not consist of directly observable categories comparable to those of the grammatical scale of rank. It is, rather, constituted of more abstract categories. Each level in the hierarchy represents a particular type of relation. Thus they cannot be directly perceived though they can be made manifest using the kind of techniques adopted in the study. Each type of relation is realised in text through selection and ordering of linguistic items which are specific to the particular text. Thus the realisations of categories at any level of the hierarchy are not themselves the elements of the hierarchy. These remain the abstract types of organisation which underlie the different realisations. At the same time, realisations at any level enter into relations characteristic of the next higher level and in this sense the constituency relation can be said to obtain among the levels. A level, then, consists of the class of relation appropriate for the units which are realisations of the type of relation at the next lower level.

On this basis a hierarchy of units of organisation can be established. In the discussion of text reduction procedures in chapter three, the lemma emerged as the minimal unit of analysis. Below the lemma the area of interest relevant to answering the questions posed here is left. The lemma is a type of organisation obtaining among words which are felt to have a fundamental semantic identity despite syntactically conditioned variation. Thus it is an abstraction comparable to the phoneme, for example. It has no substantial existence as such but can be inferred to underlie a variety of surface phenomena. A particular word can be said to be a realisation of a lemma but the lemma itself is unobservable. It is thus the fundamental level of relation in the hierarchy.

Lemmata were seen to associate in collocations. It must be recalled from chapter three that in this study the term collocation denotes an abstract notion. Collocation has been viewed throughout as the relation which allows two linguistic items to co-occur within a certain span. Thus collocation is the category of relation for the realisations of the class of organisation at the level of the lemma.

In chapter five I described how it is possible to identify lexical networks on the basis of repeated instances of collocation. These can be seen as a higher order of organisation bringing into relation particular realisations of collocation. The structure of the hierarchy is thus maintained. Networks in their turn permitted me to detect patterning extending over complete textbooks. The categories which suggested themselves at this new level I called sequential, synoptic and isolated segments. All three categories operate at the same level of generality and are members of the class 'segment'. The segment, then, is the type of relation appropriate for realisations of the category of network. Segments are constitutive of and themselves organised by 'macrostructure', which is the highest level of textual organisation identified by the study.

Thus the hierarchy can be diagrammed as in figure 8.25 below:

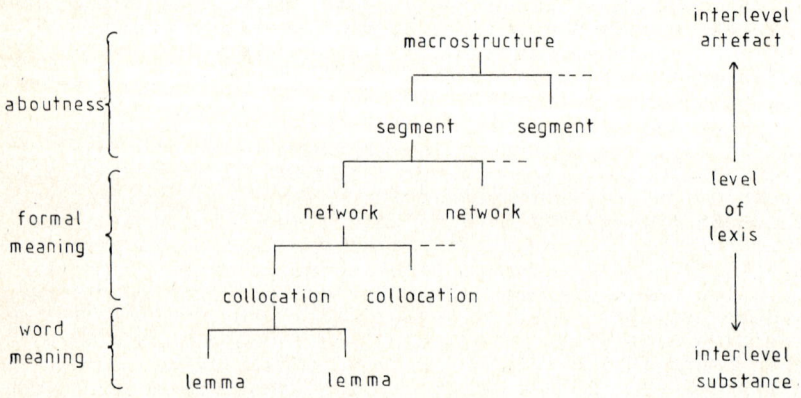

Figure 8.25

At all levels, except the lowest, realisations may combine iteratively to create a category of the next higher level. A collocation may only be of realisations of two lemmata. There is in principle, however, no restriction on the number of collocations which may constitute a network or the number of networks which may contribute to the structuring of a segment. Here the limit is defined in terms of strength of association. A higher level category is identified at that point where continuation of the process of association of realisations at the lower level would result in a failure to distinguish between intra-unit and inter-unit strength of association.

In terms of the Firthian scheme of levels of linguistic analysis, the categories operate on the lexical level with those at either extreme of the hierarchy interfacing to other levels of analysis. Thus macrostructure can be viewed as a feature operating at the interlevel between lexis and the level of context of situation. Similarly, at the other extreme, the lemma functions at the interlevel between the linguistic system of the word and the level of morphology.

Finally, the scheme posited in figure 8.25 has the advantage that it allows for a neat correlation between the different levels and various kinds of meaning. Word meaning enters into the scheme of analysis through the lemma. Formal meaning is accounted for at the levels of collocation and network. The kind of meaning which gave rise to this enquiry and which I call aboutness is associated with the higher levels of segment and macrostructure.

It is now possible to see more clearly the reason that a hierarchical Cluster Analysis procedure gives acceptable results when applied to the data extracted from the corpus. I suggested in the course of the discussion of Cluster Analysis in chapter four that it might not be unreasonable to suppose that the kind of structures I wished to investigate in text might be describable in terms of a hierarchical organisation. At that stage, however, the suggestion was speculative. It can now be seen that there exists a plausible structural compatibility between the textual phenomena which have been investigated and the methodology and that this correspondence can be asserted not merely in general terms but in detail.

8.6 Conclusion

After having considered in the last chapter the nature of textual organisation within the chapter, in this chapter the findings of the study at scales from the chapter as a whole to the complete textbook have been discussed. First, the evidence provided by the study for structuring at the level of the chapter was presented. This then led to the development of the notion of similarity of networks. On this basis it proved possible to establish links among similar networks found in different chapters. In this way it was shown that lexical networks not only organise text on the intermediate scale of the chapter but also give rise to a global structure for text.

Thus the study furnished convincing evidence for the validity
of the notion of macrostructure. Consequently the theoretical
position established in the first part of this book was
justified and the methodology developed in the second part was
shown to be effective in revealing large-scale structuring.
These findings also enabled the status of the chapter to be
reconsidered from which it emerged clearly that, in science
text at least, it is a largely conventional category.

Macrostructure was then discussed in terms of the segmentation
of the text that it reveals. Three types of text segment were
recognised, the sequential, the synoptic and the isolated
segments. It was argued that each fulfills a characteristic
function in science text. This claim was substantiated by
interpreting the macrostructure of each science text in these
terms. It was shown that the segmentation of the texts
accounts for intuitively reasonable ways of conceptualising the
various subject matters and, in particular, that the
macrostructures correspond well to the authors´ own perceptions
of the way in which their texts are structured.

The outlines of a general theory of macrostructure were then
developed. It was claimed that all the observed forms of
macrostructure could be accounted for in terms of the operation
of two principles underlying an author´s perception of his
subject matter. These are the principles of serialisation and
differentiation.

Finally, on the basis of the findings it was shown how a
theoretical model for text analysis could be established. It
was argued that the descriptive categories used in the analysis
are hierarchically related within the level of lexis. Each
level represents the class of relation obtaining among
realisations of the relation defined by the next lower level
in the hierarchy. It was also seen that different internal
levels within the hierarchy relate to different kinds of
linguistic meaning.

The findings considered in this chapter prompt a further set of
questions. The discussion has hitherto confined itself to the
implications of the results for the science texts in the
corpus. It will be recalled, however, that a number of non-
science texts were also included in the corpus for purposes of
comparison. Thus the question is raised of the extent to which
the findings of this chapter also apply to the non-science
texts. Is macrostructure restricted to science text only or is
it equally a feature of the non-science texts? If the latter
is the case, it could then be argued that it arises from
general constraints on the use of language <u>in extenso</u>. If,
on the other hand, the study were to produce no clear evidence
for macrostructure in these texts, then it would be reasonable
to enquire whether the existence of macrostructure can be
viewed as a defining characteristic of science text. The next
chapter considers how far the findings of the study clarify
these issues.

CHAPTER 9

TEXT STRUCTURE AND TEXT TYPOLOGY

9.1   The Range Index

At the end of the last chapter I raised the question whether macrostructure should be regarded as a defining characteristic of science text or whether it is a structural feature of all text. It has been seen that the lexical networks responsible for the existence of macrostructure in science text are constituted principally of lemmata underlying ´content´ words. The possibility exists, then, that macrostructure is essentially a function of scientific terminology. On the other hand, it is an open question at this stage whether in non-science text classes of vocabulary might be found which play a similar role to that of the technical lexis of science text. It could be, for example, that vocabulary carrying the major themes and imagery in a literary work will show a similar tendency to form systematic patterns of association. It might then give rise to a notion of macrostructure analogous to that discovered in science text. This is an empirical question which forms the starting point of the next stage of the enquiry.

In order to test this hypothesis an analysis of the three non-science texts included in the corpus was undertaken using an identical procedure to that described in chapters three and four. It was necessary, then, to devise a means of characterising the degree of macrostructural organisation of a text so that the results from the science and non-science texts could be compared.

The basis of macrostructure is the extent to which the collectivity of nodes in a text tends to select the same set of collocates throughout the text. The more restricted is the set of collocates of each node, the more similar will be the lexical networks found in different text intervals and hence the more marked will be the macrostructure of the text. This assumes, of course, that a reasonable proportion of the nodes collocate with each other. If this condition is not met, then there will be few networks of any sort in the text. I refer to this basic concept of restriction as opposed to freedom in the choice of collocates as ´range´, a term I take from McIntosh (McIntosh 1961). McIntosh uses it to denote the collocational potential of a node, that is the set of different collocates with which a node may potentially collocate. I use it with reference to the actual set of collocates of a node observed in a text. It follows that what is required to establish relative tendencies to macrostructural organisation is to compare different texts with respect to the range of their node lemmata.

To do this the notion of range was quantified and a ´range index´ developed which allowed a value for range to be assigned to each collocating lemma in a text. Consideration of the fundamental statistics of collocation suggested a relatively straightforward way in which this could be done. The range index was designed to embody a relation between the total number of distinct lemmata with which a lemmatised node collocates and the total number of collocations into which the node enters. Thus the index measures the number of different collocates as a proportion of the total collocations for a given node. The greater the number of distinct collocates and the fewer the actual instances of collocation, the more ´freedom´ the node enjoys in its choice of collocates. Conversely, the fewer the number of different collocates and the higher the total frequency of collocation, the more restricted is the node in its collocational behaviour.

The summation of the frequencies of collocation of node ´i´ with all its collocates can be represented symbolically as follows:

$$\sum_{j=1}^{n_i} f_{ij}$$

where ´f_{ij}´ is the frequency of collocation of node ´i´ with collocate ´j´ and the summation is performed over all the ´n_i´ collocates. The subscript to ´n´ indicates that the value of ´n´ depends on the value of ´i´, that is which node is involved. This simply recognises that different nodes have different numbers of collocates. This operation must be repeated for each of the ´p´ text intervals; the summed frequencies of collocation must themselves be summed for each text interval ´k´:

$$\sum_{k=1}^{p} \sum_{j=1}^{n_i} f_{ijk}$$

It is now possible to define an index of the variability of the choice of collocate made by node ´i´ in the text as a whole. Letting s_i stand for the total number of distinct lemmata collocating with node i, what is required is the ratio between s_i and the summed frequencies of collocation:

$$V_i = \frac{s_i}{\sum_{k=1}^{p} \sum_{j=1}^{n_i} f_{ijk}}$$

Clearly, the higher the value of this ratio, that is the more distinct collocates there are relative to the total occurrences of collocation, the more variable the node is in its choice of collocates and conversely for lower values of the ratio.

As a matter of taste, I chose to let high values of the statistic indicate greater consistency in the selection of collocates and therefore defined the range index to be the complement of the above ratio:

$$R_i = 1 - V_i$$

This index has the advantage that two of its important properties can be stated immediately. The upper and lower limits of the values that can be taken by R_i can be specified. Given that it was stipulated in the study that only cases where the frequency of collocation reaches at least two would be accepted, then the minimum value of R_i will occur when node 'i' collocates in a text with minimum frequency (ie twice) with a single collocate. In this case R_i takes the value 0.5. The maximum value will tend to unity in the limit as the value of V_i becomes vanishingly small, that is as the total frequency of collocations of node 'i' becomes much greater than the number of different collocate types.

It was realised that this index, although conceptually and computationally straightforward, is not without possible problems. First, the frequency of the node might affect the value of the index. High frequency nodes, for example, might be advantaged by the decreasing availability of new collocations. Secondly, the value of the index for low frequency nodes could be exaggerated as a consequence of the integral steps in which word frequencies augment. The relative change in V from 1/2 to 1/3 is far greater than the difference between 50/100 and 50/101 although, in a sense, the same phenomenon of one additional occurrence of a collocation has occurred in both cases. Thirdly, it is possible that the value may be dependent on the length of the text. As the text length increases, the increase in the number of occurrences of a node will tend to outstrip the incrementation of vocabulary and as a result the number of available new collocates diminishes. In this case the value of R_i tends to increase.

In summary, the preceding considerations suggested that the range index might not be independent of the characteristics of the frequency distribution of types in the given text. In this case it would simply represent a characterisation of the

frequency distribution. In fact, however, this is not the
case. It proved possible on the basis of the range index to
distinguish among texts with similar frequency distributions
and to group texts with dissimilar frequency distributions.
The evidence for this will be presented in section four.
Moreover, as far as the present study is concerned the
possibility that the value of the index might depend on text
length was irrelevant. It was used to compare only texts
containing similar numbers of running words. It was not,
therefore, considered necessary to try to develop a more
complex measure until the possibilities of this simple index
had been exhausted.

Having established a method for comparing the degree to which
texts exhibit macrostructure, it is now appropriate to present
the results of the study for the non-science texts. These will
be discussed in the next section and then in section three
compared with those for the science texts using the range
index.

9.2   Macrostructure in Non-science Text

The results for the non-science texts showed that a certain
amount of patterning of lemmata is detectable at the level of
the chapter. At the same time, however, the findings indicate
that neither the extent of the patterning nor the interest of
the lexical networks discovered match those of the science
texts. There are several points of difference between the
nature of the networks revealed in the non-science texts and
those already discussed for the science texts.

First, there is an overwhelming tendency for lexical networks
in the non-science texts to be organised into ´chains´. These
are relatively loose associations of lemmata in which no lemma
collocates with more than two items and there is no intercollocation. A typical example from THF is

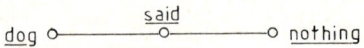

Graph 9.1

In these texts the tendency towards a restricted amount of
intercollocation of the collocates of a nuclear node noted in
chapter seven becomes paramount. In THF, for example, there is
only one instance of a network with any intercollocation and
only two further networks which display an internal structure
which is not a chain.

A similar trend is found in TMM. Only nine of the eighty-seven
networks identified in this text are not chains. Of these a
mere two display intercollocation. There is somewhat greater

evidence in MRSD of more extensive patterning, but even here the networks rarely achieve a level of complexity comparable to the average network in a science text. Moreover, the great majority of the networks in all the non-science texts are simple chains, that is straightforward pairings of lemmata. Only exceptionally, then, is lexical association detectable in these texts beyond the regular co-occurrence of two items.

Secondly, a consequence of the greater simplicity of the networks in the non-science texts is that they provide less obvious clues to the nature of topic. It is virtually impossible to predict the content of the narrative, and still less the principal themes, of either THF or MRSD from the evidence of the lexical networks. To some extent it is possible retrospectively to interpret the lexical networks given prior knowledge of the texts but there is certainly no support for the relatively clear relationship between lexical networks and subject which was found to obtain in the science texts. This is a most important finding which will be considered in detail in the next chapter.

The results for TMM, however, suggest that there is some relation between the themes discussed in the text and the structure of the lexical networks. Again, I do not believe that the networks of TMM actualise the topic in quite the unequivocal way of the science texts but they are more readily interpretable than those in the two novels. TMM, then, can be conceived of as lying midway between the novels and the science texts on some scale of ´interpretability of networks´. Again, possible reasons for this will be discussed in the next chapter.

Thirdly, the results suggest that to a greater extent than in the science texts, networks in non-science texts reflect conventional associations in the language. Networks are predictable from knowledge of the language system rather than predictive of the subject matter. In such cases very little extra information is provided by the network as a whole than is obtainable from one of its members. Some typical examples are given below:

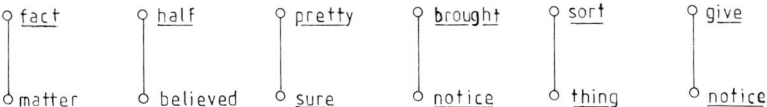

Graph 9.2 Conventional Networks in THF

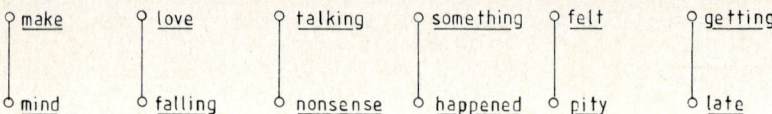

Graph 9.3   Conventional Networks in MRSD

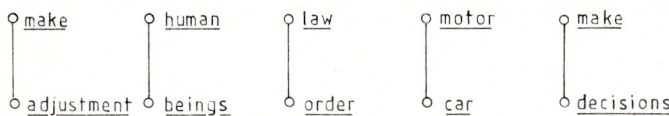

Graph 9.4   Conventional Networks in TMM

Fourthly, the proportion of nuclear nodes is much higher in the non-science texts than in the science texts, reaching between 50% and 70% of the total. In other words, there is almost no evidence for a restricted set of organising lexical items responsible for the structuring of the cognitive content of these texts. It is thus not surprising that there is insufficient information in the lexical patterning on which to base a prediction of content.

Finally, as far as the novels are concerned, there is a particular extension to the trend just noted towards conventional networks. A great number of the networks in both novels involve proper names, titles and the lemma said. This finding points to the importance of the simulation of conversation in structuring the novels.

If, as is suggested by this finding, the presentation of interaction is critical to the organisation of the novels, it might be expected that this would be reflected in the macrostructure of these texts. In both THF and TMM, however, there is virtually no evidence for macrostructure. There is very little similarity of networks across text intervals and as a result no indication of significant chapter linkages. A further major finding of the study, then, was that the patterns of association in these texts that can be revealed by the methodology are local rather than global. The implications of this finding will be considered in the next chapter.

In contrast, MRSD does display a certain degree of macro-structural organisation. This is presented in graph 9.5 below. Although Virginia Woolf does not call the sections of her novel chapters, I shall for convenience refer to them as such. Using

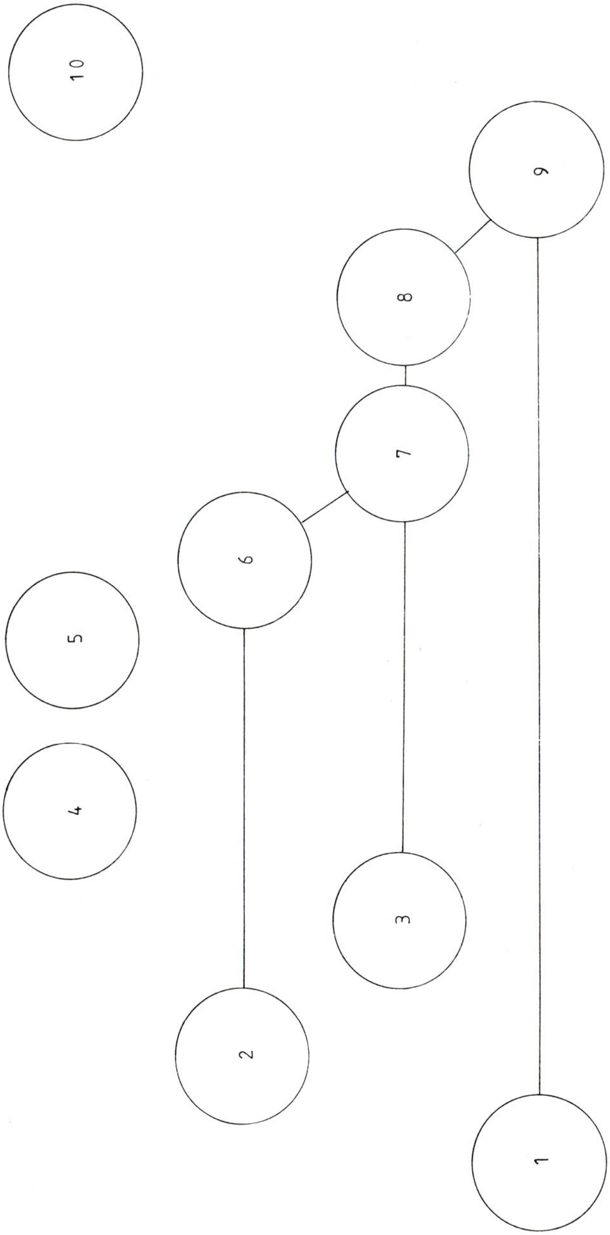

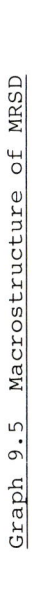

Graph 9.5 Macrostructure of MRSD

the apparatus developed in the last chapter, it can be seen that the macrostructure of MRSD consists of the following segments. Chapters four, five and ten are isolates. Chapters three and nine form a synoptic segment. There are three sequential segments composed of chapters one, seven and eight, chapters two, six, seven and eight and chapters three, seven and nine.

I do not propose to offer a full interpretation of this macrostructure. To do so would take me beyond the boundaries of text analysis proper and into the area of literary criticism. I shall confine myself to drawing attention to the central role played in the macrostructure by chapter seven. It figures as a common element in each of the sequential segments. This appears to be entirely consistent with subjective impressions of the novel. Chapter seven is appreciably longer than any of the other chapters in MRSD. This seems to indicate its critical role in structuring the novel. In it the principal sub-plot, which concerns Septimus Warren-Smith, reaches its culmination and is integrated with the main plot. Thus one of the major themes of the novel, the contrast between the vacuous lifestyle of Mrs Dalloway and her set and the real tragedy of the fate of an apparently insignificant ex-soldier from the trenches of the First World War, is achieved.

There is thus evidence in the macrostructure of MRSD which suggests that it might be as interpretable as the macrostructures of the science texts. It rests, however, upon a very different basis from those of the science texts. The macrostructure of MRSD depends crucially upon the similarity of networks containing proper names and titles. When these lemmata are excluded from the analysis, the apparently rich macrostructure of MRSD vanishes and all that remains is a tenuous link between chapters seven and eight. This can be confirmed by inspection of the information on significant chapter linkage contained in appendix six.

Such macrostructure, then, as was discovered in any of the non-science texts appears not to arise from the actualisation of subject matter in its direct projection through lexical networks, as happens in the science texts. It occurs, if at all, through a quite distinct mechanism. Various possible explanations for this will be briefly considered later, but the main theoretical discussion of this finding will be deferred to the next chapter.

Texts have thus been observed which display a pronounced macrostructure. This was the case of the science texts. Texts have also been observed in which no macrostructure was detectable, such as THF and TMM. Finally, a text has been investigated which proved to be somewhat equivocal. At face value there is considerable evidence of macrostructure in MRSD but this macrostructure, unlike those of the science texts, is firmly tied to a very narrow, non-conceptual base. These findings suggest the possibility of using the range index to establish a typology of texts. Thus consideration can now be given to an approach to the issues relating to text typology which were raised in chapter two when text linguistics and the Firthian view of language were surveyed.

9.3 Towards a Typology of Texts

Range indices were calculated for each node investigated in the five science texts and the three non-science texts. The proportion of nodes from the set investigated for which an index could not be calculated, since in all texts some nodes do not enter into any repeated collocations, was noted. The distribution of values of R was then plotted for each text as a cumulative relative frequency plot. By plotting the proportion of the total number of collocating nodes accounted for by each value of the range index rather than the absolute totals, any effects arising from the different numbers of nodes in each distribution were eliminated. This enables valid comparisons of the shape of the distributions to be made. It proved convenient to use a probability scale for the plot for the sake of clarity. The curves for the different distributions were thereby kept reasonably separate. It was also found that using a logarithmic scale for the values of R, thus plotting log(R) against the cumulative probabilities, resulted in distributions which were almost linear in form. The advantage of this approach is that on the transformed scale the standard deviations, which are represented by the slope of the lines, appear approximately equal for all eight texts. The differences between the distributions can then be described simply in terms of the mean. Texts are thus characterised by shifts in the mean of the distribution but the overall dispersion remains constant.

The R distributions thus obtained are given in Graph 9.6 on the next page. These distributions represent an abstract characterisation of the lexical macrostructure of the texts. I take these results as constituting convincing evidence of the validity of a text typology based on the degree to which collocational behaviour engenders macrostructure.

The first feature distinguishing science from non-science text is the percentage of nodes from each text which do not contribute to the distributions. These figures are given in appendix eight where it is revealed that they range from a minimum of 1.6% for CREL (ie 98.4% of the nodes investigated in CREL display some tendency to enter into significant collocations) to a maximum of 52.4% in THF (that is, less than half the nodes investigated collocate regularly). The percentage of non-collocating nodes is consistently higher for the non-science texts.

There is thus immediate evidence for the distinctiveness of science text. The vocabulary of science text forms an interlocking system where, in Saussure's words, "tout se tient", to a far greater extent than in the other texts I have examined. The scientific author uses, or is constrained to use, a relatively closely interrelated set of mutually defining

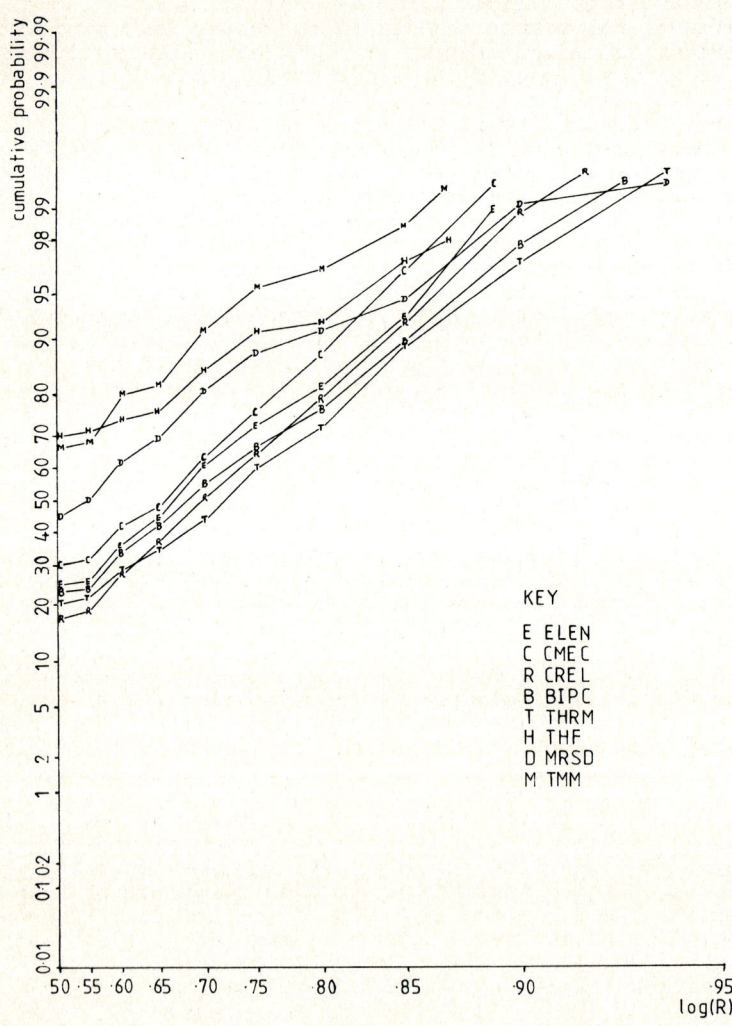

Graph 9.6 Distribution of Values of R for Eight Texts

terms. In contrast, the literary author or the scientific populariser does not appear to be similarly constrained. He has more freedom in his choice of vocabulary; the selection of a particular term does not entail to the same extent any commitment to other terms or to pre-determined patterns of use.

A second feature of these results which reveals a marked differentiation of science from non-science text in terms of collocational behaviour is revealed by the shape of the distributions. In the science texts a far smaller proportion of the nodes is accounted for by low values of the range index. It should be noted that between 36% and 50% of the collocating nodes in the science texts are accounted for by values of the range index in excess of 0.70 whereas the corresponding figure for non-science text is between 9% and 22%. Thus not only do a greater percentage of nodes enter into regular collocational patterning in science text than in non-science text but they do so to a measurably greater degree. It is also noteworthy that the differences among the non-science texts are greater than among the science texts. The science texts appear remarkably similar whilst the others are less homogeneous. This raises several interesting points.

First, it emerges at this level of abstraction that the individualities of the macrostructure of different science texts and distinctions in the choice of vocabulary disappear to reveal a striking uniformity of all the science texts in the corpus. The graphs for the five science texts are located in a relatively tight grouping. This is a remarkable result. I have argued that macrostructure projects subject matter. Nor do I think it would be seriously questioned that the selection of vocabulary is largely determined by the choice of subject matter, at least as regards the content words which principally account for the existence of the lexical networks with which I have been concerned. Yet despite the lexical and macro-structural disparity inherent in subjects as different as electronics and chemical reaction engineering, classical mechanics, thermodynamics and physical chemistry, there appears to be a global uniformity in the use of lexis. The proportions in which the vocabulary forms patterns of association with differing degrees of regularity remains comparatively stable independently of the identity of the items themselves. Thus a science text is recognisable as such irrespective of its particular vocabulary or subject matter. There appear to be constraints on the construction of science text which transcend the author's choice of topic or his use of particular items from the terminology of his field. This result is of major significance and its implications will be discussed in the next chapter.

Secondly, although graph 9.6 clearly indicates that the structuring of the non-science texts is appreciably weaker than for the science texts, it still shows that a few nodes at least enter into fairly consistent associations. If there should prove to be any feature that these nodes, or proportions of them, have in common, this may provide a clue to the

differences between the two classes of text. Inspection of the
data for the non-science texts reveals that a large number of
the lemmata at higher values of R are proper nouns or titles
such as <u>Lady</u> and <u>Sir</u>. In MRSD, for values of R equal to or
greater than 0.70 the proportion of such nodes is a
surprisingly high 47% while in THF it reaches the quite
remarkable figure of 80%. The lemma <u>said</u> also figures
prominently at the high end of the distribution with an index
of 0.84 in MRSD and 0.87 in THF. There is, on the other hand,
nothing particularly suggestive about the remaining nodes in
the distributions and they would not, for example, sustain the
notion that they represent carriers of the principal images or
themes in their respective novels. This finding thus confirms
the observation made in the last section that it is references
to the main characters which most obviously contract consistent
patterns of association in the novels.

Thirdly, these results provoke the question whether the
phenomena represented here are best conceived of as polarised
or located on a cline. The issue is whether the distribution
of values of the range index for a given text will tend to
approximate to one or other type represented here by science
text on the one hand and by novels and popular science text on
the other or whether texts can be located at different points
on a continuum between the extremes of the two classes of text
I have identified. There is a further possibility that neither
of the classes of text I have examined in fact constitutes the
extremes of the distribution. It is conceivable, for example,
that legal texts might show even greater homogeneity of
collocational patterning than the science texts.

These questions can be settled only by empirical investigation
but the following <u>a priori</u> considerations seem relevant. The
situation in lexis may be expected to be different from that of
grammar. In grammar polarities are to be anticipated. The
business of grammar is to reveal systematicity in language and
systems imply clear cut choices. In any given instance a word
can belong to one word class only. Whilst an item in the
lexicon may potentially belong to a number of word classes, as
soon as it is instantiated in text, grammar must be able to
assign it uniquely to a particular category on pain of
admitting a threat to the integrity of the whole system.
Grammar is uncomfortable in the presence of exceptions. There
is no reason to suppose, however, that lexis operates in the
same way. The difficulty of attempting to draw hard and fast
distinctions became apparent in chapter three when the
procedures for text reduction were discussed. The likelihood,
then, is that a clear dichotomy is not to be expected in the
classification of texts on the basis of their collocational
structure but that there exists a continuum from most to least
lexically structured.

The data from the study tend to support this view. The
distributions appear to form two principal groups with the five
science texts on the one hand and TMM and THF on the other
whilst MRSD occupies the middle ground. This means that the

patterning of lexical usage in MRSD is more easily detected than in either the novel by Greene or in the work of popular science but that it is still not as pervasive as in the science texts. This seems entirely reasonable. It is to be expected that the self-consciously literary work will exhibit a greater systematicity in the structuring of its vocabulary than either narrative fiction, albeit good narrative fiction, or the relatively wide-ranging and informal survey of the sociological impact of a particular technology. The point, then, is that there is some evidence for a continuum of collocational structuring. This finding can be interpreted as supporting the notion that a text typology can be established in terms of the degree of macrostructural patterning exhibited by the texts.

To what extent, then, do the findings constitute evidence for a genuine typology? The crucial issue is whether the R distributions support an interpretation in terms of a causal mechanism. If this is not the case, there remain only two logical possibilities. Either all texts are structured in essentially similar ways or the observed variation among the R distributions has to be considered as the product of purely random factors having no explanatory value. The first possibility has been eliminated by the data which clearly indicate that there are differences among the distributions which require explanation. This leaves the possibility that the differences are attributable to purely chance fluctuations in the collocational patterning.

If the second hypothesis is correct, then there would be no principled way of distinguishing between the collocational behaviour of a randomly ordered 'text' from that of a genuine example of natural text. This suggests that a means of testing the hypothesis would be to compare the observed R distributions with that obtained from the analysis of a text in which the order of words has been randomised. In such a text the occurrence of collocation would be a matter of chance. Consequently, if there proved to be no clear difference between the R distribution of the randomly ordered text and the observed distributions, the conclusion would have to be drawn that the R distributions are meaningless. The prospect of a text typology on this basis would then disappear.

The first step towards testing the hypothesis was the creation of an equivalent random text. An equivalent random text is one formed by randomly selecting words from the frequency distribution of an actual text where the selection is determined by treating the frequencies of occurrence as the estimates of population probabilities. A random number generator may be used to pick out words in accordance with these probabilities and to create a text in which the order of words is random but the distribution of words into frequency classes is typical for texts of the type under investigation. The technique has been described by Muller. Referring to a text in which a particular noun has a relative frequency of 0.18, he says

"Or on the other hand we reason from the language of the text to the parent population of which the text is a sample and the characteristics of which are only known through this text. In this case we accept 0.18 as the best estimate of the probability of occurrence of the substantive in the knowledge that this estimate is bound to be inaccurate because of fluctuations due to sampling. We are thus led to the construction of a random sample as a case of sampling with replacement, since the population is an infinite one." (Muller 1973 p112 my translation)

So that the test would not unintentionally favour either of the putative classes of text, two equivalent random texts were constructed using a simple BASIC program. One run took ELEN as the estimate of the probabilities of occurrence with the resulting randomised text identified as ELENRND. The second random text used TMM as the basis and is known as TMMRND. Values for R were calculated for the collocating lemmata in both of these texts. The graph of the distribution of values of the range index for ELENRND is presented in graph 9.7 superimposed on the plot for the other texts for purposes of comparison. It is not possible similarly to reproduce the graph of TMMRND for reasons which will shortly become clear.

Two points need to be made about the distribution for ELENRND. First, the number of nodes entering into the distribution is greatly reduced. Whereas in the original text only 8% of the vocabulary set investigated failed to display some tendency to collocational patterning, in the equivalent random text almost one third of all nodes do not enter into any regular associations. Collocational organisation in the randomised text is far less widespread than in the original. Secondly, the location and shape of the graph of ELENRND is important. These features clearly reveal that a far greater proportion, indeed a majority, of the lemmata are accounted for by the lowest value of the range index. Some 70% of all lemmata fall in the range 0.50-0.59. In other words, the tendency to collocational patterning is much weaker than in the original text.

It proved impossible to plot the graph of the R distribution for TMMRND for the reason that every lemma contributing to it had an R value of 0.50. That is, all the collocating lemmata are accounted for by the minimum value, a fact that cannot be represented on a probability plot. Further, nearly 80% of the lemmata investigated failed to achieve any value for R. In other words, four-fifths of the lemmata in the equivalent random text simply show no significant tendency to enter into collocations.

These findings reveal that differences between the distributions for the genuine texts and the equivalent random texts are sufficiently great to exclude beyond any reasonable doubt the possibility that the distributions for the genuine texts are

TEXT STRUCTURE AND TEXT TYPOLOGY 211

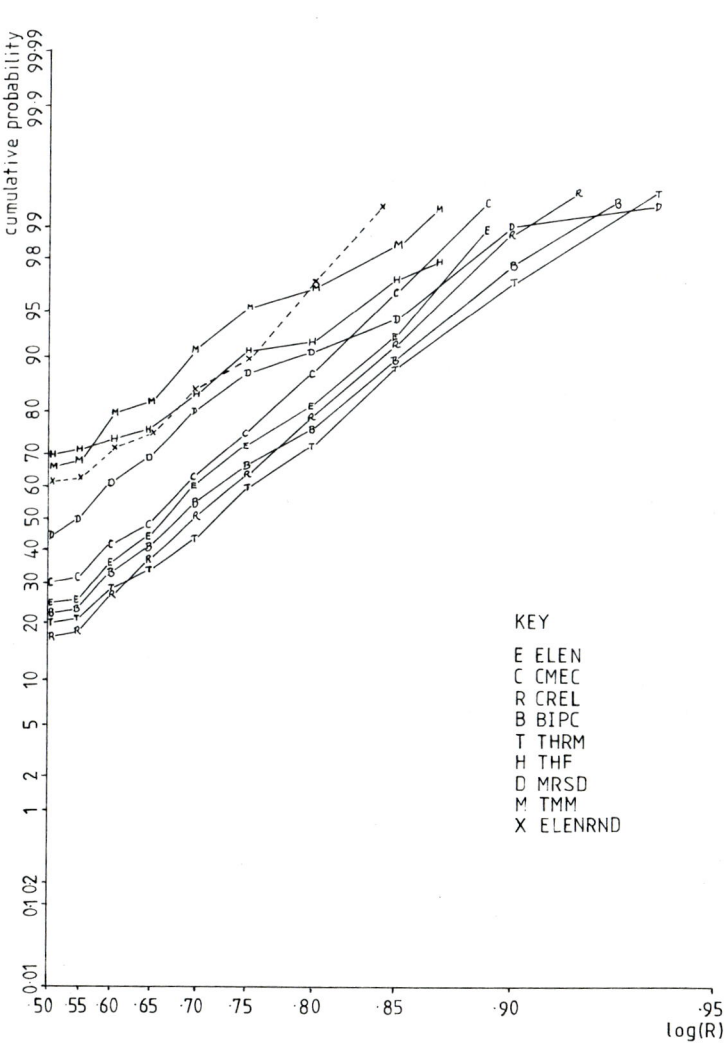

Graph 9.7 Distribution of Values of R for a Randomised Text

the products of chance factors. These distributions are
clearly attributable to a causal mechanism. Consequently, the
distributions can be regarded as offering a plausible basis for
a typology of texts.

There remains, however, a further possibility which must now be
considered. Although it has been shown that the R
distributions cannot be explained as produced by chance, it is
still quite conceivable that the differences among the various
R distributions can be explained in terms of the frequency
distributions of the texts alone. Indeed, it is suggestive
that the R distributions observed for the two random texts were
themselves distinguishable. If the two random texts can be
separated in this way, it can perhaps be inferred that this is
attributable to the one known characteristic in respect of
which they differ. This is the distribution of frequencies of
types in the texts used to generate the equivalent random
texts. This means that the possibility exists that the values
of the range index depend on the frequency distribution of
types in the texts and that in consequence the degree of
macrostructural patterning can be more simply accounted for on
this basis. In other words, although it has been shown that
the R distributions differ systematically rather than randomly,
this may be on account of systematic differences among the
frequency distributions which determine the degree of
collocational patterning. A causal mechanism has been shown to
be operative, but it has not been demonstrated that this
mechanism is in fact collocational. The question, then, is
whether the mechanism accounting for the typology is one of
lexical density. If this were the case, the plots of the R
distributions would simply be a reflection of differing
proportions of word classes in the different texts.

A number of considerations seem to me to be plausible reasons
for rejecting the view that collocational patterning, and hence
macrostructure, is entirely determined by the characteristics
of the frequency distribution. First, there is the evidence
provided by the differing proportions of lemmata which display
collocational behaviour. If the frequency distributions are
the determining factor, then it may be expected that there
would be a readily perceivable correspondence between the
parameters of the distributions and the proportions of
collocating lemmata. I reproduce in table 9.1 the basic
statistics relating to the frequency distributions of the texts
together with the data on collocating lemmata arising from this
stage of the study. The texts have been ordered according to
increasing mean of the frequency distribution to make the
comparison clearer. It can be easily seen from inspection of
the table that there is no obvious relation between the two
series of figures. Nor is there any better correspondence if
the texts are ordered according to the standard deviation of
their frequency distributions. In other words, the
characteristics of the frequency distributions cannot be said
to determine unequivocally the extent to which collocational
patterning will be found in a given text.

	mean of fr.dis.$\bar{x}$	s.d. σ	% colls	mean of R dis.$\bar{x}$	s.d. σ
TMM	8.0	70.0	64.8	0.55	0.09
MRSD	8.4	65.5	85.0	0.60	0.12
THF	9.2	62.7	47.8	0.57	0.11
BIPC	13.6	110.8	90.0	0.68	0.13
CREL	14.9	95.8	98.4	0.69	0.12
ELEN	18.6	131.1	92.0	0.67	0.13
CMEC	19.1	142.7	90.9	0.65	0.12
THRM	20.1	154.0	93.8	0.70	0.14

Table 9.1

Secondly, the evidence of the frequency distributions predicts a different ordering of the R distributions. The ordering of the means of the R distributions does not correspond to the order of the means of the frequency distributions. This is also confirmed by the figures in table 9.1. The most obvious point of difference is that the frequency distributions cannot account for the degree of collocational patterning in MRSD. There is nothing distinctive about the frequency distribution of MRSD as compared with the other non-science texts. Nor can the ordering of the R distributions of the science texts be explained in this way. It is completely different from the order of the means of the frequency distributions of these texts.

A final consideration is provided by the observation that much of the difference between the frequency distributions of the science and non-science texts is attributable to the increased number of low frequency nodes, and particularly hapax legomena in the non-science texts. If the frequency distributions are truncated at a lower cut off level of eight occurrences, all the distributions look very similar. It is thus precisely with respect to those items which are least likely to enter into regular collocations and which 'dilute' the lexical density of the texts least that the two types of text differ most.

On these grounds, then, I think it is justifiable to reject the frequency distribution of types as the underlying causal mechanism explaining the form of the R distributions. At the same time, it must be recognised that the frequency distribution represents an ultimate constraint on the structural possibilities of text. A text cannot display a greater degree of collocational patterning than the frequencies of occurrence of its constituent words allow. To this extent, the investigation of any linguistic feature in a text other than the properties of the frequency distribution itself will be unable to isolate the 'pure' phenomenon. It will always be 'contaminated' by the frequency class characteristics of the vocabulary of the text.

Nevertheless, I think it can be justly claimed that over and above any differences attributable to distinctions among the frequency distributions of the texts in the corpus, their collocational organisation also seems to be different in degree. The range index distributions have justified themselves as summarising the overall collocational behaviour of the texts rather than any more general characteristics. Consequently, I conclude that it is possible to claim that the plots in graph 9.6 constitute evidence for a typology of texts on the basis of their tendency towards macrostructural organisation.

9.4 Further Structural Evidence for a Text Typology

Suggestive evidence has been produced in favour of the view that a typology of text can be established on the basis of differing tendencies to collocational patterning in different classes of text. This evidence is supported by further findings which clearly reveal the existence of differences between the science and the non-science texts in terms of their overall lexical structuring. These findings concern the distribution of nuclear nodes through the texts and the way in which differences in this feature show up in the extent to which chapters can be considered as structural units.

It was suspected that there might be interesting differences among the texts in the corpus in the point at which the nuclear nodes are introduced. In order to investigate this possibility the number of new nuclear nodes introduced in each text interval was plotted for each text. The resulting graphs for the science texts were presented in chapter seven section three on page 142. It was concluded from inspection of these graphs that most of the nuclear vocabulary of science texts has normally appeared by the second or third chapter. After that, new nuclear nodes are introduced increasingly rarely. BIPC was the only science text to differ at all markedly from this pattern and this was readily explicable in terms of the special preparatory function of the first three chapters.

The graphs for the non-science texts present a quite different picture. The addition of new nuclear nodes to the total is distributed much more evenly through the text. More precisely, there is little evidence of the kind of ´front bias´ to the distribution evidenced by the science texts. Moreover, in contrast to the science texts where there is no obvious relation between the introduction of nuclear nodes and the lexical macrostructure, there is some indication that such a relationship exists for the non-science texts. In MRSD, for example, there appear to be two main points of introduction at the first interval and then later around intervals six and seven. This corresponds to the intuitively perceived organisation of the novel mentioned earlier. The first interval initiates the narrative whilst intervals six and seven correspond to the climax of the plot immediately before and during Mrs Dalloway´s party. It may be, then, that the point of introduction of nuclear nodes, in literary text at least, is reflective of the progression of narrative. Thus this finding provides additional confirmation for the view that the organising principles of the two classes of text identified in this study are quite distinct.

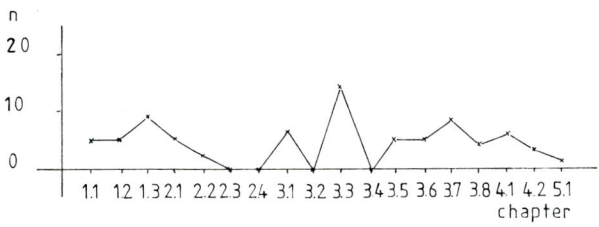

Graph 9.8   THF Distribution of Nuclear Nodes

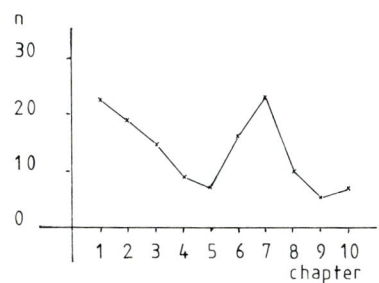

Graph 9.9   MRSD Distribution of Nuclear Nodes

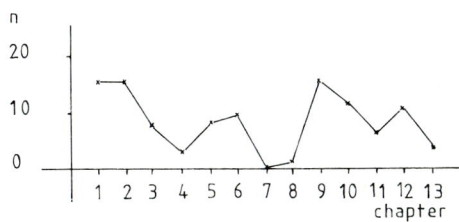

Graph 9.10   TMM Distribution of Nuclear Nodes

These findings are also compatible with my earlier results. A reasonably steady incrementation of new items in each text interval reduces the chances of the lexical similarity among intervals on which the notion of macrostructure is based. It has already been noted that there is relatively little tendency to macrostructural patterning in the non-science texts. The inability to detect any significant macrostructure has as its corollary the result that the chapter appears in non-science text as a viable structural unit. It will be recalled that in chapter eight section three it was concluded that in science text the chapter has to be regarded as a largely conventional category. In contrast, the evidence suggests that in modern literature at least, the chapter divisions have largely lost sight of their origins in convention. In THF and MRSD chapters appear to be motivated by internal considerations relating to topic and focus of the narrative.

It is perhaps not surprising that literary authors should treat the chapter boundary (or its equivalent in terms of the segmentation adopted in particular texts) in this way as a legitimate structural device and seemingly adopt a less arbitrary attitude to the segmentation of their texts than do the scientific writers. I suggest that the literary author is far more aware of the fact that he is writing in a conventional form than is his scientific colleague, for whom exposition is all, and is as a result consciously concerned to turn the constraints of the convention to artistic effect. As Sinclair puts it

> "poets complain of the shackles of language but are expert in exploiting their bondage" (Sinclair 1983a pp3-4).

Thus whereas in the science texts the chapter had to be regarded as an heuristic device, in the non-science texts chapter divisions correspond to structural units. Consequently, the adoption in this study of the chapter as an analytical unit might have been expected to throw light upon the organisation of plot or narrative. This has indeed been seen to be the case.

9.5 Conclusion

In this chapter I have discussed the possibility of using the notion of macrostructure as the basis for establishing a typology of texts. A technique was developed, based on a statistical measure called the range index, in terms of which the tendency of a text towards macrostructural organisation can be characterised. Application of this technique to the texts in the corpus revealed that the non-science texts are quite distinct in this respect from the science texts. Whilst the science texts, as was observed in the last chapter, display pronounced and readily interpretable macrostructural organisation, the non-science texts in general exhibit only weak and comparatively trivial collocational activity. There was some slight evidence for a gradation of degrees of macrostructure insofar as MRSD appears to be more structured than the other non-science texts. It was clear, however, that the macrostructure of MRSD rests upon weaker collocational foundations and a narrower lexical base than do those of the science texts. In general, then, the non-science texts show little tendency to macrostructural organisation and such macrostructure as was revealed by the study does not lend itself to ready interpretation as constructive of aboutness in the same way as the macrostructure of the science texts.

This is a convenient point at which to review the ground that has been covered before an attempt is made to pull the various strands of the investigation together in the final chapter. In the first part of the book a theoretical vantage point from which text analysis can be undertaken was established. This position had direct implications for the kind of methodology which is required and the elaboration of an appropriate analytical technique occupied the second part of the book. In part three the findings arising when an analysis on this basis of a mixed corpus of science and non-science texts was undertaken have been presented and discussed. In chapter seven, the relationship between syntagmatic patterns of association and term meaning was articulated through the notion of lexical network. This led to the description of the macrostructures of the science texts in chapter eight and a discussion of the possible principles which underlie them. In the present chapter means for quantifying the degree of macrostructure displayed by a text have been developed and the possibilities for categorising texts on this basis discussed.

It is now time to reflect upon the overall significance of these findings in two perspectives. The discovery of macrostructure in science text has confirmed the theoretical argument developed at the outset that perception of large scale structuring is a major factor contributing to the sensation of aboutness. Large scale regularities in lexical patterning appear to be a major device whereby science texts create their subject matter and hence construct a particular reality. But it has also been seen that the same does not hold of non-science text. Yet it would not be denied that literary texts, for example, can be said to be about something. The first fundamental issue raised by the present investigation, then, concerns the epistemological status of text and the problem of aboutness in literature.

The consideration of this problem will raise the second major area of interest. This is the extent to which the techniques developed in this study, and by extension the methods of linguistics, are capable of investigating the very issues which they raise. Thus in a fundamental way, this enquiry raises questions concerning the scope of linguistics and the extent to which issues of importance can be handled within conventional approaches.

It is a consideration of these issues which occupies the final part of this book and which will bring this particular stage of the investigation of text structure to a conclusion.

PART FOUR

ABOUTNESS REVIEWED

CHAPTER 10

TEXT, IMAGE AND REALITY

10.1 The Problem of Macrostructure

In the last chapter it was seen that the tendency of a text to display macrostructure arising from collocational patterning could form the basis of a text typology. It was apparent that the science texts differed markedly from the non-science texts in this respect. Indeed there was very little evidence of macrostructure to be found in the non-science texts and such as there was appeared to arise from a mechanism quite different in kind from that operating in the science texts. Several notions offer themselves as candidates for explanatory mechanisms for these differences. I shall suggest, however, that none of the ideas to be discussed in this section proves to offer an entirely adequate explanation.

The first plausible explanation for the apparent lack of macrostructure in non-science text and its presence in science text is that elegant variation is not a feature of the latter. This is an aspect of text which is taken as characteristic of literary texts. It is assumed that the literary writer will tend to avoid the monotony of repetition and seek to ´enrich´ his creation by judicious use of alternative means of expression. Consequently, the argument would run, a notion of macrostructure which depends on repetition of identical lexical items could not be sustained with regard to literary text. The crucial element of stylistic variation would not be taken into account and as a result it would be impossible to exhibit the existence of global patterns of association.

Science text, on the other hand, may be expected not to concern itself with such niceties of style and positively to use lexical repetition where appropriate. The often repeated claim for the ´precision´ of scientific language rests, I suspect, on this notion. A rose is a rose is a rose and would smell quite differently if given any other name in a textbook of botany. It is claimed that unique senses attach to scientific terms and that consequently the identical term will be used whenever the same sense needs to be evoked. As a result, it becomes feasible to detect large scale patternings based on such lexical repetition.

There is probably an element of truth in this argument, particularly as regards the eschewing of avoidable repetition in literature. I suggest, however, that the case is far from established and that the considerations upon which it is based are simplistic. It may be true that rather than resort to repetition, the literary author will rely upon implicit relations among the senses of words and expect his reader to make the connection. Imagery often operates in this way as do traditional rhetorical devices such as metonomy. But a counterargument can be developed based on the consideration that where a writer wishes to evoke similar impressions in his reader on different occasions, there has to be a stability in his use of language which must be detectable. There is no true synonymy. The question then becomes to what extent repetition is ´avoidable´. If the terms carrying the imagery are not identical, their contexts will in some respect be similar. And if this is true, then it is not unreasonable to suppose that the functional similarity of such terms will be revealed by their membership of similar lexical networks. The alternative, if the use of elegant variation is pushed too far, is to run the risk of incomprehensibility.

It can also be argued that there is a similar lack of cogency in the argument based on the notion of ´precision´ in scientific language. Sufficient evidence of variability in the composition of lexical networks has already been produced to render unsatisfactory the view that assigns a unique and immutable sense to every element of scientific terminology. It is also possible to show that a form of lexical variation operates in science text. There seems to be a hierarchy of degrees of generality in terminology such that, depending on the detail required at a given point in the text, the same event can be referred to as, for example, a ´body´, ´particle´, ´nucleon´ or ´neutron´. Similarly, the scattering of particles may be as a result of a ´process´, ´impact´ or ´elastic collision´. Thus the possibility exists that variation may occur rather than repetition even in science text. If, then, the argument to explain the lack of macrostructure in literary text is valid, it is by no means totally obvious why it should not also apply to science text.

An alternative explanation might be sought in a rather different aspect of style which has its reflection in the category of span. It might be surmised that an increase in the size of span for the non-science texts would result in the discovery of more widespread patterns of association and thus lead to a notion of macrostructure not dissimilar to that developed for science text. Were this to prove the case, it would not, however, be appropriate to conclude that, since macrostructure had thereby been shown to be a feature of all text, there no longer remained a special need to explain its existence in science text. For all that such a finding would do would be to shift the locus of the problem. The need to adopt different span sizes in order to reveal macrostructure in different types of text would now require explanation.

There is a further feature which appears to differentiate non-science from science text and which might consequently

provide a basis for an explanation. One finding of the study
which I have not yet commented upon is that self-collocation,
that is collocation of one token of a type as node with another
token of the same type as collocate within the span, seems to
occur more frequently in some of the non-science texts. The
distributions presented in the graphs of values of the range
index in the last chapter were calculated without taking self-
collocation into account. If, however, the values of R are
recalculated to include the frequencies of self-collocation,
an interesting result emerges. Whereas in general this makes a
difference of at most one or two points for a few nodes in the
science texts, it can change appreciably the values of R for a
considerable number of nodes in the novels and consequently
affect to some degree the shape of their distributions. These
are all perceptibly shifted in the direction of an increase in
collocational structuring.

The phenomenon of self-collocation was noted by Sinclair
(Sinclair et al 1970). He makes a suggestive observation:

> "Evidently self-collocation will be a common occurrence
> in the spoken language and is probably more important as
> a characteristic of a certain kind of text than for the
> theory of lexis as such" (Sinclair et al op.cit. p82).

Unfortunately, the relative unimportance of self-collocation in
science text cannot serve as the foundation for an explanation
for the existence of macrostructure. Since the overall effect
of self-collocation in the non-science texts is a tendency to
increase the values of the range index for the nodes affected,
this phenomenon tends to increase the possibility of
macrostructure rather than decrease it.

A final explanatory possibility is that there may be sufficient
overall difference in the number of running words in the text
intervals of the two classes of text to have the effect that
networks will only be consistently detected in one class of
texts. In other words, the fact that macrostructure is
detectable in the science texts might be attributable to the
decision to accept the chapter as interval. If chapters in the
science textbooks are consistently and significantly longer
than in the non-science texts, then there will be more
opportunity for the detection of lexical patterning. This
would reveal itself at the level of the whole text as macrostructure.

There does indeed appear to be a tendency for chapters in the
science textbooks to be somewhat more extensive than in the
non-science case. It is not possible, however, to elevate this
tendency to the status of an explanation of the existence of
macrostructure. The statistics for the text intervals show
clearly that there is no simple correlation between text type
and length of chapter. There is not much to choose, for
example, between TMM, which is one of the collocationally
weakest of texts in the corpus, and CMEC, which has a marked
and readily interpretable macrostructure.

None of these possibilities, then, offers itself as a plausible explanation for the fact that macrostructure was only identified to any significant degree in the science texts. Clearly, a deeper explanation has to be sought. I suggest that the clue lies in the nature of the reality which is projected by the text. This notion has profound implications and it will be possible here only to sketch the outline of a possible approach to the problem. This I shall attempt to do in the next section.

10.2 Aboutness in Literature

It has been seen that the notion of aboutness in non-science text does not depend on the global patterns of association that I have called lexical macrostructure. If the different nature of aboutness in the two classes of text can be characterised, it may be possible to explain why macrostructure is such a prominent feature of science text and why it cannot be detected by my procedures in non-science text. I propose, then, to begin this final stage of the investigation of aboutness by exploring what it means to ask what a work of literature is about. This section is speculative in nature. Rather, therefore, than attempting a sustained analysis of a relatively short and structurally simple literary text, in order to focus the discussion I shall begin by considering a text which has kept literary critics occupied for at least three and a half centuries. What is entailed when one asks what 'Hamlet' is about?

A variety of plausible responses spring immediately to mind. The subject of 'Hamlet' could be described as a study of procrastination; or the paralysing effect of reflection upon action; or the tragic consequences of melancholia; or the human condition; or all of these and more besides. One view of 'Hamlet', which was influential in its day, was put forward by the Shakespearian scholar A C Bradley. Shakespeare criticism has, to be sure, advanced since Bradley's day and perhaps few modern critics would subscribe to Bradley's views. But Bradley happens to ask the right questions, as the schoolboy doggerel reminds us:

> I dreamt last night of Shakespeare's ghost
> Sitting for his Civil Service post.
> Shakespeare answered very badly
> Because he hadn't read his Bradley.

Thus Bradley's lecture on 'Hamlet' suits my purpose.

Bradley addresses himself to the question of what the play is about. He first makes a crucial point:

> "Suppose you were to describe the plot of <u>Hamlet</u> to a person quite ignorant of the play, and suppose you were careful to tell your hearers nothing about Hamlet's character, what impression would your sketch make on him? Would he not exclaim: 'What a sensational story!

Why, here are some violent deaths, not to speak of
adultery, a ghost, a mad woman, and a fight in a grave.
If I did not know that the play was Shakespeare's, I
should have thought it must have been one of those early
tragedies of blood and horror from which he is said to
have redeemed the stage'? And would he not then go on
to ask: 'But why in the world did not Hamlet obey the
Ghost at once, and so save seven of those eight lives?'"
(Bradley 1974 p70)

Bradley then continues by claiming that

"This exclamation and this question both show the same
thing, that the whole story turns upon the peculiar
character of the hero." (ibid p70)

One may choose to object to Bradley's view that the whole of
'Hamlet' can be explained by analysing the character of the
principal protagonist. The valuable point, however, in
Bradley's argument is that he regards the aboutness of 'Hamlet'
as a peculiarly complex phenomenon only indirectly relatable to
the text of the play by means of techniques of interpretation.
No straightforward linguistic correspondence should be
anticipated between a description of the major themes of the
play and their dramatic mise en scene.

For science text it has been argued that aboutness can be seen
as arising from the creation of generalised conceptual systems
through the large scale lexical configurations of the text. It
is impossible to make a similar claim for literary text.
Erlich in his study of Russian formalism reminds us of
Tolstoy's view of his paraphrasers:

"Sklovskij and Ejxenbaum quoted on several occasions
Tolstoj's sarcastic dig at his critics who managed to
sum up in a few sentences the 'meaning' of Anna
Karenina. "Ils en savent plus que moi", wrote Tolstoj
about his brash 'paraphrasers' in a letter to A.Straxov.
"As for me", he continued, "if I were asked what Anna
Karenina was about, I would have to write the book all
over again."" (Erlich 1980 pp240-241)

In contrast to the non-paraphrasability of literary text, the
examination crib is a familiar device for paraphrasing science
text.

Thus the distinction made by the narratologists between 'theme'
and 'story' is crucial. For the connection between text and
the reality projected by it is mediated in literature through
at least one additional layer of symbolism. The investigation
of lexical patterning can at most point to story, leaving the
relations among story, theme and the world of phenomena largely
to inference. Furthermore, 'story' as opposed to 'theme'
progresses, that is, narrative embodies time. As a result it
is precisely those aspects of the narrative text which are
most mutable which are susceptible of observation by the

procedures used in this study. Consequently, the likelihood of detecting macrostructure is limited. The point has been made with gentle irony by Italo Calvino in one of his novels (Calvino 1982).

I am thus suggesting that the additional layers of symbolism which distance a literary work further from experienced, phenomenological reality than science text account for the inability to detect macrostructure in the non-science texts investigated. It can be hypothesised that this distancing arises because the aspects of reality represented by the poetic imagination cannot be actualised directly by language. They can only be alluded to by means of hints, clues, images and symbols. In the words of Polonius, literary writers "by indirections find directions out". It is in this sense that the ´meaning´ of any art form is spoken of. The ´meaning´ of music, for example, is its expression of aspects of experience which can only be evoked, not described in words. Hence, also, the centrality of metaphor in poetry. Ultimately, it is impossible to say what is: it is possible only to say what it is like. For literature there is no such thing as the ´naked truth´ and if the attempt were made to present it as such, the result would not be literature. In literature, as in life, as Eliot observed "human kind cannot bear very much reality".

This is easily seen by considering the truth value status of various classes of text. Erlich makes a crucial distinction with regard to literary text:

> "great works of literature, though not ´truthful´ in the literal sense of the word, may be conducive to truth, as they often yield crucial insights into the human predicament" (op cit p208).

Thus it cannot be expected that the ´truth´ of literature will be accomodated within any simple version of the correspondence theory of truth as it is described, for example, by Warnock (Warnock 1974). Yet this is not such an unreasonable requirement as it may seem. Tarski has shown that even for as unlikely an object as a formal language it is possible to develop a notion of truth modelled on the correspondence theory (Tarski 1956, 1974). Is it, then, beyond the wit of man to demonstrate that literature can have a truth-preserving relationship to ´reality´?

It cannot be objected that correspondence theories are necessarily inadequate in the light of the arguments in their defence put forward by Warnock and Davidson and the telling observation by Bradley and Swartz that the correspondence or ´simple´ theory is logically prior to alternatives such as the coherence or pragmatic theories (Warnock op cit, Davidson 1974, Bradley and Swartz 1979). Yet if, for example, Tarski´s scheme is adapted, a formula such as

> ´fraility, thy name is woman´ is a true sentence only if fraility thy name is woman

fails, not as a feminist would have us suppose because it does not correspond to the facts, but because it is not clear with what facts precisely the sentence is being brought into correspondence.

As Davidson points out, the correspondence theory of truth deals only with the literal sense of language and it is the literal sense only which can be investigated by the kind of objective procedures developed in this study (Davidson op cit). The truth of literature, however, is not literal truth but literary truth and consequently it cannot be related to reality by any straightforward philosophical theory of correspondence. Literature, to borrow an important concept from Russell, is not ´verifiable´ by any process

> "which involves confrontation of the statement with the evidence" (Russell 1980 p79).

The same consideration suggests, however, that science text may well be verifiable in Russell´s sense and that in consequence its truth value can be established within the correspondence theory. The basis of scientific method is precisely the testing of theory against experimentally determined evidence.

There is a problem here too, however. It is probably an over-simplification to assume that science text is any more ´true´ to the facts than is literature, or rather to assume that it is known precisely what the facts are. The typical data of science text are not empirical but ideal. It was seen in chapter one that the objects it studies are often mathematical constructs rather than objective realities. The view that scientific knowledge arises from a continuous process of accumulation of facts achieved by selfless workers dedicated to the pursuit of truth by objective methods is no longer tenable, if, indeed, it ever was. Kuhn has suggested that science progresses by the periodic overthrow of current orthodoxies (Kuhn 1970). Popper views scientific knowledge as essentially provisional and progress in science as the disproving of hypotheses (Popper 1979). Koestler has drawn attention to the imaginative content of much scientific investigation and the role chance has played in the development of theories (Koestler 1964). Even the anonymous researcher is discovered to be a stereotype, as Watson´s account of the discovery of the structure of DNA reveals (Watson 1970). Finally, Lakatos crucially points out that even observation is based on theory. The ´facts´ from which the scientist is supposed to generalise are thus theory dependent rather than objectively given (Lakatos 1978).

Warnock himself raises the problem of generalisations which cannot refer to particular and so verifiable instances. Consequently, one must admit that

> "that metals expand when heated can be said to be strongly confirmed, to be much-tested and not falsified, but not to be true." (Warnock op cit p18)

It does, as Warnock implies however, make sense to say that such a generalisation is supported by inferences from empirical data that have as yet not been shown to be false. The data are publicly available and therein lies a fundamental difference between science and non-science text. The world in which the generalisations of science are true is more closely related to the world of phenomena, within which scientific experimentation is conducted, than is the world created by the statements of literature.

There is a possibility, then, that the essential difference between science and non-science text can be explicated in terms of their status with respect to different 'possible worlds' and the relationships between the possible worlds they postulate and the actual world. For present purposes, it is convenient to distinguish among W_1, the actual world; W_2, the world of subjective experience; W_3, the world of idealised science and W_4, any representative of the fictive worlds of literary creation. It is in W_1 that people act, 'do science', and interact as social beings. In W_2 each individual synthesises a unique world view. In W_3 the generalisations of science are made and in W_4 the action of fiction takes place.

With this apparatus, it can be argued that for science text the following relationship obtains

$$W_3 \ R \ W_1$$

where R is the relationship of verifiability. For literature, in the simplest case, there is an initial relationship

$$W_4 \ R' \ W_2$$

where R' indicates that the primary relationship is established between the fictive world and the world of personal experience. Thus the non-literal truth of literature can be verified only by intuition. The reason that such truth is non-literal is now apparent. The actual world is not an argument of the relationship, or rather it enters only indirectly through the fact that intuition is born of personal experience within the actual world. Thus for literature the relations are

$$W_4 \ R' \ W_2 \ R'' \ W_1$$

The relation R is given by public knowledge of the findings of science whereas the relationships R' and R'' depend upon the reader's experience. They are thus not available to public inspection except to the extent that any successful interaction requires a ground of shared experience. In summary, it can be said that science text is a metastatement to science whilst literary text is not a metastatememt in the same sense.

To return to the considerations with which I initiated this discussion, 'Hamlet' can be said to project aspects of reality locatable not in W_1 but in W_2. And what is true of 'Hamlet' also holds for the literary texts I have investigated, THF and

MRSD. It is also the case for TMM, which is not so much about the microchip as about the less tangible concept of the future ´impact´ of the microchip on society. The status of the author´s views cannot be determined by direct appeal to W_1. His argument must be mediated by W_2, that is, by the reader´s introspective evaluation of the degree to which his personal interpretation of W_1 corresponds to that presented by the writer.

It is the existence of W_2 and the role it plays with respect to W_4, the world of fictive reality, that licences literary criticism. This distinction has been exploited to comic effect by Vladimir Nabokov in his novel ´Pale Fire´, which provides an excellent illustration of many of the notions I have been discussing (Nabokov 1962). ´Pale Fire´ is the title of

> "a poem in heroic couplets, of nine hundred ninety-nine lines, divided into four cantos" (sic) by "John Francis Shade". (op cit pl3)

It is also the title of the book by Nabokov which includes the poem in a critical edition by ´Charles Kinbote´ who, according to the index, is

> "an intimate friend of S, his literary adviser, editor and commentator" (ibid p242).

Through the critical notes the personality of the editor increasingly encroaches upon the interpretation of the poem until, by the end of the commentary, the respective roles of poet and editor have been reversed. Nabokov exploits with great skill the relationship between the possible world projected by the poem and that in which the commentary is located. But this is only possible because there is no final court of appeal in W_1, no intractable empirical evidence to verify one view and discredit the other.

The simple $W_4 \ R´ \ W_2 \ R´´ \ W_1$ schema proposed above is elaborated by Nabokov. A clue is given by the ambiguous status of the title ´Pale Fire´, which alerts the reader to the technique of a ´text within a text´ and alludes to Shakespeare. There are at least two fictive worlds, $W_4´$, within which Kinbote and Shade have their existence, and $W_4´´$ projected by Shade´s poem. The relationships between these worlds and to W_1, in which Nabokov the novelist operates, are complex. In Sinclair´s terms, there is a bewildering richness of sub-report (Sinclair 1983a). Nabokov in ´Pale Fire´ the novel reports that Kinbote has prepared a critical edition of Shade´s poem. The commentary to the poem is a further report which leads in two directions. On the one hand it points to the poem and on the other to events in Zembla, the fictive land from which it transpires that Kinbote was or imagines himself to be exiled. The commentary thus reports that Shade reports what is represented in ´Pale Fire´ the poem. It also reports that certain characters exist in Zembla who themselves report.... and so on. ´Pale Fire´ the novel thus constructs a number of

different realities which are only indirectly related to the
'real' world of phenomena. From these the statement that
Nabokov is making must be intuited.

It seems to me probable that the simpler nature of the
relationship between text and reality in science text leaves
its trace in the text as macrostructure. I therefore view my
results as providing strong confirmation of the position
briefly propounded by Ellis:

> "in fiction, on the contrary (where 'the poet lieth not,
> for he affirmeth nothing') the thesis creates a
> secondary universe (in some complex relation,
> referentially or non-referentially, to the primary
> universe), which is one reason for the greater
> complexity needed in the contextual analysis of literary
> utterance". (Ellis 1966 p92)

It is gratifying that no less a commentator than Kibote himself
is of the same opinion. In his critical comment to line 130 of
Shade's poem he emphasises

> "the basic fact that 'reality' is neither the subject nor
> the object of true art, which creates its own special
> reality having nothing to do with the average 'reality'
> perceived by the communal eye." (Nabokov op cit p106)

This is not to say that for science text the relation is
simple. From the discussion of the Firthian notion of levels
of meaning in chapter one it should be evident that even for
science text the relationship between language and the actual
world is highly complex. Nor does the conclusion reached here
deny the possibility of macrostructure in non-science text. It
merely suggests that in this case it is necessary to look
elsewhere than to lexical patterning. This helps perhaps to
explain why narrative structures, for example, are so difficult
to identify, as Sinclair has observed (Sinclair 1981).

10.3   The Scope of Linguistics

It was seen in the preceding section that the findings of the
enquiry reported in part three of this book raise questions of
a fundamental nature concerning the relation of text to reality
and the ways in which different kinds of text structure
reality. A preliminary discussion of the issues involved was
undertaken using concepts derived largely from philosophy. It
is not clear whether linguistics alone is capable of resolving
the issues. It is my belief that a far greater amount of
sustained and detailed observation of text needs to be
undertaken before this particular question can be given an
answer. Linguistics, with the observational power that is now
potentially provided by the computer, is on the threshold of
becoming truly scientific. But it may be that there is a basic
limitation to the techniques of such a scientific linguistics
whereby they are capable of raising questions which they are

incapable of answering. I propose to bring my study to a close with a brief consideration of this issue.

My concern with the relation between text and reality is a reflection of a more fundamental issue. This is the relation between the ´analogue´ and the ´digital´ in human communication. The ´analogue´ is a convenient shorthand way of referring to such properties as continuity, gradation and indivisibility. The ´digital´ is the province of the discrete, the analytic and the rational, of oppositions which are frequently binary and, most significantly, of the possibility of negation. The world of phenomena is essentially analogue. Nature knows no categories. Much of human thought, however, is digital in nature. And from this stem some crucial problems in epistemology.

In order to understand the environment and hence to survive in it, man structures the world of phenomena. He structures it socially by means of institutions and, more fundamentally, by institutionally recognised categories, such as roles. He structures it scientifically through the elaborate systems of categorisation embedded in scientific theories. And in a reflexive relation to both activities, he structures it through language by means of the conventional categories of a particular linguistic system. In other words, digital processes are a fundamental means by which order is imposed upon the continuum and understanding achieved.

This is not to say that analogue processes of thinking or expression are impossible. Nearly all music, most painting and much literature are precisely an attempt to avoid the digitalisation of the analogue. One reason, however, that avant-garde or ´concrete´ poetry, for example, often appears strange is because both intrinsically and in much of its function of publicly articulating understanding, language is moulded to man´s need to impose structure on his experience of the analogue world of phenoma rather than replicate it. The result, of course, is a distortion. This is the price that must be paid for the power conveyed by analytical schemes of thought. It was perhaps only a slight exaggeration that led George Boole to entitle the work in which he virtually invented modern symbolic logic ´The Laws of Thought´ (Boole 1854). The present study has been concerned with investigating one way in which language contributes to the imposition of structure.

At this point interesting and disturbing questions begin to become apparent. There is a danger that the plausibility or familiarity of the structure thus created through language will be taken as evidence of its reality rather than as either a necessary and convenient working hypothesis or, perhaps, a potentially dangerous falsehood. Common sense or paradigmatic views become firmly entrenched and extremely difficult to question even when they no longer provide an adequate framework for action. The history of science, of course, is replete with instances and Dingle´s questioning of relativity theory and the difficulty he had in getting his views discussed seriously, whether they were reasonable or misguided, is but the most recent example of a common phenomenon (Dingle 1972). The risks are considerable, encompassing the problem of ideology and what Leech in his study of the English used in advertising refers to as "strategic semantics" (Leech 1966). In a yet more fundamental way it concerns the manner in which the prevailing ´discourse´, to use Foucault´s term, determines the permissable categories of thought (Foucault 1970).

It is issues of this sort which lie below the surface of the present study and which need to be resolved for a study of this nature to reach a satisfactory conclusion. But I am doubtful of the extent to which purely linguistic methods can be used to elucidate such questions. The issues involved relate to the social construction of the ´episteme´ and are not, as general semanticists of Hayakawa´s persuasion suppose, essentially linguistic (Hayakawa 1974). Nor is the problem simply the Sapir-Whorf hypothesis writ large. The prevailing discourse can be replaced and has been historically. Thus the problem raised by the present study is that it has postulated a notion of linguistically constructed subject matter but in order to develop a critique of that notion, which is when philosophically interesting issues begin to be raised, it would be necessary to step outside the bounds of linguistics.

There is thus a kind of Godelian paradox about this enquiry at its most fundamental level. The approach I have adopted has the potential of raising issues which cannot be answered within the approach. The digital methodology which was adopted necessarily in order to have a methodology at all can go some way towards investigating aspects of the use of language which I believe are critical to understanding how man locates himself in the world but is ultimately inadequate for conceptualising a relationship which has the analogue as one of its terms. It may be that the human sciences will forever in this way elude all attempts to elaborate rigorous methodologies.

I do not believe, however, that this means that the quest for rational explanation in linguistics is pointless. On the contrary, I consider a primary aim should be to bring ever increasing areas of linguistic behaviour within the scope of rigorous statement. The present study has been an attempt to do precisely that in an area which had appeared hitherto unpromising in this respect. But in the process it has become clear that linguistics is ultimately circumscribed by the need for interpretation. Either that, or it must abandon its claim to be a science.

10.4 Conclusion

Despite the likelihood of this kind of ultimate limitation on the explanatory power of linguistics, it is worth reviewing in these concluding remarks the progress made in this study towards understanding an important aspect of text structure. In the first part of this book, I outlined a theoretical view of language. This suggested that more emphasis could be placed

on the graphic substance and the essentially arbitrary nature
of language and emphasised the way in which meaning
consequently arises from formal organisation. This led to the
development in the second part of the book of a methodology for
the investigation of text. In the third part, the methodology
was applied to a corpus consisting of five science and three
non-science texts in order to explore how far it was possible
to proceed towards understanding text in the light of the
theoretical principles.

In some respects, considerable progress was made. It proved
feasible to demonstrate the existence of structures in text
which are not susceptible of direct observation and which can
be identified on purely formal criteria. These structures
appear to play a major role in the projection by the text of
subject matter and hence help to account for the sensation of
aboutness. For certain types of text, these structures proved
to be more or less recurrent within the limits of reasonable
variation. As a result, it was possible to discern the global
articulation of these texts and on this basis to postulate a
scheme of text classification. The science texts could in this
way be formally distinguished from the other texts. It proved
possible to propose a mechanism which accounts for all the
observed varieties of textual articulation in terms of the two
underlying parameters of integration/differentiation and
serialisation/parallelism. This led to to a consideration of
the different status of the subject matter in the two broad
classes of text and of the relations obtaining between the
world of the text and the actual world. Thus the formal view
of text adopted here proved instrumental in investigating the
important question of how structure is imposed on phenomena by
language.

This last point I consider to be of the utmost importance. I
argued in the first part that there can be no justification for
undertaking a formal analysis for its own sake or for adopting
the "text-crushing" procedures associated with computational
analysis merely because they become obligatory when studying
long texts. If the present study has any lasting value, it may
well lie in the demonstration that questions posed at a high
level of generality, such as the question implied by viewing
the notion of subject matter as problematic, may imply for
their investigation analyses conducted at some or all of a
number of congruent levels, including the fundamental level at
which strings of graphic characters are treated as such. At
the same time, it has been recognised that further issues might
thereby be raised which escape the grasp of linguistic enquiry
at any level.

These gains notwithstanding, much still remains to be done to
further understanding of text within the perspective adopted
here. There are a number of ways in which the methodology used
needs further investigation and refinement. I consider that
the use of Cluster Analysis has been entirely justified by the
insight it has afforded into hitherto uninvestigated properties
of text. But it should not be forgotten that it is an

essentially heuristic procedure. It is of some importance to examine the extent to which it is possible to reduce the heuristic content of the methodology in favour of increasingly algorithmic procedures. Other varieties of Cluster Analysis could be evaluated. Clumping techniques, for example, might represent a viable approach to homograph separation. The solutions obtained by any Cluster Analysis technique could be submitted to the evaluation methods proposed by Gnandesikan to see whether their robustness can thereby be measured (Gnandesikan et al 1977). More ambitiously, there is a need to explore more rigorously than was possible here whether an adequate probabilistic model of text can be developed. In chapter four I gave reasons for believing that probabilistic models are unlikely to prove satisfactory. But this line of reasoning needs to be examined further. Certainly, were it to prove possible to develop an appropriate probabilistic model of text, this would represent a major contribution to text linguistics.

Even accepting the Cluster Analysis technique used in the present study, there is still scope for useful investigation of what might constitute the optimum definition of interval and span. In the absence of solid theoretical reasons, the choice of chapter for the former and plus and minus four orthographic words for the latter were decisions determined here largely by pragmatic considerations. Further methodological progress might also come by exploring more thoroughly the application of the theory of networks to collocational data derived from texts, particulary as they might help with the understanding of probabilistic structures. Networks of the type I called ´chains´ in the last chapter, for example, are formally identical with Markov chains. In general, then, it seems to me that the degree of formalism achievable in the description of the kind of empirical phenomena I have investigated can potentially be greatly increased. I see no reason at present that the statement of lexical behaviour and the macrostructural properties of text should not reach a level of rigour comparable to that obtained in, for example, the more mathematical treatments of grammar.

There is one obvious way in which the theoretical concerns of this kind of study can be extended. The analysis could be broadened to include other categories of text. In this way a more extensive investigation of the notion of macrostructure could be obtained and the proposed typology of texts more widely tested. Similarly, further study of other science texts would prove valuable in testing the hypothesis of the dimensions of serialisation and integration. But perhaps the most important and fascinating outstanding theoretical question concerns the nature of the mechanism operating in literary text which allows inference from what may be called pseudo-reference to particulars of philosophical generalisations. It would be interesting to learn how it is that there are more things dreamt of in Horatio´s philosophy than are in heaven and earth, or in text at least.

If there is thus scope to expand the objects of investigation, it is also desirable to examine in greater detail some of the linguistic phenomena which have emerged as significant in the course of this study. The crucial category of collocation would in particular repay more sustained investigation. Use, for example, could be made of the techniques of the present enquiry to illuminate the formative principles of scientific terminology. A scheme for categorising collocations along the lines that I have proposed elsewhere might lead both to a system for the formal identification of functional vocabulary classes and to a more delicate description of macrostructure (Phillips 1983).

The present study, then, besides leading to substantive findings, has the merit of suggesting a large number of further lines for investigation. I believe that it contains the seeds of what Lakatos refers to as a "theoretically progressive" research programme (Lakatos 1978). If this assessment should prove to be valid, then I shall consider that the study has been completely justified.

APPENDICES

APPENDIX 1

CORPUS STATISTICS

This appendix contains a statistical characterisation of the corpus. Table A1.1 presents the basic vocabulary statistics of the texts. The total vocabulary of each text (the number V of types) and the number of running words constituting each text (the number N of tokens) are given together with the mean and standard deviation of each frequency distribution. From these figures, the extent to which the texts differ quantitatively in respect of their vocabularies can be judged.

Statistical details of the sampling of lemmata for investigation are given in Table A1.2. The figures are reasonably self-explanatory. The following points, however, should be noted. First, the ratio of number of eligible lemmata to number of lemmata in the frequency band remains more or less constant for all texts. That is to say, the coverage of the frequency band represented by the eligible lemmata is much the same throughout the corpus. This increases the validity of comparing results from different texts. Secondly, the figures for the means and standard deviations allow the frequency distributions of the selected lemmata to be compared with the frequency distributions of the eligible lemmata from which they were drawn for each text. The extent to which the shapes of the two distributions are similar reflects the accuracy with which the random sample characterises the population from which it was extracted. It can be seen from inspection of the table that in general the match is excellent.

	ELEN	CMEC	CREL	BIPC	THRM	THF	MRSD	TMM
Number of tokens (N)	60363	63068	48124	62001	66644	62003	65730	60383
Number of types (V)	3252	3309	3235	4555	3321	6767	7834	7291
Mean type frequency ($\bar{x}$)	18.6	19.1	14.9	13.6	20.1	9.2	8.4	8.0
Standard deviation (σ)	131.1	142.7	95.8	110.8	154.0	62.7	65.5	70.0

Table A1.1

	ELEN	CMEC	CREL	BIPC	THRM	THF	MRSD	TMM
Upper cut-off freq.	291	310	236	305	328	305	323	297
Lower cut-off freq.	10	10	10	10	11	10	11	10
No. words in freq. band (a)	621	711	586	713	646	702	631	725
No. eligible lemmata (b)	362	448	316	405	392	411	358	422
Ratio a/b	1.7	1.6	1.9	1.8	1.7	1.7	1.8	1.7
No. of lemmata selected	199	198	190	200	209	210	207	210
Mean freq. eligible lemmata	34.9	37.1	34.8	35.1	43.0	27.8	34.0	23.7
Mean freq. selected lemmata	35.4	38.1	35.7	37.6	41.8	25.7	34.2	23.5
S.D eligible lemmata	37.1	43.1	35.4	40.1	48.3	28.5	33.8	20.3
S.D selected lemmata	38.8	45.0	36.7	46.1	47.6	28.6	31.0	18.3

Table A1.2

APPENDIX 2

SELECTED LEMMATA

This appendix contains listings of the lemmata selected for investigation in the analysis of each text. Each lemma is preceded by its frequency of occurrence in the text. This figure represents the conflation of the individual frequencies of occurrence of the morphological variants constituting the lemma.

SELECTED LEMMATA: ELEN

19	Account	205	Device	73	Know
21	Accurate	52	Differential		
21	Achieve	40	Diode	130	Large
29	Active	24	Direction	28	Layer
13	Actual	25	Discrete	14	Look
14	Admittance	25	Doped	62	Loop
21	Alternative	37	Draw	138	Low
803	Amplifier	17	Drift		
25	Amplitude			52	Magnitude
60	Analysis	18	Earth	19	Main
49	Appear	64	Effect	208	Make
15	Appendix	35	Effective	33	Method
101	Applied	32	Electron	31	Model
22	Arrangement	25	Elements		
83	Assume	17	Enough	16	N-channel
25	Available	12	Ensure	41	Need
21	Avoid	67	Equal	78	Network
		19	Expect	16	No-load
99	Base	11	Expense	26	Node
39	Become	29	Explain	15	Noise
92	Bias	90	Expression	25	Non-inverting
26	Block			30	Normal
10	Bridge	52	Factor	55	Note
		19	Full		
61	Calculate	23	Feed	19	Occur
48	Called	211	Feedback	13	Once
52	Capacity	43	Field-effect	43	Operational
21	Capacitance	37	Figure	38	Order
93	Capacitor	44	Find	46	Oscillation
23	Carriers	13	Finite	60	Oscillator
58	Case	65	First		
17	Certain	52	Following	37	P-N
108	Change	43	Follower	25	P-type
35	Channel	59	Form	45	Parallel
100	Chapter	352	Frequency	31	Parameter
45	Choose			69	Part
743	Circuit	245	Given	22	Particular
37	Compare	45	Greater	11	Peak
123	Component			60	Performance
21	Conductance	33	Half	19	Phase-shift
115	Connect	212	High	27	Plot
89	Consider	25	Hole	133	Power
33	Construct			10	Practical
26	Contain	19	Ideal	13	Practice
20	Correct	30	Identical	25	Problem
		20	Important	33	Product
29	Data	30	Improve	29	Property
27	Decibel	34	Increase		
18	Decrease	15	Independent	27	Range
19	Denominator	12	Inductance	17	Rate
36	Depend	17	Inductor	43	Ratio
25	Derive	510	Input	15	Reason
78	Describe	38	Inverting	92	Related
42	Determine	26	Isolation	17	Relatively

APPENDIX TWO

16	Remember	14	Sign	25	Tuned
91	Required	283	Signal	50	Typical
152	Resistor	34	Silicon		
21	Respect	35	Similar	19	Unwanted
36	Respectively	62	Simple	292	Use
50	Result	23	Single	61	Usually
39	Reverse	11	Sinusoidal		
10	Right	23	Small	184	Value
31	Rise	19	Space	55	Vary
14	Round	55	Stable	17	Various
		24	Suitable	541	Voltage
34	Say	81	Supply		
19	Second	23	System	25	Want
43	See			20	Watt
31	Separate	61	Temperature	46	Well
19	Set	13	Thermistor	60	Write
66	Shift	17	Total		
14	Short	240	Transistor	50	Zero
27	Shunt	13	True		

SELECTED LEMMATA: CMEC

61	Accelerate	12	Confine	21	Exist
42	Act	155	Conservative	39	Explicit
62	Amplitude	123	Consider	61	Expression
145	Angle	165	Constant	43	External
268	Angular	34	Contain		
60	Apply	15	Continuous	68	Fact
15	Approach	38	Convenient	231	Find
55	Approximate	24	Coriolis	10	Finite
55	Arbitrary	108	Correspond	42	Follow
59	Assume	27	Couple	460	Face
25	Attract	12	Critical	102	Frame
		50	Cross-section	38	Free
12	Blow			74	Frequency
252	Body	17	Degree	184	Function
		34	Density		
16	Cancel	61	Describe	20	Generate
12	Cartesian	26	Detector	142	Given
225	Case	59	Difference	84	Gravity
180	Centre	35	Dimension	38	Great
84	Chapter	24	Dipole	13	Gyroscope
22	Characteristic	206	Direction		
105	Charge	33	Distribution	16	Half
77	Choose			53	Hamilton
44	Clearly	152	Earth	17	Height
32	Closest	53	Easy	12	Homogeneous
62	Collision	10	Edge	27	Horizontal
40	Compared	15	Electromagnetic		
24	Complete	15	Electrostatic	29	Illustrate
22	Complex	13	Element	22	Include
13	Complicated	297	Energy	54	Independent
23	Concept	407	Equation	13	Infinity
67	Condition	50	Equilibrium	14	Information
27	Cone	14	Exact	56	Initial

27	Instantaneous	42	Possible	11	Several
24	Internal	155	Potential	28	Shape
31	Introduce	60	Precess	134	Show
23	Inverse	13	Pressure	20	Side
36	Involve	20	Previous	22	Sign
		58	Principal	87	Simple
49	Known	41	Principle	155	Small
		100	Problem	173	Solve
15	Latitude	28	Product	34	Space
32	Lead	26	Provide	39	Specify
45	Length			24	Start
27	Linear	21	Range	14	Stationary
15	Loss	43	Real	25	Subject
		18	Reason	29	Substitution
31	Magnetic	11	Recoil	46	Sum
32	Maximum	15	Reference	40	Sun
16	Mean	23	Regard	56	Surface
97	Moment	14	Region	17	Swing
		12	Release	85	Symmetry
35	Neglect	31	Remains		
78	Normal	46	Require	19	Tend
17	North	48	Respect	73	Term
		37	Rest	21	Theory
145	One	13	Return	25	Third
163	Orbit	27	Rocket	76	Total
25	Order	185	Rotate	48	Transform
11	Orthogonal	10	Round	31	Type
39	Pair	26	Satellite	66	Uniform
16	Parallel	30	Satisfy		
35	Part	29	Say	37	Vanish
63	Pendulum	15	Scalar	47	Vary
114	Period	13	Scale	106	Vector
16	Phase	62	Scatter	16	Volume
15	Physics	61	Second		
18	Pivoted	35	Section	36	Way
31	Place	10	Semi-major	19	Well
142	Point	29	Separate	12	Wholly
30	Positive	10	Series	10	Words
42	Possible	60	Set	38	Work

SELECTED LEMMATA: CREL

14	Activation	87	Batch	20	Classified
22	Actual	18	Beaker	15	Complex
20	Adiabatic	61	Become	78	Component
20	Affect	22	Behavior	59	Composition
35	Allowable			161	Concentration
14	Alone	38	Calculate	81	Conditions
65	Analysis	26	Called	12	Connected
13	Appreciable	74	Case	120	Consider
11	Appropriate	41	Catalyst	21	Constant
17	Average	19	Certain	20	Constant-volume
		104	Change	23	Consumed
44	Balance	19	Chart	31	Contacted

APPENDIX TWO

24	Corresponding	34	Initial	24	Refer
		96	Integration	118	Relative
125	Data	56	Intermediate	63	Represent
18	Decrease	22	Introduce	62	Require
36	Dependent	29	Involve	22	Respect
60	Design	27	Irreversible	16	Rule
55	Desired	31	Isothermal	42	Run
48	Determine				
19	Develop	50	Know	61	Same
39	Differential			25	Say
20	Difficult	60	Large	31	Scheme
30	Directly	29	Leave	17	Searching
24	Disappearance	52	Liter	70	See
82	Distribution	11	Little	49	Separate
28	Drop	75	Low	26	Set
15	Duty			19	Shift
		53	Make	72	Simple
29	Effect	37	Measure	40	Situation
61	Elementary	41	Mechanism	12	Sketch
50	Energy	73	Method	30	Slope
15	Engineering	48	Minimum	25	Slow
229	Equation	274	Mixed	17	Solid
62	Equilibrium	38	Molecule	32	Space-time
12	Equimolar	34	Multiple	14	Special
19	Equipment			28	State
80	Example	64	Need	16	Steady-state
20	Excess	12	Nonelementary	49	Step
15	Exothermic	41	Note	55	Stoichiometry
40	Expression	12	Nth-order	29	Straight
		49	Number	72	Stream
13	Fact			31	Study
45	Factor	68	Optimum	35	Suggest
19	Fall	24	Over-all	14	Suppose
17	Fermentation			163	System
47	Figure	21	Partial		
21	Final	34	Particular	234	Temperature
283	Find	27	Path	19	Theory
99	First	54	Performance	25	Thermodynamics
18	Fixed	26	Place	38	Three
70	Fluid	52	Plot	109	Time
143	Follow	68	Present	41	Total
10	Forward	67	Pressure	13	Transfer
14	Free	51	Procedure	62	Treatment
		42	Proceed	16	Turn
65	Gas	196	Products	130	Two
68	General	11	Progress	90	Type
223	Give	50	Progression		
36	Graphical	24	Proper	15	Uniform
26	Great	15	Proportional	58	Unit
				13	Unused
13	Heterogeneous	26	Question	201	Use
				29	Usual
33	Ideal	23	Rapid		
12	Independent	66	Ratio	97	Value
29	Inert	1167	React	18	Variable
22	Information	14	Rearranging	37	Vary

44	Various	43	Way	11	Zero-order
16	Vessel	13	Whole		
		10	Word		

SELECTED LEMMATA: BIPC

14	Ability	13	Depression	19	Infinitely
18	Accomplished	49	Derived	18	Information
17	Acetate	127	Determine	32	Initial
371	Acid	84	Dilute	14	Intrinsic
21	Act	133	Dissociation	14	Introduce
141	Activity	35	Dissolved	372	Ion
40	Actual			24	Isoelectric
38	Affect	17	Easily	15	Isoionic
64	Amino	46	Effect	13	Isolated
12	Ammonia	20	Effective	40	Isothermal
11	Amphiprotic	17	Electrical		
26	Anion	66	Electrolyte	74	Low
24	Appear	24	Electrophoresis	12	Left
58	Applied	16	End	67	Level
35	Approximately	27	Enthalpy	27	Line
14	Arithmetic	190	Entropy	73	Liquid
12	Arrhenius	231	Equilibrium	20	List
26	Atmospheric	90	Example	11	Little
17	Attraction	31	Exergonic	18	Long
17	Available	33	Explain		
		55	Express	27	Manner
255	Base			44	Manometer
29	Biochemical	50	Fact	35	Material
12	Bronsted	21	First	15	Mathematics
		35	Fixed	13	Metabolic
86	Calculate	22	Flask	39	Method
37	Cation	47	Fraction	94	Mixture
68	Characteristic	21	Freezing	57	Mole
101	Charge				
80	Chemical	264	Gas	29	Nature
19	Colligative	29	Gibbs	24	Need
40	Common	16	Glycine	78	Negative
36	Completely	71	Great	53	Neutralisation
81	Component	129	Group	22	New
270	Concentration			28	Normal
58	Condition	11	Haemoglobin		
53	Conjugate	11	Half	23	Occupied
309	Constant	11	Heading	92	Order
23	Content	47	Heat	20	Organisation
34	Contribution	14	Henry	21	Osmosis
20	Converted	27	Hydrogen	39	Overall
21	Corresponding	40	Hydrolysis		
30	Coupled			20	Perform
49	Curve	26	Identical	23	Phosphate
		18	Illustrate	37	Possess
21	Decimal	11	Impermeable	21	Potential
96	Define	34	Important	26	Power
26	Density	21	Index	92	Present
33	Depend	24	Indicator	58	Proceed

APPENDIX TWO   247

84	Product	44	Simple	16	Treatment
15	Progressive	18	Size	31	True
65	Proportional	14	Slope	19	Turn
43	Pure	62	Small	32	Type
		21	Solid		
91	Quantity	116	Solute	132	Unit
		503	Solution	17	Unity
26	Raise	12	Space		
13	Rate-limiting	51	Spontaneous	418	Value
31	Real	139	State	28	Van
20	Remain	39	Step	71	Vapour
26	Require	26	Structure	12	Vessel
25	Result	11	Sucrose	11	Virtually
10	Resultant	15	Suitable	113	Volume
45	Reversible	17	Suppose		
10	Right-hand	28	Surroundings	122	Water
		169	System	46	Way
53	Salt			41	Weight
32	Saturated	37	Table	30	Written
28	Separated	271	Temperature		
42	Show	86	Term	49	Yield
29	Side	14	Three		
14	Sign	30	Total	34	Zero
24	Significant	23	Transfer	22	Zwitterion
11	Silver	14	Transition		

SELECTED LEMMATA: THRM

40	Absolute	26	Concerned	34	Discuss
18	Acceleration	55	Conclude	19	Distance
45	Actual	25	Connect	20	Drive
82	Adiabatic	15	Conservation	30	Drop
151	Air	142	Constant		
38	Ammonia	25	Constant-	37	Electrical
44	Analysis		pressure	18	Elevation
13	Answer	24	Continuity	111	Engine
46	Approach	218	Control	11	English
159	Assume	20	Convenience	23	Entire
45	Available	52	Cooling	188	Equation
		16	Corresponding	82	Equilibrium
31	Behaviour	13	Critical	23	Essential
28	Block			22	Evacuated
58	Body	22	Data	23	Evident
11	Book	168	Defined	29	Exactly
15	Bottom	22	Degree	32	Exists
		20	Depend	15	Exit
56	Call	38	Describe	25	Extensive
50	Carnot	44	Designate		
48	Certain	17	Desired	22	Fact
64	Chapter	128	Determine	29	Factor
15	Classical	23	Development	23	Figure
17	Clausius	39	Device	26	Filled
18	Closed	65	Diagram	11	Finite
18	Coefficient	18	Diameter	195	First
30	Compare	88	Difference	28	Fitted

33	Fixed	15	Mole	69	Remain
207	Flow	56	Molecular	19	Remove
123	Follow	11	Motion	12	Rest
12	Frame	49	Move	76	Result
15	Freeze				
32	Fuel	35	Necessary	170	Saturated
		22	Negative	125	Second
47	General	31	Negligible	29	Separation
22	Generator	26	Normal	57	Simple
25	Gravity	20	Nozzle	13	Single
		12	Nuclear	17	Slightly
12	Hand			48	Small
663	Heat	13	Objective	32	Solve
30	Helium	50	Occur	184	Specific
12	Hour	30	Opened	28	Spring
		24	Order	20	Standard
98	Ideal	20	Output	38	Steady-flow
25	Imply			224	Stream
32	Important	20	Particular	12	Stops
20	Impossible	20	Passes	134	Substance
107	Increase	28	Path	39	Superheated
15	Inequality	22	Performance	29	Suppose
132	Initially	11	Pin	104	Surroundings
70	Integral	33	Pipe		
92	Internal	121	Piston	164	Tables
13	International	53	Place	156	Tank
35	Introduce	58	Plant	579	Temperature
90	Involve	12	Plus	24	Thermal
30	Isothermal	208	Point	16	Thermoelectric
		17	Positive	19	Thermometer
51	Know	30	Possible	364	Transfer
		92	Power	16	Tube
13	Later	21	Present	149	Two
223	Law	65	Problem		
98	Leave	712	Process	47	Undergo
125	Let	51	Product	115	Unit
20	Level	184	Property	191	Use
93	Line				
211	Liquid	60	Quantity	104	Value
34	Long	30	Quasi-	31	Various
61	Low		equilibrium	48	Velocity
28	Low-			65	Vessel
	temperature	30	Raise	36	View
		13	Ratio		
18	Macroscopic	11	Readily	23	Way
17	Manner	15	Reason	70	Weight
281	Mass	69	Refer	13	Wire
32	Mean	111	Refrigeration	507	Work
57	Measure	17	Region	100	Write
17	Membrane	215	Relation		
12	Minimum	29	Relative	74	Zero

APPENDIX TWO

SELECTED LEMMATA: THF

16	Able	14	Dicky	14	Large		
25	Act	15	Dog	63	Last		
22	Add	18	Donck	27	Leak		
24	Afraid	14	Doubt	28	Let		
78	Africa	21	Dream	21	Light		
20	Age	15	Drop	86	Little		
24	Agent			101	Left		
17	Agreement	32	Easy	36	Live		
22	Answer	28	End	113	Long		
15	Aim	34	Enough	25	Lose		
18	Arrive	11	Escape	61	Love		
		18	Evening				
54	Begin	13	Every	18	Malteser		
45	Believe	13	Everything	48	Married		
11	Berkhamstead	24	Expect	13	Matter		
13	Big	18	Explained	13	Maurice		
60	Bit	23	Eyes	70	Mean		
50	Black			19	Member		
56	Book	40	Face	34	Mind		
16	BOSS	14	Fact	18	Minute		
17	Bottle	15	Family	28	Moment		
24	Box	44	Father	22	Morning		
28	Break	20	File				
12	Briefcase	12	Fine	49	Name		
33	Bring	10	Five	27	Next		
19	Business	12	Foreign	16	Nobody		
		37	Forget	28	Note		
54	C	33	Friends	47	Nothing		
72	Call			25	Notice		
25	Car	47	Girl	24	Number		
46	Care	85	Give				
33	Carson	13	Gold	15	Officer		
22	Catch			52	Opened		
40	Certainly	23	Half	11	Outfit		
13	Chance	41	Happen	18	Outside		
25	Change	37	Hargreaves				
10	Childhood	19	Hate	22	Paper		
10	Chinese	10	Hell	27	Past		
14	Church	35	Help	15	Picnickers		
13	Colin	19	Hold	28	Place		
16	Colour	50	Home	31	Play		
164	Come	13	Hotel	16	Please		
21	Cornelius	36	Hour	14	Pocket		
12	Corner	48	House	24	Police		
18	Country	16	Human	23	Poor		
54	Cynthia			19	Port		
		27	Idea	13	Pour		
200	Daintry	10	Ill	19	Pretty		
17	Darling			12	Prison		
18	Daughter	10	James	16	Private		
250	Davis	16	Job				
18	Dentist			27	Question		
15	Department	47	Keep	16	Quick		
16	Desk						

24	Remus	26	Son	52	Tried
23	Return	12	Soon		
12	Round	30	Sort	26	Uncle
10	Run	14	Special	36	Understand
		12	Square		
35	Safe	15	Stairs	10	View
532	Said	18	Station		
106	Sam	18	Stay	50	Wait
28	Sat	20	Stop	38	War
29	Section	19	Story	40	Watson
43	See	83	Suppose	90	Way
89	Seem	57	Sure	13	Wedding
19	Sense			25	Weak
40	Serious	28	Table	12	Whole
18	Service	83	Talk	35	Wife
30	Shoot	41	Telephone	15	Window
17	Shop	17	Thank	35	Wonder
29	Show	69	Thing	43	Work
26	Side	24	Three	18	World
16	Sign	17	Tonight	45	Worry
32	Silence	31	Troubled	29	Worst
49	Sir	20	Trout	29	Write
27	Sleep	31	Trust		
42	Small	35	Truth		

SELECTED LEMMATA: MRSD

16	Absurd	24	Clock	24	Fine
29	Admirable	17	Cold	20	Five
36	Age	247	Come	52	Flower
31	Air	54	Course	52	Friend
48	Alone			15	Front
27	Arm	13	Daisy	25	Full
17	Aunt	80	Day		
25	Awful	30	Dear	23	Garden
		20	Deep	91	Get
50	Beauty	23	Dinner	61	Girl
43	Become	14	Direct	80	Give
32	Bed	21	Doctor	15	Glove
17	Bedroom	27	Dog	80	Good
17	Big	11	Don	16	Grass
20	Bird	35	Dr	73	Great
46	Body	19	Drawing-room	28	Green
27	Book	56	Dress	35	Grey
25	Bourton			37	Grow
38	Bradshaw	19	Ellie		
12	Brain	13	Evelyn	20	Hair
14	Bright	28	Everything	27	Happened
23	Brush	12	Exquisite	46	Happy
64	Bruton			16	Hard
		60	Face	48	Hat
34	Call	53	Falling	37	Head
31	Care	180	Feel	20	Heaven
20	Certain	15	Figure	40	Help
20	Chair	20	Filmer	16	Henderson

64	Holmes	29	Paper	18	Son
100	Home	39	Partly	36	Sort
59	House	89	Party	52	Sound
78	Hugh	163	People	120	Stood
		48	Perfect	92	Still
25	Keep	183	Peter	25	Stop
65	Kilman	18	Pity	29	Straight
31	Kind	27	Place	81	Street
		22	Playing	32	Striking
144	Lady	33	Power	17	Summer
42	Last	12	Pretty	15	Sweet
28	Late	14	Proportion		
60	Laughing	58	Put	48	Table
22	Leaf			113	Take
38	Letter	17	Queer	89	Talk
31	Lying			19	Tear
149	Life	21	Reason	11	Terrace
35	Lighted	27	Red	20	Thinner
280	Like	53	Remember	12	Thirty
43	London	16	Repeated	38	Truth
36	Long	35	Respect	39	Turned
213	Look	33	Rest	32	Two
20	Loss	54	Rezia		
121	Love	43	Right	15	Upstairs
17	Lovely	16	Ring		
35	Lunch	43	Ran	35	Wait
				77	Walsh
183	Make	39	Same	53	Wanted
166	Man	548	Said	25	War
35	Mind	17	Sea	16	Water
103	Miss	14	Seat	35	Wave
70	Moment	14	Second	78	Way
39	Mother	226	See	32	Wear
29	Motor	82	Seem	12	Westminster
37	Move	70	Septimus	29	Whitbread
117	Mrs	19	Set	57	White
		17	Shakespeare	46	Whole
43	Name	13	Short	36	Wife
25	Nature	17	Shot	56	William
26	Nice	40	Side	134	Woman
50	Night	18	Silver	42	Words
19	Nobody	25	Simply	22	Work
11	Nonsense	98	Sit		
84	Nothing	14	Six	76	Year
16	Nurse	22	Smith	77	Youth
		24	Smoke		
27	Odd	23	Sofa		
57	Once	78	Something		

SELECTED LEMMATA: TMM

22	Ability	16	Adjust	16	Answer
22	Accept	10	Alone	21	Appropriate
33	Achieve	23	American	38	Argument
16	Actual	29	Animal	35	Automatic

19	Available	13	Five	19	Name
		33	Force	23	Nature
18	Base	43	Form	47	New
41	Beginning			17	Notion
23	Beings	29	General	129	Number
50	Big	20	Generation		
27	Bit	12	Giant	27	Obvious
16	Brief	54	Give	12	Office
58	Build	81	Go	15	Old
		66	Good	43	One
97	Calculation	24	Govern	44	Operate
30	Call	62	Great	22	Order
34	Car	63	Growth		
30	Case			15	Pace
16	Cash	34	Hand	39	Paper
10	Census	13	Hard	43	Part
82	Change	19	Hold	43	Particular
38	Cheaper	29	Huge	25	Pass
35	Chip	137	Human	24	Pattern
112	Come			71	People
20	Commercial	21	IBM	36	Period
21	Common	50	Important	29	Personal
25	Company	39	Individual	64	Possible
26	Component	89	Information	14	Pound
31	Concept	11	Input	20	Principle
16	Consequence	13	Instruction	81	Problem
26	Continued	26	Invention	75	Processing
43	Cost	25	Involve	50	Produce
48	Course			26	Profession
33	Crime	15	Japan	159	Program
				17	Push
35	Day	88	Know	35	Put
34	Decision				
74	Different	18	Language	33	Question
36	Difficult	17	Law	23	Quick
30	Display	34	Lead		
		25	Learning	37	Range
37	Education	17	Let	18	Reach
32	Effect	67	Long	34	Read
22	Efficient	11	Lovelace	72	Really
17	Effort	21	Low	41	Realism
31	Employed			32	Reason
14	Ensure	185	Machine	17	Recent
12	Entity	21	Major	16	Relative
27	Equipped	133	Make	41	Robot
10	Everything	70	Man	13	Role
14	Exact	40	Market	20	Routine
50	Example	33	Mechanical	24	Rule
15	Exercise	24	Medical		
15	Expensive	30	Microprocessor	62	Say
		22	Mind	63	Science
36	Factor	13	Minute	13	Sense
26	Feature	16	Modern	71	Set
27	Fed	43	Money	11	Short-term
13	Field	22	Motor	19	Single
60	Find	54	Move	48	Size

APPENDIX TWO

26	Skilled	73	Teaching	29	Understand
49	Small	21	Tell	11	Unlikely
24	Space	30	Test	96	Use
24	Speak	98	Thing		
11	Spectacular	83	Think	18	Valve
58	Speed	30	Today	20	Various
19	Start	21	Tortoise	14	Vast
12	State	22	Total		
16	Step	12	Tradition	25	Want
50	Stored	19	Transistor	106	Way
20	Strength	16	Trend	15	Wheel
11	Stupendous	13	Trivial	33	Whole
14	Surface	10	Trouble	104	Work
41	Switching	27	Turing	119	World
		39	Turn	65	Written
19	Tackle	53	Two		
17	Tapeworm			74	Year

APPENDIX 3

ELEN DENDROGRAMS

The dendrograms in this appendix are given as examples to illustrate the first stage in the interpretation of the results of the collocational analysis of text. From these dendrograms the graphical representation of lexical networks is derived by collating the clustering information they contain with the implicit structural data in the listings of frequencies of collocation output by CLOC. For ease of interpretation, the lemmata have been identified on the dendrograms by name. CLUSTAN normally uses numerical identifiers. In addition, a horizontal broken line has been added to the graphs indicating the cut-off level beyond which further clustering is not recognised in the interpretation of the analysis. As explained in chapter four, the cut-off level was specified as that value of the criterial statistic at which the procedure begins clustering items which show no empirical association. The 'ragbag' cluster was not taken into consideration when determining the cut-off level. It can be seen from the dendrograms for ELEN that there is no difficulty in identifying the 'ragbag' cluster. In each chapter, it is the large cluster of nodes grouped at a single value of the criterial statistic.

CHAPTER 1

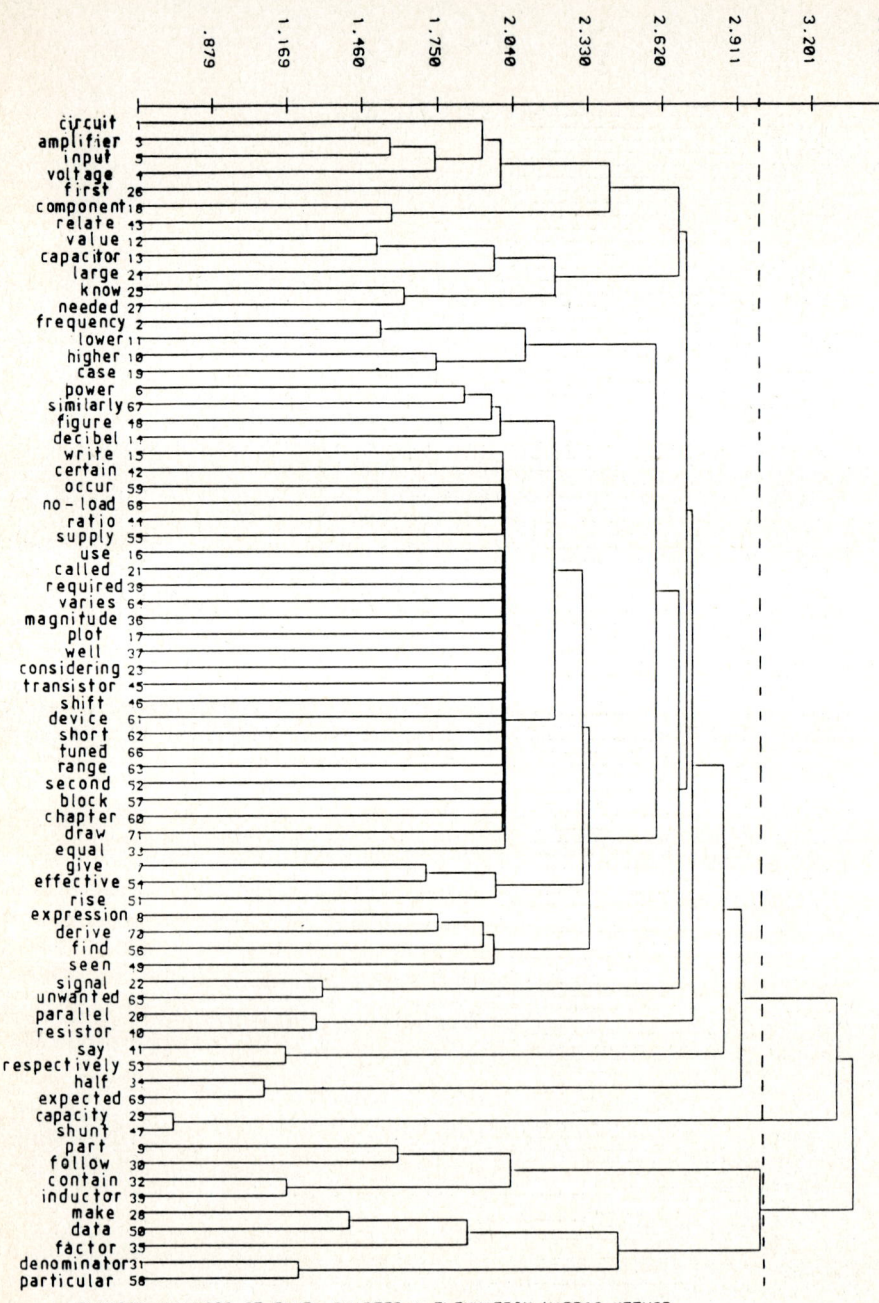

CLUSTER ANALYSIS OF 71X71 CHAPTER 1 ELENMATRIX WARD'S METHOD

APPENDIX THREE 257

CHAPTER 2

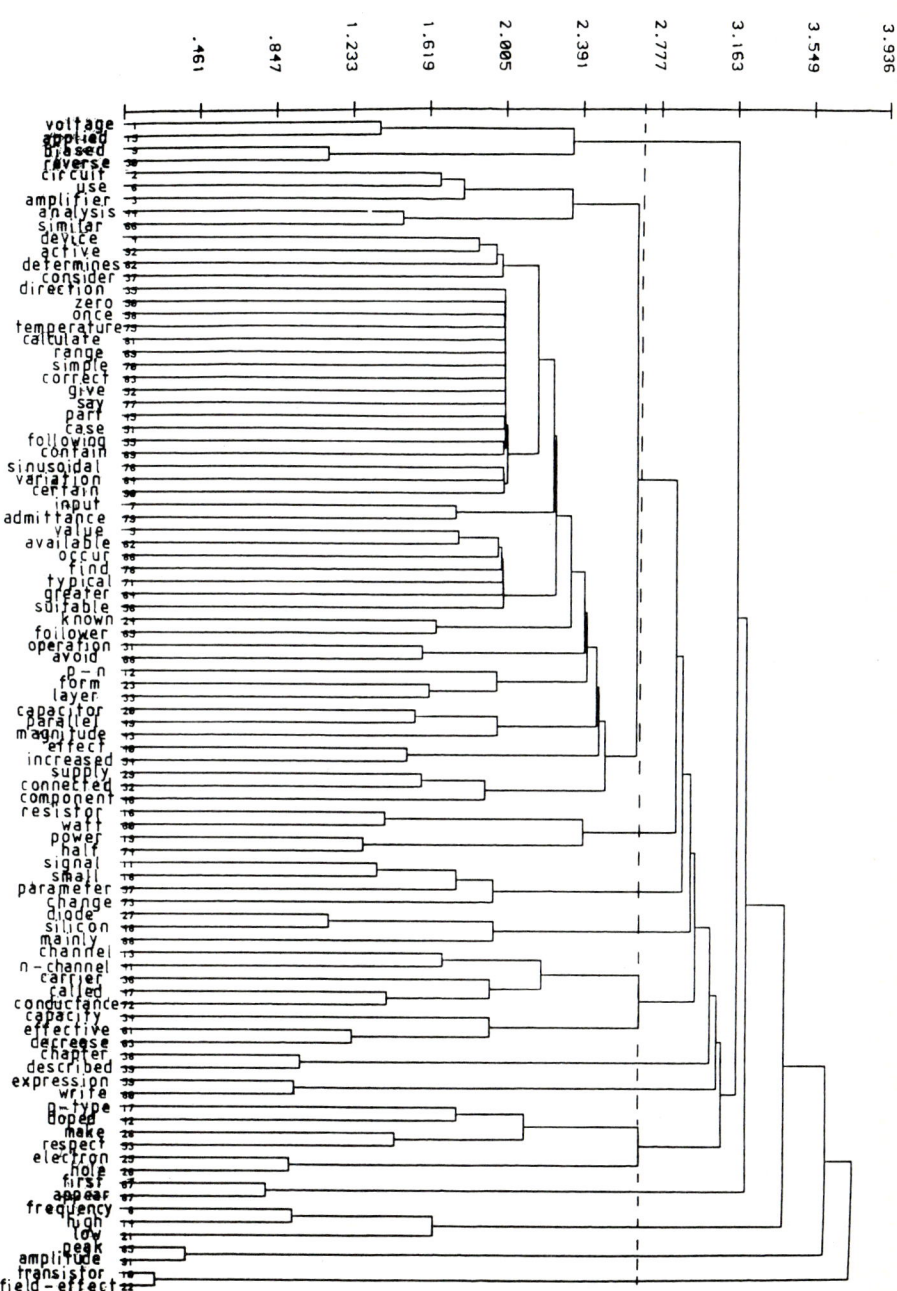

CLUSTER ANALYSIS OF 92X92 CHAPTER 2 ELENMATRIX WARD'S METHOD

QUIZ 1

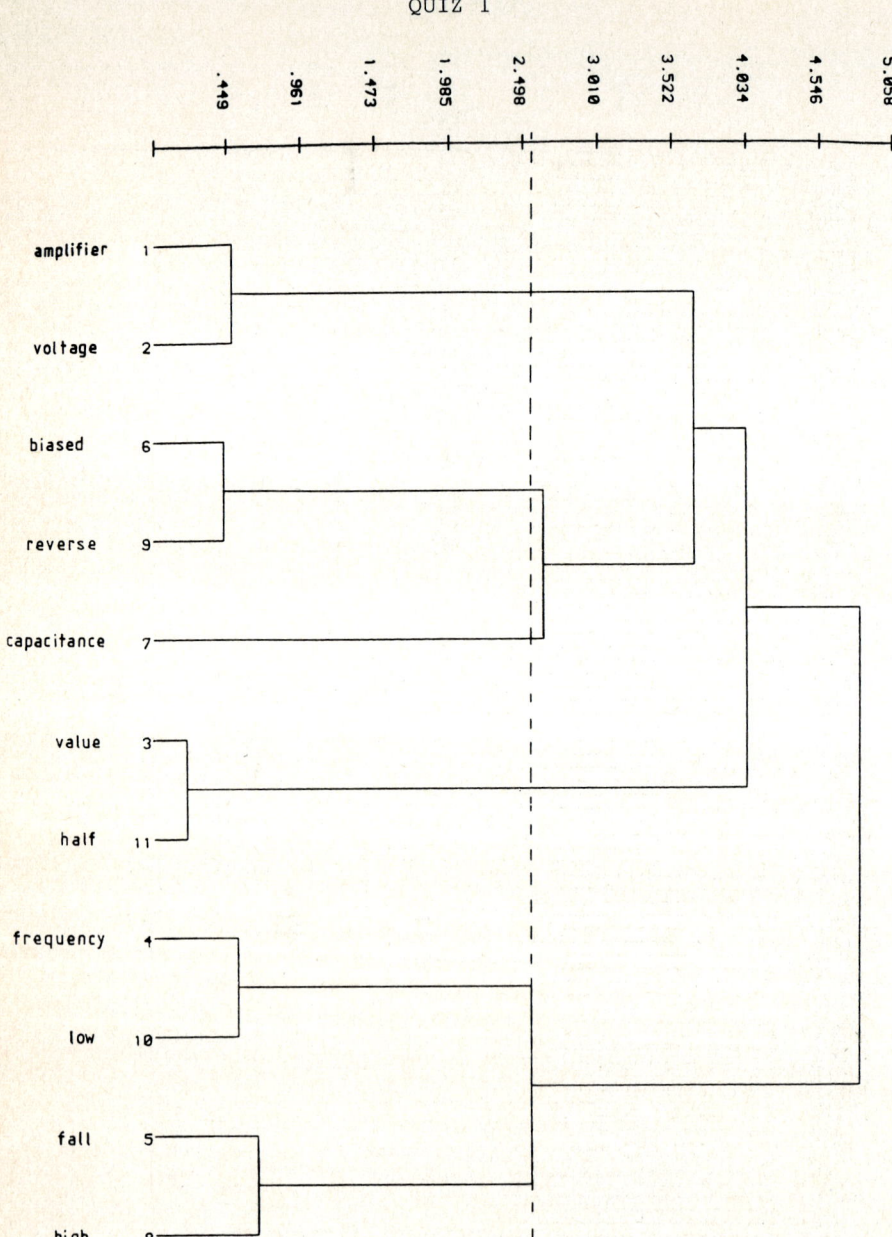

CLUSTER ANALYSIS OF 11X11 QUIZ 1 ELENMATRIX WARD'S METHOD

APPENDIX THREE

CHAPTER 3

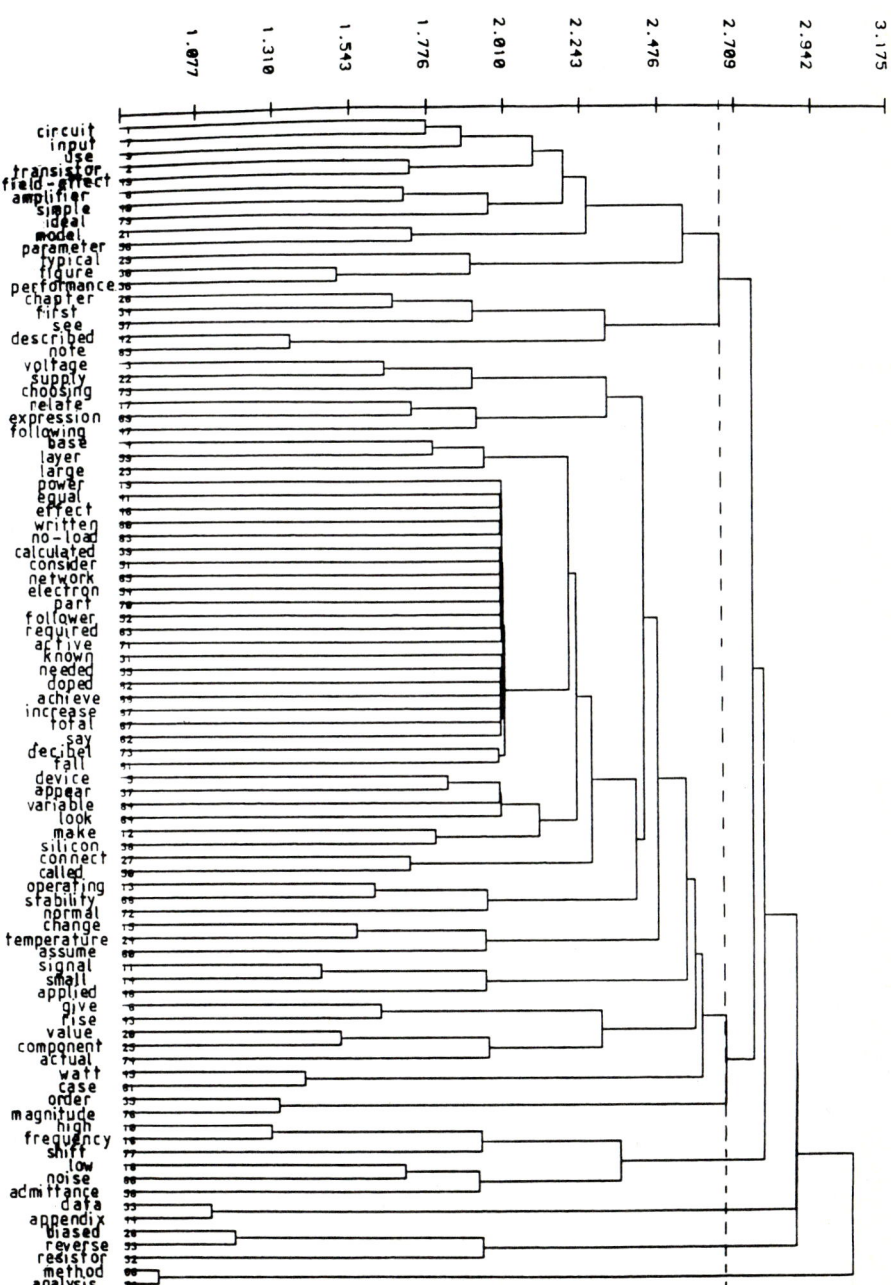

CLUSTER ANALYSIS OF 88X88 CHAPTER 3 ELENMATRIX WARD'S METHOD

CHAPTER 4

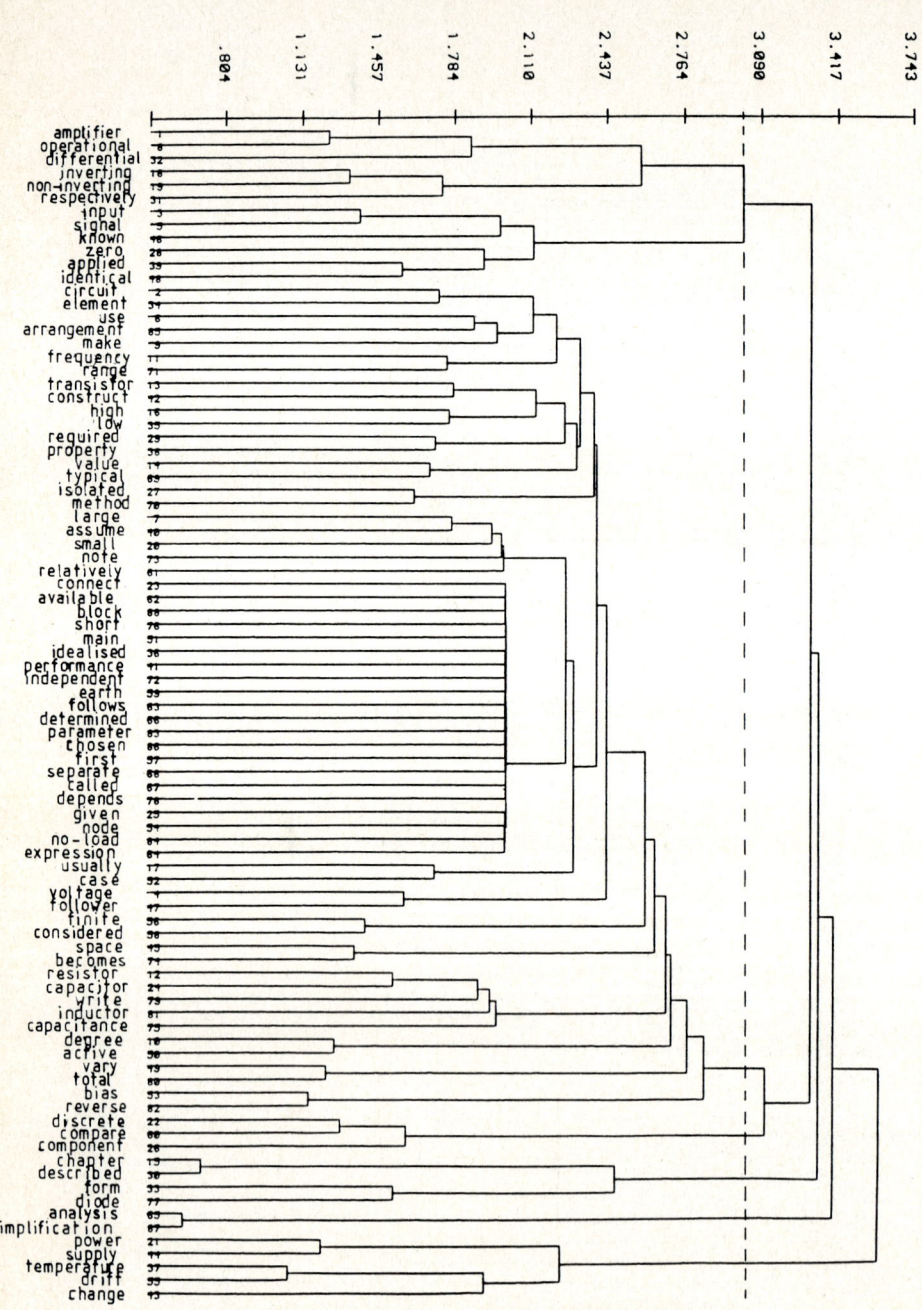

CLUSTER ANALYSIS OF 88X88 CHAPTER 4 ELENMATRIX WARD'S METHOD

APPENDIX THREE   261

QUIZ 2

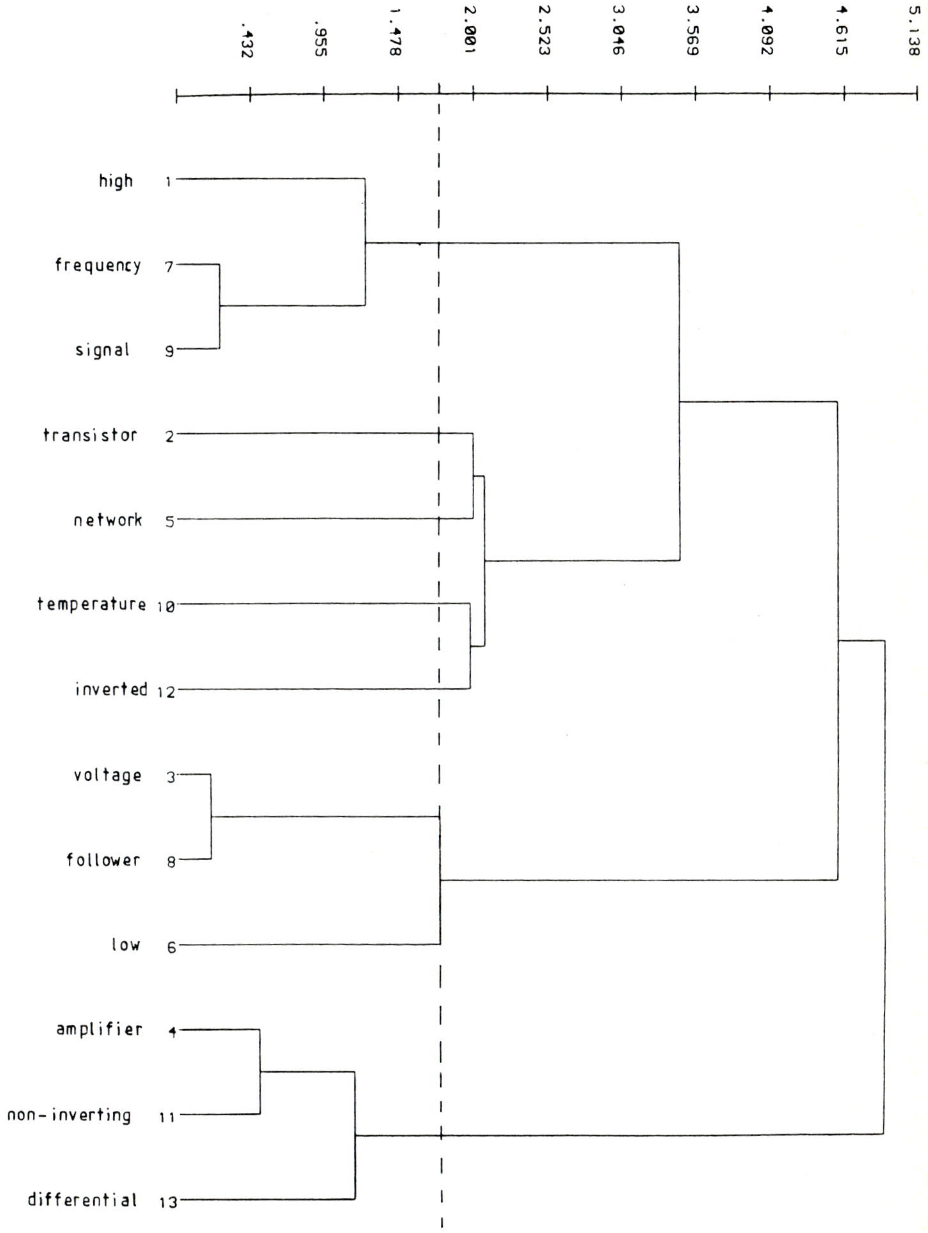

CLUSTER ANALYSIS OF 13X13 QUIZ 2 ELENMATRIX WARD'S METHOD

CHAPTER 5

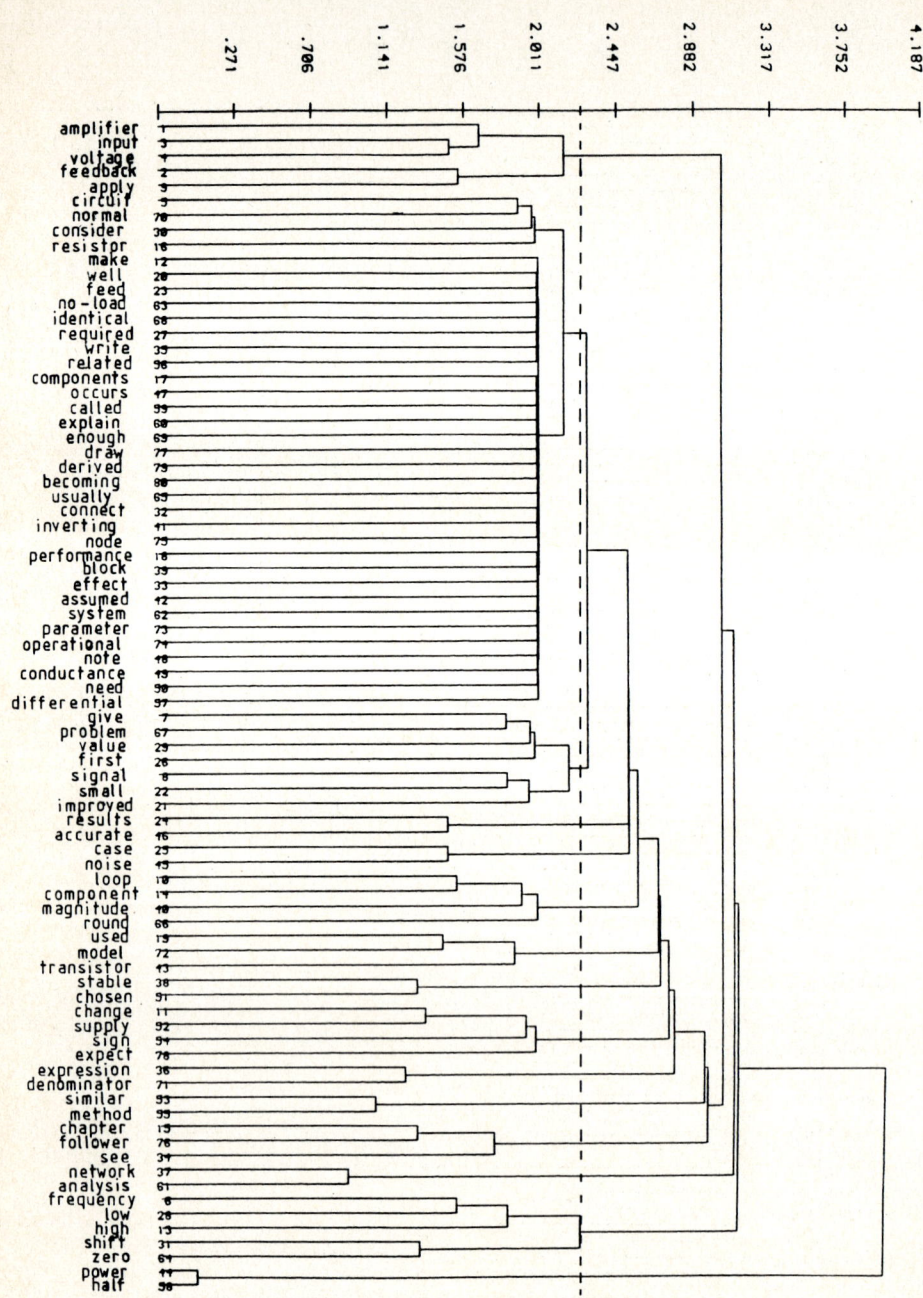

CLUSTER ANALYSIS OF 80X80 CHAPTER 5 ELENMATRIX WARD'S METHOD

APPENDIX THREE

CHAPTER 6

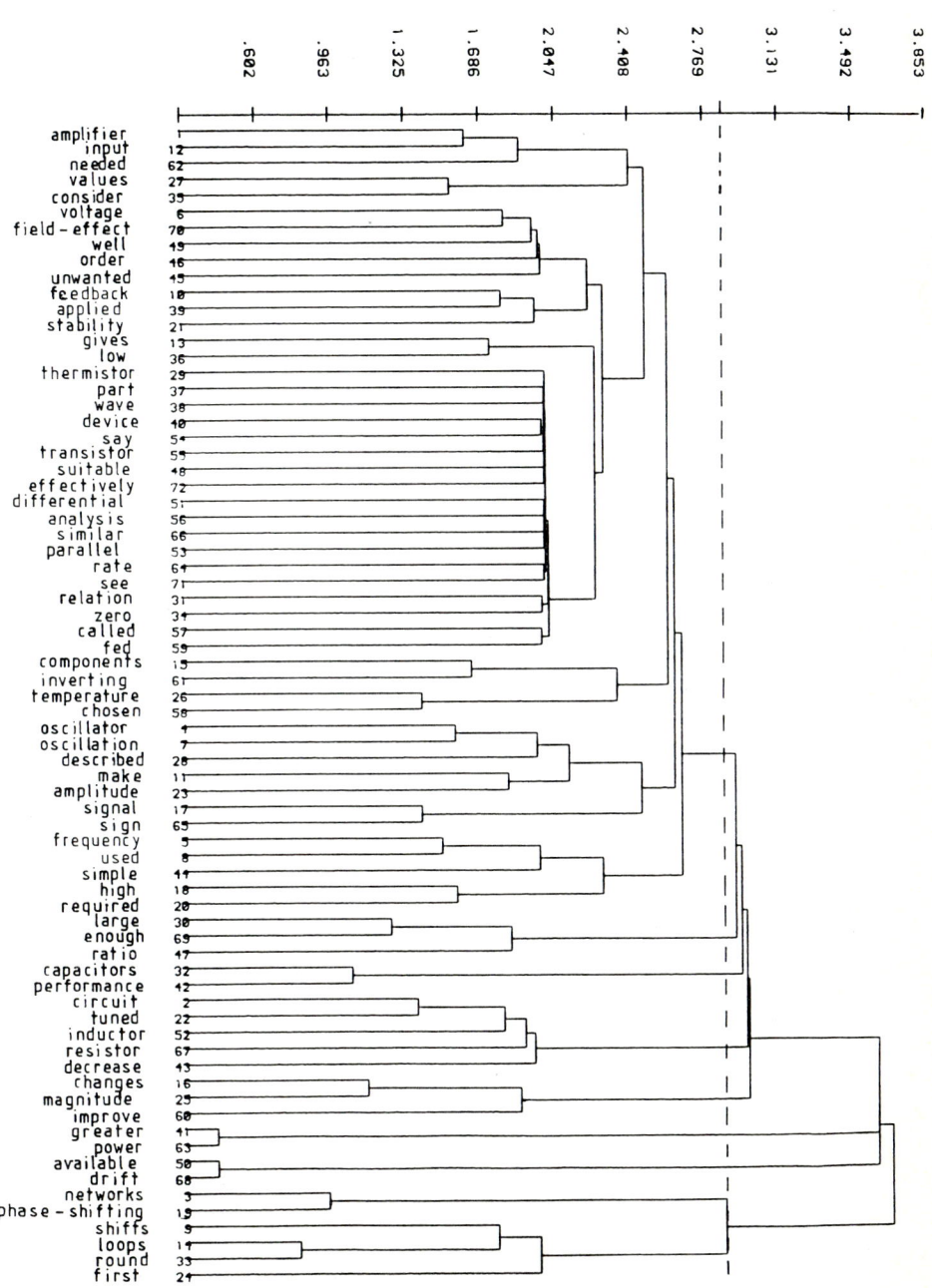

CLUSTER ANALYSIS OF 72X72 CHAPTER 6 ELENMATRIX WARD'S METHOD

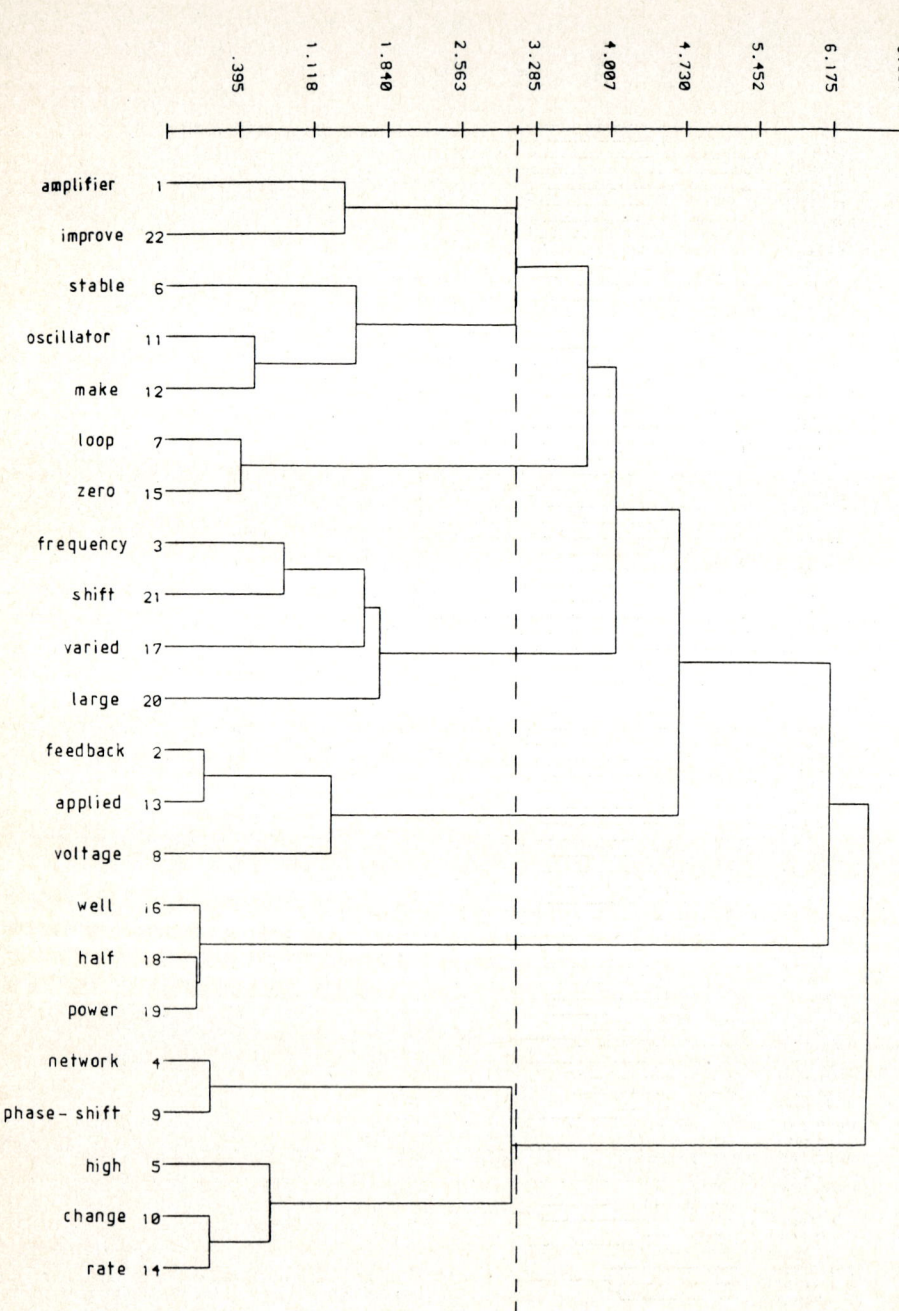

CLUSTER ANALYSIS OF 22X22 QUIZ 3 ELENMATRIX WARD'S METHOD

APPENDIX THREE

CHAPTER 7

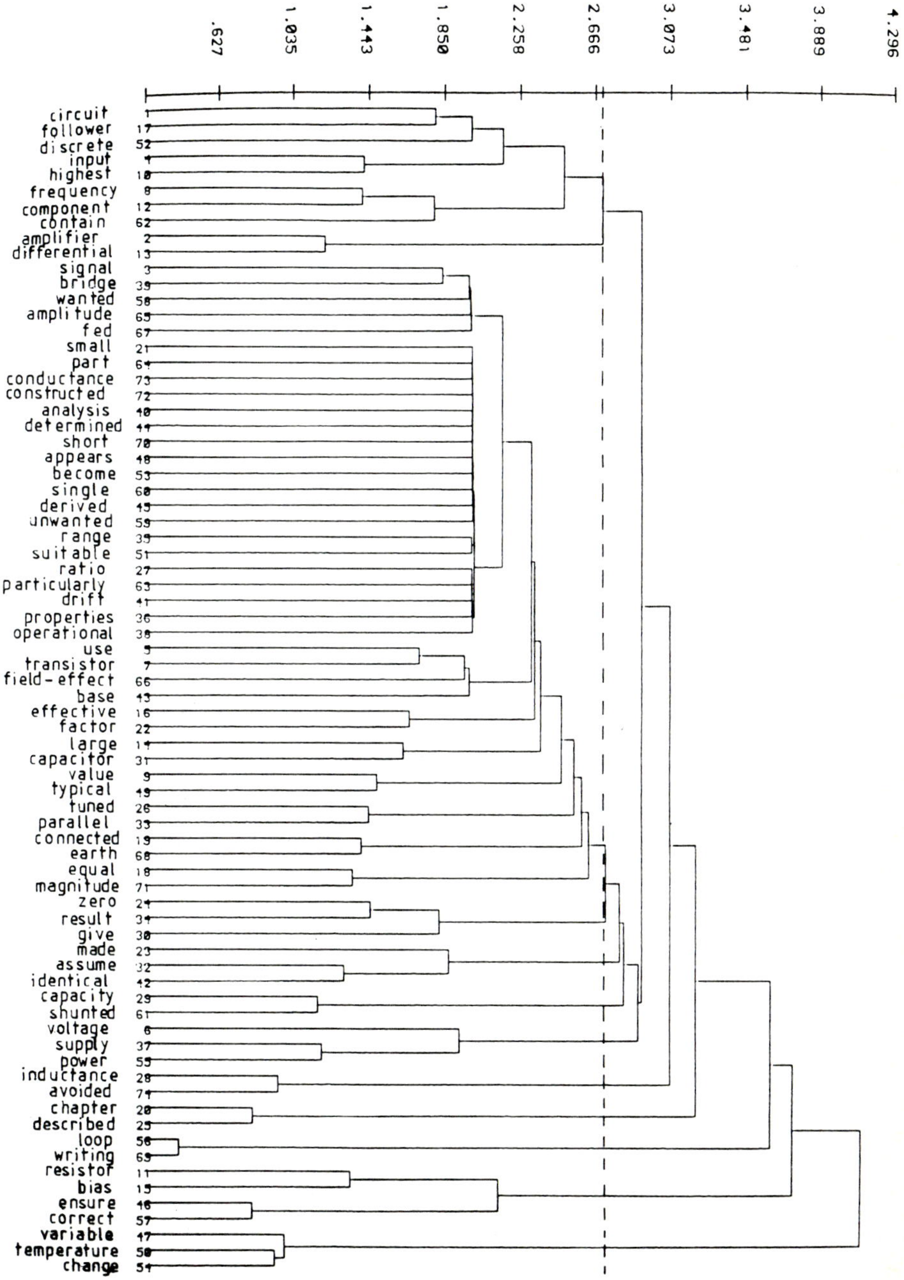

CLUSTER ANALYSIS OF 74X74 CHAPTER 7 ELENMATRIX WARD'S METHOD

APPENDIX 4

LEXICAL NETWORKS IN THE SCIENCE CORPUS

This appendix presents the lexical networks discovered in the science texts in the corpus. For reasons of space it is not practical to use the graphical representation developed in chapter five. They can be found in this form elsewhere (Phillips 1983). Instead, the lemmata composing the networks are simply listed with the nuclear nodes being indicated by underlining except in the obvious case of two member networks. The information in this appendix can usefully be compared with the listings of selected lemmata given in appendix two in order to assess the extent and the nature of the structuring discovered in the data.

ELEN

CHAPTER 1

Capacity	Parallel	Large
Shunting	Resistor	Value
		Capacitor
Half	Low	Need
Expected	<u>Frequency</u>	First
	Case	<u>Circuit</u>
Say	High	Know
Respectively		Input
	Derive	Amplifier
Data	Find	Component
Factors	<u>Expression</u>	Voltage
<u>Make</u>	Seen	Related
Following		
<u>Parts</u>	Effective	Similarly
Containing	<u>Rise</u>	Figure
Denominator	Give	<u>Power</u>
Inductors		Decibel

CHAPTER 2

Transistor	Similar	Known
Field-effect	Analysis	Follower
	<u>Circuit</u>	
Amplitude	Use	Change
Peak	Amplifier	<u>Small</u>
		Signal
First	Operation	Parameter
Appears	Avoided	
		Parallel
Make	<u>Frequency</u>	<u>Capacitor</u>
Respect	<u>High</u>	Magnitude
<u>P-type</u>	<u>Low</u>	
Doped		Active
Holes	Supply	Determine
Electrons	<u>Connected</u>	<u>Device</u>
	Component	Consider
Expression		
Write	Silicon	Occur
	<u>Diode</u>	Available
Chapter	Mainly	Find
Described		<u>Value</u>
	Capacity	Typical
Half	Carrier	Suitable
<u>Power</u>	Effective	Greater
Resistor	<u>Called</u>	
Watt	Conductance	<u>Voltage</u>
	<u>Channel</u>	<u>Bias</u>
Effect	Decrease	<u>Applied</u>
Increased	N-channel	<u>Reverse</u>

APPENDIX FOUR

QUIZ 1

Low
<u>Frequency</u>
<u>Falls</u>
High

Value
Half

Amplifier
Voltage

Bias
Reverse

CHAPTER 3

Method
Analysis

Data
Appendix

Ideal
Amplifier
Simple
Model
Parameter
<u>Circuit</u>
Transistor
Notes
Input
Described
Figure
Using
Field-effect
Typical
Chapter
First
See

Order
Magnitude

Watt
Case

Looking
Variable
<u>Device</u>
Appear
Silicon
Made

Expression
<u>Related</u>
Following
Voltage
Supply
Choose

Reverse
<u>Bias</u>
Resistor

Give
Component
Rise
<u>Value</u>
Actual

Change
<u>Temperature</u>
Assume

Small
<u>Signal</u>
Applied

Shift
High
Frequency
Low
Admittance
Noise

Stability
<u>Operating</u>
Normal

Layer
<u>Base</u>
Large

CHAPTER 4

Analysis
Simplification

Chapter
Described
<u>Diode</u>
Formed

Reverse
Bias

Power
Drift
Supply
Temperature
Change

Applied
Identical
Zero
Known
Signal
Input
Operational
Amplifier
Inverting
Non-inverting
Differential
Respectively

<u>Discrete</u>
<u>Compared</u>
<u>Component</u>

Method
Range
Construction
Frequency
Isolation
Circuit
Transistor
Made
Use
Low
Required
Property
Arrangement
High
Value
Typical

Varies   Usually   Assume
Total   Case   Small
                              Large
Device   Resistor   Note
Active   Write   Relatively
               Capacitor
Space   Inductor   Finite
Becomes   Capacitance   Consider

Voltage
Follower

                QUIZ 2

Non-inverting Frequency   Follower
Amplifier   Signal   Voltage
Differential   High   Low

                CHAPTER 5

Power   Case   Model
Half   Noise   Use
                              Transistor
Network   Results
Analysis   Accurate   Normal
                              Consider
Expression   Small   Circuit
Denominator   Signal   Resistor
               Improved
Zero   Given   Amplifier
Shift   Problem   Feedback
Low   First   Applied
High   Value   Input
Frequency   Voltage

               Sign
Follower   Supply
Chapter   Change
See   Expect

                CHAPTER 6

Performance   Need   Enough
Improve   Component   Large
               Value   Order
Transistor   Chosen
Field-effect   Amplifier
               Capacitor   Inverting
Phase-shifting Resistor   Input
Network   First
Shift   Made   Consider
Round   Fed
Loop   Amplitude   See
Magnitude   Signal   Tuned
               Oscillator   Circuit
               Use   Simple
               Describe   Parallel

APPENDIX FOUR 271

High   Decrease   Change
<u>Stability</u>   Ratio   <u>Temperature</u>
<u>Frequency</u>   Device   Power
<u>Oscillation</u> <u>Voltage</u>
Great   Well
                    Feedback
                    Applied
                    Required

                    QUIZ 3

<u>Well</u>   Change   Improve
<u>Half</u>   Rate   <u>Amplifier</u>
<u>Power</u>   <u>High</u>   <u>Stable</u>
                    Phase-shift   <u>Oscillator</u>
<u>Feedback</u>   Network   Make
<u>Applied</u>
<u>Voltage</u>

                    CHAPTER 7

Loop   Contain   Effective
Write   Differential   Factor
                    Frequency
Chapter   Component   Make
Described   <u>Circuit</u>   <u>Assume</u>
                    Discrete   Identical
<u>Temperature</u> Amplifier
<u>Change</u>   High   Voltage
<u>Variation</u>   Follower   <u>Power</u>
                    Input   Supply
Capacity
Shunted   Parallel   Use
                    Tuned   <u>Transistor</u>
<u>Bias</u>   Field-effect
<u>Ensure</u>   Value   Base
Resistor   Typical
Correct   Bridge
                    Large   Want
Equal   Capacitor   <u>Signal</u>
Magnitude   Amplitude
                    Result   Fed
Connected   <u>Zero</u>
Earth   Give

CMEC

CHAPTER 1

Given	External	Direction
Body	Known	Vector
Small		Case
	Theory	Problem
Electrostatic	Electromagnetic	
Attractive		Acting
Fact	Constant	Second
Force	Respect	Third
Really	Exist	Satisfy
Consider	Frame	
	One	Different
Introduce	Reference	Places
Concept	Charge	
Acceleration	Positive	Conservative
		Central
Point	Section	
Space	Previous	
Assume		

CHAPTER 2

Force	Collision	Equilibrium
Periodic	Problem	Point
Applied		Starts
	Initial	Rest
Phase	Conditions	Body
Maximum		Second
Amplitude	Finite	
Small	Remains	Arbitrary
Scale		Constant
	Pendulum	Choose
Find	Angular	
Independent	Frequency	Energy
	Vary	Function
Consider		Potential
Case	Part	Well
Critical	Real	Illustrated
	Solution	
Given	Equation	Centre
Approximately	Corresponding	Directed
	Homogeneous	Substitution

CHAPTER 3

Force	Problem	Following
Central	Solve	Chapter
Conservative		Case
	Vector	
Second	Product	Specified
Term		Function
	Constant	Find
	Direction	Easy

APPENDIX FOUR

Small
Order
Variation
Arbitrary
Vanish
Stationary

Dimension
Fact
Angular
Moment
Independent

Corresponding
Energy
Potential
Given
Point
Surface

CHAPTER 4

Period
Orbit
Equation
Side

Find
Shape

Direction
Specified

Surface
Earth
Assume

Point
Charge
Positive

Gravitational
Constant
Case
Arbitrary
Attractive

Total
Cross-section
Corresponding
Angle
Scatter
Distribution
Angular
Range
Maximum

Conservative
Central
Force

Mean
Free

Initial
Conditions

Approach
Closest

Way
Simplest

Types
Possible

Energy
Potential
Function

CHAPTER 5

Gravitational
Acceleration
Third
Term
Coriolis
Force
Order
Neglect

Rotating
Frame
Reference

Equation
Find

Body
Point
Orbit

Swing
Precess
Direction
Given
Angular
Constant
Clearly

Vector
Consider

Magnetic
Uniform

Compared
Show
Amplitude
Small
Blow
Angle

Earth
Surface

Frequency
Difference

Pressure
Region

Simply
Pendulum

Energy
Potential

Problem
Involving

CHAPTER 6

Force
Phase

Term
Linear

Cases
Simple

Uniform
Distribution
Density
<u>Charge</u>
Symmetry
Total

Electrostatic
Gravitational
<u>Potential</u>
Show
Energy

Solve
<u>Problem</u>
Equilibrium

Uniform
Gravitational
Potential
<u>Energy</u>
Total
<u>Angular</u>
Amplitude

Find
Transform
<u>Frame</u>
Way

Subject
Work
External
<u>Force</u>
Total
Moment
Sum

Central
Internal
<u>Angular</u>
Conservative
Orbital
Equation

Acting
<u>Earth</u>
Assume

Approximately
<u>Earth</u>
<u>Surface</u>
Centre

Equation
Space

Fact
Precess

Period
Rotation

Normal
Vector

CHAPTER 7

<u>Angle</u>
<u>Scatter</u>
<u>Maximum</u>

Direction
Specified

Corresponding
<u>Cross-section</u>
Case

Period
Orbital

CHAPTER 8

Bodies
Apply

Accelerate
Initial
<u>Rocket</u>
Find

Rotation
Period

Point
One

Small
Compared

Problem
Chapter

Satellite
Close

<u>Direction</u>
One
<u>Pointing</u>

Dipole
Moment

Volume
Element

Way
Complicated

Detector
Set

Solve
Problem

Consider
Explicitly

Separate
Completely

Approach
Closest

Distribution
<u>Density</u>
<u>Uniform</u>
<u>Gravitational</u>
Sun
Fact

Frame
Choice

Pairs
Cancel

<u>Energy</u>
<u>Function</u>
<u>Potential</u>
<u>Corresponding</u>

APPENDIX FOUR

CHAPTER 9

Type	Vector	Edge
Pivoted	Angular	Uniform
Body	Equation	
Given		Principal
	Energy	Moments
Symmetry	Potential	
Rotational		Pendulum
	Products	Simple
Centre	Vanish	Length
Respect		
	Period	Forces
One	Small	Real
See		Assumption
Find	Terms	Internal
Horizontal	Expressions	

CHAPTER 10

Rotating	Small	Total
Body	External	Moment
Principal	Point	Sun
Freely	Force	
	Gravity	Describes
Show	Applied	Vector
Simply	Acting	Instantaneous
Angular		
Neglect	Case	Space
	Symmetric	Cone
Direction		Round
Constant	Chapter	
Equation	Problem	Satellite
Find		Orbit
	Gyroscope	
Known	Uniform	Choose
Angles		Convenient
Specified	Precessional	
	Period	

CHAPTER 11

Solve	Work	Find
Show	Conservative	Angular
Equation	Type	Possible
Side	Force	Precessional
	Moment	
Homogeneous	Corresponding	Pendulum
Function		Period
Explicit	Terms	
	Vanishes	Symmetric
Independently		Body
Arbitrary	Pivot	Point
Variations	Case	
Small	Constant	Energy
Consider	Linear	Potential

Condition
Requires

Frame
Rotating

Principle
Hamilton

Electromagnetic
Charged

Problem
Described
Chapter

Rest
Release

CHAPTER 12

Normal
Solution
Find

Swing
Pendulum
Second
Amplitude

Stationary
One
Started

Equation
Characteristic

Phase
Maximum

Real
Part

Linear
Set

Conditions
Initial

Function
Homogeneous

Frequency
Angular

Subject
Force
Periodic

Energy
Potential

Conservative
Equilibrium

Arbitrary
Constants
Involve

Rest
Released

Pair
Coupled

CHAPTER 13

Required
Angular
Conservation
Lead

Direction
Vector

Type
One
Degree
Described

Frame
Reference

Equation
Set

Explicit
Contains

Potential
Energy
Function
Hamilton
Case
Return

Finding
Well

Pair
Second
Cancel
Third

Constant
Simply

Generated
Corresponding
Transformations
Differ

Symmetry
Rotational
Expression

Problem
Force
Solve
Central

APPENDIX FOUR

CREL

CHAPTER 1

Information	Steps	Heterogeneous
Needed	Treatment	System
		Solid
Equilibrium	Variables	Fluid
Constant	Affect	Unit
Temperature	Transfer	Design
Pressure	Become	Equipment
Composition		
	Desired	Classification
Chapter	Product	Reaction
Determined		Engineering
	Given	
Catalysts	Thermodynamics	
Present	Two	

CHAPTER 2

Composition	System	Complex
Dependency	State	Intermediate
Temperature	Equilibrium	Step
Given	Concentration	
Pressure		Product
	Constant	Three
Energy	Example	Molecule
Activation	Two	Number
	Reaction	
Use	Nonelementary	Searching
Measure	Type	Shifted
	Elementary	Known
Free	Consider	Mechanism
Follows		General
	Corresponds	Involves
Expression	Equation	
Found	Stoichiometric	

CHAPTER 3

Units	First	Rearranging
Liters	Step	Becomes
		Difficult
Excess	Directly	Fact
Great	Proportional	
		Catalyzed
Analysis	Proceed	Solid
Method	Appreciable	
Integral	Temperature	Pressure
Differential	Low	Total
	Shift	System
Same		
Composition	Values	Initial
	Calculated	Conditions

Zero-order
Gas
Number
Inert
Present
Product

Example
Consider
Irreversible
Overall

Plotted
Time
Data
Required
Set
Runs
Making

Partial
Drops
Charge
Concentration
Independent
Following

Paths
Two
Questions

Slope
Straight
Given
Components
Three

See
Mechanism
Suggest

Relatively
Way
Simple
Case

Study
Batch
React
Constant-volume
Place

Type
Equation
Find
Disappearance
Constant
Adiabatically
Equilibrium
Isothermal

CHAPTER 4

Two
First

Differential
Made

Whole
Batch
Reactor
Types

CHAPTER 5

Solid
Catalyzed

Graphical
Figure
Representation

Equimolar
Product

Component
Balance

Composition
Uniform

Variation
Temperature
Pressure
Drop

Given
Needed
Duty

Special
Case
Equation
Performance

See
Plot

Changing
Systems
Used
Situation

Expression
Becomes
Integration
Simple

Batch
Constant
Fluid
Elementary

Stream
Two
Mixed
Steady-state
Reactor
Leave
Ideal
Gas

Space-time
Appropriate
Time
Measure

Actual
Conditions
Same

Directly
Final
Data
Follow

APPENDIX FOUR

Solid
Catalyzed

Ideal
Set

Case
Special

Elementary
Irreversible

Factor
Designs

Reactor
Concentration
Change
Mixed
Liter

Run
Time
Batch
Value
Find
Low
Drop

Equation
Performance
Develop

Product
Distribution

Sketch
Referring

Change
Progressive

Analysis
Three

Large
Excess

Appreciable
Proceed

Needed
Determine

Same
Treatment

Composition
Final
Fixed

Ratio
Optimum
Conditions

Duty
Give
Directly
System
Whole

Procedure
Graphical
General

Equipment
Separation

Follows
Proceeds
Temperature

CHAPTER 7

Data
Initial

Expression
Allow

Equation
Differential

Optimum
Design
Multiple
Behavior

Fermentation
Catalytic

Scheme
Contacting
Proper

Minimum
Find
Rearranging

Expression
Balance
Total
Figure

Class
Large
Excess

Respect
First
Considered

Desired
Stream
Component
Distribution
Product
Two
Example
Unit
Introduced

Scheme
Method
Use
Chart

Elementary
Sets
Follow
Reactor
Low
Conditioned
Mixed
Concentration
Methods
Beakers
Two
Same
Ways

Leaving
Composition
Knowing
Stream
Separate
Unused

Balance	Little	Constant
<u>Give</u>	Variable	<u>Values</u>
Temperature	<u>Time</u>	Various
Type	Figure	
Molecular		Certain
	Consumed	<u>Components</u>
Ratio	Example	Respect
<u>Use</u>	<u>Find</u>	
<u>Batch</u>	Present	Rule
Treatment		<u>Intermediate</u>
		Desired
	CHAPTER 8	
Suppose	Isothermal	Step
Inert	Exothermic	Needs
	Two	
Measured	Minimized	Ideal
Units	<u>Reactor</u>	Type
	Mixed	<u>System</u>
Batch	Total	Example
Run	Given	Pressure
	Space-time	Gas
Stream	Duty	
Leaving		Treated
	Performance	Consider
Distribution	<u>Equation</u>	Case
<u>Product</u>	Represents	<u>First</u>
<u>Desired</u>	Note	Three
Final		Larger
	Falling	
Component	Progression	Follow
Solid	Low	Directly
	Optimum	
Activation	Allowable	Average
<u>Energy</u>	<u>Temperature</u>	<u>Data</u>
Balance	Use	Chart
<u>Equilibrium</u>	Procedure	Ratio
<u>Constants</u>	General	<u>Find</u>
<u>Thermodynamics</u>		Scheme

APPENDIX FOUR

BIPC

CHAPTER 1

Characteristic	Slope	Fraction
Greater	<u>Line</u>	<u>Common</u>
	Curve	Terms
Power		
<u>Negative</u>	Defined	Long
Index	<u>Equation</u>	<u>Constant</u>
Values	Mathematical	Example
Corresponding		

CHAPTER 2

Space	Units	Concentration
Left	Derived	Solution
Sign	Quantities	Mole
Decimal	Calculation	Solute
Table	Example	Gas
Listed	Write	Power
		<u>Constant</u>
		Value

CHAPTER 3

Manometer	<u>Density</u>	Quantity
Flask	<u>Weight</u>	Occupied
	<u>Vapour</u>	Van
Space		<u>Gas</u>
Available	Mole	Actual
	<u>Total</u>	Volume
Solution	Mixture	Equation
Heat		Real
	Low	Apply
State	Temperature	
Solid	<u>Constant</u>	Contents
	Value	<u>Liquid</u>
	Negative	Proportional

CHAPTER 4

Acids	Heat	Freezing
Bases	Required	Depression
Electric	Chemical	Sucrose
Ability	Potential	Mixed
Significantly	Effect	<u>Present</u>
Level	Common	<u>Solutions</u>
		<u>Infinitely</u>
Fraction	Raised	<u>Dilute</u>
Mole	Power	

Volume   Defined   Application
Unit   Temperature   Law
Negative   Water   Suppose
Charge   Normal
                                Actual
Gas   Weight   Value
Equilibrium   Solute   Calculate
Salt   Concentration
Identical   Corresponding   Determined
                                Total
State   Impermeable
Solid   Completely   Colligative
Pure   Dissociate   Contribution
Vapour
Liquid   Equation   Electrolyte
Introduced   Osmosis   Ion
                Explanation   Activity
Saturated   Terms
Silver   Dissolving   Constant
Product   Results   Truly
                                Proportionality

                CHAPTER 5

Steps   Example   Mixture
Three   Shown   Ability
                Calculate
Negative   Easily   Dissociation
Power   Constant
                Acid   Equilibrium
Expressed   Base
Hydrolysis   Conjugate   Pure
                                Water
Ion   Present   Produce
Concentration   Total
Hydrogen   Temperature
                Dilute   Unit
Quantity   Solution   Value
Small   Equation
                Written   Type
Curve   Applicable   Bronsted
Appears   Salt
                                Neutral
                                Cation

                CHAPTER 6

Water   Equilibrium   Cations
Pure   Constant   Anions

Acid   Group   Electrophoresis
Amino   Dissociable   Performed

Effect   Weight   Material
Gibbs   Small   Suitable

APPENDIX FOUR

Side
Contributed

Values
Identical

Charge
Negative
Fixed

Ionized
Completely

Available
List
Table

Liquid
Pure
Water
Solute
Saturated
State
Activity
Unit
Solution
Dilute
Definition
Component
Concentration

Acid
Dissociation

Dilute
Ionic

Proceeding
Left

Reverse
Chemically
Systems
Isothermal

Solution
Dilute

Electrical
Order
Neutrality

Separated
Components
Mixture

Present
Concentration
Hydrogen

CHAPTER 7

Negative
Exergonic

Quantity
Calculate

Constant
System
Surroundings
Isothermal
Equilibrium
True
Reversible
Chemically

Fixed
Temperature
Atmospheric

CHAPTER 8

Equilibrium
Constant

Concentration
Calculate

Present
Unit
Volume

True
Negative
Value
Temperature

CHAPTER 9

Weight
Small

Character
Basic
Overall

Zwitterion
Glycine
Curve

Dilute
Applied
Solution
Isoionic

Greater
Enthalpy
Entropy
Total
Isolated

Heat
Conditions

Products
Values
Methods

Proceeds
Spontaneous
Conversion

Equation
Gibbs

Product
Coupling
Exergonic
Conditions

Terms
Components
Activities
Molal
Solute
Solution

Entropy
Determination

<u>Transfer</u>	Constant	Exergonic
<u>Greater</u>	Chemical	Coupled
<u>Potential</u>	<u>Equilibrium</u>	
Group	Components	Hydrolysis
<u>Phosphate</u>		Value

CHAPTER 10

Total	Yield	<u>Order</u>
Fraction	Mole	Zero
		<u>Overall</u>
Transition	Step	Equation
State	Rate-limiting	Defines
		Determined
Gaseous	Unit	Arrhenius
Liquid	Volume	
		Fixed
Enthalpy	Value	<u>Concentration</u>
Entropy	<u>Constant</u>	Initial
	Temperature	
Proportional		
Product		

THRM

CHAPTER 1

Later	Flows	Work
Chapter	Engine	Fuel
		Used
Result	Air	Simplified
Nozzle	Process	
	Separation	Device
Two		Thermoelectric
Different	Power	Refrigerator
	Plant	
Saturation	Nuclear	Leaves
Temperature		Steam
Cooled	Heat	Figure
Quantities	Transferred	
	Products	

CHAPTER 2

Freezing	Flow	Second
Normal	Referred	Law
Point	Involve	First
View	Control	
Macroscopic	Mass	Property
	Units	Extensive
Gravitational	Length	Value
Standard		
Acceleration	International	Level
Assume	Weights	Difference
	Elevation	Measure
Exist	Increase	Used
Various		Approach
	Single	
Constant	Mole	Liquid
Remains	Fixed	Equilibrium
	Quantity	Thermal
Piston	Defined	
Removed	Substance	Described
		Specified
Process	Steam	Velocity
Quasiequilibrium	Temperature	
	Body	Two
Absolute	Cool	Thermometer
English		Block
	Work	Let
Molecule	Heat	
Helium	Transferred	

CHAPTER 3

Slight	Approaches	Ideal
Specific	Assume	Equation
Freezing	Behavior	Solve
Increase	Low	Problem

285

Weight   Defined   Equilibrium
Molecular   Ratio   Exist
                                           Substance
Level   Heat   Simple
Drops   Transfer   Properties
                      Result   Two
Tables
Steam   Mass   Closed
                      Helium   Tank
Constant   Liquid   Bottom
Remains   Temperature
                      Saturate   Constant-
Piston   Line   pressure
Fitted   Follow   Process
                      Fact   Let

                      CHAPTER 4

Integration   Deep   Positive
Performed   Path   Transfer
                      Region   Negative
Constant   Follow   Heat
Remains   Determine   Means
                      Solve
Specified   Problem   Distance
Undergoing   Unit
                      Mass   Define
Weight   Initial   Power
Raise   Length
                      Wire   Fitted
Property   Frame   Piston
Extensive   Remove
                      Process
Equation   Quasiequilibrium   Membrane
Written   Involve   Let
                      Work   Block
Assume   Electrical
Behavior   Moving   Low
                      Simple   Equilibrium
Point   Substance   Temperature
View   Two
                      Liquid
Air   Helium
Tank   Filled

                      CHAPTER 5

First   Heat   Piston
Law   Transferred   Fitted

Classical   Chapter   Point
View   Molecular   Critical

Opened   Quantity   Equation
Slightly   Fixed   Written

APPENDIX FOUR

Ammonia
Filled
Saturated
Liquid

Extensive
Property
Two
Substance
Ways
Tank
Flows

Vessel
Evacuated

Reference
Elevation

Mass
Conservation

Ideal
Behavior

First
Law

Relative
Frame

Following
Data

Chapter
Permit

Vessel
Evacuated

Problem
Solved

Zero
Approach

Helium
Various
Point
Exit
Nozzle

Opened
Slightly

Steam
Values
Internal
Tables
Lines
Constant
Specific
Define
Assuming
Constant-pressure
Relation
Quasiequilibrium
General

Approaches
Zero
Body

Use
Unit
Thermal

CHAPTER 6

Adiabatic
Essentially
Process
Steady-flow
Continuity
Equation
Write

Engine
Output
Power
Plant
Simple

Initially
Liquid
Tank
Saturated
Steam
Leave
Line

Introduction
Unit
Work
Heat
Transfer
Assume

Occurs
Closed
Filling

Behavior
Ideal
Means

Helium
Rest
Initial
Air

Increase
Dependent
Temperature
Superheated
Follows

Process
Determine
Work
Integral

Used
Measure

Pipe
Diameter

Properties
Two

Control
Flow
Mass

Refrigerant
Ammonia
Tables

Specific
Remains
Constant

Corresponding
Air
Temperature
Coefficient

Move
Velocity
Low

CHAPTER 7

Solve
Equation

Constant
Remains

Performance
Coefficient

Entire
Fills

Power
Steam
Plant
Simple

Liquid
Helium

Chapter
Discussed

Law
First
Second
Motion

Low
Temperature
Measure

Heat
Body
Transfer
Low-temperature

Implies
Clausius

Point
View

Particular
Called
Substance
Device
Difference
Finite
Thermoelectric
Ways

Weight
Raise
Piston
Stops

Absolute
Ratio

Behavior
Approach
Zero

Thermal
Introduced

Positive
Certain
Engine
Work
Two
Produced
Carnot
Refrigerate

Assume
Surroundings
Initial
Conclusions

Problem
Result
Compare

Undergo
Membrane
Let
Block

Adiabatic
Process
Factors

CHAPTER 8

Problem
Solve

Saturated
Liquid

Piston
Fitted

Substance
Simple

Reference
Relative

Chapter
Introduced

Let
Membrane

Plus
Surroundings
Place
Necessary

Temperature
Approach
Value
Zero
Integrated
Absolute
Factor

Ratio
Described
Defined
Property
Manner
Extensive

Evacuated
Initially
Tank
Air
Small

Remain
Increases
Constant
Heat
Transfer
Assume
Specific

Inequality
Clausius
First
Law
Second
Conclude

APPENDIX FOUR   289

Suppose   Undergo   Called
<u>Engine</u>   <u>Adabiatic</u>   <u>Diagram</u>
<u>Carnot</u>   Entire   General
Refrigerator   Work
                       <u>Process</u>   Ammonia
Written   Determine   <u>Tables</u>
<u>Equation</u>   Steam
<u>Ideal</u>   Two
<u>Following</u>   <u>Important</u>
Helium   Relations

                       CHAPTER 9

Equilibrium   Approach   Isothermal
<u>Surroundings</u>   <u>Zero</u>   <u>Process</u>
<u>Temperature</u>   Minimum   <u>Adiabatic</u>
Transfer   Steady-state
Heat   Work   Continuity
                       <u>Actual</u>   Write
Engine   Performance
<u>Output</u>   Comparison   Difference
<u>Power</u>   Smaller
Plant   Velocity
                       <u>Determine</u>   <u>Steam</u>
First   Exit   <u>Leave</u>
<u>Second</u>   <u>Nozzle</u>
Law   <u>Flow</u>
<u>Relation</u>   <u>Unit</u>   Analysis
<u>Property</u>   <u>Mass</u>   Assume
Tables   <u>Availability</u>
                                             Equation
Use   Know   Integral
Air   <u>Two</u>   <u>Control</u>
                       Tanks   Results

APPENDIX 5

NUCLEAR NODE STATISTICS

In this appendix some basic statistics relating to the nuclear nodes identified in the corpus are presented. These comprise the total number of nuclear nodes in each text (N), the average number of nuclear nodes in each text interval (X), the number of distinct nuclear nodes in each text (V) and, in the case of the science texts, the number of interactive plane items, (I). The latter were identified on semantic grounds as those items the principal function of which is to refer to the discourse itself rather than to the subject matter of the text. This was done in order to arrive at an intuitive idea of the proportion of nuclear nodes in the science texts accounted for by interactive plane items and hence to assess the quantitative importance for the organisation of science text of ´content´ items operating on the autonomous plane of language. No attempt was made to identify similar categories in the non-science texts since it was not a concern of the analysis to investigate this aspect of those texts. The figures given here substantiate the claim made in chapter seven that both the total of distinct nuclear nodes and the proportion of interactive plane items which are nuclear is relatively small. There is of the order of only 100 nuclear nodes in each text and thus, although allowance must be made for the fact that the lemmata investigated were sampled from the frequency distribution, it is clear that the numbers of nuclear nodes are relatively small. Further, in the science texts at most 20% or so of the nodes are interactive plane items and this figure may be considerably less in particular cases. The inference is that whilst certain aspects of the discourse structure of these texts may be attributable to the operation of interactive plane items, the lexical structure of text is in general the responsibility of a restricted set of vocabulary items concerned with organisation on the autonomous plane.

	N	$\bar{X}$	V	I
ELEN	186	18.0	97	20
CMEC	325	25.0	127	25
CREL	219	27.0	112	16
BIPC	219	35.8	119	7
THRM	284	31.5	132	22
TMM	142	7.8	78	--
MRSD	272	27.2	134	--
THF	150	11.5	103	--

Table A5.1   Nuclear Node Statistics

APPENDIX 6

SIGNIFICANT CHAPTER LINKAGES

The patterns of linkage between pairs of chapters in each text in the corpus which achieve a significant degree of strength are presented in this appendix. The conventions used are as follows. Each graph represents the conflation into a single weighted graph of all the second-order networks linking the same text intervals. In the second-order graphs the nodes represent lexical networks and the lines stand for the relation of similarity between networks. The weight given to each third-order graph so obtained represents the number of second-order graphs conflated. It can thus be interpreted as the ´strength´ of the linkage obtaining between text intervals. A significance level of three linkages was set. Thus only those linkages between chapters which are representable as third-order networks with a weight of at least three are retained.

The macrostructures of the texts are derived from these data on significant chapter linkages. As is made clear in chapter eight, with the exception of MRSD, there is no evidence for macrostructure in the non-science texts. None of the chapter linkages in THF or TMM reaches the criterial level and thus no entries for these texts will be found in this appendix. Two tables are provided for MRSD. The first takes proper names and titles into consideration when assessing chapter linkages whereas they are omitted in the second table. There is some evidence for macrostructure in MRSD, but the data presented here clearly reveal that this is almost entirely a consequence of the distibution of proper names and titles. Such significant chapter linkage as is observable in MRSD is not, therefore, explicable as the organisation of subject matter as it is with the science texts.

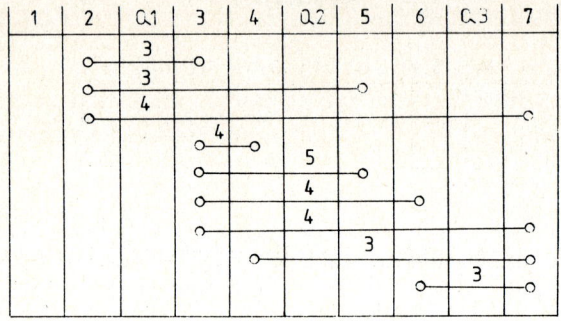

Table A6.1   ELEN Significant Chapter Linkages

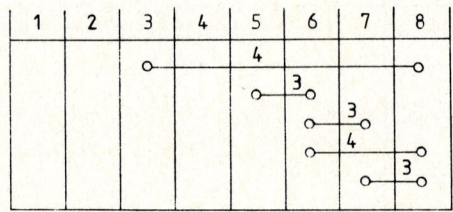

Table A6.2   CMEC Significant Chapter Linkages

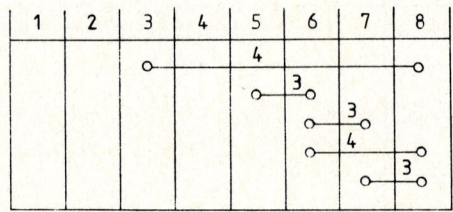

Table A6.3   CREL Significant Chapter Linkages

APPENDIX SIX 295

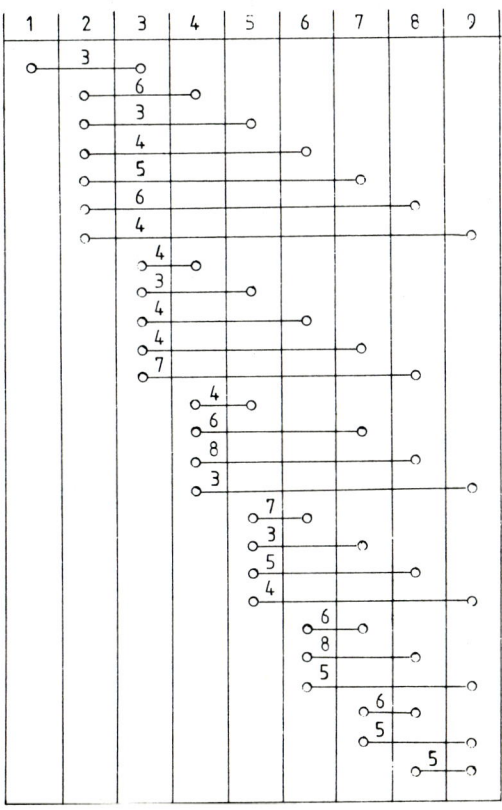

Table A6.4 BIPC Significant Chapter Linkages

Table A6.5 THRM Significant Chapter Linkages

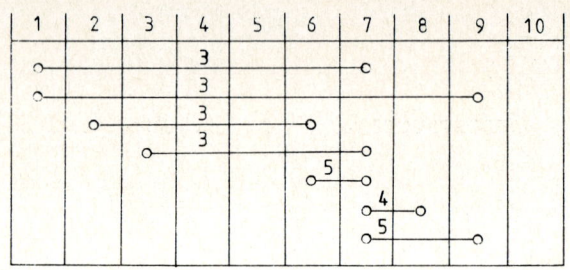

Table A5.6 MRSD Significant Chapter Linkages (including proper names and titles)

1	2	3	4	5	6	7	8	9	10
						o—3—o			

Table A5.7 MRSD Significant Chapter Linkages (excluding proper names and titles)

APPENDIX 7

MACROSTRUCTURES OF THE SCIENCE TEXTS

This appendix contains the lexical macrostructures of the science texts derived from the data on significant chapter linkage presented in the last appendix. Chapters are identified on the diagrams by their number and title. A left to right ordering across the page corresponds to the sequence of chapters in the text. No other significance should be attached to the layout of the diagrams on the page which in other respects is determined by purely topological considerations of clarity of presentation.

ELEN

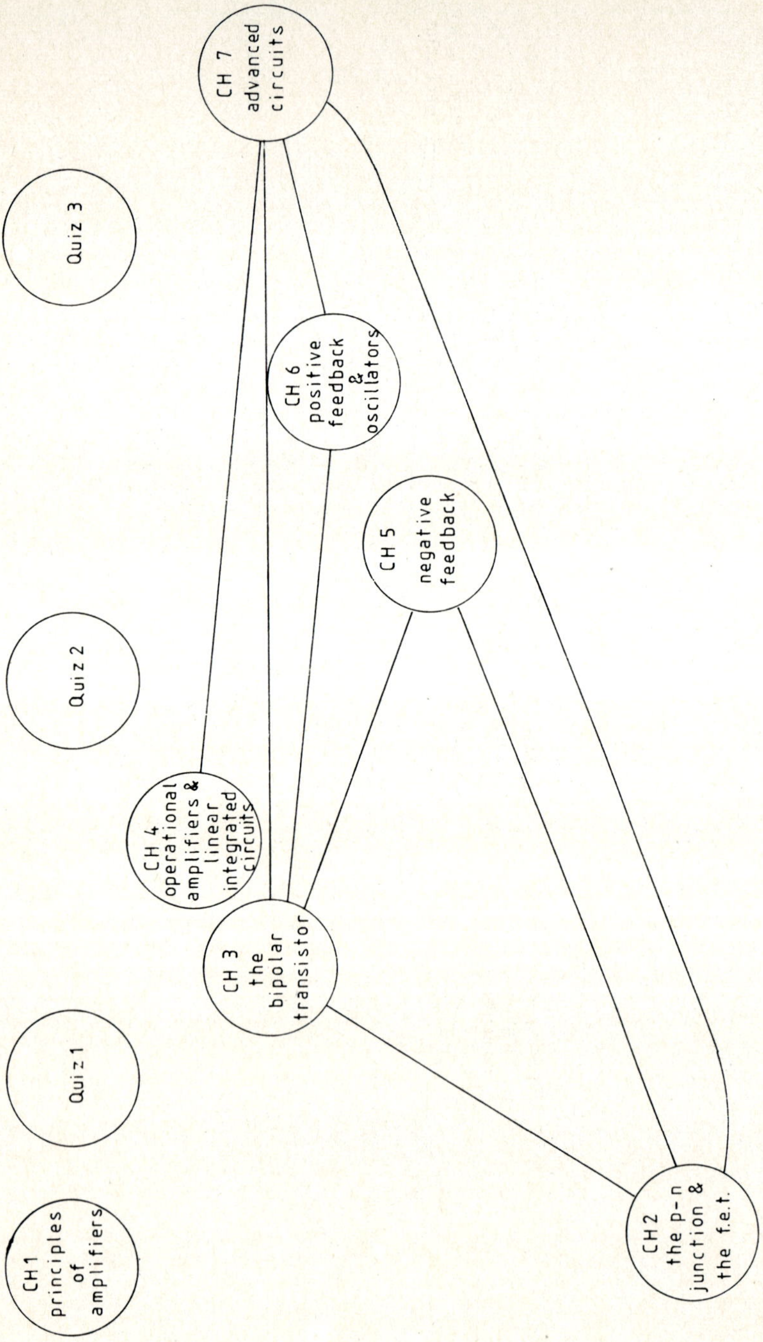

CH1 principles of amplifiers
Quiz 1
Quiz 2
Quiz 3
CH2 the p-n junction & the f.e.t.
CH 3 the bipolar transistor
CH 4 operational amplifiers & linear integrated circuits
CH 5 negative feedback
CH 6 positive feedback & oscillators
CH 7 advanced circuits

CMEC

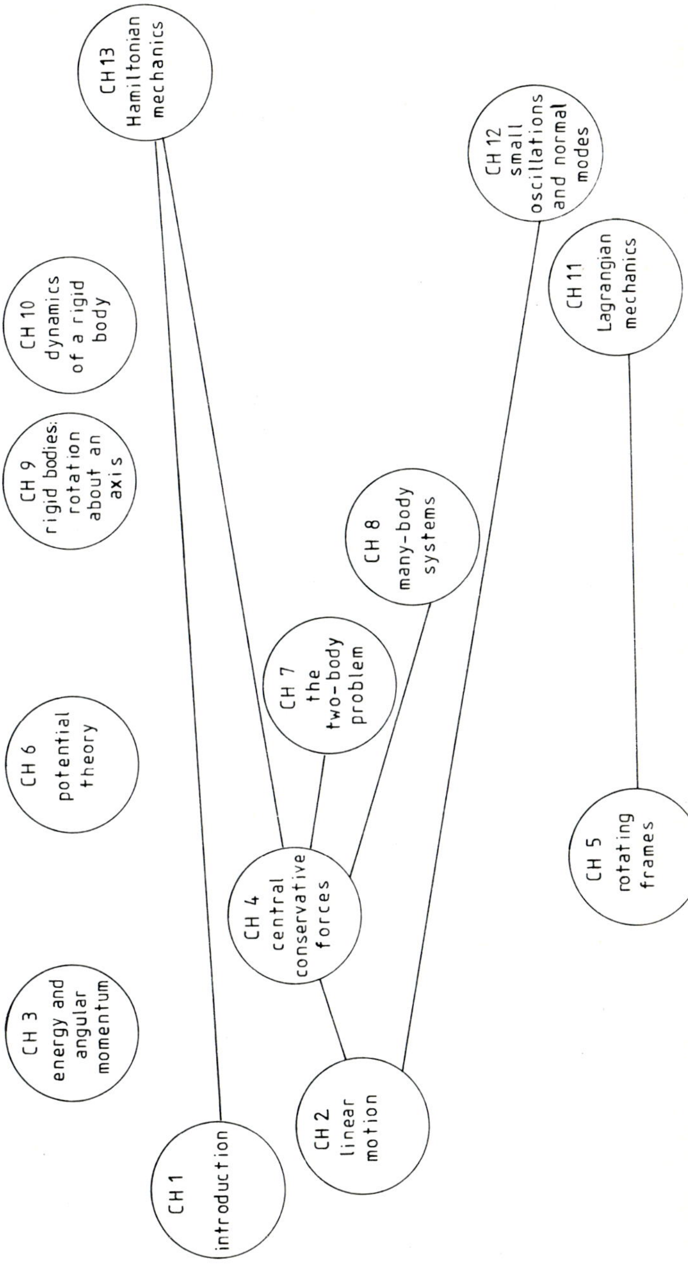
CH 1
introduction
CH 2
linear
motion
CH 3
energy and
angular
momentum
CH 4
central
conservative
forces
CH 5
rotating
frames
CH 6
potential
theory
CH 7
the
two-body
problem
CH 8
many-body
systems
CH 9
rigid bodies:
rotation
about an
axis
CH 10
dynamics
of a rigid
body
CH 11
Lagrangian
mechanics
CH 12
small
oscillations
and normal
modes
CH 13
Hamiltonian
mechanics

CREL

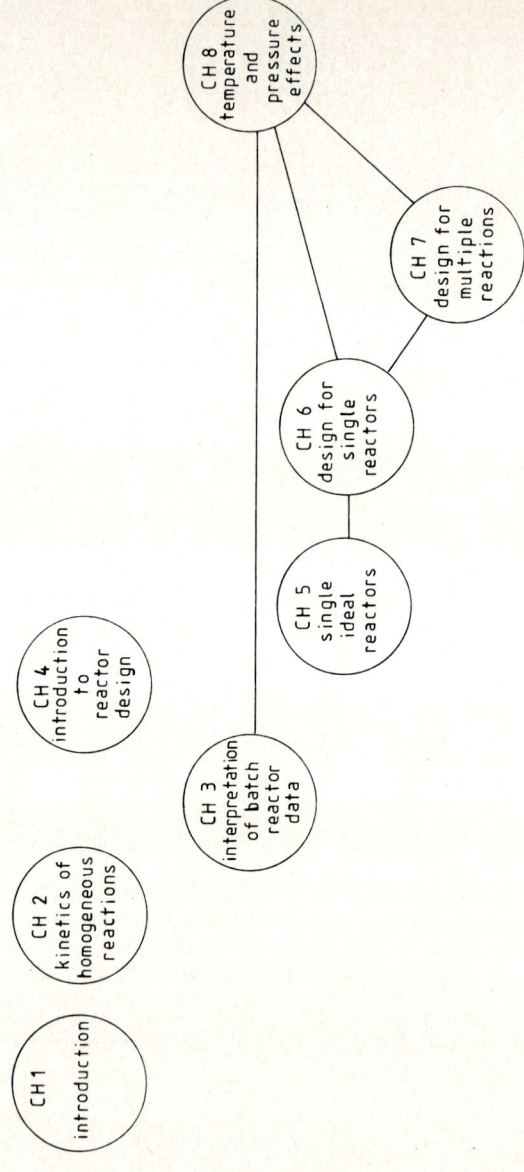

APPENDIX SEVEN 301

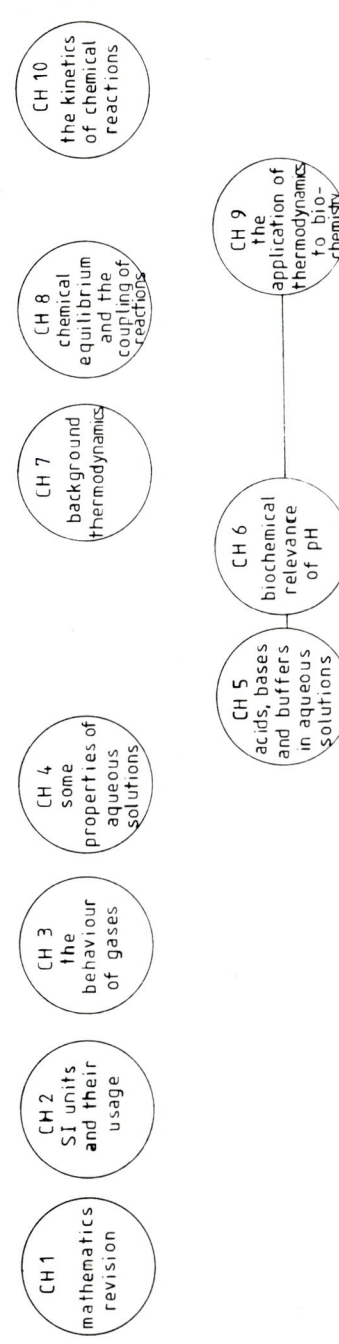

THRM

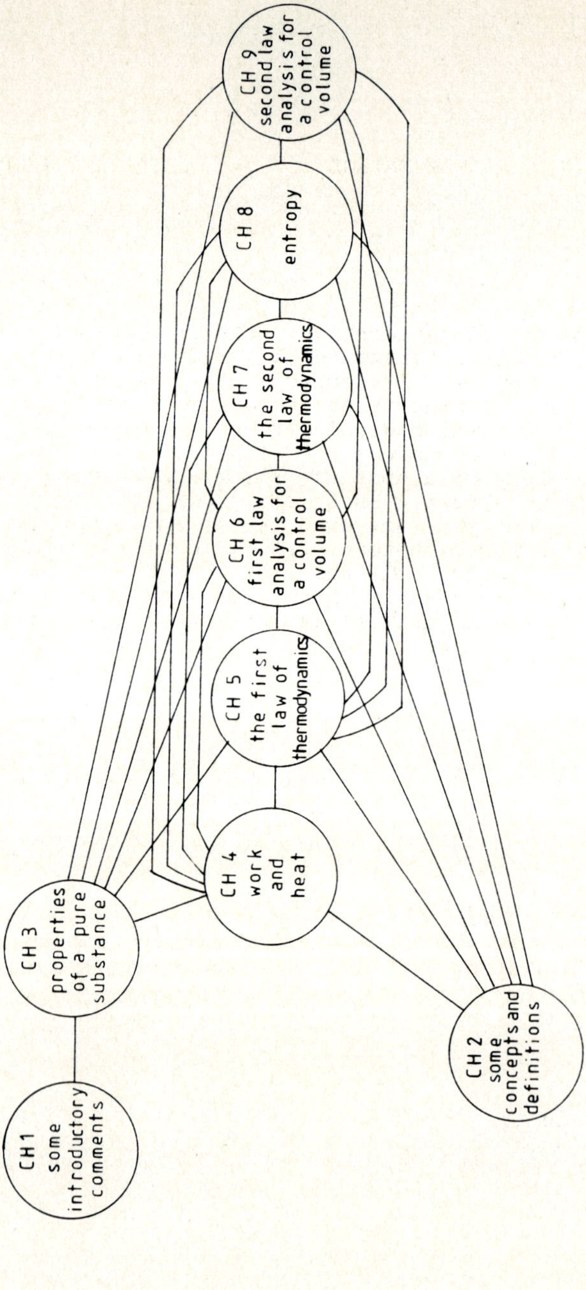
CH 1
some
introductory
comments
CH 2
some
concepts and
definitions
CH 3
properties
of a pure
substance
CH 4
work
and
heat
CH 5
the first
law of
thermodynamics
CH 6
first law
analysis for
a control
volume
CH 7
the second
law of
thermodynamics
CH 8
entropy
CH 9
second law
analysis for
a control
volume

APPENDIX 8

PERCENTAGE OF NON-COLLOCATING NODES

In chapter nine a technique for comparing the collocational behaviour of different texts was developed on the basis of which the possibility emerged of establishing a text typology. Texts were distinguished in terms of the proportion of nodes investigated which displayed collocational patterning and the distribution of values of a range index R which characterises the tendency of a node to select a consistent set of collocates throughout a text. In this appendix the percentages of nodes which do not show any evidence of collocational behaviour are presented for each text. It can be seen that the tendency for nodes to display collocational behaviour is much greater in the science texts than in the non-science texts. Thus these figures give an initial indication of the extent to which the different classes of text are distinguishable on this basis.

ELEN	CMEC	CREL	BIPC	THRM	TMM	MRSD	THF
8.0	9.1	1.6	10.0	6.2	35.2	15.0	52.2

Table A8.1 Percentage of Non-collocating Nodes in the Corpus

BIBLIOGRAPHY

1   Ahmed, H. and Spreadbury, P.J., Electronics for Engineers (Cambridge University Press, Cambridge, 1973).
2   Anthony, E.M., Towards a Theory of Lexical Meaning (Singapore University Press for SEAMEO: Regional Language Centre, Singapore, 1975).
3   Basso, K.H., 'To Give up on Words': Silence in Western Apache Culture, in: Giglioli, P.P. (ed.), Language and Social Context (Penguin, Harmondsworth, 1972).
4   Benson, J.D. and Greaves, W.S., Field of Discourse: A Theoretical Vantage Point Enabling More Effective Use of Computer Assisted Collocational Analysis, Paper presented at ALLC Conference, (1983).
5   Berger, P. and Luckman, T., The Social Construction of Reality (Penguin, Harmondsworth, 1967).
6   Berry-Rogghe, G.L.M.G.A., Collocations: Their Computation and Semantic Significance, Ph.D. Thesis, University of Manchester, (1970).
7   Bloomfield, L., Language (Unwin University Press, London, 1935).
8   Bolinger, D., The Atomization of Meaning, Language 41 4 (1965) 555-573.
9   Bolivar, A.C., Interaction in Written Text: A Discourse Analysis of Newspaper Editorials, Ph.D. Thesis, Dept. of English, University of Birmingham (in progress).
10 Boole, G., An Investigation of the Laws of Thought (1854) (Dover, New York, n.d.).
11 Borges, J.L., Pierre Menard, Autor del Quijote, in: Prosa Completa Vol.1. (Bruguera, Barcelona, 1980).
12 Bradley, A.C., Shakespearean Tragedy 2nd. ed. (Macmillan, London and Basingstoke, 1974).
13 Bradley, R. and Swartz, N., Possible Worlds (Basil Blackwell, Oxford, 1979).
14 Calderbank, V.J., A Course on Programming in FORTRAN IV (Chapman and Hall, London, 1969).
15 Calvino, I., If on a Winter's Night a Traveller (Pan Books, London, 1982).
16 Carroll, J.B., Word-Frequency Studies and the Lognormal Distribution, in: Zale, E.M. (ed.), Proceedings of the Conference on Language and Language Behaviour (Appleton-Century-Crofts, New York, 1968).
17 Carroll, J.B. et al., The American Heritage Word Frequency Book (Houghton Mifflin Company, Boston, and American Heritage Publishing Co.Inc., New York, 1971).

18. Chatfield, C. and Collins, A.J., Introduction to Multivariate Analysis (Chapman and Hall, London, 1980).
19. Clark, H.H. and Clark, E.V., Psychology and Language (Harcourt Brace Jovanovich, New York, 1977).
20. Cooper, M., An Investigation into the Notion of Structure of Written Academic Discourse, Ph.D. Thesis, Dept. of English, University of Birmingham (1983).
21. Coulson, A.E., An Introduction to Matrices 3rd. impression with corrections (Longman, London, 1969).
22. Criper, C. and Widdowson, H.G., Sociolinguistics and Language Teaching, in: Allen, J.P.B. and Corder, S.P. (eds.), The Edinburgh Course in Applied Linguistics Vol.2. Papers in Applied Linguistics (Oxford University Press, London, 1975).
23. Davidson, D., True to the Facts, in: Zabeeh, F. et al. (eds.), Readings in Semantics (University of Illinois Press, Urbana, 1974).
24. Dingle, H., Science at the Crossroads (Martin, Brian and O´Keefe, 1972).
25. Ellis, J., On Contextual Meaning, in: Bazell, C.E. et al. (eds.), In Memory of J.R.Firth (Longman, London, 1966).
26. Engels, L.K., The Fallacy of Word Counts, International Review of Applied Linguistics III 2 (1965) 213-231.
27. Erlich, V., Russian Formalism 4th. ed. (Mouton, The Hague, 1965).
28. Evans, C., The Mighty Micro (Victor Gollancz, London, 1979 and Hodder and Stoughton, Dunton Green, 1980).
29. Everitt, B.S., Graphical Techniques for Multivariate Data (Heinemann Educational Books, London, 1978).
30. Everitt, B.S., Cluster Analysis 2nd. ed. (Heinemann Educational Books for Social Science Research Council, London, 1980).
31. Fillenbaum, S. and Rapoport, A., Structures in the Subjective Lexicon (Academic Press, New York, 1971).
32. Firth, J.R., Speech (1930), in: The Tongues of Men and Speech (Oxford University Press, London, 1964).
33. Firth, J.R., The Technique of Semantics (1935), in: Papers in Linguistics (Oxford University Press, London, 1957).
34. Firth, J.R., Personality and Language in Society, The Sociological Review XLII (1950) 37-52.
35. Firth, J.R., Modes of Meaning (1951), in: Papers in Linguistics (Oxford University Press, London, 1957).
36. Firth, J.R., The Languages of Linguistics (1953), in: Palmer, F.R. (ed.), Selected Papers of J.R.Firth 1952-1959 (Longmans, London and Harlow, 1968).
37. Firth, J.R., Philology in the Philology Society (1956a), in: Palmer, F.R. (ed.), Selected Papers of J.R.Firth 1952-1959 (Longmans, London and Harlow, 1968).
38. Firth, J.R., Linguistic Analysis and Translation (1956b), in: Palmer, F.R. (ed.), Selected Papers of J.R.Firth 1952-1959 (Longmans, London and Harlow, 1968).
39. Firth, J.R., Introduction to Studies in Linguistic Analysis (1957a), in: Firth, J.R. (ed.), Studies in Linguistic Analysis (Basil Blackwell, Oxford,1957a).
40. Firth, J.R., A Synopsis of Linguistic Theory, 1930-1955 (1957b), in Firth, J.R. (ed.), Studies in Linguistic

Analysis (Basil Blackwell, Oxford, 1957).
41 Firth, J.R., Ethnographic Analysis and Language with reference to Malinowski´s views (1957c), in: Palmer, F.R. (ed.) Selected Papers of J.R.Firth 1952-1959 (Longmans, London and Harlow, 1968).
42 Firth, J.R., The Treatment of Language in General Linguistics (1959), in: Palmer, F.R. (ed.) Selected Papers of J.R.Firth 1952-1959 (Longmans, London and Harlow, 1968).
43 Foucault, M., The Order of Things (Tavistock, London, 1970).
44 Gareth Morris, J., A Biologist´s Physical Chemistry 2nd. ed. (Edward Arnold, London, 1974).
45 Geens, D., On Measurement of Lexical Differences by Means of Frequency, in: Altmann, G. (ed.), Glottometrika I (Quantitative Linguistics) (Studienverlag Dr.N.Brockmeyer, Bochum, 1978).
46 Gindin, S.I., Contributions to Textlinguistics in the Soviet Union, in: Dressler, W.U. (ed.), Current Trends in Textlinguistics (Walter de Gruyter, Berlin, 1977).
47 Gnandesikan, R. et al., Interpreting and Assessing the Results of Cluster Analysis, in: Proceedings of 41st Session of the International Statistical Institute (1977) 451-463.
48 Greene, G., The Human Factor (Penguin, Harmondsworth, 1978).
49 Gruber, J.S., Lexical Structures in Syntax and Semantics (North-Holland, Amsterdam, 1976).
50 Gutwinski, W., Cohesion in Literary Texts (Mouton, The Hague, 1976).
51 Haas, W., Zero in Linguistic Description, in: Firth, J.R. (ed.), Studies in Linguistic Analysis (Basil Blackwell, Oxford, 1957).
52 Halliday, M.A.K., Categories of the Theory of Grammar, Word 17 3 (1961) 241-292.
53 Halliday, M.A.K., Lexis as a Linguistic Level, in: Bazell, C.E. et al. (eds.), In Memory of J.R.Firth (Longman, London, 1966).
54 Halliday, M.A.K., Language as Social Semiotic (Edward Arnold, London, 1978).
55 Halliday, M.A.K. and Hasan, R., Cohesion in English (Longman, London, 1976).
56 Halliday, M.A.K. et al., The Linguistic Sciences and Language Teaching (Longman, London, 1964).
57 Harari, H., The Structure of Quarks and Leptons, Scientific American 248 4 (1983) 48-60.
58 Harary, F. et al., Structural Models: An Introduction to the Theory of Directed Graphs (John Wiley, New York, 1965).
59 Harris, Z.H., Discourse Analysis, Language 28 (1952) 1-30.
60 Hasan, R., Text in the Systemic-Functional Model, in: Dressler, W.U. (ed.), Current Trends in Textlinguistics (Walter de Gruyter, Berlin, 1977).
61 Hayakawa, S.I., Language in Thought and Action 3rd. ed. (George Allen and Unwin, London, 1974).
62 Herdan, G., Language as Choice and Chance (P.Nordhoff

N.V., Groningen, 1956).
63 Herdan, G., Type-Token Mathematics: A Textbook of Mathematical Linguistics (Mouton, 's-Gravenhage, 1960).
64 Herdan, G., The Calculus of Linguistic Observations (Mouton, 's-Gravenhage, 1962).
65 Herdan, G., Quantitative Linguistics (Butterworths, London, 1964).
66 Herdan, G., The Advanced Theory of Language as Choice and Chance (Springer-Verlag, Berlin, 1966).
67 Hockey, S. and Marriott, I., Oxford Concordance Program Users' Manual (Oxford University Computing Service, Oxford, 1980).
68 Hofstadter, D.R., Metamagical Themas, Scientific American, 244 1 (1981) 34-41.
69 Hutchins, W., On the Problem of 'Aboutness' in Document Analysis, Journal of Informatics 1 1 (1977) 17-33.
70 Jespersen, O., The Philosophy of Grammar (George Allen and Unwin, London, 1924).
71 Jones, K. and Roe, P.J., Designing English for Science and Technology (EST) Programmes in Academic Settings for Overseas Students: Problems and Perspectives, ETIC Occasional Paper (The British Council, London, 1975).
72 Jones, P.E. and Curtice, R.M., A Framework for Comparing Term Association Measures, American Documentation 18 3 (1967) 153-161.
73 Jones, S. and Sinclair, J.McH., English Lexical Collocations. A Study in Computational Linguistics, Cahiers de Lexicologie XXIII II (1973) 15-61.
74 Kahn, D., The Codebreakers (Sphere Books, London, 1973).
75 Katz, J.J., Semantic Theory (Harper and Row, New York, 1972).
76 Khatibi, A., and Sijelmassi, M., The Splendour of Islamic Calligraphy (Thames and Hudson, London, 1976).
77 Kibble, T.W.B., Classical Mechanics 2nd. ed. (McGraw-Hill, Maidenhead, 1973).
78 Kim, S., Inversions: A Catalog of Calligraphic Cartwheels (BYTE Books, Peterborough N.H., 1981).
79 Kintsch, W., On Comprehending Stories, in: Just, M.A. and Carpenter, P.A. (eds.), Cognitive Processes in Comprehension (Lawrence Erlbaum Associates, Hillsdale N.J., 1977).
80 Koestler, A., The Sleepwalkers (Penguin, Harmondsworth, 1964).
81 Kucera, H. and Francis, W.N., Computational Analysis of Present-Day American English (Brown University Press, Providence, 1967).
82 Kuhn, T.S., The Structure of Scientific Revolutions 2nd. ed. (Chicago University Press, Chicago, 1970).
83 Lakatos, I., The Methodology of Scientific Research Programmes Philosophical Papers Volume 1 (Cambridge University Press, Cambridge, 1978).
84 Leech, G.N., English in Advertising (Longman, London, 1966).
85 Leech, G.N., Semantics 2nd. ed. (Penguin, Harmondsworth, 1981).
86 Leech, G.N. and Leonard, R., A Computer Corpus of British

English, Hamburger Phonetische Beitrage 13 (1974) 41-57.
87 Lehrer, A., Semantic Fields and Lexical Structure (North-Holland, London, 1974).
88 Levenspiel, O., Chemical Reaction Engineering 2nd. ed. (John Wiley, New York, 1972).
89 Levi-Strauss, C., Structural Anthropology 2 (Penguin, Harmondsworth, 1978).
90 Longacre, R.E., The Paragraph as a Grammatical Unit, Paper presented at Symposium on Discourse UCLA (1977).
91 Lyons, J., Introduction to Theoretical Linguistics (Cambridge University Press, Cambridge, 1968).
92 Lyons, J., Semantics I (Cambridge University Press, Cambridge, 1977).
93 Malinowski, B., The Problem of Meaning in Primitive Languages, in: Ogden, C.K. and Richards, I.A., The Meaning of Meaning (Kegan Paul, Trench, Trubner and Co, Ltd, London, 1945).
94 McIntosh, A., Patterns and Ranges, Language 37 3 (1961) 325-337.
95 Mitchell, T.F., Syntagmatic Relations in Linguistic Analysis, Transactions of the Philological Society (1958) 101-118.
96 Mojena, R., Hierarchical Grouping Methods and Stopping Rules: An Evaluation, The Computer Journal 20 4 (1977) 359-363.
97 Montague, R., Pragmatics (1968), in: Thomason, R. (ed.), Formal Philosophy: Selected Papers of Richard Montague (Yale University Press, London, 1974).
98 Montague, R., English as a Formal Language (1970a), in: Thomason, R. (ed.), Formal Philosophy: Selected Papers of Richard Montague (Yale University Press, London, 1974).
99 Montague, R., Universal Grammar (1970b), in: Thomason, R. (ed.), Formal Philosophy: Selected Papers of Richard Montague (Yale University Press, London, 1974).
100 Montague, R., Pragmatics and Intensional Logic (1970c), in: Thomason, R. (ed.), Formal Philosophy: Selected Papers of Richard Montague (Yale University Press, London, 1974).
101 Montgomery, M., Some Aspects of Discourse Structure Cohesion in Selected Science Lectures, M.A. Thesis, Dept. of English, University of Birmingham (1977).
102 Moskovich, W. and Caplan, R., Distributive-Statistical Text Analysis: A New Tool for Semantic and Stylistic Research, in: Altmann, G. (ed.), Glottometrika 1 (Quantitative Linguistics) (Studienverlag Dr.N.Brockmeyer, Bochum, 1978).
103 Muller, C., Le Mot, unite de texte et unite de lexique en statistique lexicologique, Universite de Strasbourg: Travaux de Linguistique et Litterature (1963) 155-173.
104 Muller, C., Initiation aux methodes de la statistique linguistique (Hachette, Paris, 1973).
105 Muller, C., Principes et methodes de statistique lexicale (Hachette, Paris, 1977).
106 Nabokov, V., Pale Fire (Penguin, Harmondsworth, 1962).
107 Nagel, E., The Structure of Science (Routledge and Kegan Paul, London, 1961).

108 Needham, R.M., Automatic Classification in Linguistics, The Statistician 17 1 (1967) 45-54.
109 Petofi, J.S., Towards an Empirically Motivated Grammatical Theory of Verbal Texts, in: Petofi, J.S. and Rieser, H. (eds.), Studies in Text Grammar (D.Riedel Publishing Company, Dordrecht, 1973).
110 Petofi, J.S., Beyond the sentence, between linguistics and logic, in: Ringbom, H. (ed.), Style and Text: Studies Presented to Nils Erik Enkvist (Sprakforlaget Skriptor A.B., Stockholm, 1975).
111 Petofi, J.S., A Formal Semiotic Text Theory as an Integrated Theory of Natural Language (Methodological Remarks), in: Dressler, W.U. (ed.), Current Trends in Textlinguistics (Walter de Gruyter, Berlin, 1977).
112 Petofi, J.S. and Rieser, H., Overview, in: Petofi, J.S. and Rieser, H. (eds.), Studies in Text Analysis (D.Riedel Publishing Company, Dordrecht, 1973).
113 Phillips, M.K., Lexical Macrostructure in Science Text, Ph.D. Thesis, Dept. of English, University of Birmingham 1983.
114 Phillips, M.K., J.R.Firth as Computational Linguist: A Description of the CLOC Text Analysis Package in its Linguistic Context, Les Cahiers de L´Apliut 14 (1984).
115 Phillips, M.K., Text, Terms and Meaning: Some Principles of Analysis, in: Benson, J.D., Cummings, M. and Greaves, W.S. (eds.), Linguistics in a Systemic Perspective (John Benjamins, Amsterdam, forthcoming).
116 Pike, K.L., Language as Particle, Wave, and Field, The Texas Quarterly (1959) 65-76.
117 Pope, M., The Story of Decipherment (Thames and Hudson, London, 1975).
118 Popper, K.R., Objective Knowledge rev. ed. (Oxford University Press, Oxford, 1979).
119 Quillian, M.R., Semantic Memory, in: Minsky, M. (ed.), Semantic Information Processing (MIT Press, Cambridge Mass., 1968).
120 Reed, A., CLOC User Guide (Birmingham University Computer Centre, Birmingham, 1978).
121 Rieser, H., On the Development of Text Grammar, in: Dressler, W.U. (ed.), Current Trends in Textlinguistics (Walter de Gruyter, Berlin, 1977).
122 Roe, P.J., The Notion of Difficulty in Scientific Text, Ph.D. Thesis, Dept. of English, University of Birmingham (1977a).
123 Roe, P.J., Scientific Text Discourse Analysis Monographs No 4 (English Language Research Birmingham University, Birmingham, 1977b).
124 Rumelhart, D.E., Notes on a Schema for Stories, in: Bobrow, D.G. and Collins, A. (eds.), Representation and Understanding: Studies in Cognitive Science (Academic Press, London, 1975).
125 Russell, B., My Philosophical Development (George Allen and Unwin, London, 1980).
126 Sachs, J.S., Recognition Memory for Syntactic and Semantic Aspects of Connected Discourse, Perception and Psychophysics 2 9 (1967) 437-442.

127 Saussure, F., Course in General Linguistics (Collins, 1974).
128 Schmidt, S.J., Some Problems of Communicative Text Theories, in: Dressler, W.U., Current Trends in Text Linguistics (Walter de Gruyter, Berlin, 1977).
129 Shepard, R.N., The Analysis of Proximities: Multidimensional Scaling with an unknown distance function Part 1, Psychometrica 27 2 (1962a) 125-139.
130 Shepard, R.N., The Analysis of Proximities: Multidimensional Scaling with an unknown distance function Part 2, Psychometrica 27 3 (1962b) 219-246.
131 Sibson, R., Order Invariant Methods for Data Analysis, Journal of the Royal Statistical Society Series B (Methodological) 34 (1972) 311-337.
132 Siegel, S., Nonparametric Statistics for the Behavioural Sciences (McGraw-Hill Kogakusha Ltd, Tokyo, 1956).
133 Simmons, R.F., Semantic Networks: Their Computation and Use for Understanding English Sentences, in: Schank, R.C. and Colby, K.M. (eds.), Computer Models of Thought and Language (W.H.Freeman, San Francisco, 1973).
134 Sinclair, J.McH., Beginning the Study of Lexis, in: Bazell, C.E. et al. (eds.), In Memory of J.R.Firth (Longman, London, 1966).
135 Sinclair, J.McH., The Linguistic Basis of Style, in: Ringbom, H. (ed.), Style and Text: Studies Presented to Nils Erik Enkvist (Sprakforlaget Skriptor, Stockholm, 1975).
136 Sinclair, J.McH., Discourse in Relation to Language Structure and Semiotics (1980a), in: Greenbaum, S. et al. (eds.), Studies in English Linguistics for Randolph Quirk (Longman, London, 1980).
137 Sinclair, J.McH., Computational Text Analysis at the University of Birmingham (1980b), ICAME News: Newsletter of the International Computer Archive of Modern English 4 (1980) 13-16.
138 Sinclair, J.McH., Some Implications of Discourse Analysis for ESP Methodology (1980c), Applied Linguistics 1 3 (1980) 253-261.
139 Sinclair, J.McH., Frameworks for Linguistic Description, Internal Departmental Memorandum, Dept. of English, University of Birmingham (1981).
140 Sinclair, J.McH., Planes of Discourse (1983a), in: Rizvi, S.N.A. (ed.), The Twofold Voice: Essays in Honour of Ramesh Mohan (Salzburg Studies in English Literature, Universitat Salzburg, 1983).
141 Sinclair, J.McH., Chairman's Introduction to Session 4: Language and Terminology (1983b), in: Snell, B. (ed.), Term Banks for Tomorrow's World: Translating and the Computer 4 (Aslib, London, 1983).
142 Sinclair, J.McH. and Coulthard, R.M., Towards an Analysis of Discourse: The English used by Teachers and Pupils (Oxford University Press, London, 1975).
143 Sinclair, J.McH. et al., English Lexical Studies: Report to OSTI on Project C/LP/08 (Department of English, University of Birmingham, 1970).
144 Slagle, U.V., The Relationship of the Structure of Meaning to the Structure of Experienced Reality, Linguistics 138

(1974) 81-95.
145. Sonntag, R.E. and Van Wylen, G.J., Introduction to Thermodynamics: Classical and Statistical (John Wiley, New York, 1971).
146. Sweet, H., A New English Grammar (Clarendon Press, Oxford, 1892).
147. Swieczkowski, W., Word Order Patterning in Middle English (Mouton, 's-Gravenhage, 1962).
148. Tadros, A.A., Linguistic Prediction in Economics Text, Ph.D. Thesis, Dept. of English, University of Birmingham (1981).
149. Tarski, A., The Concept of Truth in Formalized Languages, in: Tarski, A., Logic, Semantics, Metamathematics (Oxford University Press, Oxford, 1956).
150. Tarski, A., The Semantic Conception of Truth, in: Zabeeh, F. et al. (eds.), Readings in Semantics (University of Illinois Press, Urbana, 1974).
151. Thomas, D., The Poems (Dent, London, 1982).
152. Thorndike, E.L. and Lorge, I., The Teacher's Word Book of 30,000 Words (Bureau of Publications, Teacher's College, Columbia University, New York, 1944).
153. Thorndyke, P.W., Cognitive Structures in Comprehension and Memory of Narrative Discourse, Cognitive Psychology 9 1 (1977) 77-110.
154. Trier, J., Uber die Erforschung des Menschenkundlichen Wortschatzes, in: Hamp, E.P. et al. (eds.), Readings in Linguistics II (Chicago University Press, Chicago, 1966).
155. Van Buren, P., Preliminary Aspects of Mechanisation in Lexis Part 1, Cahiers de Lexicologie 11 II (1967) 89-112.
156. Van Buren, P., Preliminary Aspects of Mechanisation in Lexis Part 2, Cahiers de Lexicologie 12 I (1968) 71-84.
157. Van Dijk, T.A., A Note on Linguistic Macrostructures, in: Ten Cate, A.P. and Jordens, P. (eds.), Linguistische Pespektiven (Max Niemeyer Verlag, Tubingen, 1973).
158. Van Dijk, T.A., Text and Context: Explorations in the Semantics and Pragmatics of Discourse (1977a) (Longman, London, 1977).
159. Van Dijk, T.A., Semantic Macro-Structures and Knowledge Frames in Discourse Comprehension (1977b), in: Just, M.A. and Carpenter, P.A. (eds.), Cognitive Processes in Comprehension (Lawrence Erlbaum Associates, Hillsdale N.J., 1977).
160. Van Dijk, T.A. and Kintsch, W., Cognitive Psychology and Discourse: Recalling and Summarising Stories, in: Dressler, W.U. (ed.), Current Trends in Textlinguistics (Walter de Gruyter, Berlin, 1977).
161. Ward, J.H., Hierarchical Grouping to Optimize an Objective Function, Journal of the American Statistical Association 58 301 (1963) 236-244.
162. Warnock, G.J., Truth and Correspondence, in: Zabeeh, F. et al. (eds.), Readings in Semantics (University of Illinois Press, Urbana, 1974).
163. Watson, J.D., The Double Helix (Penguin, Harmondsworth, 1970).
164. West, M. (ed.), A General Service List of English Words (Longman, London, 1953).

165 Whorf, B.L., Language, Thought and Reality (MIT Press, Cambridge Mass., 1956).
166 Wilden, A., System and Structure 2nd. ed. (Tavistock, London, 1980).
167 Wilson, R.J., Introduction to Graph Theory 2nd. ed. (Longman, London, 1979).
168 Winter, E.O., A Clause-Relational Approach to English Texts: A Study of Some Predictive Lexical Items in Written Discourse, Instructional Science 6 (1977) 1-92.
169 Wishart, D.J., CLUSTAN User Manual 3rd. ed. (Program Library Unit, University of Edinburgh, 1978).
170 Woolf, V., Mrs Dalloway (Granada, Frogmore, 1976).
171 Yule, G.U., The Statistical Study of Literary Vocabulary (Cambridge University Press, Cambridge, 1944).
172 Zadeh, L.A., Fuzzy Sets, Information and Control 8 1 (1965) 338-353.
173 Zettersten, A., A Word-Frequency List of Scientific English (Studentlitteratur, Lund, 1969).
174 Zipf, G.K., Human Behavior and the Principle of Least Effort (Addison-Wesley, Cambridge Mass., 1949).

SUBJECT INDEX

aboutness, 3f, 15f, 22, 29f, 30, 33f, 45, 101, 140, 168, 195, 224f
active prediction ratio, 98
A-item, 141, 291
antonymy, 62
appropriateness, 7
arbitrariness, 6f
autonomous plane, 23, 141, 143, 167

BIPC (A Biologist's Physical Chemistry), 107, 133f, 141f, 146, 164f, 176f, 184f, 190f, 213f, 240, 246f, 281f, 295, 301

calligraphy, 9f
chain, 200
chapter, 61, 155f, 162f, 166 215f, 223; chapter linkage, 162f, 181, 202, 269, 293f
characteristic K, 42, 58
Chinese language game, 10f
classical statistics, 67f
clause relations, 57
CLOC, 84f, 93, 111f
closed system, 54f
CLUSTAN, 77f, 83, 85f, 115
cluster analysis, 73f, 90, 110, 114, 195; clumping, 77; density search, 73, 79, 110, 115f; evaluation, 75, 77, 114f; hierarchical, 73f, 110, 195; optimisation, 77; Ward's method, 79, 83, 110, 115f
CMEC (Classical Mechanics), 107, 114f, 128f, 141f, 162f, 166f, 171f, 184f, 190f, 213, 223, 240, 243f, 272f, 294, 299
cognitive schemata, 6, 16
coherence, 15, 31
cohesion, 31, 37, 55
collocate, 44, 63
COLLOCATECONTROL, 112
collocation, 14, 31, 43, 46, 63, 111, 115, 140, 144, 195, 198f, 205, 209f, 250; collocational analysis, 15, 44f, 64, 69, 112, 115f, 212f; collocational frequency, 69, 80; collocational matrix, 80, 113
colligation, 43
completely connected graph, 96, 145f
componential analysis, 33
computational analysis, 39, 44, 47, 84f
computer programs, 111f
conceptual content, 5f, 21, 35f
conceptual structures, 3, 13, 20, 24, 32
CONCORDCOMMAND, 112
concrete poetry, 11, 231
conditioned probability, 43, 69, 160
connectivity, 96f, 144, 157; connectivity index, 96f, 144f,
content, 5f, 21, 35f
context of situation, 13f, 40, 195
contextual meaning, 13f, 148, 150
correspondence theory of truth, 226f
coverage, 21, 38
CREL (Chemical Reaction Engineering), 108, 130f,

141f, 163, 167, 174f, 184f, 191, 205, 213, 240, 244f, 277f, 294, 300
cryptography, 12
cut off limit, 86, 110, 116
cutset, 96

data analysis, 70f; data collection, 84; data reduction, 85f, 110f
decipherment, 12
dendrogram, 77, 121f, 255f
differentiation, 188f
digraph theory, 89f
directionality, 82, 98f
disconnected graph, 92, 95
disconnecting set, 96
discourse, 4, 21, 26, 143; discourse analysis, 6, 34f, 44, 106; discourse level, 34f, 55
distance, 94
distributional analysis, 13, 20f, 37, 46f, 59; distributional relations, 9, 58
DSA (distributional statistical analysis) 46f, 59

elegant variation, 221f
ELEN (Electronics for Engineers), 107, 121f, 141f, 163, 168f, 184f, 190f, 210f, 240, 242f, 255f, 268f, 294, 298
ELENRND, 210f
epistemology, 40, 231f
equivalent random text, 106, 109, 113, 209f
errors in text reduction, 56, 58
E.S.S. (Error Sum of Squares), 83, 115
Euclidean metric, 83
exclusion filter, 53f

first order graph, 161
formal system, 7, 18, 226
Fortran format, 80, 112f
frequency, 21, 37f, 45, 82, 110, 140, 199; frequency count, 38, 45; frequency distribution, 58, 86, 199, 212f
fuzzy set, 160

generative grammar, 17; generative semantics, 33
generic structure, 15
goal, 182, 185f
grammar, 18, 208
graphological level, 30, 54

Hamlet, 224f, 228
Herdan-Waring distribution, 41
hierarchical model, 192f
homography, 62; homograph discrimination, 55f, 117, 145f
homonymy, 8

I-item, 141, 291f
illocutionary force, 34
incentre, 95
information science, 29
innumber, 94f
interaction, 35, 162, 202; interactive plane, 141, 143, 165, 167
intercollocation, 97, 144, 146, 200
isolate, 182, 185, 187f, 191

langue, 8, 13, 17, 41, 47
lemma, 61, 111, 113, 121f, 157, 193f, 241f; lemmatisation, 54, 61f, 65, 85, 112
LEMMACOUNT, 112
levels of analysis, 14, 29f, 54
lexical choice, 5, 23; lexical density, 212f; lexical level, 31f, 43, 54f, 195; lexical meaning, 31, 33, 54, 148; lexical network, 100, 115, 121f, 141, 143f, 155f, 194f, 200f; lexical patterning, 15, 37, 44; lexical set, 44f, 68, 100
lexicon, 32
linearity, 3, 5, 8, 15, 41, 188
line-connectivity, 96, 144
linguistic sign, 6f, 22; linguistic substance, 3, 5, 9, 11f
literature, 12, 23, 221f, 228f
logical relations, 55

SUBJECT INDEX

lognormal distribution, 38, 41

macrostructure, 4f, 21, 36, 39, 44f, 100f, 158f, 165f, 180f, 194f, 197f, 202f, 212, 215, 221f, 230, 273f;
  macro-structure, 17f
mathematics, 7
meaning, 8, 11, 18, 24, 40;
  meaning potential, 148f, 162
medial, 181, 185f
microstructure, 58
model-theoretical semantics, 19
morphological level, 30, 54, 195
MRSD (Mrs Dalloway), 108, 201f, 208f, 213f, 216, 229, 240, 250f, 295
multidimensional scaling, 71f

narrative, 16, 214, 216
natural text, 64f
network, 98f
NEWMATRIX, 113
NEWRANDOMTXT, 113
node, 43, 63, 65f, 239, 280;
  nuclear node, 141f, 159, 202, 214f, 291f
non-linearity, 20, 167
non-science text, 197, 200f, 205f, 214, 222f, 228f
non-systemic lexis, 123
normal distribution, 68
normalisation, 80f, 113
NORMALISE, 113

OCP (Oxford Concordance Program), 84
open system, 55, 57f
opposition, 8
orthographic word, 62f
outcentre, 95
outnumber, 94f

paradigmatic organisation, 13, 32, 47
paragraph, 60
parole, 8, 13, 17, 41, 47, 82
passive prediction ratio, 98
path, 94
perception, 6

phatic communion, 12
phonological level, 30
pilot study, 114f
pivot, 182, 185f, 191
Poisson distribution, 68
polymorphemic item, 62
polysemy, 62
possible world, 228f
positional value, 5f, 43
post-structuralism, 25, 29
process perspective, 165, 181
Procrustean criticism, 74f, 116
product perspective, 165, 181
propositional content, 35f, 122
prospection, 162, 165, 181

ragbag cluster, 117, 121, 157
random sampling, 86f, 110f, 117
range, 197f; range index, 198f, 205f, 210
R distribution, 205f, 210f, 223
reachability, 94
reality, 6f, 23f, 141
redundancy, 78
reference, 23f, 26
register, 5, 14f, 31, 42
restricted language, 14
retrospective patterning, 162, 165, 181

Sapir-Whorf hypothesis, 6, 232
scale, 37f
science text, 20, 24, 106, 124f, 164, 167, 192, 205f, 214, 221f, 227f
second order graph, 161f
section, 60
segment, 165f, 194f, 204;
  isolated segment, 166f, 171, 173f, 176, 185, 204
  sequential segment, 166f, 173f, 176, 178, 185, 204
  synoptic segment, 166f, 173, 176, 185, 204
self-collocation, 80, 97, 223
semantics, 7, 33
semantic memory, 4
sense, 14, 26
sentence, 60
serialisation, 188f
signifiant, 6f, 13, 25;

signifie, 6f, 13, 25; signifier, 9
significance testing, 68f
similarity, 159f; similarity coefficient, 73, 83
simultaneity, 66, 68, 71
source, 181, 185f, 204
span, 43f, 59, 63f, 222
spectrum intersection theory, 148f
speech act theory, 18, 34
statistical techniques, 37, 42, 44, 46, 66f
stopping rule, 74, 76
story, 225
strength of clustering, 74, 141
style, 7, 15; stylistics, 42
symbolic system, 7
synonymy, 7, 222
syntagmatic patterning, 9, 13, 15, 32, 43f, 121f
syntax, 9, 17, 30, 54
systemic-functional model, 18
systemic lexis, 21, 141
subject matter, 3, 5f, 15, 20, 22f, 116, 122f, 145f, 166f, 188f, 201, 207

tagging, 65
terminology, 6, 22, 99, 222; term bank, 33; term meaning, 5f, 22, 148
TeSWeST (Text-Struktur-Welt-Struktur-Theorie), 18
text, 4f, 14; text analysis, 58, 64; text corpora, 38f, 45, 65, 105f; text and interaction, 4, 20; text interval, 5, 45, 59f, 122, 157; text and lexis, 31, text linguistics, 6, 16f; text logic, 18f; text and reality, 3, 22, 26, 226, 228f; text reduction, 53f, 58, 65; text structure, 6, 15, 17, 20, 42, 45, 47; text typology, 5f, 15, 25, 42, 204f, 214f
theme, 225
THF (The Human Factor), 108, 200f, 205, 208f, 213, 216, 228, 240, 249f
third order graph, 161, 163
THRM (Introduction to Thermodynamics), 108, 136f, 141f, 164, 178f, 184f, 189f, 213, 240, 247f, 285f, 295, 302
TMM (The Mighty Micro), 108, 200, 202, 208, 210, 213, 223, 229, 240, 251f
TMMRND, 210f
token, 21, 62, 150
truth value, 226f
type, 21, 62, 150; type-token distribution, 41
typographical patterning, 30

units of analysis, 59, 61, 192f

valeur, 8f, 13, 148
verifiability, 227f
vocabulary, 5, 21f, 57f, 143, 148, 207; vocabulary connectivity, 158

wave model, 150f
weight, 97
word meaning, 14, 33f, 62, 150, 195; word morphology, 30; word order, 12, 54
Wortfeldtheorie, 33

Zipf's law, 42

AUTHOR INDEX

Ahmed, H., 107, 163, 168f
Anthony, E.M., 148f

Basso, K.H., 12
Benson, J.D., 140
Berger, P., 24f
Berry-Rogghe, G.L.M.G.A., 44f, 65f, 68, 82
Bloomfield, L., 9
Bolinger, D., 33
Bolivar, A.C., 36, 60
Boole, G., 231
Borges, J.L., 23
Bradley, A.C., 224f
Bradley, R., 226

Calderbank, V.J., 80
Calvino, I., 226
Caplan, R., 46f, 59, 81
Carroll, J.B., 38, 82
Chatfield, C., 71, 114
Chaucer, G., 11
Clark, E.V., 4
Clark, H.H., 4
Collins, A.J., 71, 114
Cooper, M., 35, 162
Coulthard, R.M., 17, 34
Coulson, A.E., 80
Criper, C., 4
Curtice, R.M., 81

Daley, R., 43
Davidson, D., 226f
Dingle, H., 231

Eliot, T.S., 226
Ellis, J., 230
Engels, L.K., 38f
Erlich, V., 7, 225f
Evans, C., 109
Everitt, B.S., 71, 77

Fillenbaum, S., 32f, 72, 74, 77f, 83, 114, 117
Firth, J.R., 13f, 19, 25, 29f, 43, 148
Foucault, M., 12, 25f, 29, 232
Francis, W.N., 38, 62, 105
Frege, G., 14
Frumkina, R.M., 38

Gareth Morris, J., 107, 133, 164, 176
Geens, D., 45
Gindin, S.I., 60
Gnandesikan, R., 75, 114, 234
Greaves, W.S., 140
Greene, G., 109
Gruber, J.S., 33
Gutwinski, W., 37

Haas, W., 12
Halliday, M.A.K., 14f, 17, 30f, 43, 54f, 62, 193
Harari, H., 24
Harary, F., 89f
Harris, Z.S., 18, 37
Hasan, R., 15, 17f, 31, 37, 55, 62
Hayakawa, S.I., 232
Herdan, G., 10f, 37f, 41f, 62, 70, 76, 86, 158
Hockey, S., 84
Hofstadter, D.R., 11
Hutchins, W., 29

Jakobson, R., 7
Jespersen, O., 32
Jones, K., 23, 39
Jones, P.E., 81
Jones, S., 43, 45f

Kahn, D., 12
Kant, I., 6
Katz, J.J., 33

Khatibi, A., 10
Kibble, T.W.B., 107, 128f, 140, 163, 171, 173
Kim, S., 10
Kintsch, W., 16, 19, 72
Koestler, A., 227
Kucera, H., 38, 62, 105
Kuhn, T.S., 227

Lakatos, I., 183, 227, 235
Leech, G.N., 24f, 39, 149, 232
Lehrer, A., 32
Leonard, R., 39
Levenspiel, O., 108, 131, 162f, 174
Levi-Strauss, C., 25
Longacre, R.E., 60
Lorge, I., 38
Luckman, T., 24f
Lyons, J., 33

Malinowski, B., 13
Marriot, I., 84
McIntosh, A., 197
Mitchell, T.F., 43
Mojena, R., 76, 79
Montague, R., 18
Montgomery, M., 36
Moskovich, W., 46f, 59, 81
Muller, C., 4f, 32, 41f, 61f, 209f

Nabokov, V., 229f
Nagel, E., 153
Needham, R.M., 78, 87, 121

Petofi, J.S., 17f
Phillips, M.K., 24, 64, 84, 109, 115, 124, 140, 161, 235, 267
Pike, K.L., 18, 150, 153
Pope, M., 12
Popper, K.R., 183, 227

Quillian, M.R., 54, 148f

Rapoport, A., 32f, 72, 74, 77f, 83, 114
Reed, A., 84
Rieser, H., 17, 19
Roe, P.J., 20f, 26, 39, 61, 105f, 141, 157, 167, 188, 192
Rumelhart, D.E., 16
Russell, B., 227

Sachs, J.S., 4
Sapir, E., 6
Saussure, F., 5f, 8f, 13, 17, 22, 25f, 148, 205
Schmidt, S.J., 15
Shakespeare, W., 11
Shannon, C.E., 78
Shepard, R.N., 71
Sibson, R., 71, 86
Siegel, S., 70
Sijelmassi, M., 10
Simmons, R.F., 90, 148
Sinclair, J.McH., 7, 9, 12, 15, 17, 23, 31, 33f, 37, 42f, 48, 55, 63f, 66, 68f, 82, 98, 141, 148, 153, 216, 223, 229f
Slagle, U.V., 6
Sonntag, R.E., 108, 136, 164, 178
Spreadbury, P.J., 107, 163, 168f
Swartz, N., 226
Sweet, H., 32
Swieczkowski, W., 12
Swinburne, A.C., 15

Tadros, A.A., 35f, 162
Tarski, A., 226
Thomas, D., 11, 23
Thorndike, E.L., 38
Thorndyke, P.W., 16
Tolstoy, L.N., 225
Trier, J., 33
Twadell, W.F., 105

Van Buren, P., 98, 117
Van Dijk, T.A., 4f, 16f
Van Wylen, G.J., 108, 136, 164, 178

Ward, J.H., 79
Warnock, G.J., 226f
Watson, J.D., 227
West, M., 38
Whorf, B.L., 6
Widdowson, H.G., 4
Wilden, A., 40
Wilson, R.J., 89, 96
Winter, E.O., 57f
Wishart, D.J., 77, 79, 83
Wittgenstein, L., 15
Woolf, V., 108

Yule, G.U., 42, 59, 141

Zadeh, L.A., 160
Zettersten, A., 38

Zipf, G.K., 42, 45, 86